WHO WE BE

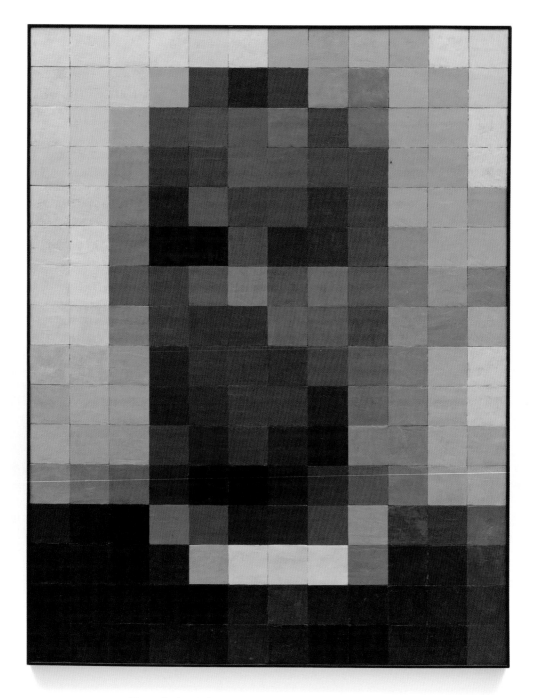

Channel 11 by Kori Newkirk. 1999. Encaustic on wood panel.
Collection of the Santa Barbara Museum of Art. Gift of Barry Sloane.

WHO WE BE

THE COLORIZATION OF AMERICA

JEFF CHANG

St. Martin's Press ⌘ New York

To great teachers:
Dicksie Tamanaha, Kathleen Dudden Rowlands, William Y.S. Lee,
Gary Delgado, Don Nakanishi, Roberta Uno & Kate Hobbs

To the memory of
Ronald Takaki and Morrie Turner

www.stmartins.com

Art direction and book design by Stephen Serrato
www.sserrato.info

Jacket design by James Iacobelli

Visit Jeff Chang online at the following Web sites:
whowebe.net
www.jeffchang.net

Library of Congress Cataloging-in-Publication Data is available upon request.

ISBN 978-0-312-57129-0 (hardcover)
ISBN 978-1-4668-5465-9 (e-book)

St. Martin's Press books may be purchased for educational, business, or promotional use.
For information on bulk purchases, please contact Macmillan Corporate and Premium Sales Department at
1-800-221-7945, extension 5442, or write specialmarkets@macmillan.com.

First Edition: October 2014

10 9 8 7 6 5 4 3 2 1

The author gratefully acknowledges permission to republish lyrics from the following songs:

"Culture War" by Arcade Fire
Reproduced with kind permission of Dounia Mikou for Arcade Fire, Quest Management.

"Me" by Erykah Badu
New Amerykah Part One: (4th World War)
Released March 26, 2008
Universal Motown Records/Control Freq Records
Thanks to Paul J. Levatino and Erykah Badu.

"I Am Here" by Savages
Words and Music by Gemma Thompson, Ayse Hassan, Fay Milton, and Camille Berthomier.
Copyright ©2012 by Pop Noire and BMG Rights Management (UK) Ltd.
All Rights Administered by BMG Rights Management (UK) Ltd., a BMG Chrysalis company.
All Rights Reserved. Used by Permission
Reprinted by Permission of Hal Leonard Corporation.
Thanks to Gemma Thompson, Jehnny Beth,
Savages, Edna Pletchetero and Dean O'Connor.

Also by Jeff Chang

Can't Stop Won't Stop:
A History of the Hip-Hop Generation

Total Chaos: The Art & Aesthetics of Hip-Hop (editor)

Contents

"The gods were fighting…. And the gods were fighting because the world was very boring, with only two colors to paint it …."

—A folktale from Chiapas retold by Subcomandante Marcos, *La Historia de los Colores*

Photo by B+ from the series *Is A Record Like A Wheel…*

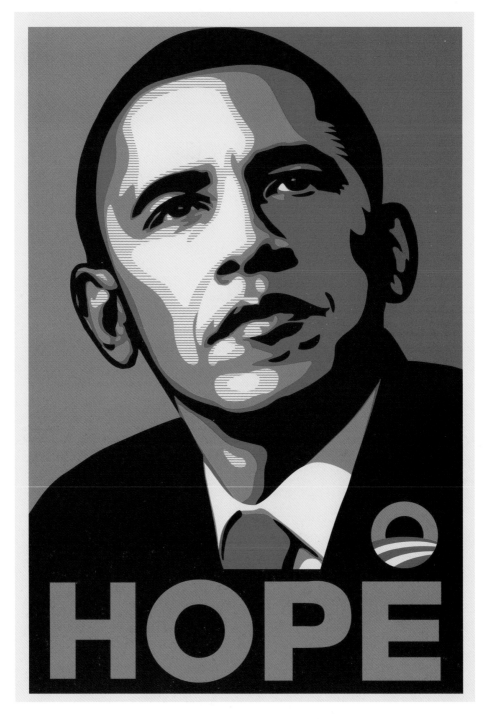

Obama HOPE poster by Shepard Fairey. 2008.

SEEING AMERICA

I

For most of 2008, the most arresting image in America was a screen print by the street artist Shepard Fairey that appeared on posters, stickers, and clothing from sea to shining sea. The image was of a Black and white man rendered in red, white, and blue. The man was named Barack Obama and the four-letter word below his image was "HOPE."

Obama was, of course, the presidential candidate who had come from the far geographic and cultural edge of the United States, its Pacific borderland in Hawai'i, to secure the Democratic Party nomination. He had run on a platform of mending a divided country. In a speech he gave in March that he called "A More Perfect Union," he offered his own biracial heritage—the unity of Black and white histories in his own body—as a symbol of empathy and reconciliation.

That address, now popularly known as the "race speech," was in some ways as historic as Martin Luther King Jr.'s "I Have a Dream" speech, delivered at the Lincoln Memorial almost forty-five years earlier. "The complexities of race in this country that we've never really worked through," Obama said, remained "a part of our union that we have yet to perfect." If Americans could move forward on race, he seemed to say, they could move forward on anything.

By then demographers had become accustomed to naming each new cohort of youths the most diverse generation the nation had ever seen. One in three Americans was of color. They formed the majority in a third of the country's most populous counties, and in forerunner states like California, Texas, New Mexico, and Hawai'i.

In 2000, voters of color made up only 19 percent of the electorate, but in 2004, more than half of all new voters between the ages of eighteen and twenty-nine were

Black or Latino. In 2008, youth and voters of color turned out in record numbers, forming the foundation of a new electorate that put Obama into office. By 2012, more than a quarter of voters were of color. It seemed apparent that an emergent majority had spoken once again at the polls, loudly.

Experts had begun projecting that sometime, perhaps as early as 2042, the United States would become "majority-minority." The notion seemed stranger with each new census—if no race was a majority, then wouldn't each be a minority? And just what would it mean for the nation?

The country in which Barack Obama could take the oath of office on the inaugural platform at the West Front of the Capitol building was most certainly not the same as the one in which Martin Luther King Jr. addressed the nation from the steps of the Lincoln Memorial. For that to have occurred, America needed to understand itself differently than it had for most of its first two centuries, which had been marked by formal racial segregation. Even after the civil rights movement enabled dramatic and sweeping legislative and judicial changes, those changes could take Americans only part of the way toward desegregation. Laws could not tell people how to see each other, how to be with each other, how to live together. They would have to find a new way of seeing America.

The United States had been historically defined by whiteness, drawn in grays, shades of white and black. But in Fairey's famous print Obama had been colorized, to coin a phrase, just as the country to and for which he had become a symbol had been colorized. Colorization describes the massive shifts that began taking place as the civil rights movement began to ebb. These shifts were demographic and would have political implications. But the most profound changes have been cultural.

This is where we begin: How has the national culture changed over the past half-century that we could elect a Black president? And, just as important, how has it not changed?

To begin to answer these questions we must address that most complicated of American words, another four-letter word: "race."

II

We can all agree that race is not a question of biology. Instead it is a question of culture and it begins as a visual problem, one of vision and visuality. Race happens in the gap between appearance and the perception of difference. It is about what we see and what we think we see and what we think about when we see. In that sense, it's bigger than personal affinities, preferences, tastes, and bonds.

Race has driven centuries of civil and cultural schisms and periodically brought the nation to the brink of dissolution. In 1952, Ralph Ellison encapsulated the central problem of race and American visuality. "I am invisible, understand, simply because people refuse to see me," his protagonist remarked in the famous prologue to *Invisible Man*. "When they approach me they see only my surroundings, themselves, or figments of their imagination—indeed, everything and anything except me."

Difference is human, and noticing difference is human. For us, it begins as babies, from our very earliest days of perception. But of course Ellison was pointing out that America's race problem came from something deeper. For whites, historically, skin tone and physiognomy signaled not only difference, but notions of superiority and inferiority. This was the way racial power worked. It went further than merely perceiving difference. It sorted difference into vast systems of freedom and slavery, commitment and neglect, investment and abandonment, mobility and containment.

Then it drew a veil over these systems. It pretended not to have even seen difference in the first place. Racism, in other words, was supported by a specific kind of refusal, a denial of empathy, a mass-willed blindness. In this context, the Other's true self might always remain unseen. The Other might always bear the burden of representation.

The musician and intellectual Vijay Iyer has compared seeing to listening. When we feel empathy for another person, he reminds us, our brain's mirror neurons fire. We understand another's pain or joy at the root level of our being. Art, music, and literature can move us in the same way.

But psychologists and neuroscientists also warn that visual racialized difference gets in the way of empathy. Between a child's curiosity about difference and an adult's perception of difference, something has changed. We have learned to be compassionate or fearful before what we see.[1]

What made the breakthroughs of the civil rights movement—the last great consensus for racial justice—possible? Iyer speculates on the history of race, visuality, and popular music in the last half of the twentieth century by asking:

> Is it possible that music-heard-and-not-seen … might have overridden the visual, racialized, culturally imposed constraints on empathy? Could the essential humanity of African Americans been newly revealed for white American listeners in the twentieth century through the disembodied circulation of "race records," by activating in these listeners a neural "understanding" of the actions of African American performers? Could a new kind of cross-racial empathy, or at least a new quasi-utopic racial imaginary, have been inaugurated through the introduction of recorded sound?[2]

Listening, Iyer suggests, may have been crucial to the making of this consensus for racial justice, the aurality of race—powerfully shaped by twentieth-century Black music— firing the national conscience. But after the civil rights movement, race became a new kind of American problem. *Seeing* became increasingly important.

With energy and urgency, artists and activists of color were pursuing their visions of a post-segregated nation, attacking the twin conditions of cultural segregation—the absence of representation and the presence of misrepresentation. The *visuality* of race—with its national history of erasure and debasement—became critical simply because people of color would no longer remain invisible.

So the new formal conditions of legal desegregation gave rise to a movement of art and ideas meant to bring about cultural desegregation. Its proponents came to name it multiculturalism. By the late 1970s, artists of color were focused on the question of recognition of *identity*—both legal and cultural. They argued that American culture had never been only white and Western, a singular, unitary, exceptional model. America had *always* been multicultural.

That is when multiculturalism began to encounter powerful resistance. As lawmakers and judges unraveled an already fragile national civil rights consensus, questions of racial justice and cultural equity combusted in the most unlikely places: urban galleries, elite museums and institutions, advertising and marketing agencies, the studio, the theater, the editorial desk—everywhere where creativity was stoked and those desires expressed; where the image, the sound, the story, the work of art was made.

Within a decade, the ideas once incubated in a tiny West Coast avant-garde caused pitched battles from the classrooms to the editorial pages to the halls of power. Opponents argued that if multiculturalists were allowed to triumph, American democracy would crumble. Four decades after Ralph Ellison's cogent articulation of America's race problem, Pat Buchanan declared the start of the "culture wars."

These wars were declared in the name of restoration. As Buchanan began his 2011 Obama-era polemic, *Suicide Of A Superpower: Will America Survive to 2025?*: "What happened to the country we grew up in?" Both questions—the first inseparable from the second—pointed to an aching imperial nostalgia, an ideal of a homogenous Christian nation, and a quaking fear of a future conditioned by cultural and racial change.

Like all wars, the culture wars were not inevitable. But in the last epoch of the twentieth century these wars erupted because demographic change and multiculturalism had prompted new discussions about democracy, particularly around contested values of expression, recognition, inclusion, and empathy. After Obama's election in 2008, the culture wars flared anew.

On the forty-seventh anniversary of Martin Luther King Jr.'s "I Have a Dream" speech, conservative talk-show host Glenn Beck gathered hundreds of thousands on the Mall in Washington and told them, "For too long, this country has wandered in darkness." Failed vice presidential candidate Sarah Palin clarified the intent of the gathering, saying, "We must not fundamentally transform America, as some would want. We must restore America and restore her honor."

The culture wars were always framed as a struggle for the soul of America, a clash of competing narratives: the story of the great America we are in danger of losing forever versus the story of a hopeful emerging America. The nation's colorization might lead to the end of American civilization or the beginning of a great national transformation. The culture wars made clear that race remained America's most troubled divide.

Both sides understood that battles over culture were high-stakes. The struggle between restoration and transformation, retrenchment and change, began in culture. Culture was where change could be thwarted, or where it might flower.

III

Culture, the great thinker Raymond Williams once wrote, "is one of the two or three most complicated words in the English language."[3] I may be about to do Williams and the community of serious scholars a grave disservice. But here goes.

Culture is the realm of images, ideas, sounds, and stories. It is our shared space. It is the narrative we are immersed in every day. It is where people find community, and express their deepest-held values, where, as Eduardo Galeano put it, "the collective symbols of identity and memory: the testimonies of what we are, the prophecies of the imagination, the denunciations of what prevents us from being" are circulated.[4] It is where what Abraham Lincoln called "public sentiment" is formed and moved, like a wave.[5]

The metaphor of the wave seems perfect for this moment of broad change. But what are we talking about, exactly? A wave is a thing, an event. We can see a wave of water breaking over a reef like the one at Pipeline on the North Shore of O'ahu or Teahupo'o on the southwestern coast of Tahiti. These waves are beautiful, monumental, and deadly if you're caught in the wrong place when it rolls through.

But in scientific and lexical terms, as the writer Susan Casey has noted, a wave is a paradox. It is not only an event—it is a motion, a process. It's the process of forces generated in the Arctic or the Antarctic, rolling from the bottom of the ocean for hundreds of miles until they gather to hit these shallow reefs. Then, boom—the famous waves at Pipe or Chopes. So a wave is an event. But it's also a process—the movement of forces, some visible above the surface, much of it unseen, rising from the bottom up.

When we talk about social change, many of us who are historians, organizers, and activists focus our intellectual energy on discrete events in time—elections, Supreme Court decisions, legislative votes, demonstrations. We privilege events—they form our story about how history thrusts forward. We alter our language to fit this worldview. Politics is hard, tangible like the earth. Culture is soft, slippery like water.

But what if we thought of change not just as a chain of events? Instead, what if we thought of change also as a process that, like the ocean itself, never stops moving? We would have to acknowledge that there is a vast world out there whose substance and drift do not always cohere into big events—but within which invisible forces are pushing back and forth, creating meanings and movements all the time.

Here is where artists and those who work and play in the culture enter. They help people to see what cannot yet be seen, hear the unheard, tell the untold. They make change feel not just possible, but inevitable. Every moment of major social change requires a collective leap of imagination. Change presents itself not only in spontaneous and organized expressions of unrest and risk, but in explosions of mass creativity.

So those interested in transforming society might assert: cultural change always precedes political change. Put another way, political change is the last manifestation of cultural shifts that have already occurred. Obama could not have been pictured as a symbol of hope if the seeds of that hope had not been planted in the culture long before.

IV

By the new millennium, multiculturalism was less a movement than a platitude. While some still claimed diversity would be the ruin of America, many of multiculturalism's former advocates had long forsaken it. To some—Aaron McGruder in *The Boondocks*, Trey Parker and Matt Stone in *South Park*, or the Martin Agency in their GEICO caveman commercials—it had become a cliché, a target ripe for parody, the last refuge of clueless hippiedom, the musty den of the PC police, the church of white guilt.

Multiculturalism had also been wholly absorbed into the mainstream. Forty years after *Sesame Street* was introduced to Public Broadcasting Service audiences, the Nickelodeon network had Dora, Diego, Little Bill, and Kai-Lan. Multiracial TV casts became so normal that audiences objected when they did *not* appear. Our visual culture had been colorized. There had never been a time in American history when nonwhite people were more visible. President Obama and his beautiful young family were the apotheosis.

Global companies and national political parties embraced diversity. Advertisers segmented market niches for nonwhites. Multiculturalism had generated a new face for global capital and what David Theo Goldberg called the post-millennial "racial state." But although difference was everywhere, it seemed to mean less than ever. So it was now worth asking: What good had colorization done?

From the height of the civil rights movement through the Cold War into a new era of globalization, the United States trumpeted the value of inclusion as central to its democracy. In response to European race riots or ethnic cleansing pogroms, we could invoke our exceptionalism. Yet the reality of race still belied the nation's image of itself.

When Barack Obama's candidacy began to gather steam in 2008, some wrote that it was a sign the rancor was finally dissipating. He was greeted as a "Black Joshua" or a "Healer-in-Chief" in the context of an America still divided on issues like affirmative action, immigration, policing, and criminal justice. In his race speech, the candidate said, "I have never been so naive as to believe we can get beyond our racial divisions in a single election cycle, or with a single candidacy." Yet in the afterglow of his historic victory, many declared that the United States had entered a "post-racial" era.

But if the image of 2008 had been Fairey's HOPE poster, the image of 2009—the year, Pat Buchanan claimed, that had "radicalized much of white America," the beginning of what some only half-jokingly called the "post-hope" era—was a picture of a Obama whitefaced into Batman's arch-nemesis, the Joker.[6] Someone had photoshopped the president's visage onto Heath Ledger's Joker, mottled his eyes black, smeared his lips and dimples bloodred into a gruesome grin. The entire picture was framed by a commie-red border and finished with the accusatory word "SOCIALISM."

The image had actually been assembled before Obama's inauguration, but it went viral during the following summer, when organized conservative opposition to his health-care reform legislation disrupted town-hall meetings across the country. Far-right Tea Party members carried picket signs depicting Obama as an African witch doctor. Redesigned food stamps featuring watermelon and fried chicken buzzed through e-mail and social networks.

The designer of the Obama Joker was a bored Palestinian American college student named Firas Alkhateeb, who during a lull on his Christmas break was sitting in front of his computer with a *Time* magazine cover of Obama, his Web browser pointed at a Photoshop how-to page. Alkhateeb's politics were left of Obama. He was a Dennis Kucinich supporter and had not voted in November. He later said he wasn't trying to make a political statement when he spent several hours that evening designing the image.

He simply posted the image to his Flickr account, and found seven months later that someone had stripped the *Time* logo and cover lines, added the "Socialism" tag, and wheatpasted posters of it all over Los Angeles, the same streets that had been ground zero for Obama HOPE. Reached by the *Los Angeles Times*, Alkhateeb fessed up but quickly added, "To accuse him of being a socialist is really ... immature. First of all, who said being a socialist is evil?"[7]

Yet by then the Joker image had gone epidemic. It pressed all of the Obama opposition's hot buttons. To call Obama the Joker was to uncover all of his pathologies and elevate them into something archetypal. He was psychotically single-minded (his obsession with health-care reform), dismissive of tradition (his callousness toward "guns or religion" Americans), and downright murderous (his alleged support for so-called death panels).

"See, I'm not a monster, I'm just ahead of the curve," says the Joker to Harvey Dent and Batman in Christopher Nolan's *The Dark Knight*. "You have all these rules and you think they'll save you…. The only sensible way to live in this world is without rules."

"Introduce a little anarchy," he says. "Upset the established order and everything becomes chaos. I'm an agent of chaos."

Tea Partiers understood themselves in that quintessential, paradoxical American way. They saw themselves as rebels, outsiders, nonconformists. But they cast themselves in the role of Batman, a vengeful Old Testament kind of hero endowed with modern wealth, skill, and technology. Through their call to austerity, disinvestment, and civic white flight, they would restore the rightful order. Obama was a screen for their projections, a worthy opponent.

"What would I do without you?" the Joker tells Batman. "You complete me."

In the 1830s white minstrels had put on blackface, creating space for the white working class to challenge the elite while keeping Blacks locked into their racial place. Obama now appeared as a dual symbol of oppression. Because of his Blackness, he was even more of an outsider—and in that sense, even more American—than them. But he was also the president. His Blackness did not just confer moral and existential claims, it was backed by the power of the state.

And so the summer of 2009 stretched into more absurdity. When, in a press conference, Obama said that the white Cambridge police who had harassed the famous African American scholar Henry Louis Gates Jr. had "acted stupidly," he caused a national uproar. Glenn Beck called Obama a "racist" who held a "deep seated hatred for white people or the white culture."[8]

Not long after, the Obama administration fired African American official Shirley Sherrod after conservative white blogger Andrew Breitbart accused her of being anti-white in a speech to the NAACP. Sherrod—whose father had been murdered by white racists—was in fact speaking candidly of how she had overcome her own prejudices against whites, and the administration hastily tried to rehire her.

It was then that Obama, who had wanted to be a symbol of reconciliation, seemed to have been restored—by those fearful of a new America—to a symbol of all things Other: he was not just Black, not just the product of miscegenation, he was also a socialist, a Muslim, an illegal alien. Behind the colorized face of hope was the whiteface demon of disorder. The Obama Joker was a lord of misrule, the triumph of the minstrel, in a show played no longer for laughs but for nothing less than the end of their America. Change the joke and revert the yoke.

The Obama Joker image enclosed the sum of all their fears while presenting the picture of confrontation. The image said: skip your empathy, screw your reconciliation, we embrace our victimhood—because a nation is not an unfinished draft in search of its missing words, it's a game, and only one can win.

V

With Obama's election in 2008, everything changed. And nothing changed. We have entered a new era in U.S. history. But how do we describe this time?

The divides remain. We live in an era in which the primary social schism is not that between so-called red states and blue states, but between those stuck on monoculturalism and a singular "American way," and those comfortable with demographic change and cultural difference; those fearful over the great America in danger of being lost forever, and those hopeful about the one being made anew; those stuck in black-and-white, and those living in color. Americans remain overly apocalyptic on the one hand and overly ardent on the other, identity-fatigued and post-racially euphoric.

Cultural desegregation *has* changed America. We can be seen as a happy rainbow country. Yet all of our social indexes show rising rates of resegregation and inequity. In other words, there is a growing gap between what we see and what we think we see. For these conditions hide in plain view. Even as our image world expands at a profound rate, making us believe that every thing worth seeing is available to us, what sits in our blind spots may be more important than ever.

There is also a growing gap between what we think and what we say. Blindness and denial—personal and systemic—often stop us from speaking at all about race. What Toni Morrison once said of American letters is true for all civil discourse: "[I]n matters of race, silence and evasion have historically ruled."[9]

Almost two decades after Bill Clinton announced that he wanted to begin a national conversation on race, we largely seem to talk about race through shallow media spectacles. We make noisy ritual of rapidly shunting to the dim wings of the image-world celebrities who reveal themselves as bigots. At the same time, illusion, acrimony, exhaustion, indirection, and muteness describe the rest of our all-but-suspended conversation. We know what *not* to say to each other, but not what *to* say.

How did we get here? The story is not to be found in the faded glories of the sixties, but in the tumultuous decades that followed, not in the civil rights movement that rendered legal segregation obsolete, but in the story of the grand triumphs and crushing failures of the American multiculturalism movement that grappled with the actual segregation that remained, and in the tumult and ruins and visions of this era after multiculturalism, a history we seem to have forgotten we have forgotten. It is to be found in the flash and the half-light, the din and the silences of the eternal culture wars.

And so, although Obama's rise provoked this inquiry, *Who We Be: The Colorization of America* is not really about the man or the politician. It is about what has happened to the ways we *see* race in this country, how they have changed and how they have not. It is about the questions that have yet to be answered and the new ones that proliferate.

Who We Be spans the last half-century of American image- and idea-makers. It talks about some of their images and ideas, and the words spun around those American images and ideas. It is an admittedly unusual dub history—written to be complementary to, and sometimes intersect with, *Can't Stop Won't Stop*. It cannot be exhaustive, but it can be suggestive.

The book begins at the end of the civil rights movement when the Republicans' Southern strategy locked into place a politics of racial distancing. It discusses the rise and fall of the multiculturalism movement. It revisits the claims for representation and recognition, the debates about the nature and future of American culture. It examines how multiculturalism's animating ideas were acknowledged, adopted, and diverted by the market and the state.

The book then moves on to look at how demographic change has impacted American arts, cultural politics, and electoral politics. It asks: Why, after colorization, has racial and cultural inequality remained largely unseen and undiscussed? It asks us to consider the fate of this still emerging cultural majority, and the fate of the nation itself.

"Images transfix," Susan Sontag once wrote. "Images anesthetize."[10] They focus our attention, and they dissolve it. They reveal things and they hide them. Each image demands a frame, and the act of framing is also the act of discarding. The writing of history can be, in a sense, the curation of images, revealing the struggle over what will be seen within the frame.

I think there is a particular reason we need history, even recent history. In the United States of America, we still tend to begin each conversation about race as if it were new, from a willed presumption of what might be called racial innocence, as if we have lived nothing and learned nothing. We presume race and identity to be fixed, not subject to any past or any future, beyond interpretation and beyond change. For these reasons they reappear time and again as unknowable irritants to a supposedly settled present.

Writing about race in America must always be a labor of recovery and faith and—yes—*hope* against the spectacle of fear and the twilight of forgetting.

The story of the colorization of America is a story worth telling because, even as it reminds us that only a painful process of illusion-burning can bring us to see things anew, it also suggests our faith in democracy is renewable. And, finally, it is a story that—at least right now—cannot help but have fewer answers than questions. Perhaps in times of massive change like this, the questions, not the answers, are the most important thing.

After the 1992 Los Angeles riots, while the bulbs flashed and the shutters clicked and the questions fired like bullets, Rodney King blinked into the lights, confused. People watched him stutter on television and made fun of him. But for a moment he held his ground like some kind of a savant or prophet.

"Can we all get along?" he asked.

We could not answer then and still cannot now. King's question reminds us how inarticulate we can be when the subject is race. If race begins as a visual problem, how do we overcome our misrecognitions and blindnesses? How do we move toward recognition, honesty, empathy, and mutuality?

A book or a work of art—culture—cannot by itself change the world, but by asking the questions that matter, it might attempt to be an act of articulation against violence, both the brutal and the casual kinds. It might aspire to starting a conversation through which together we might find common meaning, and words that free.

Jeff Chang
Berkeley, CA; Stanford, CA; and Provincetown, MA
2006–2014

Let the nation and the world know the meaning
of our numbers.

—A. Philip Randolph, *The March on Washington
for Jobs and Freedom*

PART ONE

A NEW CULTURE

1963–1979

Morrie Turner at his South Berkeley studios 2009. Photo by B+ for mochilla.com.

CHAPTER 1

RAINBOW POWER

MORRIE TURNER AND THE KIDS

For all life seen from the hole of invisibility is absurd.

—Ralph Ellison, *Invisible Man*

The night of Barack Obama's presidential victory in 2008, the eighty-six-year-old cartoonist Bil Keane called his old friend Morrie Turner, a sprightly eighty-four years old himself. Turner was working on his strip *Wee Pals* in the office of his tiny bungalow in South Berkeley, leaning over his woodgrain, worn Leitz drafting desk, tracing and embellishing the pencil outlines in India ink on Bristol board. A *Law & Order* rerun played on his tiny black-and-white television, unwatched. For Turner these were familiar rhythms, warm comfort. At that moment the last thing he wanted to see or hear was the news.

Keane's strip, *Family Circus*, had launched in 1960, the year before Obama was born. Daily he drew the antics of his suburban children in a single round panel, each installment like a portrait-miniature of white boomer wonder years. Five years later, days before Malcolm X was assassinated, months before the Voting Rights Act was signed and Watts burned, his friend's strip *Wee Pals* debuted. Its launch made Morrie Turner the first nationally syndicated African American cartoonist. Turner's strip presented an urban, multiracial group of kids figuring out how to get along. Nothing like it had ever been seen on the funny pages.

Keane and Turner had formed their close bond as pacifist World War II vets on a USO trip to Vietnam in 1967. Keane would introduce a Black boy named Morrie into *Family Circus* at about the same time Charles Schulz added Franklin to *Peanuts*.[1] Both were tributes to Turner and, in the context of the comics, small acts of desegregation. Then Martin Luther King Jr. was assassinated on April 4, 1968. Cities were on fire. Blackness was suddenly in demand. *Wee Pals* went from six newspapers to more than a hundred. For Turner, success was bittersweet. Privately, he would say that it was guilt that got him into the papers.

The hopeful children of *Wee Pals* belonged to a gentler universe. They were a vision of a post-segregated American future that still seemed so far away. So even in the worst of times Turner would labor on, certain that it was the country that needed to come around to his kids' world, not the other way around. Was Obama's candidacy a sign that that day was finally coming to pass? People had begun using a strange word— "post-racial." Did it mean racism was over? Or just images of racism? Was the word just another form of denial?

Turner had told friends he was happy that Barack Obama was running, but he was terrified Obama would be killed while trying. And now on election night he was sure a Black man, even this one, had zero chance of becoming president. His friends had invited him to election-watching parties. Morrie declined them all. Work was a shield against despair. The night would end. The campaign would be over. The kids would go on.

But at 8:00 p.m., when the polls at the seniors' center around the corner closed and the festive whoops on the block began, Turner's phone rang. It would ring all night. Old friends wanted to share the breathlessness of the moment. Into the bright streets people were swarming, delirious with music and the suddenly cantering rhythms of history. There still were not the words for all the new images.

Bil Keane had called his old friend with congratulations. Through *Wee Pals*, Keane told Turner, he had helped set America on a path to this historic moment. Turner tried to find the words to reply. Finally, he said to Keane that it was only the second time in his life he had ever felt like an American. Keane was about to ask Turner what he meant, but he stopped.

He heard Turner sobbing.

THE ANIMALS AND THE KIDS

Like many other forms of American pop culture, comics arose partly from a potent brew of racial fascination, temptation, and debasement. In 1895, two decades before D. W. Griffith's *Birth of a Nation*, Richard Outcault's Yellow Kid became the first broadly popular cartoon character. The invention of the Kid probably owed something to Charles Saalburg's *Ting-Ling Kids,* who had debuted in color a few months before the Yellow Kid's first appearance. The Ting-Lings were "Chinese" only in the way blackface minstrelsy was "Negro."

As the cartoon scholar Christopher P. Lehman put it, the funnies relied on caricature and ridicule.[2] For Blacks in the late nineteenth century and most of the twentieth, that meant the antic humiliation of slaves, mammies, and Sambos; for Chinese, the exploitation of alienness. Cartoon Blacks and Chinese were not representations of blackness and yellowness. They were representations of whiteness—the laughs were found in what whites were *not*. Once real Chinese were legally estranged by the 1882 Chinese Exclusion Act, cartoonists could tame the strangeness left behind, transform the "yellow peril" into a Yellow Kid.

Outcault drew his boy with huge ears, buck teeth, and a big yellow nightie. The result seemed a refined Ting-Ling, a simplified Chinaman. Unlike the silk suits, the Yellow Kid's taut garment—which, because the boy also wore a pretty, vacant smile, doubled as a thought balloon—needed little detail. The shaved head[3] eliminated the mandarin hat and the Manchu queue. Slant eyes were replaced by round blues.

The Yellow Kid was alien, urban, loony, and instantly accessible. He became a killer app for the tabloids, helping elevate the reps and circs of both Joseph Pulitzer and William Randolph Hearst. Outcault's creation is remembered by history because he had gone beyond Saalburg's Ting-Lings. He had shifted the focus from what whites were *not* to what whites *were*.

The Yellow Kid put the bustle and thump of the streets of New York—where immigrant, white, and Black kids were beating out a new national language of play—right onto his nightie: "Dis is a new piece we're pla'in." Yet if street culture could sometimes be leveling, the emerging national visual culture was the opposite. In the 1896 strip "The Yellow Kid's Great Fight,"[4] a Black boy—drawn with a monkey face and round white lips—was knocked out by the Kid, then humiliated by a goat. By the final frame, the goat had taken the gloves from the Black boy—he had no name, was simply referred to as "dat nigger"—and the smiling Yellow Kid's nightie read, "Dat goat took my part cause I am a kid."

Whiteness was the power to define, appropriate, and transfigure. Relocation programs, forced-assimilation projects, anti-immigration laws, and court rulings on racial classification were about defining who could be white. Jim Crow was about defining who was Black—and so it was about who could not be white. In the popular culture, whiteness acted fluidly, displacing and absorbing all the strands of non-whiteness and finally masking itself, while remaining center stage. So in the funnies, over the next half-century, the little Black Sambos and whitened Yellow Kids disappeared, and in their place animals took over the show.

Strangely—or maybe not so strangely—this development was traceable to a singular trio of a mouse, a dog, and a Kat invented by a New Orleans-born, Los Angeles-raised biracial Black genius. George Herriman's *Krazy Kat*, which ran from 1913 to 1944, was a thoroughly American invention.[5]

Krazy was a black cat in love with Ignatz, a white mouse. Ignatz repaid that with bricks to the head, which Krazy took as signs of tender affection. The white Offissa Bull Pupp expressed his own love for Krazy by chasing down Ignatz and locking him up. It was almost like the Civil War restaged as a bizarre love triangle, full of desire and philosophy and race-bending and gender-shifting and broken English and brick-throwing—race and jokes and casual brutality whipping round in circles in a bright American desert of primary colors.

Herriman played with black and white, in life and in art. His grandmother was born in Havana. His parents were listed as "mulatto" in public records and his own birth certificate read "colored." But when he died, "Caucasian" was written on his death certificate. Before *Krazy Kat*, Herriman's strip *Musical Mose* wrung laughs from the ways a blackface Mose attempted to pass for white.[6] When he invented Krazy, Ignatz, and Offissa Pupp, he broke out of minstrelsy's conventions into something new—a quintessential American story of identity, with characters whose destinies depended upon each other, where all of the hurts and laughs came through intimate moments of recognition and misrecognition.

SYBIL   WELLINGTON   PETER   OLIVER   DIZ   RANDY

But the animals that followed Krazy, Ignatz, and Pupp, especially the cartoon ones, revived minstrelsy in new ways. Felix the Cat,[7] Mickey Mouse, and Bugs Bunny picked up the big eyes and lips, white gloves, and sideways grins.[8] This "blackface design," as Lehman calls it, was efficient. Inky bodies with big eyes eliminated the need for detail and provided instant comic context.

Many of the neo-minstrel animals were endowed with yes-we-can optimism and improvisational genius and, when sound—specifically the looney merrie sound of African American music—hit the cartoons, a whole lot of rhythm. Mickey was a corked-down jazz-age mouse. Bugs was a Brooklynized Br'er Rabbit.[9] When the animals appeared with Black characters, they appeared more human than the humans, freer than the freed. Eventually the animals also erased kids of color from the funnies page, except for a few remaining Sambo characters.[10]

Blackface design and neo-minstrelsy streamlined processes in another significant way. The whitened vaudeville mouse and the urbanized trickster rabbit shouldered the rise of industrial-era entertainment empires. If a national popular culture was forged in nineteenth-century minstrelsy, twentieth-century cartoon neo-minstrelsy helped propel the development of American visual culture.

CONNIE   JERRY   GEORGE   NIPPER   ROCKY

The *Wee Pals* gang. Art from 1973 King Features promotional brochure. Courtesy of Morrie Turner.

Rainbow Power: Morrie Turner and the Kids

CONFEDERATE FLAGS AND RAINBOWS

After World War II, NAACP protests against the major studios—Warner Bros., Walter Lantz, Paramount, and others—helped end the era of neo-minstrelsy. By the 1950s, Jackie Ormes was flipping Milton Caniff's flyboy adventure scripts with *Torchy in Heartbeats*, a strip featuring the Beyoncé-esque character Torchy Brown, in search of racial justice, hot fashion, and sweet love in faraway places. Oliver Harrington, whose comic-strip character Brother Bootsie was an ordinary Harlemite dealing with the follies of racism and protest, was fleeing the House Un-American Activities Committee to join expats like James Baldwin and Chester Himes in Paris. Ormes's and Harrington's works could be read only in Black newspapers.

Original art of the first *Wee Pals* strip, published February 15, 1965. Courtesy of Morrie Turner.

If such history felt weighty, Morrie Turner's characters shrugged it off. In the first *Wee Pals* strip, published on February 15, 1965, Turner introduced three of his principal characters: Randy, an Afroed Black boy in a smart cardigan; Oliver, a clean-cut, overweight, white Spanky McFarland preppie with huge spectacles; and Turner's alter ego, Nipper, the soul of the strip—a small, unathletic Black child possessed of a gentle trickster wit.

In Alabama, civil rights demonstrators were about to march into a month of deadly clashes with white supremacists and state police. But Turner drew—and would always draw—Nipper's eyes covered by a Civil War–era Confederate soldier's hat, the better to call attention to the boy's perpetual smirk. In that debut strip, Nipper spent the first three panels parading in front of Randy and Oliver waving a rebel flag. "Obviously," Randy remarked to Oliver, "American history is not a required subject of the kindergarten class."

In later strips, Nipper would learn about the Civil War. But he chose to keep the hat. "We pardon in the degree that we love," he'd tell Wellington, a mop-topped, turtleneck-sporting white kid.

The blackface animals were gone. Instead Turner drew kids—usually in midrun on the way to play—having profound discussions about race and community. Youth—as Alain Locke, the herald of the Harlem Renaissance and the savant of Black visual culture, had once put it—speaks for itself.

The ink on the Civil Rights Act had not yet dried. The Voting Rights Act and the Immigration and Nationality Act were soon to be signed. But *Wee Pals* already belonged to the future. Oliver introduced the neighborhood kids to each other. Here was Peter "the Mexican-American," George "the Oriental,"[11] Rocky "the full-blooded American Indian," and Randy, who, Oliver paused to note, was "a Afro-American, Negro, Black, Colored, Soul Brother."

"And what are you?" Peter asked Oliver.

"Very careful!" Oliver replied.

The expanding *Wee Pals* cast would include Ralph, an "Archie Bunker-type character" who served as a narrative foil, a deaf girl named Sally, and a fireball feminist named Connie. She tormented Oliver, because the only hole in his Berkeley-raised political correctness was his gender insensitivity. It was up to Sybil Wrights, a sensitive and sensible Black girl, to check and correct Connie's temperamental excesses.

When the neighborhood baseball team needed to come up with a nickname, the boys began arguing, coming up with names that might befit a sequel to *The Warriors*. George suggested "The Yellow Dragons," Rocky "The Redskins," Jerry "The Mitzvah Boys," Randy "The Black Bombers," Paul "The Brown Destroyers." It fell to Nipper to suggest the obvious choice: "The Rainbows." Jesse Jackson might have been taking notes.

THE VALUE OF HUMOR

Morrie Turner was born on December 11, 1923, the youngest of four boys. His parents had met in New Orleans, that first great continental city of miscegeny. His mother, Nora, had attended Southern University and worked as a teacher and a nurse. His father, James, shined shoes until he secured a job as a Pullman porter, working the line to Chicago. By the time Turner was born, they had settled in West Oakland, California, not far from the transcontinental railroad terminus.

Much later, television producers—led by a young exec named Mike Eisner who would go on to build a "Disney Renaissance" on cartoon films like *The Lion King*, *Pocahontas*, *Mulan*—began adapting *Wee Pals* into a cartoon renamed *Kid Power*. They asked Turner where he had come up with the idea. "I told them I lived it. West Oakland, believe it or not, because it was the Depression, it was totally integrated," Turner said. "We were all poor—yeah, ghettoized—but there were all the races there."

From his mantle Turner would pull down a photo of his 1929 kindergarten class at Cole Elementary. The sepia photo had faded, yet the picture bore more color than the American imagination could handle for decades to come. Among the thirty-seven children, there were seven Blacks; six Mexican Americans; two Chinese Americans; a Japanese American; and the Native American girl with the heart-shaped face, the object of his unrequited crush. Some held teddy bears or rag dolls. Three of them waved American flags. Turner pointed out the friends who took him to their Portuguese festivals, Jewish synagogue events, and Chinese lunar New Year parties. "You didn't know what the heck was going on, but you knew there was a lot of food there," he laughed.

While his father was working the rails, the boys ran to the park, played games, or headed to Yosemite Gym to box. His brothers were well known in the neighborhood; elders called them "the fighting Turners" with equal parts exasperation and bemusement. Morrie preferred spending time reading *Krazy Kat*, *The Katzenjammer Kids*, and *Terry and the Pirates*, and drawing imaginary friends. When he was twelve, he wrote to Milton Caniff asking for advice on how to be a cartoonist. Caniff answered with a letter that was six pages long, typed and single-spaced.

When Turner's schoolwork wasn't going so well, he dreaded the days his father returned from Chicago. In the middle of the last beating Turner received, the boy dove under the bed and scampered like a sand crab from one end to the other until his father was laughing so hard he gave up. "I learned the value of humor that day," Turner said.

War broke out. The Japanese American family across the street disappeared. Turner graduated from Berkeley High in 1942 and was drafted. On his way to Kentucky to join the 477th Army Air Forces Bomber Group, an all-Black unit that served as one of the feeders for the famed Tuskegee Airmen, he encountered segregated facilities. At the base, hostilities ran even higher. Turner had arrived shortly after the Freeman Field

Mutiny, a proto–civil rights protest in which Black officers desegregated a white officers' club. Over 160 Black airmen had been arrested in the aftermath, and two of the group's squadrons had been inactivated.

Assigned night duty after a full day of hard labor, Turner snuck a copy of Richard Wright's *Black Boy* to his post to read, and fell asleep. A white MP shook him awake, and dragged him into military custody. Turner was charged with neglect of duty. The white prosecuting officer was determined to make an example of him. Turner spent nearly a month in the brig at Fort Knox.

As he awaited his hearing, the army assigned decorated Black colonel Benjamin Davis to oversee the 477th in an effort to reduce racial tensions. Black officers now took leadership positions, and Turner's case was dismissed. But even under Davis's leadership, it became clear to the members of the "overtrained" 477th that they would not get a chance to prove their mettle overseas. Like hundreds of thousands of other African American soldiers, Turner never saw combat. Instead, his commanding officer assigned him to draw cartoons for the *Stars and Stripes* newspaper, a job Turner was happy to take.

When Turner returned home, he married his high-school sweetheart, Letha, and took a subpoena clerk job at the Oakland Police Department that allowed him to doodle through the night shift. He began selling his work to Boy Scout and baking magazines, then to a number of mainstream magazines. He seemed to be following the career of one of his heroes, the African American illustrator E. Simms Campbell.[12]

As his cartoons began appearing in *Collier's*, *Better Homes and Gardens*, and the *Saturday Evening Post*, he decided to quit his night job. But only *Negro Digest*, which made Turner a regular contributor, purchased his work that featured nonwhite characters. Inspired by Dick Gregory and Martin Luther King Jr., Turner wanted more.

One night Charles Schulz gave a presentation at a local cartoonists' meeting on the evolution of his strip and its characters. That night Turner went home and created Nipper and a Black version of Oliver, the beginnings of an urban *Peanuts* gang. Two Black newspapers, the *Berkeley Post* and the *Chicago Defender*, picked up his new strip, *Dinky Fellas*. Soon Turner realized an all-Black strip was not going to work. He needed characters of other cultures to complete the jokes he was writing. The revised *Dinky Fellas* became *Wee Pals*. When the tiny Lew Little Enterprises syndicate picked it up, Turner was forty-one years old.

Between George Herriman's death in 1944 and Morrie Turner's national debut in 1965, the industry and the country had changed. The comics business had become huge, the form had become standardized, and the content had turned conservative. Comic strips were decades behind the social mainstream. Turner was a middle-aged man in tune with the children of Chuck Berry and Little Richard. But the funny pages were less a mirror of the tastes of children than of middle-aged men.

"I went to a Boston newspaper, I think it was the *Globe*," Morrie recalled. "I showed

"Humor In Hue" from *Negro Digest*, February 1967. Courtesy of Morrie Turner.

it to the editor. He said, 'I showed it to some *Negro* people around here. They wasn't impressed.' I said, 'Why don't you try showing it to some *Black* people?' He looked at me like, What the hell are you saying to me? I shook his hand and I said, 'Thanks for your time,' and I left."

HOW IT FEELS TO BE AMERICAN

For most of the 1960s, Turner's best customer was *Negro Digest*, later renamed *Black World*. There, his *Humor in Hue* cartoons ran between discussions on the role of Black artists in American culture, essays by John Hope Franklin and John Henrik Clarke, and poems by Nikki Giovanni and Amiri Baraka. The strips reflected the sharpening militancy in Black America.

In November 1961 Turner had drawn a strip for *Negro Digest* in which a blond girl painted a Black boy's face white and then told him, "Now Mother won't forbid our playing together!" But by the end of 1966, Stokely Carmichael and Huey Newton had stepped onto the national stage and Turner was drawing a mischievous Black boy scaring the shopping boxes out of a white matron's arms with the whisper of two words: "Black Power!"[13] As the long, hot summer drew to a close, even Turner was losing his patience. Turner's strip for the September 1967 issue depicted a boy turning from a TV western to ask his father, "Why do they call it 'colored television' when there ain't *none* on it?"

Turner directed his swelling anger at those he felt were exploiting the issue of race: white segregationists, white admen, even Black nationalists. And in his rage he seemed to have gained a level of prescience. He drew a Black psychotherapist with an African American man clad in Nazi gear on the couch. The shrink remarked, deadpan: "Your case is destined to make psychiatric history." With that strip, Turner had anticipated by over three decades Dave Chappelle's pivotal "post-racial" skit, the blind Black white supremacist Clayton Bigsby.

His cynicism was peaking when the National Cartoonists Society invited him to join a four-week USO Thanksgiving tour to Vietnam. Police incidents had sparked major riots in the inner cities of Detroit and Newark. Nearly a thousand Americans and many more Vietnamese were dying each month overseas. Turner strongly opposed the war, and antiwar demonstrations were mounting. But over the protests of friends and family members he agreed to go.

Turner landed in Saigon with five other cartoonists, all of whom were also veterans. Three were pro-war, two others, Bil Keane and Bill Sanders, were also antiwar, a perfect pollster's sample. No longer a twenty-one-year-old private grounded in a segregated company thousands of miles from the front, Turner would finally see war up close.

The artists visited an airfield where operating tables had been set up. The units had been battling to take a hill nearby. They were on their third or fourth try. Helicopters buzzed in with wounded men, arms and legs and heads riddled with shrapnel or blown to bits, clothes ripped and stained with blood, screams piercing through the roar of the choppers.

The cartoonists moved on to the hospital, where they met with the soldiers, told jokes, and drew pictures of them—soldiers' wheelchairs transformed into baby carriages with helicopter blades carrying them away. They would spend the next four weeks going through South Vietnam, dressed in army gear and combat boots like the troops, entertaining them. "You felt good about yourself," Turner recalled. "But honestly, what they had us doing was kind of stupid."

Turner was struggling to reconcile everything he was feeling. The South Vietnamese, he couldn't help but notice, were treating him with more deference than his white colleagues. "It had to have been my skin," he said. And what the hell was this war about anyway? They were *all* dying.

One afternoon Turner sat down in a quiet room to have a smoke. Nothing made sense, an unfocused rage was mounting, and he needed to clear his head. A white MP appeared. "You don't want to sit there," the MP told him. Turner bit down on his cigarette. He was almost twice the age he had been when he had been locked in the brig. He was not going down this road again. He glared at the MP.

"Why?" he asked, his back stiffening.

"Those are caskets," the MP said.

Turner sprung up and scanned the room—there were dozens of cordwood boxes, stacked three high. They were filled with the bodies of those who had fought and died and were going home. In his anger, pride, and shame, he realized that this was the first time he had ever felt fully American.

Turner wouldn't feel that way again for a long time. In four short months, his hero Martin Luther King Jr. would be dead. In seven, *Wee Pals*'s audience would increase tenfold. After that, Turner said, "I didn't know how to feel."

Racism, Albert Camus once said, is absurd. Chester Himes famously elaborated, "Racism generating from whites is first of all absurd. Racism creates absurdity among blacks as a defense mechanism. Absurdity to combat absurdity."[14]

THE KIDS GET COLORIZED

Above Turner's desk hung an original 1946 *Blondie* strip from Chic Young and an original 1965 *Gordo* strip from the pioneering Mexican American cartoonist Gus Arriola, gifts from each. Shortly after Turner's syndicated debut, Arriola decided to give the new guy some advice. He took a piece of tracing paper and copied Turner's strip. He placed big X's over all of the superfluous background Turner had drawn—the trees with their knotted bark and careful leafage, the picket fences to nowhere. Turner had wanted to impress his fellow cartoonists with his skill. But Arriola was letting him know to prepare to be doing this for a long time.

Hanging in the center of Turner's living room wall was a Sunday strip original of *Steve Canyon*, a December 7 memorial from 1969 that opened with a splash panel of an exploding Pearl Harbor battleship. It was a gift from Milton Caniff, the skilled draftsman and storyteller, one of America's most famous midcentury Orientalists, and Turner's early mentor.[15]

On one end of the wall was a 1966 strip from John Liney, who took over the duties of drawing Carl Anderson's bald-headed boy, Henry, after Anderson's death. In this strip, Henry is walking home when he passes a furniture store sign that says, "Add Some Color to Your Living Room." He encounters his father snoring in an easy chair. By the final panel, he has decorated his still snoozing father in an American Indian headdress. On the other end of the living room hung a single-panel *Graffiti by Leary* strip done by Bill Leary in the early Seventies. On a white wall someone has paint-brushed in black: "Morrie Turner Sees Everything in Black and White."

Turner actually found it vexing to move beyond black and white. The palettes for the Sunday color pages were constraining; only a pinkish tone was called "flesh." Presenting the skin tones of a polycultural cast, especially a range of Black characters, was a weekly problem. Nipper might be rendered in a muddy brown, Randy in orange, Mikki in purple. When Turner complained, the syndicate asked him, "Did you get your check?" Turner registered his protest in four panels. "Boy!" Oliver mused in the final one. "The manufacturers of flesh-colored Band-Aids would go broke in this neighborhood!"

The 1970s were about to begin. Sly Stone, the Bay Area flower child who had ooo-sha-sha'd about everyday people, was now singing "Don't Call Me Nigger, Whitey." In a decade, protests would break out in the Bronx over the movie *Fort Apache, The Bronx* and at a downtown Manhattan gallery against an exhibition of charcoal works called *The Nigger Drawings*, perhaps the Lexington and Concord of the multiculturalist art movement.

But in *Wee Pals*, Turner's vision of multiculturalism aspired to be patient, innocent, unhardened. He knew that casting kids allowed him some freedom. "If a Black *kid* was saying it, it was funny," Turner said. "But if a Black *man* was saying it, it would be fighting time." He drew five boys walking down the street, side by side, having this conversation:

Rocky: "Red Power!"
Paul: "Brown Power!"

Kid Power! paperback cover. Published July 1970. Courtesy of Morrie Turner.

Randy: "Black Power!"
George: "Yellow Power!"
Jerry: "Bagel Power!"
Randy: "Bagel Power?"

Most of *Wee Pals*'s punch lines hinged on cultural misunderstandings and mistranslations. But conflict could be defused by common sense and collective action. After one meeting of the neighborhood club, the boys counted their dues and decided to buy ice cream with the surplus. As they slurped up their reward, Diz, a Black boy sporting a black beret, kente cloth shirt, and Wayfarer glasses, said to the others, "There's gold at the end of Rainbow Power!" The idea seemed to migrate from the funnies into the movement when the Black Panthers, Young Lords, and Young Patriots announced a coalition of the same name in the summer of 1969.

By 1972, Turner had four top-selling paperback collections out and had attracted the interest of cartoon powerhouse Rankin/Bass and ABC. Suddenly there were writers, producers, voice actors, casting agents, Japanese animators, and lots of execs. There were recording sessions and toy deals and lunch boxes, an album and a stage musical, and trips to New York City for meetings in which he was given a seat at the table and the right to be ignored, which studio heads exercised often.

The *Kid Power* cartoon, named after one of the book collections, first aired on Saturday mornings in September 1972 on ABC, opposite Bill Cosby's CBS cartoon *Fat Albert and the Cosby Kids*. The cartoon lasted seventeen episodes before being canceled in an executive shake-up at ABC.

But the comic strip continued to be influential. To fill the extra space afforded by the Sunday strip, he and Letha began *Soul Corner*, a box devoted to documenting the lives of great African Americans. Turner had anticipated multiculturalism's obsession with positive representation and America's fetishization of diversity.[16]

His crossover success made him a minor celebrity. He accepted a proffer to serve on President Richard Nixon's White House Conference on Children and Youth. (It came not long after he published a cartoon in *Negro Digest* in which an Afroed woman looked up from her newspaper to ask her husband, "You mean President Nixon will only listen to me if I'm silent?") He often traveled with John Madden and Daryle Lamonica's Oakland Raiders. It was nearing the end of the era in which newspaper cartoonists were rock stars.

Soon, he said, "I was no longer alone representing the race." During the eighties, with the rise of multiculturalism, Black cartoonists made breakthroughs, including Ray Billingsley (*Curtis*), Robb Armstrong (*Jump Start*), and Barbara Brandon-Croft (*Where I'm Coming From*). All three had substantial success by *Wee Pals* standards. Both *Curtis* and *Jump Start* were featured in over two hundred papers, double the number *Wee Pals* had at its peak. Morrie's kids still dressed the same way they had always dressed, played the way they had always played, spoke about the things they had always spoken about. Turner finally felt free to be just a cartoonist, without the modifier "Black."

THE PRICE OF CROSSING OVER

In April 1999, Aaron McGruder, a prodigy from Maryland's Black suburbs, launched *The Boondocks*. In that uniquely hip-hop-generation kind of way, he seemed to want to impress people and piss them off at the same time. *The Boondocks* had one of the most successful syndicated comic strip launches ever, opening in 160 newspapers. But soon enough, some readers began complaining the strip was "racist," "angry," "gangsta-oriented garbage."

Six weeks after the launch, his modest Web site's guestbook had exploded in flames, with commenters debating interracial marriage, racial stereotypes, whether the strip was anti-white, whether it harmed Black children's self-esteem. McGruder seemed both satisfied and worried. He said, "I will regularly do whatever the hell I want to do."

But he also added, "You try not to let it affect your work. You hope it doesn't, but at the same time when you look at some place, like, damn, if I lose Chicago I lose three million readers on Sunday alone...." McGruder embodied the opportunity and ambiguity of the post-multicultural moment. When the *Chicago Tribune* and dozens of other newspapers dropped *The Boondocks* over reader complaints, McGruder was twenty-five years old.

Turner noticed McGruder's strips—as his had been—were meticulously plotted and lavishly drawn. He remembered the way white editors had regarded *Wee Pals* with disdain or disinterest, and sometimes disgust. He recalled how Caniff, Schulz, and Arriola had encouraged him. So he wrote a letter to McGruder to pass on the kind of advice he had once received. "Keep the faith," Turner concluded, his standard parting words to good friends. McGruder did not reply. Perhaps he was overwhelmed. Perhaps he was just busy. By the end of the year, *The Boondocks* had matched the readerships of *Curtis* and *Jump Start*. At its peak it appeared in three hundred newspapers.

In a time of turmoil, Turner's kids had been earnest and lighthearted. Their message was that everyone wanted equality, they could work it out, and no one need be uncivil in the process. McGruder's kids were products of the hypocrisies of a post–civil rights America, armed and armored with irony and attitude. Toward the failed promises of the civil rights generation and multiculturalism, the shuck-n-jive of hip-hop capitalists, the fake racial innocence of the nation, they declared their right to be hostile.

McGruder's kids lived in a suburb that had long passed the racial tipping point. But they were hemmed in by clueless white exurban America on one side and aimless mixed-up urban America on the other. Turner's kids had aspired to a dream of equality and harmony. McGruder's kids mocked the dream, but their bravado also seemed to mask a profound sense that something dear had been lost. What was the price of crossing over? More money, more problems, more confusion about those problems?

On a rainy evening in 2007, I was scheduled to interview McGruder before a standing-room-only crowd at San Francisco's Jewish Community Center. I brought Morrie Turner backstage so that they could meet for the first time. They greeted each other with a warm hug.

They had a lot in common. Both dressed like cartoonists—they seemed to have put on whatever wasn't stinking up the hamper that morning. McGruder, whose father was an air traffic controller, told Turner that he might have been a pilot had he not decided in high school to do comic strips. Although he had famously "censored" his own strips with "The Adventures of Flagee and Ribbon" to mock the jingoistic, patriotic fervor after 9/11, McGruder spoke passionately of wanting to work on George Lucas's then-long-rumored Tuskegee Airmen project, *Red Tails*. Turner took hold of McGruder's arm, telling him, "I was in the 477th." McGruder's jaw dropped.

Turner asked whether McGruder was bringing back the comic strip. It was a sincere question, but Turner may not have understood it was also loaded. No cartoonist had ever attained the kind of star status McGruder had. *People* magazine had named him one of the country's most eligible bachelors. In a Wolfe-ian *New Yorker* profile, he was portrayed as a latter-day Black Panther mau-mauing an audience of uptown white liberals.

In 2005, *The Boondocks* became the cornerstone of Cartoon Network's Adult Swim programming. McGruder had long fled his own Maryland boondocks for the twilight velocity of Los Angeles, where he kept an office full of Bruce Lee and Star Wars memorabilia and a staff of young hip-hop heads who helped him create his half-hour shows. When the TV series debuted, McGruder had already been subcontracting most of the artistic duties of the daily strip. In March 2006, the syndicate began reruns. By September, the syndicate announced that McGruder had ended the strip.

"Newspapers are dying. No one reads them anymore," McGruder told Turner. "I had to think about my career."

After our onstage interview, McGruder took a seat in the lobby to sign books and DVDs for hundreds of fans. Turner entertained a group of young Black and white cartoonists. As the lines wound down, I brought McGruder over and we snapped some photos for posterity. The two cartoonists clasped hands again. "Keep the faith," Turner told McGruder. Then he pulled his old body up, leaned on his walking cane, and started toward the parking garage elevator. McGruder slipped his hoodie over his head and stepped alone into the wet night to find the chartered limousine that would take him back to his hotel.

A year later, a dozen young Black, Latino, and white cartoonists—led by Cory

Thomas (*Watch Your Head*) and including Lalo Alcaraz (*La Cucaracha*), Darrin Bell (*Candorville*), and Keith Knight (*The K Chronicles*)—held what they called a "Sunday comics page sit-in," using their strips to protest the continuing lack of cartoonists of color in the newspapers.[17] After *The Boondocks* left the comics pages, a *Washington Post* Writers Group study found that of the 238 comic strips in syndication, only 17 were drawn by cartoonists of color or featured characters of color. More than three-quarters of the 1,413 newspapers surveyed did not run a single one of those strips.[18]

But McGruder surprised many by taking the side of the newspaper editors. He had always seen himself as a realist, not an idealist or a radical. "Despite the hurdles and the issues of race, I was given more than a fair shot," McGruder said. "It's like [the cartoonists are] the Black passengers on the *Titanic* protesting to get to the top deck, and overlooking the fact that the whole ship is sinking."

In 2003, when Turner turned eighty, he received a Lifetime Achievement Award from the National Cartoonists Society. It was not clear that there would still be a National Cartoonists Society when McGruder turned eighty. It seemed even less clear that the country might ever be able to discuss race in the way the *Wee Pals* did—with empathy, humor, and hope.

One summer day in 2009, over his favorite meal, a waffle at Lois the Pie Queen in North Oakland, Turner discussed whether President Obama's election had changed the way Americans saw race. He had been watching these screaming white protestors on his digital cable color television, but feeling like he was back in 1961. They didn't look so different from the screaming white protestors he had watched on his old black-and-white. He was thankful he had been able to see a Black man elected to the presidency in his lifetime. But what had changed? Was America still an ideal worth dying for, worth hoping for?

"It used to be that lower-class whites wanted to keep Blacks down because they had certain jobs that were theirs. But that's gone 'cause there's no profit in it," he said. "But yet prejudice still remains. Why?"

For almost half a century, day after day, Turner had drawn his children asking variations of the same question. What other question was so absurd, so rich in comic potential? What other question was there to ask?

Sunday strip, September 16, 1984. Courtesy of Morrie Turner.
The Mackites, of course, are the Oakland Athletics.

Rainbow Power: Morrie Turner and the Kids

CHAPTER 2

AFTER JERICHO

THE STRUGGLE AGAINST INVISIBILITY

I wondered, when that vengeance was achieved,
What will happen to all that beauty then?
—James Baldwin, *The Fire Next Time*

At the end of September 1956, the nation was still only beginning to deal with the impli-cations of the far-reaching *Brown v. Board of Education* decision, a Jericho moment when the walls trembled, made imaginable by the clarion calls from the culture: the Southern Black church, pop radio, the baseball diamond.

It would still be almost eight years before a civil rights bill would reach President Lyndon B. Johnson's desk. By then it was clear that even if "separate but equal" had been declared dead before the law, true integration would require much more. Culture would yet need to move the nation forward out of formal segregation toward its colorized future.

That future lay far ahead. At the end of September 1956, the young preacher Martin Luther King Jr. had been heading the tiny Dexter Avenue Baptist Church in Montgom-ery, Alabama, for only twenty-eight months. It had been only ten months since the local

←Previous page: *Die* by Faith Ringgold. American People Series #20. 1967.
Oil on canvas, 72 × 144 in. In the Artist's Collection represented by ACA Galleries, NYC.
© Faith Ringgold 1967.

NAACP chapter secretary, Rosa Parks, had refused to give up her seat on a public bus to a white man, the precipitating event of the Montgomery Bus Boycott. It had been just eight months since King had been arrested and his home bombed by white supremacists.

Boycotts were spreading across the South. Some municipalities were explicitly outlawing segregation, but Montgomery's white elite vowed to hold the line. King, as the head and spokesperson of the Montgomery Improvement Association, had suddenly become a national, even international, figure. He toured the United States to explain the Association's cause and raise money for their efforts, to tell the nation why he and the civil rights marchers found it "more honorable to walk in dignity than ride in humiliation."[1] So it was that King found himself the single Black passenger on an airplane flight to Norfolk, Virginia, on September 27.

When his connecting flight departed from Atlanta it developed generator trouble and was forced to turn back. King had begun a conversation with a white passenger, a moment that King found significant—two men connecting across the gap of segregation—and as they deplaned and headed back into the terminal they were informed that repairs would take three hours. They were handed lunch tickets to the airport's restaurant, the Dobbs House.

This concession was already notorious—its "Song of the South" theme was hard to miss. A portly, white-bearded Black man in an old suit sat out front next to a high bale of cotton, a low table set before him with a box of cigars and a dinner bell. His job was to greet guests, and sometimes entertain them with a tune or a tale.

A March 1955 issue of *Jet* featured a picture of this smiling "Remus Alfonso Smith" with a caption that concluded, "Negroes, using airport facilities during airport stopovers, have termed [this] sight 'disgusting.'"[2] When King retold this story to audiences, he admitted that it outraged him. "He's the symbol of a *dying off*," King would say, "an order which is passing away, and every time I look at him I see that."[3]

At the host area, the headwaiter separated King from his white companion and led King to a small, curtained compartment in the rear of the restaurant. Realizing what was happening, King declared he would rather starve than eat under such conditions. He went back to take a seat in the main dining room. There he waited vainly to be served. In the Dobbs House, King was no fearsome civil rights firebrand, the scourge of the racist white South. He was just another invisible man.

King grew angry. The white hostess was apologetic, declared herself embarrassed. Some of the Black waitstaff quietly told him they would serve as witnesses if he were to file a lawsuit. He went to find the manager. And this incident—which, by the standards of his community's fight to integrate the buses of Montgomery, was so small and insignificant—led to an epiphany for King. It became a central story in many speeches he would give in the years before the March on Washington.

The manager told King that he was bound by the laws of the state and the ordinances of the city. King argued that interstate travel had been desegregated, that the law required he be seated in the main room. But the manager still refused to budge. "We can't serve you out here," the manager told him placatingly, "but now, everything is the same. Everything is equal back there. You will get the same food. You will be served out of the same dishes and everything else. You will get the same service as everybody out here."[4]

"I know that I shouldn't get angry," King replied to the Dobbs House manager. "I know that I shouldn't become bitter, but when you put me back there something happens to my soul.[5]

Then he offered some cutting sarcasm. "Now I don't see how I can get the same service. Number one, I confront aesthetic inequality," he said, signifying on the Dobbs House's antebellum plantation chic. "I can't see all these beautiful paintings that you have around the walls here. We don't have them back there."

When King retold this part of the story, he raised roars of laughter. (We can only wonder what kind of racist kitsch decorated the Dobbs House walls.) But King was serious about aesthetic inequality. He had been profoundly moved by Mamie and Kenneth Clark's famous beauty-standard experiments, in which Black children, given a choice, had chosen white dolls to play with over Black ones. Even if *Brown v. Board of Education* had moved Blacks closer to formal equality, they were still far from realizing true equality in a society that remained culturally segregated.

"You see, equality is not only a matter of mathematics and geometry, but it's a matter of psychology," King told his audiences. "It's not only a quantitative something, but it is a qualitative something. And it is possible to have a quantitative equality and qualitative inequality."[6]

The impact of segregation, he was arguing, goes far beyond the reach of the law. The segregated is utterly dehumanized, reduced to the status of an object, "a thing to be used, not a person to be respected."[7] But the act of segregation distorts the vision of everyone living under its regime. It "scars the soul of both the segregated and the segregator," King said. "It gives the segregated a false sense of inferiority and it gives the segregator a false sense of superiority."

King had been forcibly separated from his white traveling companion and their entire conversation had been disrupted. He was left alone with the shames and rage borne of invisiblity. Separation prevented trust, reconciliation, and redemption. It denied the possibility of mutuality and the creation of a beloved community.

Through this experience, King would tell his audiences, he came to understand the deeper wisdom of the *Brown v. Board of Education* decision. "Segregation has always been evil," King would say, "and only the misguided reactionary clothed in the thin garments of irrational emotionalism will seek to defend it. Segregation is both rationally inexplicable and morally unjustifiable."[8]

King would not eat that afternoon at the Dobbs House. Not long afterward, he would again be refused service at the same restaurant under similar circumstances. By the start of the 1960s, Black civil rights leaders and attorneys were filing discrimination lawsuits against the chain that would finally prove successful. In the new decade, the Dobbs House chain would replace its zip-a-dee-doo-dah with "South Seas" exotica—tikis and rattan, leis and palms.

By then the civil rights movement had taken a turn toward fuller political enfranchisement. But past the strictures of de jure segregation, there still lay the actual facts of segregation, and that question was as much a question of culture as of politics, as much a question of cultural representation as of political representation.

IN THE WHITE GALLERY

Nineteen sixty-three was the year of the Birmingham campaign, the year the Civil Rights Act was introduced, and the year of the March on Washington for Jobs and Freedom. It was the year that George Wallace declared, "Segregation now, segregation tomorrow, segregation forever." It was the year that James Baldwin responded, "Color is not a human or a personal reality, it is a political reality."

In 1963, Faith Ringgold knew of only one Black artist, Jacob Lawrence, who showed at a gallery on East 57th Street, then the center of the art world. Yet Ringgold had made up her mind that she wanted to be regarded as a serious artist. So she and her second husband, Burdette "Birdie" Ringgold, packed up her still lifes and landscapes—her subjects then, she said, were "trees and flowers"—and went downtown to East 57th Street to see the gallerist Ruth White, who specialized in French-style works.

Ringgold had a way of dealing with life's obstacles. Her mother, Willi Posey, a fashion designer, had taught the asthmatic child to draw and paint, and reminded her that her grandfather, the son of slaves, had been a teacher. Once, Faith had asked her mother where all the young men coming out of the subway station at the end of her block in Harlem were going every day. She was told they were headed to the City College of New York, and the little girl made up her mind that someday she was going there, too.

When Ringgold enrolled there in the 1950s, she was told that the School of Liberal Arts's art department allowed only men to matriculate. Making art was not women's work. Teaching was. So she registered in the School of Education to major in art and minor in teaching. That was how she dealt with problems.

As the 1960s began, Faith Ringgold was an art teacher; a single mother of two daughters, Michele and Barbara Wallace; and now that the males-only rule had been rescinded, one of the first African American women to receive a master's degree in art from City College. In 1961, while in Paris with her mother and daughters on a failed search to find expatriate artists of the Harlem Renaissance, she decided making art was her life's work.

"I realized if that was true, I was going to have to give it all I had," she said. "Being a woman and being Black too was going to be a problem so I had better be highly focused. I had better be ready."

So there Faith Ringgold was in Ruth White's gallery in 1963. White looked at Ringgold's paintings—derivative of Picasso, the Impressionists, and the rest—and asked her, "Do you know where you are?"

Ringgold said, "Yes. I am on East 57th Street."

White said, "You cannot do this."

Faith and Birdie walked out of the gallery with the words ringing in their heads. *You cannot do this.* "What do you think she meant?" Birdie asked.

For years afterward Faith would speak of this encounter in present tense, as if it was still happening. "I'm on the line here," she would say. "I got to turn into a blues singer. I got to take that bad experience and turn it into something good."

"I think what she meant is, Here we are in the sixties, the beginning of the most challenging period of American history, and your future is on the line and you're painting still life and landscapes like you're a European person?

"That's what she means. You don't just become an artist to paint a pretty picture. It's a powerful way of documenting a time, a period, and a people."

"And so I said, 'Well, thank you, Ruth White. I really appreciate it.'"

THE SPIRAL

As the March on Washington neared, many of New York's leading Black visual artists—including Norman Lewis, Hale Woodruff, Emma Amos, Richard Mayhew, and Charles Alston—began gathering at Romare Bearden's studio to discuss the issues of the day: the American civil rights uprisings and the African anticolonial struggles, Negritude and nonviolence, African art and abstraction, what it meant to be a Negro and a Negro artist in that time.

With the exception of Amos, the entire group was middle-aged and male. Most had come of age with the Harlem Renaissance or the Federal Art Project of the Works Progress Administration. All were highly accomplished and profoundly overlooked. Norman Lewis had been a pioneer of Abstract Expressionism, was represented by the powerful Willard Gallery, and was recognized by Willem de Kooning and Ad Reinhardt as one of their most influential peers. But, the critic Elsa Honig Fine wrote, "At openings, the wealthy art patrons were more likely to ask him for a drink than to discuss his aesthetic theories."[9]

The group named itself Spiral, evoking, in Woodruff's words, "the Archimedean one;

because from a starting point, it moves outward embracing all directions, yet constantly forward."[10] It was an image of perfect, natural form: the embodiment of beauty, diversity, organicity, inevitability. Perhaps Spiral's name also reflected a kind of reclamation.

Ellison, a friend of Bearden, had his hero in *Invisible Man* warn, "Beware of those who speak of the spiral of history; they are preparing a boomerang." By the early 1960s, Ellison was writing, "American history is caught again in the excruciating process of executing a spiral—that is, returning at a later point in time to an earlier point in historical space," with the South as "the point of maximum tortuousity."[11] But by choosing this image, the artists seemed to suggest that if the forces arrayed against the freedom struggle wanted to plunge history downward and backward, Black art could help reverse that course. They envisioned a circular movement progressing upward to encompass the whole.

The group would never mold a manifesto. They were unable to adopt the kind of lockstep discipline demanded of their political counterparts in the civil rights movement. They had aesthetic and strategic disagreements, not to mention the usual cat-scratch of egos. But they understood that expression was the key for achieving self-determination, and that itself was worth the strife of collectivity.

At best they shared a desire to confront, as Ellison would write later of Romare Bearden's stunning post-Spiral collages, "a distorted perception of social reality," "a stubborn blindness to the creative possibilities of cultural diversity," and "the prevalence of negative myths, racial stereotypes, and dangerous illusions about art, humanity, and society." Ellison continued, "[T]he true artist destroys the accepted world by way of revealing the unseen." In the same way, Bearden and the Spiral artists would reveal themselves and their people not just through their unmasking of racial injustice but through their demonstration of artistic mastery. They would "bring a new visual order into the world."[12]

In 1965, Spiral opened a gallery at 147 Christopher Street where they mounted an exhibition of works executed in only black and white. The centerpiece was Lewis's *Processional*, a sweep of bold strokes of white suggesting marchers moving across the dark scrim of history, an advance of joy, hope, and progress. It would do nothing else of consequence. In 1966, the year SNCC declared itself the vanguard of Black Power, signaling a new era in which secular militancy would replace King's spirit-driven nonviolence, the gallery quietly closed.

PICTURING THE STRUGGLE

Spiral's significance was not lost on Ringgold. She had made it a point to attend every Black artist's show opening to introduce herself to all of her elders. "They would sort of thin out," she chuckled at the memory. "Like, 'Oh, here she comes. See ya later, man.'"

Once, when Ringgold asked Romare Bearden if she could come to a Spiral meeting, he politely brushed her off. "One day your art will find its own friends," he told her. Ringgold was disappointed. But, she said, "I needed them desperately. I was going to make sure that I had a connection with these people because I'd been deprived of any connection with Black artists."

Ringgold knew that they had been defined by their delicate dances on the razor edge of the color line. "They were struggle-bound. They were angry," she said. "They were afraid to be thought of as angry." She wanted to explore that emotional chroma, what had defined it, how it might be transformed. In the American People paintings she set out to paint that generation's painful racial drama in flat, depthless colors. *Between Friends* depicted a white matriarch staring mutely past an eager-to-please young Black woman, the personal made political.

By 1967—when, in an increasingly desperate urban America, it seemed that every stretch of hot weather and bad policing brought the threat of riots—Ringgold's canvases and ambitions had grown. On the wall-size *The Flag Is Bleeding*, she superimposed the American flag—"the only truly subversive and revolutionary abstraction one can paint," she had said—over a white woman linking arms with a Black man and a white man.[13] The stars partly hid the first, besieged man. He covered a stab wound with one hand and wielded a threatening knife with the other. The stripes were spattered with his blood.

In *Die*, the last painting in the series, a shocking race riot scene—its slashing, splaying bodies echoing Jacob Lawrence's Migration series *No. 52*—offered neither Blacks or whites respite from the violence. Nineteen sixty-seven marked the fiftieth anniversary of the East St. Louis riots Lawrence had painted, the year of the Newark and Detroit riots, and the year that Republican presidential hopeful Richard Nixon began voicing the desire of the "silent majority" for a return to law and order. Were hope and reconciliation even imaginable anymore? She called her style "Super Realism."

Color had long been an issue for Ringgold. At City College, she had caused snickering among her fellow students with her paintings of dark-skinned models. In the classical chiaroscuro method, lighter colors were supposed to convey light and foreground, darker to show shadow and depth. But in order to spotlight her dark-skinned subjects, Ringgold reversed the process. Her paintings looked inside out to her peers, who sneered at her work behind her back. But she knew from her experimentation that darker colors tended to reveal other dark colors better.

In her Black Light series, she painted six faces arranged from darkest skin to lightest and called it *The American Spectrum*, a sharp retort to the chiaroscuro tradition. The capstone of the series featured another flag. Hidden within its stars were the letters "DIE." The stripes reconfigured themselves into the word "NIGGER." She called this one *Flag for the Moon: Die Nigger*, and it preceded Gil Scott-Heron's recording "Whitey on the Moon" by just a few months.

These works finally secured her the serious attention from critics, peers, and elders that she had sought. Yet the paintings did not sell. "We want to see something that's restful and nice to the eyes," one man told her. "I don't want your painting screaming at me from the wall." But for Ringgold the history of art, the history of generations, indeed the history of America, was the history of lines drawn by color.

THE RISE OF THE SOUTHERN STRATEGY

In 1964, Democrats had controlled the South since Reconstruction. But in the debate over segregation, many Republicans saw an opportunity to challenge blue rule. The party's presidential nominee, Senator Barry Goldwater, had supported previous civil rights bills, a position in line with the Northern moderate leadership of the party. But by the summer, Goldwater had taken up the states' rights cause and voted against the landmark Civil Rights Act.

By adopting this position—that segregation should be determined not by the feds but by the states—they appealed to a broad front opposed to civil rights—from fringe-right extremists who believed the civil rights movement was a pro-Communist, anti-Christian conspiracy to working-class whites bitter that they had been forgotten by Northern cultural elites. This "Southern strategy" might lose them the West and parts of the North. But they might keep New England and the Rockies and parts of the Midwest, and lock up a "solid South" with the states of the former Confederacy, a coalition that might dominate for years to come.

At the same time, Alabama's segregationist governor George Wallace stormed into the Democratic primaries to run a three-state protest campaign. Only a month after declaring his candidacy, Wallace won 34 percent of the Democratic vote in the historically progressive northern state of Wisconsin. In Indiana, he grabbed 30 percent of the vote, and in Maryland, 43 percent. President Lyndon Johnson instinctively understood Wallace's appeal. He told his aides, "George Wallace makes these working folks think whatever is happening to them is all the Negro's fault."[14]

Johnson would be triumphant that summer. He secured the Democratic nomination, and on July 2 he signed the Civil Rights Act. Yet on the evening of his greatest legislative victory, he brooded. He told his aide Bill Moyers, "I think we just delivered the South to the Republican Party for a long time to come."[15]

The evidence would not be clear for another four years. On November 3, Johnson won 44 states and the District of Columbia, amassing a stunning 486 electoral votes, the most lopsided victory in the history of presidential elections. But for the next forty years, Johnson's premonition held stubbornly true.

By the time the 1968 election rolled around, Wallace's second presidential run—this time as an independent—once again forced the parties to align themselves in relation to the white backlash. Vice president and future Democratic presidential nominee Hubert Humphrey went to Georgia to take pictures with Lester Maddox, the new governor whose main qualification for office, historian Rick Perlstein wrote, "was having chased Negroes from his Atlanta fried-chicken emporium after passage of the Civil Rights Act with a pistol and a pickax handle."[16]

Richard Nixon had long aligned himself with the Republicans' Northern moderate leadership on the question of states' rights and the Southern strategy. His support for the 1957 Civil Rights Act had earned him the praise of Jackie Robinson and Martin Luther King Jr. But now that he was the Republican nominee, Nixon decided to reevaluate his stance. A twenty-seven-year-old expert in white ethnic voting patterns named Kevin Phillips played a central role in his rethinking.

Phillips's analysis was counterintuitive. Goldwater had secured just five states outside of his home state of Arizona, but they were Southern states that had been intractably Democratic for years: Louisiana, Mississippi, Alabama, Georgia, and South Carolina. In the memo that landed him a job with Nixon's campaign, ambitiously titled, "Middle America and the Emerging Republican Majority," Phillips argued that Goldwater's vanquishing augured Republican renewal.

Victory, Phillips believed, turned on mobilizing white working people. He called them "the great, ordinary Lawrence Welkish mass of Americans from Maine to Hawaii." They had once voted for the New Deal in order to direct their anger at economic elites. But amid this long economic boom, Phillips argued, they were now ready to target those whom they saw as *cultural* elites.

Who were these new elites? Northeastern liberals, the longtime enemy of George Wallace's imagining. In a piece for *Reader's Digest* drafted by his speechwriter Pat Buchanan, Nixon made his own case. "Just three years ago this nation seemed to be completing its greatest decade of racial progress," he said. "Why is it that in a few short years a nation which enjoys the freedom and material abundance of America has become among the most lawless and violent in the history of the free peoples?"

Race riots, he argued, were "the most virulent of symptoms to date of another, and in some way graver, national disorder—the decline in respect for public authority and the rule of law in America." Liberals had created a culture of "permissiveness toward violation of the law and public order."[17] The primary beneficiaries were the cultural elite's pet demos: baby boomer youths and minorities.

Race, and to a lesser extent youth, provided Republicans with a shot at complete national voter realignment, an enduring red majority. "All the talk about Republicans making inroads into the Negro vote is persiflage," Phillips would say. "From now on, Republicans are never going to get more than 10 to 20 percent of the Negro vote and they don't need any more than that."[18]

Only half-jokingly he told another reporter, "Republicans would be shortsighted if they weakened enforcement of the Voting Rights Act. The more Negroes who register as Democrats in the South, the sooner the Negrophobe whites will quit the Democrats and become Republicans. That's where the votes are."[19]

Nixon believed that people did not vote their hopes, they voted their fears. They liked to be flattered into thinking they were voting their principles. If white working-class voters feared that postwar wealth was being redistributed away from them to Blacks, the Southern strategy gave them a target and a justification.

In the spring of 1968 Nixon met with Senator Strom Thurmond and won the segregationist's support. As Thurmond assured hard-liners Nixon was really on their side, he worked on more moderate whites who found Wallace distasteful, but not his agenda. Nixon added a new line to his stump speeches. "At least half" of Wallace's supporters were not racist, he said, "A lot of them are just terribly concerned about the problem of law and order."[20]

The message to whites—which was meant, said one campaign strategist, to be stated "between the lines" and "in regional code words"—was clear as a kill.[21] Like Wallace, Nixon's agenda absolved whites of the sins of history, and restored white privilege. The difference was aspirational. By voting Nixon, they could show they were better than that old bellowing Wallace fool.

Nixon understood that in the long run he needed to change the entire civil discourse. The civil rights movement had reshaped the national conversation about race. It had begun to build a new cultural consensus that supported the exercise of federal power for racial and economic justice with a capacious morality. The Southern strategy was, by no means, a fait accompli.

In the beginning Nixon's "silent majority" was a theory in search of evidence. The writer Barbara Ehrenreich has argued that there was little proof of a massive white rightward shift during the late sixties. Indeed the period marked a high point of cross-racial labor organizing. Whites who worked in closest contact with Blacks did not form the angry core of Phillips's new conservatism—they were, in fact, the most disposed *toward* racial integration.[22]

But the media-awkward Nixon seemed to have his sweaty finger on the pulse of the media establishment, which had loudly discovered working-class white America.

Exposed first in Michael Harrington's *The Other America*, the white poor remained under-represented through the decade. "In the sixties, it was hard to find a blue-collar worker in the media at all," Ehrenreich wrote.[23] But by 1969, the media had bought Nixon's narrative, and an enduring blue-collar stereotype was born. She continued:

> Professional authority was under attack; permissiveness seemed already to have ruined at least one generation of middle-class youth. And so, in turning to the working class, middle-class observers tended to seek legitimation for their own more conservative impulses. They did not discover the working class that was—in the late sixties and early seventies—caught up in the greatest wave of labor militancy since World War II. They discovered a working class more suited to their mood: dumb, reactionary, and bigoted.

The mood was set at the top. Nixon told his aides, "You have to face the fact that the *whole* problem is really the Blacks. The key is to devise a system that recognizes this while appearing not to." Their job, he added, was to "get rid of the veil of hypocrisy and guilt and face reality."[24] Realignment depended on the right's ability to detach questions of justice from questions of race.

When Nixon spoke of law and order, Blacks heard unmitigated support for the same police who had fire-hosed civil rights protestors and brutalized their communities, whose protection of racist elites and indifference to basic dignities had helped fueled the rage of the urban riots. "I'm all for law and order," said one woman from the NAACP, "but he is trying to get the support of the white backlash people."[25] Nixon had a cool and ready response: "Law and order is not a code word for racism. Black Americans have just as great a stake in law and order."[26]

Meaning had slipped away. Everything was encoded. One could signal racial denigration and division in the same moment he denied he was doing so. In the years to come, it would be more difficult than ever to find reconciliation and renewal, to start a real discussion about race.

On November 5, 1968, seven months after Martin Luther King Jr.'s assassination had set off days of despair and nights of fire in the nation's inner cities, Wallace took the forty-six electoral votes in Goldwater territory, the heart of the Deep South. But Nixon ran the rest of the table from coast to coast.

His victory signaled that a major shift had begun. For marginalized minorities in particular, the state was shifting, as scholar Vijay Prashad would put it, from a responsive one to a repressive one. The Southern strategy would dominate national politics for the next forty years. Jericho had fallen. New walls had risen quickly.

But if Nixon was correct that his party's dominance depended on neutralizing a Black progressive agenda, the right would still need to address the cultural shifts that had made that agenda viable. It would have to somehow undo the puissant words of King, Ellison, Baldwin, Hansberry, and Hurston, silence the uniting sounds of Berry, Cooke, James, Robinson, and Simone, eclipse the penetrating images of Lawrence, Bearden, Saar, Douglas, and Ringgold. It would need to deconstruct the emerging language, aurality, and visuality of race. During the post–civil rights era, battle lines would increasingly move from the political front to the cultural front.

WHAT REMAINED UNSEEN

As the sixties roared to a close, Black artists were debating form, content, and social responsibility with increasing urgency. But no matter their politics or their aesthetics, they all shared the condition of invisibility and they were increasingly unwilling to tolerate this condition. They would no longer be unseen. They would demand recognition.

In October 1968, the Museum of Modern Art (MOMA) opened a benefit exhibition dedicated to Martin Luther King Jr.'s memory. But no Black artists had been invited. Only after community outcry were Faith Ringgold, Jacob Lawrence,[27] and a handful of others asked to participate. Their paintings were hung in a room away from the main show. Days later the Whitney Museum of American Art opened a major survey exhibition on painting and sculpture of the 1930s without any Black artists included.

Frustrated, the trustees of the new Black artist–focused Studio Museum in Harlem called an emergency meeting at the offices of *Artforum* magazine to discuss what to do. The curator Henri Ghent agreed to organize for the Studio Museum a show of Black artists from the 1930s—including Henry Ossawa Tanner, Lawrence, Bearden, and Woodruff. Dramatizing the Whitney's snub, the show would be called *Invisible Americans: Black Artists of the 1930s*.

But Ringgold felt they needed to go further. She argued to the meeting's attendees, "A public demonstration at a major museum protesting the omission of Black artists is long overdue in New York City."[28] On Sunday, November 17, thirty artists marched on the Whitney Museum, beginning two years of demonstrations against three of the most important institutions in the American arts.

Farther up Museum Mile, Thomas Hoving, the young Upper East Side-born, Princeton-educated director of the Metropolitan Museum of Art had announced a blockbuster exhibition called *Harlem on My Mind: The Cultural Capital of Black America, 1900–1968*.[29] Hoving's chief curator, Allon Schoener, would install multimedia "information environments" featuring six hundred photographs and slides,[30] films, and sound recordings immersing museum visitors in a simulacrum of Uptown. The real thing was just two miles up Madison Avenue, a world away.

Behind the scenes some Met trustees were loudly unhappy about the notion of doing a "nigger show."[31] But Hoving told a reporter, "We want to do anything we can to help whites understand more of what the black community's about."[32] Later in his memoir, he wrote, "Through 'Harlem,' the museum would pay its true cultural dues. It would chronicle the creativity of the downtrodden blacks and, at the same time, encourage them to come to the museum."

While the exhibition featured Black photographers, musicians, poets, and performers, it excluded Black visual artists. Instead the Met only allowed them a panel discussion. The politics of protest had only enabled this absurd arrangement: the artists' art could not be seen, but the artists could be seen talking about not being seen.

With Bearden moderating, they took the Met to task, discussing Ellison's other truism about Black invisibility: *they see everything and anything but me*. Jacob Lawrence said, "I don't know of any other ethnic group that has been given so much attention but ultimately forgotten."[33]

On January 16, 1969, the day that *Harlem on My Mind* opened to previews, the newly founded Black Emergency Cultural Coalition (BECC) began a picket in the gathering dusk at the base of the steps to the Met.[34] The Met protest made the issue of Black artists' invisibility an urgent topic among the art-world elite. The underground paper *The East Village Other* warned: "The art world is about to enter the stormiest period it has ever known."[35]

While the BECC was forming uptown, a multiracial group of downtown conceptualists who shared an interest in radical politics—including Carl Andre; Lucy Lippard; Hans Haacke; Tom Lloyd; and Ringgold and her daughters, Barbara and Michele Wallace—began the Art Workers' Coalition (AWC) downtown. Artists brought a wild mix of ideas to the open meetings. Some called for a copyright and royalty system that would allow artists to profit from auctions and resales of their work. One proposed that New York museum research departments be repurposed to serve the Vietcong army.

Finally the AWC chose the MOMA as its target for radical democratization. Some demands, such as support for fields like installation art or film, increased educational materials, community outreach, and free admission, would soon be accommodated. Other rejected ideas would take root later in alternative galleries like the downtown gallery Artists Space.

Still other ideas seemed too radical for the art world altogether. In April 1969, Tom Lloyd and Faith Ringgold wrote a letter signed by the United Black Artists Committee calling on the MOMA to create a Martin Luther King Jr. Wing for Black and Puerto Rican art.[36] Galleries had been reserved, they noted, for "the exhibition of Dutch, Russian, Italian, Austro-Germanic, and other ethnic and national contributions." Why not American minority artists? In advance of the Committee's first scheduled "evaluation tour," for which buses from Harlem would bring dozens of community members to demonstrate inside the museum, MOMA officials hurriedly installed paintings from Jacob Lawrence's Migration series.

The proposal for the wing fizzled, but two years of protest had made an impact. The 1970 Whitney Annual included Betye Saar and Barbara Chase-Riboud, the first Black women to be shown in the museum. The Whitney announced a show entitled *Contemporary Black Artists in America*—although when artists learned that a white male, Robert Doty, would curate it, they protested it, too. For the 1971 season, MOMA announced shows for Richard Hunt and Romare Bearden.

But the vogue for artists of color peaked. In 1969, Benny Andrews had told *New York Times* reporter Grace Glueck, "We're a trend like Pop and Op. We're the latest movement. Of course, like the others, we may be over in a year or two."[37] He was right. "Between 1966 and 1973 there were thirty major exhibitions of African-American art," the scholar and curator Sharon F. Patton would note. "The rest of the 1970s, however, were disappointing. There was less than enthusiastic institutional sponsorship of exhibitions, many galleries and artist groups dissolved, and artists often 'disappeared.'"[38]

In this the end of the 1960s was no different than the end of the close of the Works Progress Administration, the drying-up of a fertile field. "The more hell we raised, the more some people got their work bought, got inside, got their big show," Ringgold said. "But the history of this country, in respect to Black people, has been a series of backslidings." How might an integrated nation be imagined if much of it remained invisible? What would it take for the unseen to be seen?

SAVING AMERICA'S SOUL

Exactly a year before his death, Martin Luther King Jr. had taken to the pulpit of the Riverside Church in Harlem to deliver what would be one of his most excoriated talks, the very opposite of his "I Have a Dream" or "I've Been to the Mountaintop" talks, the "Beyond Vietnam" speech. King had decided to side with the antiwar movement, and in this talk, he meant to outline why he had taken such a controversial position, why he had chosen to confront "the fierce urgency of now," why "the path from Dexter Avenue Baptist Church … leads clearly to this sanctuary tonight."

Many people—Black and white—had told King that fighting to end the war would hurt the cause of Black freedom. King believed that they misunderstood the nature of the cause. The struggle against segregation, the struggle to end an unjust war, and the struggle against poverty were all part of the struggle for freedom.

When President Kennedy first focused on alleviating poverty, historians Frances

Fox Piven and Richard Cloward wrote, it was "a way to evade civil rights demands while maintaining Black support."[39] By 1967 all of the liberal commitments—to the poor, to African Americans, to people of color—seemed paper-thin. King had come to believe that liberal politicians were pitting jobs against civil rights, class against race. And the war loomed as the biggest threat to everyone's freedom.

At Riverside Church, King noted that President Johnson's War on Poverty had given way to the Vietnam War. He said he could not tell the young Black radicals to put down their rifles and Molotov cocktails for nonviolence if he did not oppose the violence America was inflicting on the world. More important, militarism was the "enemy of the poor." It was a "cruel irony," he said, that Black and white boys who would never attend the same schools together were being sent to kill and die together, absurdity taken to the level of a global tragedy.

"We watch them in brutal solidarity burning the huts of a poor village," he said, "but we realize that they would never live on the same block in Detroit."

He reminded his audience that the Southern Christian Leadership Conference had taken "To Save the Soul of America" as its motto. And he quoted Langston Hughes:

America never was America to me,
And yet I swear this oath—
America will be!

King called on the gathering to consider it the height of "compassion and nonviolence" to understand "the enemy's point of view, to hear his questions, to know his assessment of ourselves." And then he pushed them further, to reach for a deeper universalism. He asked Americans to consider the voices of a much different, more expansive silent majority than the one that Nixon claimed, one that extended to the world. Then he himself took on those voices:

I speak as a child of God and brother to the suffering poor of Vietnam.
I speak for those whose land is being laid waste, whose homes are being destroyed, whose culture is being subverted.
I speak for the poor of America who are paying the double price of smashed hopes at home and death and corruption in Vietnam.
I speak as a citizen of the world, for the world as it stands aghast at the path we have taken. I speak as an American to the leaders of my own nation.

These, King said, were revolutionary times. While there were immediate political stands to be made, conscientious objections to be stated, ceasefires to be declared, negotiations to be undertaken, and reparations to be made, these actions would not by themselves make a more just world. Nor would they be enough to cure the "deeper malady within the American spirit." King had come to see "racism, materialism, and militarism" as the forces driving the nation's march toward war. He said, "I am convinced that if we are to get on the right side of the world revolution, we as a nation must undergo a radical revolution of values."

From the early days of his ministry at Dexter Avenue Baptist Church to the night he took the pulpit at Riverside Church, King had called for nonviolence, not as a mere strategy for civil rights reform, but as the basis for this revolution of values. Nonviolence and redemption were the animating principles of what King called "the beloved community," his central unit of change. Undergirded by values like recognition, inclusion, and empathy, the beloved community would not seek peace through war, but peace through peace. Herein lay true freedom. Forging the beloved community was the beginning of building a new world.

"One day we must come to see that the whole Jericho road must be transformed so that men and women will not be constantly beaten and robbed as they make their journey on life's highway," he said that night at Riverside Church. "Our only hope today lies in our ability to recapture the revolutionary spirit and go out into a sometimes hostile world declaring eternal hostility to poverty, racism, and militarism."

Here was a higher calling for the culture, a muezzin's cry at dawn, the faint line of orange against the purple horizon of a new day. But in the thunder and bluster of the coming decades of the culture wars, it would go largely unheard.

From *Rainbow Power*, 1973. Originally published in 1971. Courtesy of Morrie Turner.

After Jericho: The Struggle Against Invisibility   **53**

Stills from "Buy the World":
Coke teaches the world to sing in perfect harmony, 1972.

CHAPTER 3

"THE REAL THING"

LIFESTYLING AND ITS DISCONTENTS

Every advertisement is an advertisement for success.
—Andy Consumer, from a 1925 magazine campaign to educate consumers
about advertising

From the turgid summer of 1971 through the terrible autumn of 1972, TV newscasts must have seemed unrelenting: millions marching to stop the war, prisoners attacked at Attica, the Watergate scandal and the Pentagon Papers, the Manson and Serpico and My Lai trials, guns in Munich, bombs in DC, and troops in Derry. Pain and hatred and misery. Where was the harmony, sweet harmony? It was in the ad-break, in a commercial for Coca-Cola.

The spot begins with a woman, eyes as blue as her tunic, lip-synching a strange lyric, "I'd like to buy the world a home, and furnish it with love." There is an even weirder second line, about growing apple trees and honeybees and snow-white turtledoves.

The camera pans across rows of young singers smiling with the rising sun—Spanish, Swedish, Nigerian, Nepalese, dressed in a dashiki, a kimono, a dirndl, a Nehru, a turtleneck. Together they lip-synch, "I'd like to teach the world to sing in perfect harmony." Each holds a green glass hobble skirt bottle in their right hand, one branded in English script, the next in Arabic, another in Thai. "I'd like to buy the world a Coke," they sing, "and keep it company." The camera pulls up to an aerial view, revealing two hundred singers aligned on a green hillside like an open fan, a youth chorus of the world.

"It's the real thing—Coke is," they sing in unison, "what the world wants today."

It was a sweet and earnest-seeming commercial that made no kind of sense. So Coke wanted to buy a home for the world? Who could sell such a home? Why was the home even for sale? Was it being foreclosed? Did snow-white turtledoves even exist? If you put the birds in the same trees as the bees, couldn't they get stung in their eyes and die? The most effective commercials are bound only to the laws of desire.

The commercial, first aired on July 8, 1971, had been conceptualized by Bill Backer, a McCann-Erickson executive who had been searching for a way to rebrand Coke. Backer wanted "a big basic idea—one that would involve the entire United States market for Coca-Cola,"[1] everyone regardless of race, color, class, or creed. The jingle he and his team wrote would come to be known as "I'd Like to Teach the World to Sing."

The campaign's code name was "Buy the World," the budget for this commercial alone was nearly $1.3 million in 2013 dollars, and through it Coke might have a shot at more than just glass-bottle redemption.[2] Imagine in a season of racial division, imperialist deception, capitalist malaise, and national despair the whole world gathered upon a hill sharing a fizzy brown drink. It might look like a picture of renewed American faith.

At the same time, Los Angeles radio DJ Tom Clay's six-minute version of the Burt Bacharach song "What the World Needs Now Is Love" was climbing toward the top of *Billboard* and a million singles sold. A French horn traced the melody. The all-girl Blackberries sang of love—not just for some, but for everyone. Then Clay added the sounds of a drill platoon and gunfire, Martin Luther King Jr.'s final "Mountaintop" speech, and raw broadcast clips from the assassinations of John F. Kennedy and Bobby Kennedy.

Clay began and ended the song with a clip of an interview with a guileless child:

Clay: What is segregation?
Child: I don't know what seggeration is
Clay: Uh, what is bigotry?
Child: I don't know what biggery is.
Clay: What does, uh, hatred mean?
Child: I don't know what it is.
Clay: Uh, what is, uh, prejudice?
Child: (Inhales) Um. I think it's when somebody's sick.

Maybe sugary sentiment really could conquer blood anxiety. But if Clay said that the world needed love, sweet love, Coke was saying that the world just wanted a cola. Buying a Coke was like buying the world shelter and peace.

The hilltop commercial was among the first that Coca-Cola shot in full color. More importantly, it was perhaps the nation's first colorized one—an unusual advertisement that admitted a possible multicultural future beyond whiteness.

THE LIFESTYLING OF AMERICA

Back at the beginning, when Coca-Cola had been first introduced in the late 1800s, it faced the question that would bedevil all marketers of the coming era of mass production: Who in the world would want this stuff?

Americans needed to be convinced that this brown sugary liquid was delicious, healthful, and quenching, better even than water. The copy for one 1905 print ad boasted of its attributes:

> It Relieves Fatigue and Is Indispensable for Business and Professional Men, Students, Wheelmen, Athletes. It Relieves Mental and Physical Exhaustion.
> Is the Favorite Drink for Ladies when Thirsty, Weary, Despondent.

But medicinal appeals could go only so far. By 1913, Coca-Cola was spending at least a million dollars a year transforming the word "refreshment" from an emotional state into a craved commodity.[3]

In Coca-Cola's early years, over seven thousand imitation brands tried to cut away slices of its massive market share. There was an Afri-Cola brand marketed to Blacks. And there was also a Klu-Ko Kola brand marketed not just to whites, but the apparently underserved hooded supremacist niche.[4] Advertising helped maintain Coke's status as "the universal drink," the market leader for racists, antiracists, and everyone in between.

Indeed it made Coke into a symbol of America itself—freckled Norman Rockwell boys, rose-cheeked Bradshaw Crandell girls, and jolly Haddon Sundblom Santa Clauses. According to legend, rum and Coke had been the invention of U.S. soldiers in Cuba in the early 1900s, who called the drink "Cuba Libre." A World War II soldier said, "If anyone were to ask us what we are fighting for, we think half of us would answer—the right to buy Coca-Cola again."[5]

As America ascended the world stage, the drink bubbled up with it. In 1945, the company sent representatives and large shipments of the product to the United Nations Charter meeting in San Francisco. During the Cold War, more copycat colas from Mexico to Germany folded before the imperial red American can. Coca-colonization broke through the Iron Curtain and disrupted Arab and Asian markets.

French and Italian leftists protested Coke as a symbol of Yankee hegemony. Guerrillas everywhere filled the bottles with gasoline, stuffed them with cloth, lit them, and flung them at tanks and government buildings—proto-IEDs called Molotov cocktails. One security-conscious company exec assigned to a volatile Latin American country was heard to say, "Coke bottles can be pretty bad in riots. They're such handy, wonderful things to throw."[6]

By midcentury Pepsi had emerged from the niche cola scrum as Coca-Cola's main challenger. It had come out of its second bankruptcy during the Great Depression, and survived through the Second World War by positioning itself kind of like crack, a low-price downmarket alternative—you could get twice as much drink for the same nickel. But after the war, price inflation forced Pepsi to compete directly with Coke.

The history of consumerism in communities of color is surprisingly tied to the history of aggressive second-place competitors. Like other future upstarts—Nike, Apple, Fox TV—Pepsi concentrated on the market leader's underserved segments. If at their peaks Reebok, Microsoft, and Coke advertised with broad appeals, challengers needed a different kind of approach. They experimented with the content of their ads and the structure of their staffing.

Pepsi began mixing old-school product-attribute marketing with what would come to be known as lifestyle marketing. Its agency BBDO designed ads that spoke less to what the drink offered—great taste and low calories—and what the drink did—quench, refresh, relax—than what the drink *represented*—status, leisure, modernity. In print-ad illustrations, gorgeous young couples mixed at cocktail parties or lounged beside resort pools. "You're one of the Sociables," the copy said. The company's new commercial jingle went "Stay young and fair and debonair / Be Sociable, have a Pepsi!"[7] Every laborer, housewife, and striver could buy this world.

In 1947 the company hired a pioneering group of young Black marketers.[8] Although the group was short-lived, its success was apparent. In parts of the South, Pepsi became known as the "nigger drink," a development partly explained by the fact that some of Coke's bottlers had long been aligned with White Citizens' Councils.[9] When African Americans began boycotting Coca-Cola for exactly this reason, the company's frustrated ad director, Delony Sledge, was heard to complain, "For God's sake, just let us go on selling Coca-Cola to anyone who's got a gullet we can pour it down."[10]

Belatedly, Coke enlisted endorsements from Satchel Paige, Floyd Patterson, and the Harlem Globetrotters.[11] But their marketing seemed careless and inconsistent. In the November 1959 issue of *Ebony*, a full-page Coke ad shouted "Coke with Franks!" and showed a white woman's hand pouring a glass in front of four different hot dogs. The copy offered up recipes for hot dog toppings and proclaimed unironically, "So Good in Taste... In Such Good Taste..."[12] How was this supposed to flatter African Americans?

In the same issue, Pepsi's ad depicted a young Black woman presenting a birthday cake to her friend's husband, flanked by her husband and his wife. The giftee stood mostly outside of the frame, but it was hard not to miss his presence: a Black man's single hand resting on a golf bag. "They do nice things for others," read the copy. "Have fun with The Sociables."[13] Pepsi had placed its product at the center of the post-segregated good life, heralding the coming triumph of segmented marketing.

Between 1950 and 1960, Pepsi increased its sales more than sixfold to $157 million.[14] Its ads seemed to be touching desires much deeper than comfort and distinction. In the February 1960 issue of *Ebony* an ad featured two well-dressed Black couples singing around a piano. The copy read "Have a Pepsi anywhere … at play, at home or at your favorite soda fountain."[15] On the first of that month, a group of North Carolina A&T students took seats at a Greensboro Woolworth's lunch counter to try to do just that. They were refused food and refreshments. Yet they stayed, holding the breakthrough sit-in of the civil rights movement. Suddenly the simple act of buying and sharing a soft drink in a public facility seemed almost revolutionary. Unlike Coke, Pepsi had positioned itself on the right side of history.

In its first major TV campaign, launched in 1963 just weeks after the March on Washington, Pepsi focused on Kennedy youth, the rising baby boomer generation. Here were fast, stylish young Americans zipping down Disneyland's Matterhorn or scootering through golden California hills—carefree, confident New Frontier optimists.[16] Shot with soaring helicopter cameras and zooming handhelds, framed askew and jump-cut like French New Wave, the commercials shouted excitement. "Come alive!" beckoned twenty-two-year-old singer Joanie Sommers, in a voice described as "like wind through sugar cane."[17] "You're in the Pepsi Generation!"

Coke responded with the bland slogan "Things Go Better with Coke," replacing the even blander "Be Really Refreshed." The admen at McCann-Erickson desperately wanted Coca-Cola to take on the Pepsi challenge. Bill Backer and Coca-Cola ad director Sledge often argued. "Let's not go back to defining what (Coke) *is*, 'the greatest taste ever known to man,' et cetera," Backer would tell Sledge. "Let's talk about what it does *for* people."[18]

A paradigm shift in the consumer economy had begun. Pepsi had staked its future on youth, women, and African Americans—vanguard buyers who embodied postwar optimism and the largest reserves of unmobilized demand. Meanwhile, Coke was still aiming for the median American—the white, middle-aged suburban professional, the mirror image of the image-makers themselves.

The main question the Pepsi Generation commercials answered was not "Why do you want this drink?" It was "Who the hell wants to be old?" A drink was now more than a drink. It represented a lifestyle. Pepsi sold drinks by selling youth, which was no longer a mere biological condition, but an emotional condition enabled by the products of youthiness. If you felt young and hip, then you, too, could enjoy "the official drink of today's generation."

Business scholar Stanley C. Hollander once asked, "Was there a Pepsi Generation before Pepsi discovered it?"[19] There was not. Lifestyle marketing was less about persuasion than seduction, less about necessity than aspiration, less about reason than mood, less about ego than id. It was about the notion that, in the words of one beverage industry insider, "We *are* what we drink."[20] Capitalism sped toward the twenty-first century on this closed logic: you are what you buy, and what you buy defines who you are.

Advertising would provide you with the signs needed for the making of you: your desires, ambitions, and dreams, the entire conscious and unconscious thrust—the styling—of your life. Bill Backer would later call the youths in his commercial "a chorus of a hundred I's wishing the same wish."[21] Consumerism would teach the world, harmonize the world, buy the world.

THE REAL (AMERICAN) THING

By the time that the Civil Rights Act had passed, Morrie Turner's *Wee Pals* had its national debut, and the United Farm Workers had begun its grape boycott, Coke was beginning to get the point. They still had a squeaky clean young singer named Anita Bryant as their "Ambassadress of Goodwill."[22] But they expanded their use of radio, print, and television spots by the likes of Aretha Franklin, Marvin Gaye, Diana Ross and the Supremes, and Ray Charles.[23]

More than just the consumer economy, the culture had shifted, and they knew it. On the day Martin Luther King, Jr. was assassinated, Coca-Cola president Robert Woodruff was sitting in the White House with President Lyndon B. Johnson. Immediately Woodruff arranged for Coretta Scott King to fly back to Atlanta on his personal jet.[24]

The sixties would soon be over, but not Coca-Cola's troubles. In Florida, Cesar Chavez and the UFW was striking its Minute Maid company over its poor treatment of Black migrant workers. Environmentalists were pushing Coke to recycle its bottles and reduce waste. The company was being targeted for doing business in apartheid-ruled South Africa.[25] Federal Trade Commission lawyers were charging the company with false advertising and antitrust violations. Ralph Nader was in Congress attacking the company for "pumping syrupy brown drinks into people's stomachs."[26]

But Coke's biggest problem was that the Pepsi Generation campaign had softened its hold on the leading demographic—the soft-drinkers of the future. After the "Things Go Better with Coke" campaign, Sledge began to trust Bill Backer's instincts. McCann-Erickson's market research had found—surprise!—that young boomers hated insincerity and inauthenticity. So they created a new campaign based on an old slogan from 1942, another war-torn year: "It's the Real Thing."

Conceived during the fall of 1968, the Real Thing commercials would incept the drink into a new dream of America, in which divisions between young and old, counter-culture and mainstream, Black and white, poor and rich, liberal and conservative had been resolved.[27] In this era of fragmentation and unrest, it was time for the universal drink, like Brand U.S. itself, to reassert some alpha swag.

McCann-Erickson went to an earlier grand dream of one America, the social realist vision of the cultural front, which had found expression through Franklin Delano Roosevelt's Depression-era jobs programs for artists. The Works Progress Administration and Farm Security Administration had employed virtuoso artists, writers, and photographers like Stuart Davis, Thomas Hart Benton, Orson Welles, and Gordon Parks. From Dorothea Lange's *Migrant Mother* to Zora Neale Hurston's collections of Black folklore, Social Realism advanced the themes of inclusion, struggle, and triumph that would come to be associated with the "American Century."

But Social Realism would be increasingly hounded and suppressed. Lange, whose government assignment had once been to create images that would support the case for FSA programs, now found her images of the internment of Japanese Americans being impounded by the army. Paul Robeson's promising radio, musical, and theatrical career was derailed. The long culture war that began with the formation of the House Un-American Activities Committee in the late 1930s, and climaxed with the Hollywood Blacklist—framed as a battle between capitalist democracy and New Deal socialism, national patriotism and Communist subversion—ended the high period of Social Realism.

Now at the start of the 1970s, McCann-Erickson was sending teams of photographers and art directors again into the great land. Their mission was to capture—or to stage—slices of American life far from the cultural battlefronts. The earliest Real Thing spots, which began airing in 1969, were montages of these images.

One Real Thing spot was called "Friendly Feelings," a subtle turnabout of that fog-of-war phrase "friendly fire." The images included teenagers taking a break from fixing a roof, a boy and a girl dancing in a wheat field, a young woman cutting her husband's long hippie hair. It included two close-ups of a Black family, a mother and daughter and a father and son, both parents enjoying a bottle of the brown sugary stuff. The jingle concluded, "Coca-Cola, it's the real thing, like friendly feelings."

Social realism had depicted images of everyday people to urge a better future. It moved the unseen into the frame in order to mobilize disenchantment with inequality. Capitalist realism reappropriated this radical act of seeing in order to induce trust and satisfaction. The idea was that all our aspirations could be contained within the frame.

Where Social Realism conveyed heroic struggle, capitalist realism traded in sentimental acquiescence. Here was what the anthropologist Renato Rosaldo had called "imperialist nostalgia," that condition "where the people mourn for the passing of what they themselves have destroyed."[28] Capitalist realism seemed to say, "Things have always been good. *We* have always been good." In this sense the notion was not very realistic at all. But it would become the sunrise gleam of Reagan's morning, the "living tapestry" of Thatcher's No Alternative, the abundant eternal Now of the End of History.

In the closing voiceover of "Friendly Feelings," a narrator declared, "A bottle of Coke has brought more people together than any other soft drink in the world."[29] Bill Backer and the young staff at McCann-Erickson finally were ready to meet BBDO's challenge. But they also seemed to want to address something deeper: what it meant to be an innocent American bumbling through a suddenly very big and dangerous world.[30]

In the early 1600s, Puritan leader John Winthrop outlined an aspiration for the new colony at Massachusetts Bay. He called upon New England to become the "city on a hill" of Jesus's Sermon on the Mount. As the 1960s dawned, John F. Kennedy revived the idea. Ronald Reagan later used it to exorcise the nation of the demons of that decade. American exceptionalism patinated into creation myth—baptismal, purifying, God had shed his grace on thee. "The eyes of all people are upon us," Winthrop had written. Everyone in the world wanted our lifestyle economy. We simply wanted to share it.

Walt Disney introduced his last great amusement at the 1964 New York World's Fair. With funding from Pepsi and using his latest "audio-animatronic" technology, he unveiled an exhibit featuring the children of the nations of the world. Early in its conception, Disney's Imagineers wanted to have the kids singing their nation's anthems. But Disney felt that the competing songs would turn the exhibit into a boat ride through Babel. Instead he insisted that each animatronic child be synched to a single jingle—born in America, sung first in English. So the songwriters came up with a melody and line that stood: "Though the mountains divide and the oceans are wide, it's a small world after all."

Now that the Real Thing spots had displaced crisis into opportunity, Coke might wed the genius of Winthrop and Disney. The next spot would be "Buy the World."

YO, WHAT HAPPENED TO PEACE?

It was Backer who first saw the outlines of racial harmony and world peace in a green bottle of brown bubbly sugar water. His epiphany, like Martin Luther King's insight into the evils of segregation, also came out of a disrupted airline flight.

Two weeks before the debut of "Friendly Feelings," Backer was on his way to meet his songwriting collaborators in London. But he found himself grounded by Heathrow fog at the tiny Shannon Airport outside Limerick, Ireland. Passengers, mostly high-maintenance business travelers, were forced to double up overnight at an overcrowded motel, a situation accepted mostly with reluctance and not a little petulant acting out.

The next morning Backer took a seat in the airport restaurant and looked at the crowd. The night before they had been at each other's throats. Now they were all conversing in English, laughing together. And they seemed to be drinking bottles of Coke. Backer was struck by the notion that Coke was "a tiny bit of commonality between all peoples, a universally liked formula that would help to keep them company for a few minutes."[31] He started scribbling ideas on a napkin.

When Backer finally met with his colleague Billy Davis—a songwriter from Motown who had been in the Four Tops—and the rest of his team, he said he wanted "a song that treated the whole world as if it were a person—a person the singer would like to help and get to know." He read to them what he had written on the napkin: "I'd like to buy the world a Coke and keep it company."[32]

Working quickly, they got British folksingers the New Seekers to record the song and brought it to radio. Coca-Cola's bottlers hated it, company president Paul Austin thought it was *too* sentimental, and listeners were unmoved. But somehow the agency prevailed in getting more money to turn the jingle into a television commercial. A young McCann-Erickson employee named Harvey Gabor suggested an idea for the "First United World Chorus" singing the song. *Medium Cool* director Haskell Wexler signed on to direct. They returned to England to shoot, a globalized production assembling the diversity of the Old World to comfort the anxious masses of the New.

London brought bad weather so they moved to Rome. This first shoot was a disaster, a telling one.

An Italian production company brought in 1,200 young extras from local orphanages. As the sun grew hotter, the orphans were kept locked in steaming buses. By noon the bored, parched teens were rocking the buses off their axles and wolfishly eyeing the big truck full of Cokes parked at the bottom of the hill. At the top, Davis stood on a conductor's ladder, struggling to teach the united world chorus how to mouth lyrics in a language many did not speak.

For the final scene—an aerial shot of the orphans cheering alongside the united world chorus—the teens were released from their buses. They raged loud and broad across the field. A beleaguered team of marshals finally corralled and herded them into place near the chorus. There the orphans took the glass bottles they had been handed and with an angry roar began flinging them at the director's helicopter overhead. Then they stormed down the hill toward the Coke truck and tried to overturn it.

Where was the harmony? It had been interrupted by a teenage riot worthy of Black Friday. Perhaps this, too, was what American exceptionalism looked like.

The next day Wexler, still angry he had nearly been toppled from the sky to certain death over a stupid Coke commercial, fled the set, never to return. With a different crew and production company, a much smaller cast, and a different Italian location, the spot was finally completed. The "Buy the World" commercial was released in Europe, mostly to indifference.

But in the United States the TV spot found huge success. Coca-Cola was suddenly flooded with letters of gratitude and requests for lyrics and sheet music. As Tom Clay's "What the World Needs Now Is Love" fell off the *Billboard* charts, two different versions of "I'd Like to Teach the World to Sing (In Perfect Harmony)" took its place. In the end both topped the charts not just in the United States but around the world, including Europe. America was still losing the war in Southeast Asia, but it was back to winning hearts and minds at home and abroad.

In 1939, near the end of the Great Depression, Coke had run print ads entitled "The drink everybody knows…" that collected illustrations of Americans at work and at play. There were airline pilots and stewardesses, young women shoppers, baseball-playing kids, courting teens, a homemaker, a snow-shoveler. Except for a smiling Pochontas-type Indian sharing a drink with a young little rosy-cheeked cowboy, all of the subjects were white. Each illustration represented a frontier closed and a market opened. Together they pointed forward toward the affluent society and Kennedy's suburban New Frontier.

At the start of the 1970s, at the end of the long postwar boom, "Buy the World" pictured the last frontier. Each smiling young person on the Italian hill—marked by their race, nation, and culture—held a market in their hand. It was a primitive picture, to be sure, a couple hundred smiling stereotypes, a stock sheet of misrepresentations. But it was not dishonest. In the eyes of capital, nonwhites and non-Americans represented the last to be brought inside, organized, harmonized. What else did it care for representation?

Here was a plausible capitalist realist narrative of multiculturalism. As the American Century roared to a close, capitalism's destiny would belong to identity. "Buy the World" had stumbled upon a key to unlocking not just for Coca-Cola, but all of American business, the young world of the coming Global Century. From capital's dream of one America, a New World Order might be born. But it would be decades before many realized that such a world was even possible.

From *Right On!*, 1971. Courtesy of Morrie Turner.

The Real Thing: Lifestyling and Its Discontents

The cover of Yardbird's 5th edition, 1976. Top row (L–R): Lawson Inada, Joe Bruchac, Victor Cruz, Alex Kuo, James Welch, Al Young, Neil Parsons, Mei Mei Berssenbrugge. Bottom row: Frank Chin, Phil George, Ishmael Reed. Cover image permission courtesy Ishmael Reed and Al Young.

CHAPTER 4

EVERY MAN AN ARTIST, EVERY ARTIST A PRIEST

THE INVENTION OF MULTICULTURALISM

I once leafed through a photo book about the West.
I was struck by how the Whites figured in the center of the photos and
drawings while Blacks were centrifugally distant.
The center was usually violent: gunfighting lynching murdering torturing.
The Blacks were usually, if it were aWn interior, standing in the doorway.
Digging the center.

—Ishmael Reed, *Mumbo Jumbo*

Multiculturalism—what a waste of syllables. The original idea had been: Third World
thieves looting the Western art temples to repatriate their stolen legacies and making

a party of it all, an ecstatic liberation dance heralding a prismatic future. At least that had been the way Ishmael Reed described it in his giddy novel-cum-manifesto, *Mumbo Jumbo*.

Neo-HooDoo—now there was a *real* fermented agave drink of a word. If U.S. history had been different, maybe the haters would have been talking about how Neo-HooDoo was assaulting the academic enterprise, insulting serious art practice, contaminating children's minds, segregating lunchrooms, and turning America into a Negro-Chindian-Mexifornia slum-country. Instead they had multiculturalism to kick around.

Might have been a good joke on them, too. Except that even when multiculturalism was young, wild-eyed, and dangerous, it seemed destined for bland respectability, stiff-necked formality, and a particularly unforgiving senescence—set upon by goons, abandoned by its BFFs, its kin and offspring publicly protective but privately embarrassed about how it had let itself go.

We might have blamed the Canadians. In 1973, just about the time that Bruce Lee and Bob Marley were going global, Canada got official, establishing a Ministry of Multiculturalism. It was a national imposition—unappreciated by right-wingers who saw it as a safe harbor for barbarians and by Canadians of color who saw it as just another government window. Nonetheless this little innovation put the Canadians far ahead of us, their unenlightened neighbors south of the border.

So in the United States, where racial history sometimes still seemed to hang like a tire necklace and whose official policy after 1965 on all matters of cultural equity began with, "Well, we'd rather not but…," it was up to the young, wild-eyed, and dangerous writer Ishmael Reed to be the first to suggest that this doomed-to-be-regrettable word maybe wasn't such a bad idea.

GAINING MY RELIGION

Reed himself had grown into multiculturalism, out of other things. In 1962, at the age of twenty-four, the prodigy—he had started writing poetry and journalism at thirteen—moved from Buffalo to Manhattan. He quickly became the consummate hipster, back when "hipster" was still something good, a one-man transfer station between the Black Arts movement and the East Village counterculture.

Reed joined Umbra, a collective whose eponymous magazine captured the energy of a new Black literary renaissance. He roomed on East 5th with Charles Patterson, William Patterson, and Askia Muhammad Touré, who were developing what they would call the "Black Arts aesthetic" and codifying a philosophy of Black Power they would introduce in a famous SNCC position paper. Reed developed close friendships with Joe

Overstreet, Amiri Baraka, Cecil Taylor, Albert Ayler, and Sun Ra. Langston Hughes published Reed's poetry and introduced him to the big publishers.

Later he moved to a swank apartment at 79 St. Mark's Place and hung out at Stanley's Bar, where he and Walter Bowart founded one of the country's first underground newspapers, *The East Village Other*. "I'd just read Carl Jung's introduction to Milton's *Paradise Lost*," he would later recall, "where he referred to Milton's Satan, the revolutionary Satan, as the 'Other.'"[1] Somehow it seemed perfect for one who would always find solace with cultural outsiders.

He hobnobbed with Norman Mailer, Brion Gysin, and W. H. Auden. He and his partner, Carla Blank, became fixtures of the counterculture. When Woodstock happened, he was one of a small number of Blacks name-checked in the festival program (the others included Sly Stone and Jimi Hendrix). But in later accounts the East Village of the 1960s would become associated with Andy Warhol, the Velvet Underground, and the Yippies.

"We get left out of history," Reed would note. "The whole impetus for the East Village renaissance in the 1960s was the whole cultural and political Black Power thing."[2]

Reed's notion of Neo-HooDoo began taking shape after he read a Robert Tallant book called *Voodoo in New Orleans*, pulp nonfiction issuing from the symbol-rich Tremé borderland that led him toward sustained study of Yoruba language and cosmology. Not long after he was dumbstruck by Joe Overstreet's painting *Hoo Doo Mandala*. In these circles and stripes of bright oranges and blues and deep violets, forming a bull's-eye canvas pulled taut with rope, was a whole worldview.

To the untrained eye, the painting might have seemed folkish, earthbound, Mondrian through a curved lens. But here was an entirely different art history. Overstreet described the color fields to Reed as "Ve Ve," "landing strips for *loas*," the saints of Haitian syncretism.[3] Reed began to see the links between African religion—*vodun*, *santéria*, *macumba*, and *candomblé*, African American hoodoo—and the absorptive, protean creativity of Afrodiasporic music and art.

It suddenly seemed to him that all of American pop—its rhythms, its poetry, its swagger—descended from African and indigenous religion. If that were true, then perhaps the entire American tragedy of race had issued from the forcible suppression of such forms of knowledge and other more inclusive worldviews. Reed wrote a prose poem he titled "Neo-HooDoo Manifesto," 1,794 words of rapturous provocation limning the coming culture wars: uptight Christians and hidebound ideologues bent on closing the American mind in one corner, free practitioners of a forgotten faith opening up myriad new ideas for modern living in the other.

"Neo-Hoodoo believes that every man is an artist and every artist a priest," he wrote with not a little ambition, signifying on no less than Walt Whitman and his famous first-edition preface to *Leaves of Grass*. Reed concluded his "Black Power Poem" with the clang of the bell:

may the best church win. shake hands now and come out conjuring

Reed rendered the coming clash of civilizations not as a Samuel P. Huntington heaven-and-hell battle between the forces of light and dark, but as a sloppy cosmic tug-of-war between Funkentelechy and the Placebo Syndrome. His tour de force jazz-age renaissance noir *Mumbo Jumbo* and his early poetry collection *Conjure*—both published in 1972—were stuffed full of systems of thought, histories of knowledge, and aesthetic strategies that would not rigidly oppose European American norms as much as mock, humble, seduce, and jook them into awe, dialogue, or submission.

Mumbo Jumbo described the spread of a recurring epidemic known as Jes Grew, after James Weldon Johnson's sublime encapsulation of ragtime, a plague that largely took the form of spontaneous urban outbreaks of jazz and blues parties and dancing, "a Church finding its lyrics." This idea shared with the visual artists' image of the spiral a sense of organicity and inevitability.

It also smuggled in Ralph Ellison's idea about Black music's relation to time and space—that invisibility allowed one to slip down inside the break to take a look around. In 1972, Jes Grew indeed was back—rumba, samba, salsa, *nyabinghi*, New Orleans R&B, and soul were together locking into a new hoodoo moment: funk. When the scholar Rickey Vincent asked George Clinton what had inspired his P-Funk cosmology, Clinton turned the question back on him: "Have you ever read a book called *Mumbo Jumbo*?"[4]

Litany finding text—Neo-HooDoo was ancient but futuristic, African but expansive, connective and viral, spiritual, sexual, magical, and always unfinished. It was America.

ROOTING IN THE WEST

Reed would have to go west to have his own Neo-Hoodoo moment. By 1967, Reed had published his first novel, *The Free-lance Pallbearers*, to great acclaim, but feared the New York literary scene would kill him softly with an overdose of affection. Black Arts and Black Power made him cynical. "All art must be for the end of liberating the masses," he had the "neo—social realist" villain in his new novel saying. "A landscape is only good when it shows the oppressor hanging from a tree." He felt his former roommates had become separatists. Their writing merely served the new politics.

Reed thought to himself, "I want to go to the most primitive part of the country." So he and Carla packed their bags for Los Angeles. There in the shadow of the dream machines he completed this second book, a countercultural hurly-burly/hoodoo western called *Yellow Back Radio Broke-Down*. One day as he walked down from his apartment to the Echo Park library—who walked in LA?—he was surrounded by a small army of

LAPD officers. They had taken the suspicious Black pedestrian's writing notebooks for women's purses.

In the wake of the Watts riots, Alonzo and Dale Davis had opened the influential Brockman Gallery in Leimert Park to show African American artists and other artists of color, and C. Bernard Jackson had established the nation's first multicultural theater with his Inner City Cultural Center in central Los Angeles. The metropolis was a sprawling, combustible lab of political and aesthetic energy. But Reed was not yet ready for the emerging West Coast scene.

Instead he was soon lured north to Berkeley with the promise of a teaching job. The place was a perfect fit. The Bay Area was the last frontier of the visionary, the bold, and the weird. Here was where students had launched the Free Speech movement, where the Black Panther Party bought guns with money from the sales of *Quotations from Chairman Mao Tse-Tung* to college students, where Chinatown leftists battled the slumlords by organizing gangsters and artists, where Raza artists had repainted the Mission in the bright colors of *la huelga y la lucha*—the UFW grape boycott and the struggle, where the American Indian Movement had taken over Alcatraz Island, where students of color had launched their own cultural revolution.

Grassroots arts movements led by people of color were blooming across the United States, but nowhere were there the kind of proliferating, overlapping circles of artistic, political, and intellectual intensity that there were in the San Francisco Bay Area. These students, activists, and artists began with the act of naming themselves. They called themselves "Third World."

THE NEW COUNTERCULTURE

In 1967, the future novelist, poet, and playwright Jessica Hagedorn was a precocious teen rushing into the future, only three years removed from the mestizo suburbs of Manila but now deep in the Bay Area counterculture, hanging at the Grateful Dead house in the Haight-Ashbury or pretending to be a college coed at San Francisco State, smoking cigarettes on the quad and sitting in on the San Francisco Renaissance lion Kenneth Rexroth's poetry workshops.

After her father's extramarital affair was discovered, her mother had uprooted her and her two brothers from the Philippines and taken them to San Diego, then to San Francisco. She bought Jessica a typewriter, and allowed her to hang out with Rexroth and his daughter at their Haight district home, with its Cubist paintings, endless bookshelves, and its nonstop parade of visitors like James Baldwin and Amiri Baraka. Her brothers felt stranded in America. But Jessica fully embraced the new city—its buses, its bookstores, its bloom of freaks. "It was an adventure to me," she said.

She graduated from Lowell High School into the Summer of Love and moved across town to a cheap apartment on the Lower Haight because she hadn't been able to find anything in the white part of the Haight. While the national media hyped the appearance of gentle flower children, the counterculture was hurtling into darkness. A new guru named Charles Manson, just out of jail, had arrived on Haight Street with his retinue of female converts. "It got ugly fast," she recalled. "It wasn't about anything anymore but just good times and a kind of opportunism."

At the historically white institutions San Francisco State College and the University of California at Berkeley, young radicals of color energized by the Black Panthers' call to "serve the people" had formed a new kind of vanguard. They staked solidarity with the anti- and postcolonial leaders of the underdeveloped African, Asian, Pacific, Latin American, and Caribbean nations. They were colonial subjects within America forming their own movements for self-determination. Fanon, Guevara, Mandela, Neruda, Ho Chi Minh, and Malcolm X were their heroes.

They believed, as the American Indian scholar Vine Deloria Jr. wrote at the time, "The white man must no longer project his fears and securities onto other groups, races, and countries. Before the white man can relate to others he must forego the pleasure of defining them."[5] They were no longer Negro, Mexican, Oriental. They were Black, Chicano, Asian American. They would be the agents of their own freedom.

By the spring of 1968, the student of color organizations at San Francisco State formed the Third World Liberation Front. When the campus president suspended a popular Black lecturer in the fall, the Front began the longest campus strike in U.S. history, demanding the creation of a Third World College. By the end of the year, students at UC Berkeley and the College of San Mateo launched their own strikes.

The new Ethnic Studies programs at San Francisco State and UC Berkeley ushered in a kind of an intellectual renaissance. Afro-American Studies programs soon opened at Harvard, Stanford, Syracuse, Cornell, the University of Michigan, and other campuses in the wake of similar student protests. In segregated ghettos, barrios, and Chinatowns, young people of color set up storefronts for community organizing and arts projects. As the hippie counterculture entered its decadence, the new Third World counterculture was emerging.

By 1972, Hagedorn was all in, hanging out at the City Lights bookstore in North Beach, reading at the Blue Unicorn near the Haight-Ashbury, listening to Brazilian pop and free jazz at the Keystone Korner around the corner, catching film and theater at Project Artaud in Potrero Hill, digging the *muralistas* at the Galeria de La Raza in the Mission, sharing rough drafts and salsa dance lessons at the Kearny Street Workshop in the I-Hotel at the border of Chinatown, North Beach, and Financial District. Tiny publishers sprouted like poppies.

One night Hagedorn found herself at Glide Memorial Church, a progressive out-post in the Tenderloin, reading at a benefit for Chilean leftists. As she began, small on the wide stage under soaring rafters, before a standing-room audience filled with poets like Lawrence Ferlinghetti, Serafin Syquia, Janice Mirikitani, and Thulani Davis, she was nervous. By the end she had been inducted into the new scene. "Come to a meeting, sister!" a young writer told her. She wondered whether to call him brother.

From *Yardbird Reader, Volume 5*: "The Yardbird Krewe" making the scene in 1975.

The meetings were convened at Mirikitani's home and they produced Third World Communications, a collective of the daughters and sons of migrant workers and train porters and family farmers and shopkeepers and intellectuals, a group of artists deter-mined to advance a revolution of culture. In 1972, the collective produced an anthology, *Third World Women*, helping outline a new feminism that centered women of color. *Time to Greez! Incantations from the Third World*, an expansive anthology that marked the vitality of a movement of U.S. writers of color, followed in 1975.

It seemed the perfect moment for a cultural turn. With rising inflation and declining standards of living, the affluent society seemed a distant memory. Watergate and the backlash from San Francisco to Boston against busing fueled distrust in the state's ability to advance the fortunes of minorities. Rising unemployment and crime rates seemed to have become indexes of the failure of the political revolution.

So the artists turned inward. They rejected realism and dogma. They embraced the abstract, the disjunctional, the conceptual, the magical. They focused their rage on the structures of invisibility. They preached and practiced self-determination. The world revolution began with the personal revolution. Identity was their critical work. Their self-questioning turned rigorous, relentless.

Hagedorn asked herself: Didn't "Third World" signify something inferior? Why were her light-skinned Spanish relatives considered higher-class than her dark-skinned village-born grandmother? She had long discussions with Rexroth about race and American history. Was it true that Filipinos in the United States picked asparagus? That they had organized with Cesar Chavez? She wondered, how did people really see her?

It helped to try to figure this out together with others. Soon Hagedorn and Davis were helping their friend Ntozake Shange develop an experimental "choreopoem" play Shange was calling *for colored girls who have considered suicide / when the rainbow is enuff*. At Black Expo '72, they met Ishmael Reed and the poet Al Young.

MISSION IRRESISTIBLE

In the same year folklorist Alan Lomax, who had spent four decades recording the music of the African American South and the African diaspora, published a manifesto through UNESCO that he called an "Appeal for Cultural Equity." The problem of the era, he declared, was that cultural diversity had been put at global risk. "A grey-out is in progress," he wrote. "A mismanaged, over-centralized electronic communication system is imposing a few standardized, mass-produced, and cheapened cultures everywhere."

He called for "the principle of cultural equity," the protection, expression, and propagation of local, marginalized cultures. All culture was local, he argued, "Nations do not generate music." And local musics had deep importance to all of humanity:

1. They serve as the human baseline for receiving and reshaping new ideas and new technologies to the varied lifestyles and environmental adaptations of world culture;

2. They perpetuate values in human systems which are only indirectly connected with level of productivity, and they give women and men—old and young—a sense of worth;

3. They form a reservoir of well-tested lifestyles out of which species can construct the varied and flexible multicultural civilizations of the future; since they are living symbol systems, they have growth potential of their own. As such they are the testing grounds for the social and expressive outcomes of human progress.

Lomax argued that the best way to foster the preservation and growth of local musics would be to provide these cultural producers with resources and "an equitable share of media time."

"Practical men often regard these expressive systems as doomed and valueless," he wrote. "Yet, wherever the principle of cultural equity comes into play, these creative wellsprings begin to flow again."[6]

Cultural diversity, Lomax was arguing to global leaders and thinkers, was every bit as important as biodiversity. Although he was not at all involved with the young counterculturalists in the Bay Area, he had perfectly described the founding notions on which they had built one of the most fertile cultural ecosystems anywhere.

Ishmael Reed and Al Young had founded a journal called the *Yardbird Reader* to "publish the finest work by Afro-American artists without regard to ideological or aesthetic affiliation." But by the second issue, they were championing the new multiracial counterculture. *Yardbird* featured Hagedorn, Shange, and Davis, as well as writers like Victor Hernández Cruz, Leslie Marmon Silko, June Jordan, Terri McMillan, and Frank Chin. With Reed's help, Chin, Shawn Wong, Jeffery Paul Chan, and Lawson Inada published *Aiiieeeee!*, the first anthology of Asian American writers.

Reed was captivated by the ardor in these bars, cafés, nightclubs, galleries, and black-box theaters, all these young voices eager to explode form, passionate to reveal the unseen and tell the untold. He knew what a movement felt like, and *this* felt like a movement. Why couldn't this movement transform the entire country? Just as ragtime and jazz had sprung forth from New Orleans, this latest outbreak of Jes Grew might spread across the country from the Bay Area.

Reed's friend, the writer Toni Cade Bambara, was telling her growing audiences in this nascent movement—becoming aware of themselves as they gathered in cafés and bookstores and lecture halls—that the work of the artist was to make revolution irresistible.[7] It had not yet been named a *multicultural* revolution—but there the word was, flickering like a grand yearning, a mass becoming, an end to the monoculture, the true arrival of a post-segregated nation.

And so Reed, an adept of the neological arts, plucked it down and put it into circulation. In a December 12, 1975 cover story interview of the *Berkeley Barb*, Reed announced the movement:

The multi-cultural movement is the movement of the Seventies. In the
Sixties you had the Black Arts group, which was very narrow and Black;
and the counterculture movement, which was very narrow and white.
Now you have the multi-cultural movement, which is mixed up. This is the
wave of the future for the whole country.[8]

An editor had inserted a hyphen into the word, as if to highlight how paradoxical it
seemed then to think of culture as *multi*. How could a culture—one that, by definition,
sought to melt, absorb, unify—be *multi*?

Reed was describing multiculturalism as the next step in the great American march
to freedom. The civil rights movement had been concerned with bringing down legal barriers to integration. The multiculturalism movement would concern itself with bringing
down cultural barriers. The turn from politics to culture would pivot around the concept
of difference.

Civil rights activists had attacked differential treatment under the law, the engine
of racial segregation and inequity. But multiculturalists believed that the play of cultural
difference might undo those same conditions. The law could set only the basic terms on
how we were to interact. The multi-culture was the place where we might actually create
a new nation.

In this context, the very notion of integration became something of a loaded word
for the multiculturalists. The central question in *Brown v. Board* had been, "[D]oes segregation of children in public schools solely on the basis of race, even though the physical
facilities and other 'tangible' factors may be equal, deprive the children of the minority
group of equal educational opportunities?" In arguing that it did, the Warren Court
argued that segregation always implied "the inferiority of the negro group." Formal integration had been delivered under the shadow of the white man's burden.

Integration meant one thing in education, public accommodations, and housing. In
culture, it meant another. It implied cultural inferiority as much as structural inequality,
unequal distribution of ability as much as unequal access to opportunity. From the majority's point of view, the new freedom afforded by *Brown v. Board* left a person of color with
a single option: assimilation.

But after the assassinations of Malcolm X and Martin Luther King Jr., after the cities
burned, after the white backlash and as benign neglect set in, many had come to agree
with Malcolm X's critique of the March on Washington from over a decade before. In his
November 1963 speech, "A Message to the Grassroots," he had said:

It's just like when you've got some coffee that's too black, which means it's
too strong. What d'you do? You integrate it with cream. You make it weak.
If you pour too much cream in, you won't even know you ever had coffee…[9]

These artists would never go back to that. In a brief, funny, but pointed retort to "'quali-fied' racial missionaries unmindful of booby traps in racist language" who had "begun to describe *Yardbird*'s projects as 'integrationist,'" Reed wrote, "[T]he super-race phase of American art, whether advocated by yellows, blacks, browns, or whites, men or women is through!"[10]

Instead, they would begin at the point where the law had ended and the multi-culture began. They would refuse the kind of integration that changed just the minority for the actual cultural exchange—"a fact of everyday ordinary existence in the complex civilization in which we live," Reed wrote—that transformed everyone.

The future of desegregation was not just about reaching mere numerical diversity. It was about fostering radical diversity, the wild protean sort. It was about what might flower when people could really meet across the lines. The cover of the fifth volume of the *Yardbird Reader*, rendered in day-bright Oakland A's yellow and green, featured the collective caught as they laughed at someone's wisecrack. They looked simultaneously hip and welcoming. In this colorized vision of American renewal, everyone could share in the joy.

At the end of *Invisible Man*, Ellison's nameless narrator had concluded, "Our fate is to become one, yet remain many—This is not prophecy, but description." Now Reed told his interviewer, "This country has a historical destiny to change the world. It started off as an experiment, and there have been a lot of setbacks, but I think it can work."

He said, "I think we can start a new culture...."[11]

In the coming decade this little avant-garde from the far Left Coast would no longer be invisible, would find its ideas taken up by intellectuals and a new generation of students, would be described as a new threat to the Union, a force that might bring down American civilization. In their name opponents would assemble to declare the opening of the culture wars.

But when Reed had wanted to announce the arrival of the American multicultural-ism movement outside of the West Coast underground press, he had to do it in the Paris newspaper *Le Monde* for the utter disinterest at home. Word of the big ambitions of this small group of dreamers had not even reached the other coast. Over a decade after the formal legal breakthroughs of the civil rights movement, there was still no national lan-guage through which to describe a post-segregated American future. Words still failed.

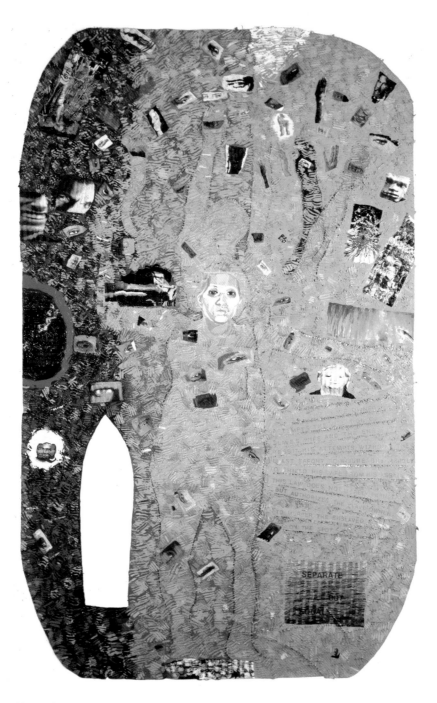

Autobiography: Water/Ancestors/Middle Passage/Family Ghosts by Howardena Pindell, 1988.
Acrylic, tempera, cattle markers, oil stick, and polymer on paper. 118 × 71 in.
Collection of the Wadsworth Atheneum Museum.
Gift of The Ella Gallup Sumner and Mary Catlin Sumner Collection Fund.

COLOR THEORY

RACE TROUBLE
IN THE AVANT-GARDE

What I'm getting at is that we're all more or less niggers and slaves,
teachers and students alike.

—Jerry Farber, *The Student as Nigger*

In February 1979, the downtown New York gallery Artists Space opened an exhibition featuring a group of young white postmodern artists that included a twenty-three-year-old who chose to use only his first name, Donald—as if, like generations of self-mythologizing young urban newcomers before him and since, he might rush into his American future by casting away his past.

His surname was Newman and he had come to the sooty punk streets of lower Manhattan from the crisply sodded suburban tracts of Southern California. He had been studying at the California Institute of the Arts, a short freeway ride from his family home, where the eucalyptus trees were still taking root in the Valencia soil and teachers like John Baldessari were still overturning received wisdoms. It was the tail end of the era that had produced the "CalArts Mafia," a clique of precocious alumni headed for super-stardom. Very quickly, Newman was accepted into the prestigious independent study program at the Whitney Museum in New York.

Donald was like a rocket launched at two. He arrived at Penn Station and headed straight to the front desk at Artists Space, where he name-dropped Baldessari and

CalArts and asked, "Do you have any place for me? I was told you would take care of me." That first night, he slept on the floor of the gallery.

He had arrived downtown at a splendid time. In the city, venues for young artists such as The Kitchen, PS 1, Franklin Furnace, and White Columns were springing up. Artists Space was a special nexus of fresh energies. When the nonprofit alternative space opened in 1973 on the northern fringe of Soho with funding from the New York State Council on the Arts, its mission was to allow artists of a new generation to introduce their unknown, unrepresented peers to the world. It would be streetwise, egalitarian; singular in the flood of new galleries, workshops, community centers, artist collectives, and museums surging against an art world, cofounder Trudy Grace said, "locked up and controlled by critics, curators, and dealers."[1]

Outside the galleries, Donald could hear the first screams of the new in bars, clubs, and galleries from the Bowery through Soho across to Tribeca. The first punks—as they came to call themselves—intended to defy all the gestures and conceits of the old countercultures. They were opposed to everything, even opposition. "Mass movements are so un-hip," said Legs McNeil, a cofounder of *Punk* magazine. Liberation movements were, he said, "the beginning of political correctness, which was just fascism to us. Real fascism. More rules."[2] Of his peers, Joey Ramone sang, "What they want, I don't know. They're all revved up and ready to go!"[3]

At night Donald began hanging in musty clubs and airy lofts. He wore bondage pants and T-shirts screen-printed with pictures of penises. He dyed his spiky hair blue. He found himself at parties with the Sex Pistols and he joined a girlfriend in a band that called itself the Erasers. They practiced in an old bank vault in the basement of the Fine Arts Building at 105 Hudson Street in Tribeca, where Artists Space had moved their gallery. Donald befriended the assistant director, Paul McMahon, a ferociously smart and witty artist, musician, and curator who bridged the art and punk crowds. McMahon agreed to visit him at his Whitney program studio.

Donald had been creating seven large triptychs, five feet high by seven feet long, combining black-and-white photography with charcoal drawings. He rendered these works in gray, black, and tan tones, and flush-mounted the center sections with plexiglass, a trick that mirrored back the viewer as much as it revealed the art underneath.

The images were indistinct, jarringly juxtaposed—a nighttime flash of brownstone windows, a forest and a creek starkly rendered in black and white, a fragile Ad Reinhardt shadow; aspens and abstractions in a bank of snow, a chimney blowing smoke into a dusk sky, thin lines arcing into an eclipse. Their large Rauschenbergian fields of light, dark, and reflection were alluring and distancing at once. They hoarded meaning.

At that moment in the small corner of the art world that McMahon and Donald called home, Conceptualism was still king. When the conceptualists emerged in the 1960s in an affluent society awash in material things and a global village aflood in images, they shared a fervent belief that art should be more than just seen. Some of them intended to save art by removing it from oppressive systems of war, racism, and capital, and transporting it back into the mind. They hoped to accomplish, as the critics Lucy Lippard and John Chandler put it, "the dematerialization of the art object."

Sol LeWitt distilled the movement into seven words: "Ideas alone can be works of art."[4] Art was not just about making things, but making things happen. Embedded in these ideas was the radically democratic possibility that everything could be art and everyone could be an artist. Conceptualism made it sexy to be smart again.

To the younger crowd, there were two kinds of conceptualists. John Baldessari represented the cool kind. He once assigned his students to fill gallery walls with the text—"I will not make any more boring art." In one of his works, *What Is Painting*?, he copied text from an instructional art manual: "Do you sense how all the parts of a good picture are involved with each other, not just placed side by side? Art is a creation for the eye and can only be hinted at with words." Here was a "painting" made with nothing but words, a picture of letters just placed side by side.

The other conceptualists were those whose ideas on power and liberation had led them to form alternative galleries like Artists Space. In 1969, Lucy Lippard's friend Carl Andre had called on fellow artists to free themselves from the capitalist imperatives of the art world, to withdraw their work from all galleries, museums, exhibitions, and commercial relationships in order to form a "true community of artists." Then in 1972, Andre made an installation entitled *Equivalent VIII*, consisting only of 120 bricks stacked on the ground, that he sold to the Tate in London for a large sum.[5]

McMahon didn't find this funny. He thought it was hypocritical. Even worse, these "rich Marxists" were now the ones keeping new artists and ideas under their thumbs. They were part of the old guard he wanted to overthrow.

McMahon and his peers had been the beneficiaries of a national expansion of collegiate arts programs launched to absorb the young baby boomers. They came from CalArts, the Whitney program, and SUNY Buffalo, where enterprising students like Robert Longo and Cindy Sherman had broken off to form the Hallwalls Contemporary Arts Center. They armed themselves with Baldessari's technique of appropriation, and applied it not just to the history of art but to the rising ocean of images in which they had been raised.

They were all revved up and ready to go. They didn't want bricks. They wanted the flood of stimuli, Pop with passion. They wanted their meta and their mystery, too. In 1977, Douglas Crimp—with the enthusiastic support of McMahon and Artists Space director Helene Winer—organized an exhibition at Artists Space called *Pictures*. McMahon and his colleagues would come to be called "the Pictures Generation." To them the history of art was the collision of generations.

McMahon knew that Donald Newman had a fine pedigree. And now in Newman's studio, blown through with charcoal dust, McMahon thought he might have that extra something else, too. Winer and McMahon scheduled a show of the young man's still unnamed works for the winter of 1979. What they liked about his works was exactly what they wanted Artists Space to be about. They were engaging and rough around the edges, fresh and inscrutable.

On the night of February 16, 1979, when Artists Space opened the doors to the young artists, there was a massive blizzard. From then to the end of the month nothing of note happened, not even any reviews. But what happened next became an odd augury for the coming decade, as if a small cast of close friends and colleagues at the outer edge of the New York art world were in a dress rehearsal for the national opening of the culture wars.

Perhaps an artist's greatest fear is to have his work go ignored. And perhaps in the era of punk upheaval the act of simply hanging these works in a downtown gallery and inviting visitors to contemplate their useless beauty seemed too easy. So Donald—a handsome young white man with a bright future—had chosen to call the seven pieces in his first exhibition *The Nigger Drawings*, and that's where all the troubles began.

PICTURES AND WORDS ABOUT PICTURES

About a month before *The Nigger Drawings* was to open, Ragland Watkins, who had replaced Paul McMahon as assistant director at the Artists Space, met with Donald Newman to prepare the announcement cards for his show. It was the first time Watkins learned that Donald did not want to use his last name and the first he heard of the title. "He said it was because it was about blackness," Watkins said. "I did question him a little bit about it. Not very aggressively."

Watkins had grown up in San Francisco with "a raging bohemian bar-owner, a wild crazy lesbian" for a mother, Peggy Tolk Watkins, whose Tin Angel and Fallen Angel nightclubs had been the hub for the West Coast proto-multiculti bohemia of the 1950s. Then he had moved to tiny McComb, Mississippi, to live with his father, a Southern architect whose work designing government buildings and Black colleges marked him as a liberal just as the civil rights movement was beginning.

In 1961, students at McComb's high school were jailed for supporting SNCC's voter registration campaign. The Ku Klux Klan began an intimidation campaign, forcing white civil rights supporters to leave town. In the two months after 1964's Freedom Summer, McComb saw a dozen racially motivated firebombings. "I knew the people who were doing the cross burnings, and I knew the people who were trying to put it all together," Watkins recalled. "I had a strong sense of race and words you do and do not say."

He told his boss Helene Winer that he thought they might have trouble on their hands. She felt that the title was stupid and Donald's dropping his last name was silly. But if that was what the artist wanted to do, so be it. "We were interested in freedom of speech," Watkins said. "I think she thought, 'Well, maybe it's shocking, but art is shocking.' We were supposed to be a cutting-edge space."

One day a reporter from *Art Workers News* called Watkins and asked him about the title. Watkins said Donald's drawings were an act of self-identification, "the portrait of an artist as a nigger."[6] He had overheard Donald saying to someone that the title had come to him because he was too broke to afford the materials to frame the pieces in the way they deserved, and he repeated that to the reporter.

But even as Watkins defended Donald publicly, he felt ambivalent. "There are words and then there are contexts," he said many years later. "There are no bad colors in the visual arts. It's only in combination, it's only in context they become disagreeable, and I think the same is probably true for words."

Paul McMahon saw nothing wrong with the title. "It was not a racist statement. Donald's not racist. Nobody at Artists Space is racist," he said. "What Donald did was that he exposed a generational rift."

Like Watkins, McMahon had grown up in a household with ties to the music scene—his mother had booked artists like Pete Seeger and Woody Guthrie. He had grown up in Cambridge, Massachusetts, as the only white kid at the Bobby "Blue" Bland shows. "I hung out with Black people and when I saw one white face in the mirror I was very angry toward that white face until I realized it was me," he said. "I had a self-hatred thing, and thinking I was Black was part of it."

Once he had aspired to becoming a lead guitarist in a rock band. But at Pomona College he took a jazz appreciation class with a young Black professor named Stanley Crouch who disabused him of the notion, told him that whites would never be qualified to play the blues. With that McMahon stopped playing his guitar and began focusing on art, leaving a largely Black world for a largely white one.

That was about the time he met Helene Winer. She was the only woman on the art department faculty, and was sometimes asked to pour tea for the male faculty members, an insult she refused. Winer had an uncluttered mind, a no-nonsense nature, and an affinity for young mavericks. She began to mentor McMahon, in whom she saw a gangly, gregarious, long-haired undergrad with a talent for finding where the action was.

After college McMahon started a wildly successful exhibition night at the modest after-school arts center where he taught in Cambridge, Massachusetts, luring big names like Sol LeWitt, Dan Graham, Laurie Anderson, and many of the CalArts Mafia to show their work and party. He had made fast friends of the like-minded self-starters from Hallwalls. In 1976, Winer hired McMahon at Artists Space. They committed themselves to showing young artists and questioning the organization's radical legacy.

At its founding, Artists Space had incorporated two Art Workers' Coalition demands that MOMA had rejected—the idea that artists should curate fellow artists and the formation of an artist registry, an open-source bank of slides of any artist who wanted to do a show, from which artists could democratically select shows. Both proposals were meant to break the exclusivity of the art world. In its early years, the system worked. Barbara Kruger, Jonathan Borofsky, Laurie Anderson, and Adrian Piper got early Artists Space shows, as did United Graffiti Artists, the first gallery graffiti exhibition ever.

Winer and McMahon hated this process. McMahon joked, "I was thinking of doing a show called 'Former Lovers, Relatives, and People I Owe Money To.'"[7] They felt Artists Space exhibitions often lacked coherence, context, and—what would soon become the art world's most loaded word—*quality*.

Reverting to the traditional selection process would break the power of the old guard, allow for more competition, and make room for the next generation. These young artists had, Winer said, "new ideas and that happy energy and ingenuity to get the job done without great financial demands."

Hallwalls's Cindy Sherman became Artists Space's front-desk receptionist. Others picked up odd jobs around the office. Soon they were helping consult on exhibitions and select artists for the shows. They felt like insurgents. They were helping move the center of the art world from to 57th Street to Soho.

On July 7, 1977, McMahon left the staff to focus on his music and art.[8] But he did not go far. He and his close friends had helped turn the Artists Space loft in Tribeca's Fine Arts Building into a floating world of shows, concerts, and parties. Susan Wyatt, the youngest staff member, remembered being thrilled that her circle of art-geeks had suddenly become so cool. She said, "It was kind of ridiculous and lame and we thought it was wonderful."

A POP HISTORY OF A TROUBLESOME WORD

In 1964, the comedian and activist Dick Gregory had written that he and his fellow civil rights marchers were trying "to change a system where a white man can destroy a Black man with one word. 'Nigger.'"[9] But Southern segregationists weren't the only ones with a fondness for the word. Northern antiracists and avant-gardists—from Harlem Renaissance patrons to the Beatniks to the White Panthers, from Carl Van Vechten to Allen Ginsberg, Norman Mailer to John Sinclair—had used "nigger" in a different way, to define their own identity politics. Were they doing this in poetic solidarity, a joining of arms for the battle? Was it racial innocence, a mask of cool bought at a discount?

By the early seventies, following civil rights activist and teacher Jerry Farber's galvanizing essay "The Student as Nigger," the underground papers were buzzing with manifestos for the "Hippie as Nigger" or the "Artist as Nigger."[10] As feminism spread, John Lennon and Yoko Ono wrote a song, "Woman Is the Nigger of the World," with no apologies to Zora Neale Hurston's character Janie Crawford's famous line, "De nigger woman is de mule uh de world so fur as Ah can see."[11] There would be Lenny Bruce, Ralph Bakshi, and Blaxploitation movies.

Downtown artists and Artists Space board members Vito Acconci and Dennis Oppenheim appropriated Black talk for the "authentic" soundscapes in their installation art meant to bring the street into the gallery.[12] When punk laureate Lester Bangs left the Motown of Berry Gordy and the MC5 for the Bowery of Richard Hell and the Ramones, he appeared in a black leather jacket and a black T-shirt with white iron-on letters that read, "Last of the white niggers."[13]

All this was part of a very old process dating back to when a scrum of rebel colonists stormed three ships in Boston Harbor, some costumed as Indians, some masked by lampblack, and proceeded to toss the cargo overboard. The Boston Tea Party was, the historian Philip J. Deloria wrote, "a generative moment of American political and cultural identity."[14] This righteous uprising, this spectacle of misrule, this first minstrel show was less a love poem to the Other than a romance of the Self—destroying, creating, breaking things open.

Two hundred and five years later, working-class heroine Patti Smith—her bandmate Lenny Kaye had said they thought of themselves as "the White Panther Party, New York Division"[15]—brought the romance to stomping, ecstatic heights. "In heart I am an American artist and I have no guilt," she howled on their 1978 album, *Easter*, as if in an amphetamine rush. The band then tore into their biggest anthem and as they squalled to a climax, she growled, "Jimi Hendrix was a nigger, Jesus Christ and Grandma too. Jackson Pollock was a nigger! Nigger niggerniggerniggerniggernigger nigger!"

"Rock N Roll Nigger" was the name of this song, burning on the righteous confusion of rebellion with rejection that had powered so much twentieth-century American art. For the white avant-garde, "Nigger" was the darkness at the edge of town, the last sign out of civilization on the highway to freedom. "Outside of society," she sang, "they're waiting for me!"

Donald loved the song. Perhaps it consecrated his newfound circle of punk heretics, sacralized his rebellion, his own freedom run. "Patti Smith talks about 'rock-and-roll niggers' and people call each other 'nigger' all the time," he said. "I was just using the word as poetry."[16]

THE LETTER

Two and a half weeks after the opening of *The Nigger Drawings*, on Monday, March 5, 1979, a letter arrived at Artists Space addressed to Helene Winer and signed by a cross-section of Black and white artists. It read:

> OPEN LETTER TO ARTISTS' SPACE
> A white artist exhibiting abstractions at Artists' Space from February 16 to March 10 has titled his show "The Nigger Drawings." We assume this was chosen as some sort of puerile bid for notoriety, but we are amazed that the staff of Artists' Space has lent itself to such a racist gesture. Surely it must have occurred to you, if not to him, that this was an incredible slap in the face of Black and other artists, of Black audiences and of everyone connected in any way with one of our leading alternative spaces. Did anyone object to these antics, or is social awareness at such a low ebb in the art world that nobody noticed? The appalling title is an abuse of the esthetic freedom artists allegedly enjoy in this society. We hope some sort of explanation from you is forthcoming.

At the bottom of the letter, Lucy Lippard had scribbled a note: "Helene—Sorry about this but *how* could it have gotten by?"[17]

Winer was stunned. She knew many of the signers very well. She was working with Lippard on a show of British leftist art. Carl Andre was an early Artists Space supporter. Faith Ringgold had shown there. Other Black artists had signed the letter—Black Emergency Cultural Coalition cochair Cliff Joseph, Tony Whitfield, and Howardena Pindell. Winer was most horrified that Pindell's name was on the list. She had thought of Pindell as a close friend.

The only daughter of a courts administrator and a teacher, Howardena Pindell had grown up in the segregated Germantown and Chestnut Hill neighborhoods of Philadelphia. Her parents—both of whom held multiple degrees—had started her in weekend art classes at a young age. A gifted student, she had graduated from her all-girls high school early, in part as an escape. "I would be held back from certain kinds of classes or have my artwork hidden when there were competitions," she told the art historian Kellie Jones. "I couldn't call that sexism."[18]

Pindell left for Boston University, where she won a scholarship and became the only Black student in the art school. "There was a very clear sense of what you could and couldn't do," she said. She could not share a dorm room with a white friend. She could not run for student office. She joined Delta Sigma Theta, a Black sorority. But she could not find relief there from her alienation. She became one of the top students in the art program. But a rich parent of a white student attempted to offer the school an endowment if it could convince her to leave the school.[19] Pindell cultivated her own solitariness.

After receiving her MFA from the Yale School of Art, Pindell began working at the Museum of Modern Art in 1967 and rose to become an assistant curator of prints and illustrated books. When the BECC protests began, she watched with interest, and through her friend Lucy Lippard quietly began attending Art Workers' Coalition meetings. When others realized that she worked at the MOMA and began to distrust her intentions, she stopped coming.

Pindell had met Winer when she was in London as a young museum assistant, and the two became fast friends. They were similar—brilliant, decisive, uncompromising. After Winer moved back to New York City to begin working at Artists Space, Pindell had subleased then eventually passed on her downtown apartment to Winer. Now Pindell was helping to lead the protest against Artists Space.

Pindell had become aware of Donald's exhibition through a young Black woman named Janet Henry. Slender and tender-eyed, Henry was about a decade younger, born to a family of artists. She had worked as education director at the Studio Museum in Harlem and then joined Linda Goode Bryant, who had established the Just Above Midtown gallery to show contemporary African American art. Teaching children to make art was Henry's greatest joy.

"How I conceive of the world—I realize it's kind of Pollyannaish," she said. "Why would you do things that are evil and mean to people? I can't fathom that and I can't understand people who do."

In January 1979, Henry received the announcement card for *The Nigger Drawings*. Staring at Donald's half-tone pine tree, trying to make sense of it, she became curious. "I looked at it and said, 'I wonder if this is a Black person doing something about *that word*,'" she recalled.

But when she visited Artists Space, Henry took in Donald's works with increasing anxiety. Here were images of a doorway, a nebula, an inverted upside-down scene of a man playing a trumpet for children on a boat, large dark fields of charcoal. What was Donald trying to say? Did he actually understand what the word meant? She walked over to her friend Cindy Sherman and soon the Artists Space staff had gathered around her. Why, she asked them, are these pieces called *The Nigger Drawings*?

Someone—she couldn't remember who—told her that perhaps it was because the artist liked to use charcoal and often got it on his hands and face. Someone else—she couldn't remember who—brought her pictures of some of Donald's other works. It was the thing artists might do for other artists in a gallery like this in the middle of a quiet, unbusy afternoon.

But Henry's head was already loud with noise. She could not process what they were telling her, what all these pretty pictures were for, why this wall in the main gallery of this downtown alternative space had the words "The Nigger Drawings" emblazoned across it. She left the studio gasping for air. She found herself in the subway, heading as fast as she could to West 57th Street to the Just Above Midtown gallery. Henry recalled, "I came in there babbling." Linda Goode Bryant got Henry to calm down and tell her story. Then Goode Bryant began making calls.

Pindell and Lucy Lippard began composing the "Open Letter to Artists Space." Henry and Goode Bryant initiated a letter-writing campaign to James Reinisch, the head of the New York State Council on the Arts. NYSCA still provided over 60 percent of Artists Space's operating funds. Under the name of the Black Emergency Cultural Coalition, the group that had protested the Met a decade before, they began to lobby NYSCA, whose members included Romare Bearden, and the National Endowment for the Arts to cut off Artists Space's funding.

By the end of the same Monday, March 5, that the Open Letter had arrived, Helene Winer had also received an urgent telegram from NYSCA:

WE WOULD LIKE TO EXPRESS THE COUNCIL'S DISTRESS AT THE POOR TASTE USED IN SUCH A CHOICE OF TITLES. WE BELIEVE ART SHOULD BRING PEOPLE TOGETHER AND NOT BE DIVISIVE AS SUCH TITLE BECOMES, PARTICULARLY SINCE IT IS UNRELATED TO THE CONTENT OF THE WORK.

(Signed,)
THE NEW YORK STATE COUNCIL ON THE ARTS[20]

First there had been the pictures. Then followed words about the pictures, hot with appeal, accusation, and outrage. All week the letters poured in.

Linda Goode Bryant wrote that the word "nigger" was simply the reminder of a childhood marked by "the stench of southern jails, cocked guns, dog bites, and the ever present red screaming cries of 'nigger.'"[21] In her letter to NYSCA's Reinisch, Janet Henry wrote as if she was also responding to Winer, Watkins, and Sherman in the way she could not when she was breathless in the gallery. "Alright, then," Henry wrote, "why not *Black Drawings*? Charcoal is black, uncomplicated, straightforward BLACK. The word Nigger is neither."[22]

Henry wrote that when she had stood in the gallery, she felt that "no matter how good you get, no matter how much you are needed, you ain't what we are and therefore will never drink from the same fountain we do. You will also put up with anything we choose to sling in your face."

She concluded, "Seems like somebody's asking for a fight."[23]

A RACE CONVERSATION, PART 1

Donald was unrepentant. He fired off his own broadside to the signers of the Open Letter, comparing himself to D. H. Lawrence, Henry Miller, and William Burroughs. He wrote in a third-person passive voice: "It would be presumptuous to consider that the artist's titling of his work 'The Nigger Drawings' was an explicitly racist gesture."[24]

But Winer removed the title from the gallery wall. Then she closed the gallery for a day, to give the staff a reset. Still, when they returned, the calls continued, the letters piled up. NYSCA and NEA officials were hinting that the organization's funding would be reduced. Board members were losing patience. The staff was fearful of Black protests. Winer had begun fearing for the organization's survival.

On the day the exhibition closed, she sent out a public letter of apology.[25] She then appealed to her allies to send letters of support to NYSCA and the NEA. She asked Donald not to make any more media statements. But when the *Village Voice*'s Richard Goldstein came calling, Donald gave an interview, telling Goldstein, "A lot of what fed this controversy is that my art is real. I'm not some punk who sat down and scrawled these things. There's an intelligence operating here."

"All you moralists," Donald said. "It takes an amoral kid like me to make things move."

Goldstein returned to his desk and pounded out a piece he called "The Romance of Racism": "The romance is that 'nigger' no longer refers to race, that anyone can be a nigger under the right circumstances and that artists—those jaunty explorers on the frontiers of consciousness—are niggers in spades."[26]

The article hit the stands three weeks after the show had closed, but the controversy was yet to crest. Twenty-four artists signed a letter to the *Voice*, including most of the original signers of the Open Letter; Benny Andrews, who had led the protest at the Met in 1969; and prominent artists Leon Golub, David Hammons, and Sol LeWitt. They accused Goldstein of falling for Newman's "self-promotion stunt."

"Typical of social practice in the art world, racism appears in chic packages," they wrote. "[M]any in the art world lull themselves into believing that *in an art context* racism isn't racism: it's art."[27]

THINGS FALL APART

On April 7, Newman responded with another public letter, all but naming Andre, Lippard, and LeWitt as aggressors on the wrong side of what he called an "artistic generation gap":

> It was these same people who, in the sixties when government support of the arts was being debated, warned against the danger of censorship; particularly with respect to any government programs designed to support and nurture the avant-garde. What happened?...

> I have the good fortune, if only by virtue of age, to be a product rather than a part of that art world whose processes have led these people to such a protest (against me). I am at worst a Frankenstein of it.[28]

Then he finally gave his explanation for the title. "To the degree that I consider that 'nigger' is a prejudicial term, my use of it in the title is a means of locating the viewer within the dichotomy that exists between the titling of the art and the actual content of the drawings." Newman had intended, he said years later, to "create something beautiful, place it next to something ugly, and stick the viewer in the middle."[29]

But *The Nigger Drawings* had succeeded only in dividing the avant-garde along racial lines. Publicly Winer backed Donald. "He felt [the title] had an esthetic complexity, it was metaphorical," Winer told the *Washington Post*. "I was surprised that everyone who was offended saw it only in the absolute, slur meaning."[30]

"At this point, 'nigger' is a broadly used adjective that no longer simply refers to Blacks in a pejorative context," she told Goldstein. "People are neutralizing language. These words don't have quite the power they used to—and that seems like a healthy thing."

Finally she nodded to the pop culture. "If anyone has perpetrated the use of that term, it's Black people. They can't use it to the degree that they do and then disallow its use by whites. I mean we do have some sort of culture exchange."[31]

Douglas Crimp, the managing editor of the leftist art journal *October* and the curator of the *Pictures* exhibition, argued that categorically calling any use of the word "nigger" was ridiculous. Worse, attacking Artists Space's funding was censorship "from those pretending to defend a liberal cause."[32] He said, "It's damaging to think about the political issues and not the work."[33] He circulated his own petition in support of *The Nigger Drawings*, free expression, and full funding for Artists Space. Laurie Anderson, Rosalind Krauss, and Roberta Smith signed on.

In an *Art in America* piece, Smith gave the art a favorable review. She wrote that

Donald's critics seemed to have an unsophisticated understanding of aesthetics. Worse, she said, they misunderstood artistic freedom.

"Certain opponents of the work's title have objected to its use by a 'white artist' in reference to 'abstractions,'" she wrote, "suggesting that it might have been all right for a black artist to have used it for nonabstract work. It is peculiar to declare a word off-limits and even more peculiar to declare it off-limits to some people and some work and not others. Making something taboo is, among other things, to ask that the taboo be broken." [34]

But the meaning of the words and the work, Donald's critics insisted, went beyond what was in the frames. "The decline of the civil rights movement in the 1970s has been accompanied by a resurgence of both covert and explicit racism," the art critic Alan Wallach wrote. "The style of our age is what the French unabashedly call *'le style ret-ro'*—a style with built-in nostalgia for the 1940s when whites ruled the world and blacks were kept in line with racist violence."[35]

The stakes were not only aesthetic, they argued, but structural. Their protest was about misrepresentation *and* lack of representation. The art historian Carol Duncan wrote, "This demonstration is about whose images become visible, not the freedom to make images."[36] Less than 4 percent of artists who had shown at Artists Space were Black.[37] A survey of forty of the city's most important galleries found that only 27 percent of the represented artists were women, 3 percent Asian, and 2 percent Hispanic. Less than 1 percent were Black.[38]

Artists of color were showing on the periphery of the art world: Linda Goode Bryant's Just Above Midtown on West 57th Street, Joe Overstreet's Kenkeleba House on the Lower East Side, Basement Workshop in Chinatown and Jamaica Arts Center in Queens, the Bronx Museum of the Arts, El Museo del Barrio in Spanish Harlem and the Studio Museum in Harlem. "The attitude was, 'Let's just do it ourselves,'" said Janet Henry. "The other part of that was white artists were saying, 'You don't belong down here anyway.'" Winer admitted to Goldstein that she felt unqualified to curate a show of artists of color at Artists Space.[39]

Given how deeply so many of the principals on both sides knew each other, the fight had become personal. "He wants intimacy," Howardena Pindell said of Donald. "I don't want to give him intimacy." She might have also been feeling the same about Winer.

Here at the far edge of mass consciousness, the dispute unraveled like a family clash—innocence and intimacy lost, small slights and major injustices accumulating unredressed, the staking of ground and the planting of flags, the messy collision of grand histories. No one could imagine how portentous it all would be in the end.

A RACE CONVERSATION, PART 2

In the handful of black-and-white pictures of the event that remain they appear, Black and white, sitting on the floor in a circle—fixed and intent and listening as if they are still connected by their debts to each other. But on the drugstore cassette of the event, their voices can be heard flaring, coarse and outraged.

The ballpoint scrawl on the tape label reads "Tape of Protest at Artists Space." It is somehow appropriate that this cassette and these pictures, kept by the Black artist and filmmaker Camille Billops, are incomplete, at best impressionistic.[40] Sometimes when Americans talk about race the images and the words refuse to correspond. History makes us heedless. Desire makes us deaf.

The moment is Saturday, April 21, 1979. In three years, downtown will become mythic Downtown, the sounds of hip-hop in strobing, miscegenating dance clubs that kiss the morning. But that point lies beyond the horizon, yet unimaginable.

Two weeks before, the Black Emergency Cultural Coalition had sent Artists Space a telegram announcing their intention to visit the gallery the following Saturday. They planned to conduct an "evaluation tour," the kind of protest that Faith Ringgold and Tom Lloyd had brought to the MOMA in 1969. Winer and the staff panicked. They sought counsel from board members. They sent unanswered telegrams to the Coalition begging for explanations. Finally Winer decided to lock the doors and stay home.

On the cold, rainy morning of April 14, the Coalition had arrived, choked themselves into the small lobby, and realized no one would be answering their door buzz. They moved out to the rain-drizzled street and the gathered media. Under a banner that read "Black Artists Locked Out of Artists Space," Benny Andrews, who had been born to a Georgia sharecropper, told the crowd, "I came from the South, where 'nigger' was burned into the skins of people who were lynched."[41]

So on the twenty-first, a few dozen protesters filed into the Artists Space gallery and arranged themselves in a circle on the floor. The staffers, reluctant and discomposed, followed Bob Blackburn, a former Artists Space board member and a Black artist who had signed on to the protest, into the gallery. There were graying men and young women, a mother with a baby, a few downtown journalists. Some supporters of Donald had arrived, too.

On the cassette, some voices are identifiable. Many more have been rendered faceless and nameless by time.

Blackburn opens the meeting by addressing Winer. "This is not an attack on Helene," he begins, in the etiquette of confrontation. He acknowledges that as a former board member, he should have remained more involved with Artists Space. But why, he wants to know, did she lock out the demonstrators the previous week?

Winer replies, "We couldn't get any answers from members of the Coalition as to the nature of the event."

"Why," Blackburn asks, "would a gallery like this fear people like us so much that they would think we would do something?"

And then, from the circle: *Why wasn't there an apology? Artists Space is an alternative space. You have a larger responsibility not just to this one artist but to the community. Do you show other Africans' work? Do you object to our objecting to this?*

Ragland Watkins wedges in a question: "What is the nature of the complaints?"

It wasn't so many years ago that they used to lynch niggers and that was considered OK. Would you have done a Kike show? How about the "Kike Drawings"? Is this indicative of the gallery's attitude toward minority artists?

As Winer answers the crowd quiets. "Well, it is indicative of our policy toward censorship and control of an artist's work and it certainly has nothing whatsoever to do with our exhibition policy in terms of who we show. If there's a particular show, we treat it the way we treat every exhibition that occurs here."

Pindell murmurs. Camille Billops is in disbelief. "You're not free to have a 'Kike Drawings,'" she shouts. "Artists are free to do anything in their studio but you know you can't do that with public funds because they come down on you. You just try to do that. You're full of shit. You know it. You know what power is."

"We did issue an apology," says Winer. "Apparently we made a mistake in a certain sense which was not anticipating what the response would be or how the feelings were. I'm saying that that is what is ignorance on my part or stupidity or a variety of things that you could call it, not to know what that would mean."

Her voice now wobbles with doubt, as if she has begun checking out of the conversation. The baby wails. The clamor rises. Finally the noise on the cassette recedes, clarifies into two voices—Winer's and a man's, white and Black.

Did you ever ask yourself how Afro Americans would respond to this? Be man enough to say damn it, I did it, this is what I feel, I know about you people, think what you like. And you think we're childlike.

"That is clearly not the case!"

What we've gotten so far is a verbal apology—which absolutely means nothing.

"Well what do you want? What exactly do you want?"

Because along with that apology the same practices, the same discriminatory practices still exist in this gallery that exist in the whole art system in this country. A truly constructive apology would be one in which you would consciously sit down and figure out ways to make this, truly make this an alternative space it's supposed to be, to truly address yourself to the question of Black artists. Then I might be persuaded that you were genuinely sorry.

A pause. The low hiss of the tape deck.

She nods. Perhaps she is agreeing, perhaps she is parrying. Maybe it is a reflex, a pulse of empathy or of loathing. It rankles him.

And this head-shaking nod—"Oh, I'm so sorry, we'll try in the future not to do it." You will *try in the future* not *to do* precisely *what you've been doing all along—which is* excluding *Black artists from a* dialogue.

Another woman's voice, coarse and petulant, issues from the bounds of the circle.

It's just a word.

Someone responds, *If you speak English you* know *what that word means.*

It could lose its meaning.

Someone asks, *What does it mean to you?*

The woman speaks louder, snarling and angry and low.

It's just what was lying around the culture.

The pitch of her voice rising, her words gathering velocity.

For you to tell me what it means when it's being used in so many contexts that I can't say it only means this and therefore it can't be used again....

Let me tell you what it means to Black people! It means castration. It means hanging....

This is not a Black community.

Another pause.

What? What did she just say?

She repeats, louder, with an edge.

This is not *a Black community.*

The din again. The voices.

Oh here we go. This is our *community! This conversation is over. What are the neutral meanings of "nigger"? What else can it mean but "nigger"? This is a multi, this is a multi, this is a multi...* The man wants to be heard. *This is a multiracial community, this is a multiracial* country *here.*

So what's the matter with using that term?

It's not our term it's your *term.*

No it's not my term! I didn't invent the fucking language.

It's not a Black-invented term, it's a white-invented term.

Who cares? WHO CARES?

We do! The community.

I'M NOT *trying to take responsibility for* ALL THIS.

▲

A week later, the Artists Space staff released its final public letter on the matter. "We wish to expand our programming to include more artists active in other communities. The way in which we can do this is to see more work or to have it brought to our attention," it read.

"Our concern is a result of an increased awareness that a large community of artists are not approaching us."[42]

Howardena Pindell, Camille Billops, and Benny Andrews went to Washington, DC, to meet with NEA officials to discuss the exclusion of artists of color from artist grants. They left with promises to increase the number of artists of color on peer selection panels.

Winer made amends with the NEA. She promised NYSCA that Artists Space would add more people of color to the board, meet with artists of color to increase representation, and do more exhibitions with other organizations in different communities. She hired the young Black artist Tony Whitfield, who said he had been an unwilling signer of the March 5 letter, to pursue artists of color for the program.

Ragland Watkins weighed the episode with a mixture of professional duty and personal regret. "We were very proud of what we were doing and we were doing a good job, and suddenly we fucked up," he said. The *Nigger Drawings* episode had brought him back to McComb, feeling stuck in the middle as history raged all around him.

"Coming where I came from, I believe totally in freedom of speech," he said. "But let me put it this way: I believe in good manners."

He reached out to Janet Henry and tried to convince her to do a show at Artists Space. Together they visited a movie set where Donald Newman was acting, perhaps to seek to some sort of closure. Henry thought he "looked like a junior executive on his day off," and decided she didn't want to meet him. Later Henry wrote a note to Watkins, thanking him for his courtesy and explaining why she could not in good conscience ever accept a show at Artists Space.

A month later, Lucy Lippard's exhibition, *Some Art from the British Left*, opened in the same gallery where *The Nigger Drawings* had shown. Of the seven artists Lippard had chosen for the show, four were women, two had recently been involved in a censorship controversy in a London gallery, and one was a Black artist prominent in the antiracist movement there. The title was spray-painted onto a wall near the gallery entrance.

Donald Newman, once the rocket launched at two, saw his career briefly ride higher. All the media hype had made him a minor sensation. By the end of the year, he had followed Julian Schnabel and Ross Bleckner to Mary Boone's gallery. Charles Saatchi bought three of *The Nigger Drawings*. Bruno Bischofberger exhibited him in Switzerland and bought more of his work. Newman then moved to Annina Nosei, the gallerist whose list included Keith Haring and Jenny Holzer and who once had the young Jean-Michel Basquiat in her basement painting canvases as fast as he could. Some in the Artists Space clique felt Newman was not getting attention for his work, but for his notoriety.

But as Schnabel, Basquiat, and Haring blasted off, Newman did not. Critic and gallerist Mitchell Algus wrote that the downtown art world had been invigorated by Donald's "reckless punk posture," a move that temporarily eclipsed "the earnest, mid-century obsessed post-conceptualism" of the Pictures Gen artists and challenged "the art world's newly evolving, ambivalently liberal, ethical order." But soon enough, when the art was separated from its title, Donald's work "began to seem thin and worse, mild-mannered."

Algus wrote, "Perhaps this is the inevitable fate of the precocious sophomore. It was the context after all, not the art, that had changed."[43]

At the end of April 1979, in the same *Village Voice* issue where Richard Goldstein trashed Artists Space and Winer in a second editorial, punk critic Lester Bangs's piece "The White Noise Supremacists" appeared, an indictment of the downtown scene's racism and a ringing personal mea culpa.

Bangs wrote of drunken escapades improvising blues lyrics in front of singers like David Ruffin and Bobby Womack about wishing he "wuz a nigger / Then my dick'd be bigger." He wrote:

> [T]o this day I wonder how many of them hated my guts right then. Because Lenny Bruce was wrong—maybe in a better world than this such parlor games would amount to cleansing jet offtakes, and between friends, where a certain bond of mutual trust has been firmly established, good natured racial tradeoffs can be part of the vocabulary of understood affections. But beyond that trouble begins—when you fail to realize that no matter how harmless your intentions are, there is no reason to think that any shit that comes out of your mouth is going to be understood or happily received. Took me a long time to find it out, but those words are *lethal*, man, and you shouldn't just go slinging them around for effect.[44]

In 1982, the year hip-hop blew onto the downtown scene like a fresh wind, Newman quit the art world to become a computer programmer.[45]

Helene Winer left Artists Space to cofound Metro Pictures gallery. With its roster of Artists Space vets like Robert Longo, Cindy Sherman, Richard Prince, and Jack Goldstein, Metro Pictures would become one of the most influential. But when she wanted to represent David Hammons, he refused. It was a reminder that she had once gotten it wrong.

Years later she would say that that she had not understood that the protest "was really about this fairly exclusively white art world, not the title of the show." She said, "It could have been a really productive thing, where everyone would have ended up feeling pretty good. I knew all these people. It wasn't like I was some distant white person and that they couldn't get in the door or something."

"And we could have just planned something, and made a big statement...."

Winer had little occasion to speak to Howardena Pindell again. Not long after *The Nigger Drawings* Pindell left the MOMA. Her time there had been marked with sudden disinvites to the museum's exclusive social events. Now it ended with loud whispers among staff that she had turned into a Black female Jesse Helms. She was a censor, the art world's version of a snitch.

"Never mind that women and Blacks and people of color were censored *out of the system*," Pindell said, "the issue was: you're censoring a white male artist."

Pindell felt voiceless. Up to that point she had done conceptual pieces constructed meticulously from tiny paper circles she had hand-punched, colored, and sometimes numbered—as if she were fragmenting and reassembling herself into bits of order. She had drawn and numbered arrows on color photographs she had taken of televised sports contests. The arrows made the blurry images seem like maps of ocean currents. They swirled into impossible, impenetrable systems. They moved against each other.

But in 1979, her art changed. She survived a life-threatening auto accident. Her new art helped her recover her presence, her memory, the very sound of herself.

She made a video art piece entitled *Free, White and 21*, in which she split herself in two: playing herself earnestly describing her personal experiences with racism, then donning a blond wig to rejoin, "You ungrateful little—after all we have done for you. You know we don't believe in your symbols, they are not valid unless we validate them. And you really must be paranoid."

She began making large self-portraits, collaged and sewn canvases whose surfaces rippled with intensity, bristled with weaponized words—*Imposter, We Will Not Listen to You, How Dare You Question*. In some of the paintings of her Autobiography series from 1987 through 1990, her face and body seem to be carried away by that river of suggestion, that shimmering toxic wash. But the images also suggested a refusal to be submerged.

Artists Space would move on, remaking itself as a major supporter of new artists exploring multiculturalism and identity. When former intern Susan Wyatt became executive director in the late eighties, the organization came under national attack by cultural conservatives who attacked an exhibition on the AIDS crisis entitled *Witnesses: Against Our Vanishing*, and called for the defunding of the NEA. Suddenly the *Nigger Drawings* protest appeared both as a distant moment and a shuddering portent.

In years to come, after the national language had found the words to describe the fight, some might come to debate whether this moment had marked the birth of "hipster racism" or "political correctness." But before that, just around the bend, there would be protests over images and stereotypes, marches and shouting matches over school curricula, many more words over quality and exclusion, the lines distinctly drawn, the engulfment of all into obsessive disputes, post and riposte increasingly ritualized, hyperbole and spectacle the ascendant modes.

"'Freedom for me, or freedom for him!' is a current theme which is running throughout this society," Linda Goode Bryant had written in her letter from the early days of the *Nigger Drawings* protests. "Perhaps naively, I still believe in freedom for all."[46]

Now the future's staring back at me like a vision
from the past....
Oh we know the culture war
We don't know what it's for

But we've lived your Southern strategy
We know it's never gonna last

—Arcade Fire, "Culture War," *The Suburbs*

PART TWO

WHO
ARE
WE

1980—1993

Students protest at Stanford University for more faculty of color, ethnic studies classes, and stronger action against hate incidents, May 15, 1989. Fifty-six were arrested. From left: Cheryl Taylor, Gina Hernandez, Richard Suh. Photo by Chris Eisenberg. ©The Stanford Daily.

CHAPTER 6

THE END OF THE WORLD AS WE KNOW IT

WHITENESS, THE RAINBOW, AND THE CULTURE WARS

> The culture wars over art are really battles that the dominant culture stages with itself.... But the culture wars over race are more about whether former outsiders will ever be given a new status, either inside the mainstream or, at least, closer to the inside.
> —Michele Wallace, "The Culture War within the Culture Wars: Race"

Harvey LeRoy "Lee" Atwater was a son of the South, the kind of infectiously loud and rude American boy obsessed with conquest. He wore his gold-buttoned blue coat, blue tie, and khakis with a bully swagger. He taunted his enemies, told lies about them little and big, treated the world like it was his sideline to stalk, firing up his players and working the refs. When he won, he let out a scream and put on a smile that looked like a grimace.

When he lost, he was still trying to figure out how to win. During the 1980s he almost never lost.

Lee Atwater loved Black music. Growing up he had admired people like Steve Cropper, the Southern blue-eyed bluesman from the famous Stax studio band who had cowritten "In the Midnight Hour" and "Knock on Wood" and backed Otis Redding, Booker T. Jones, and Sam & Dave. After Atwater got George Herbert Walker Bush elected the forty-first president—politics was Lee's chosen adult sport—his first act was to organize an inaugural party that he told the media, without any irony, would be "the Woodstock of rhythm and blues."

On the appointed night he appeared onstage in his gold-buttoned blue coat, blue tie, and khakis, accessorized with black Ray-Bans and a red Fender. Then, in front of his heroes Cropper, Ronnie Wood, Stevie Ray Vaughan, B. B. King, Percy Sledge, Carla Thomas, and Chuck Jackson, he took the mic—whites and Blacks together, American music, good rocking on the nation's grandest stage.

When Lee Atwater played the blues, he frowned, pursed his lips, and jutted his chin forward. He got on his knees and fell back like a believer catching the spirit. He exploded into a manic dance that ended in James Brown splits. He screamed and made that grimacing smile. If it all looked like something you might have seen before, maybe it was—Atwater playing Michael J. Fox playing Marty McFly playing his parents' desegregated 1955 high school dance in *Back to the Future*.

This neocon boogie made perfect sense. Reaganites had tried to evoke imperialist nostalgia—transfiguring the memory of the thing destroyed into beautiful, romantic delusion. Native American author David Treuer called the phenomenon "kill the Indians, then copy them."[1] Ishmael Reed summed up the performance in a word: "Blackface."[2]

After the party, Atwater returned to his new job, running the Republican Party, where he would mentor an operative named Karl Rove and plant the idea in the head of the president's son—a young, smiley, former frat boy like himself—that Junior, too, had a bright future in politics. Atwater had arrived on the big stage by helping to mastermind the post-Watergate resurgence of the Republican Party. Neoconservatives were reviving Richard Nixon's Southern strategy, and Atwater was the perfect person to take the reins. Who better understood power in America than a white boy who aspired to the heavenly soul of a bluesman and the earthbound entitlement of a good ole boy?

The facts of Atwater's career are the weird stuff of American irony. When he graduated from high school, his band the Upsetter's Revue had been offered an opportunity to hit the road backing Lee Dorsey, the New Orleans R&B singer who would soon have a regional hit entitled "Yes We Can." The song began:

Now is the time for all good men
To get together with one another
Iron out their problems and iron out their quarrels
And try to live as brothers

Instead Atwater enrolled in Newberry College and took his first political internship with Strom Thurmond, the diehard segregationist who had fathered a daughter with his family's Black maid.

Harry Dent, the architect of Nixon's Southern strategy, became Atwater's mentor. In 1980, at the age of twenty-nine, Atwater stopped a Democratic congressional challenger in South Carolina by arranging for anonymous phone calls to white voters letting them know that the candidate was a member of the NAACP. Impressed, the Reagan administration came calling, and so began Atwater's rapid rise.

He believed that the best way for the party to cement a coalition of segregation-sympathetic "populists" and market-minded "country clubbers" was to exploit "social issues."[3] He told the journalists Thomas and Mary Edsall how he did this: "In the 1980 campaign, we were able to make the establishment, insofar as it is bad, the government. In other words, big government was the enemy, not big business."[4]

More to the point, Atwater's new Southern strategy would wrap the iron fist of pro-corporate policy in the velvet glove of anti-Black racism. He explained to political scholar Alexander Lamis and an unidentified newsman:

Atwater: As to the whole Southern strategy that Harry Dent and others put together in 1968, opposition to the Voting Rights Act would have been a central part of keeping the South. Now [the new Southern strategy] doesn't have to do that. All you have to do to keep the South for Reagan is to run in place on the issues he's campaigned on since 1964 ... and that's fiscal conservatism, balancing the budget, cut taxes, you know, the whole cluster.

Questioner: But the fact is, isn't it, that Reagan does get to the [1968 candidate George] Wallace voter and to the racist side of the Wallace Voter by doing away with Legal Services, by cutting down on food stamps...?

Atwater: You start out in 1954 by saying, "Nigger, nigger, nigger." By 1968 you can't say "nigger"—that hurts you. Backfires. So you say stuff like forced busing, states' rights, and all that stuff. You're getting so abstract now [that] you're talking about cutting taxes, and all these things you're talking about are totally economic things and a byproduct of them is [that] Blacks get hurt worse than whites. And subconsciously maybe that is part of it. I'm not saying that. But I'm saying that if it is getting that abstract, and that coded, that we are doing away with the racial problem one way or the other. You follow me—because obviously sitting around saying, "We want to cut this," is much more abstract than even the busing thing, and a hell of a lot more abstract than "Nigger, nigger."[5]

Just as with the old, the new Southern strategy counted on racial dissociation to work. The 1980s were, the Edsalls would write, a period in which Republicans skillfully "consolidated, updated, and refined the right-populist, race-coded strategies of Wallace and Nixon." They added, "The race and tax agenda effectively focused majority public attention onto what government *takes*, rather than onto what it *gives*."[6]

Mad that they put in basketball courts and not tennis courts at your local park? Angry your school-age kids were being bused to the inner city? Suspicious your hard-earned money was going to support welfare moms, junkies, and gays? Certain the job at the downsizing plant went to an unqualified person of color over you because of affirmative action? Atwater was saying: we feel your pain.

And he understood: defunding legal services and food stamps might slam poor whites, too, but if *they* thought it hurt minorities *more*, that might be enough to make them vote Republican. In this way the 1960s divide between Wallace voters and Nixon voters—those comfortable with naked racial appeals versus those who were not—was reconciled. Southern strategy 2.0 meant never having to say "White Power."

These new abstractions demanded a new class of encrypters and code talkers, and as the historian David Roediger wrote, "The Republicans, it must be said, knew the codes better than the Democrats."[7] The Heritage Foundation's 1984 edition of *Mandate for Leadership*, the essential conservative politician's playbook, stated the cultural imperative clearly: "For twenty years, the most important battle in the civil rights field has been for the control of language."[8] After the civil rights movement, the *Mandate* authors wrote, Americans were clearly for "equality," "opportunity," and "remedial action," and against "racism," "discrimination," and "segregation." They concluded, "The secret to victory, whether in court or in Congress, has been to control the definition of these terms."[9]

Over the next thirty years the right would experiment at containing and reversing the advances of the civil rights movement—claiming and subverting its moral language, repackaging old racial superiority theories in the new language of "color-blind justice," encoding attacks in racialized narratives and imagery, denying both difference and inequality. The nation's race conversation itself would pass from clarity into kudzu.

The Republicans had learned a lot since George Wallace had first mobilized white rage against the Northeastern liberal establishment. Two decades later, Atwater was working for a son of that establishment, the former oilman and CIA chief George H. W. Bush. As the summer began, Bush was in big trouble, double digits behind Massachusetts governor Michael Dukakis. Atwater faced a major problem: how could he generate working-class white sympathy for a stiff-necked blue-blood millionaire?

Violent crime in Massachusetts had dropped 13 percent during Dukakis's administration.[10] The campaign needed an image that would eclipse the facts. Then *Reader's Digest* published a story about a man named Willie Horton. Horton was a Black felon imprisoned for life in Massachusetts, who, after disappearing from a weekend prison furlough, had kidnapped, stabbed, and beaten a white suburban couple in their home, raping the woman. Atwater told Republican operatives in a private meeting, "If I can make Willie Horton a household name, we'll win the election."[11] At the same time he told his staff that the issue with Horton "was crime, not color."[12]

In the fall an independent conservative political action committee ran an attack ad featuring a grainy black-and-white police lineup photo of Willie Horton in full ragged Afro and unclipped beard. The ad was primitive in look and primal in message: a slide show of images of Horton, Dukakis, and Bush; the words "kidnapping," "stabbing," "raping" flashing under a picture of a handcuffed Horton; the conclusion—"Weekend Prison Passes: Dukakis on Crime."

Publicly Atwater denied having anything to do with the TV spot. He told journalist Eric Alterman that he had asked campaign groups not to use photos of Horton in their ads. "I defy you to find any other campaign I have done where race has become the issue," he taunted. "Race, politically, is a loser."[13]

Historians would forever debate whether Atwater masterfully plotted this turn or completely lost control of his strategy and operatives. Either way the proof was in the results: Dukakis never recovered from the Pandora's box of racial and sexual anxieties that the Horton ad had unleashed. "Here we have," Kevin Phillips wrote, "the nation's leading preppy—an ornament and offspring of the Establishment—winning as a barefoot populist."[14] Bush's victory not only turned the word "liberal" temporarily into a political millstone, it secured the continuing neoconservative realignment of America.

Plunged into despair, some liberals began to train their sights on multiculturalists, feminists, and queers, whom they said had destroyed the left with identity politics. Class, they said, was the real issue, not race or gender or sexuality. But, really, it was all of the above. Why had working-class white Americans—after half a century of strongly supporting strong government, social programs, and economic reform—turned so strongly against their own clear economic interests? What really was the matter with Kansas? It was the culture wars, stupid.

As a political gambit to realign the American two-party system, the Southern strategy had succeeded beyond its architects' imaginings. But it also needed continual care and feeding. As the demographics of the nation shifted profoundly, the culture wars would continue to mobilize voters against the emerging America.

For Atwater, there would be a painful postscript. A month after Bush's inaugural bash, he was appointed to Howard University's board of trustees. He seemed humbled by the nomination. He said he was eager to lecture to the predominantly Black student body, to perhaps teach this new generation something about politics.

Yet the students, whose leaders included Ras Baraka, the son of Amiri and Amina Baraka, and Karma Bene Bambara, the daughter of Toni Cade Bambara, had not forgotten. They closed down the university with a five-day strike. Hundreds took over the administration building and disrupted the annual university convocation. Saying that he was "deeply saddened" that he had not had a chance to dialogue with the students, Atwater quickly resigned.

It was the end of the 1980s, a decade in which almost every day felt like a battle for the heart of America.

THE FEAR

In his first inaugural address in 1981, President Ronald Reagan had said, "We're not, as some would have us believe, doomed to an inevitable decline." Yet as the eighties closed, traditionalists' faith in American exceptionalism was being tested. They invoked metaphors of endings: the fraying of America, the disuniting of America, the closing of the American mind, the twilight of common dreams.

What had happened in between? The arrival of the most diverse generation in history and the outbreak of the culture wars.

These wars, like all wars, began with no name. They were partly the product of a free-floating white anxiety, unloosed by Reagan's economic restructuring and attack on the welfare state. Barbara Ehrenreich named this new complex of anxieties afflicting the middle class. The middle class, she wrote,

> is afraid, like any class below the most securely wealthy, of misfortunes
> that might lead to a downward slide. But in the middle class there is another
> anxiety: a fear of inner weakness, of growing soft, of failing to strive, of
> losing discipline and will.... Whether the middle class looks down toward
> the realm of less, or up toward the realm of more, there is the fear, always,
> of falling.[15]

The fear of falling would catalyze a suburban arms-race meritocracy, with its contradictory ethic of self-management and binge consumption, its harder-better-faster-stronger mode of presentation, even its structured leisure of twenty-four-hour fitness, reality TV, and youth soccer leagues.

The fear would also spread like a thunderhead over the heartland. Reagan's disastrous farm policies caused food prices to plunge and real estate prices to rise. At nickel auction prices family farms passed into the hands of large agribusinesses at an astonishing rate. At the peak of the crisis in 1986, family farms were foreclosing at a rate of two thousand per week, the fastest since the Great Depression. A whole way of life seemed to be disappearing. Outbreaks of violence and suicide—not just among farmers, but even their bankers and federal lenders—accompanied the despair.[16]

"You don't talk free trade to a man with an empty belly," said one agricultural economics expert. "You feed him."[17]

Yet in their 1984 reelection ad, Reagan's image managers offered only a voice intoning "It's morning again in America," and pictures of Rockwellesque imperialist nostalgia—saccharine, gauzy, sentimental.

Across calm daybreak waters a fishing boat sails past the city-on-the-hill out to sea. Suited men and women march to their office jobs. An elderly man steers his tractor backward in the dawn's half-light. A newsboy tosses the morning paper onto green lawns. A family carries a rug into their newly purchased picket-fenced white home. A young couple gets married before a weeping, happy, gray-haired mother. Flags are raised over a log cabin, a firehouse, and a country home, and as each is run up the pole, two white-shirted boys, a fireman, and a family patriarch look up to the Stars and Stripes and smile.

"It's morning again in America," the voice says, "and under the leadership of President Reagan our country is prouder and stronger and better."

Against unrest and despair, these were images of comfort and stability, a soft utopia of restored order. No dislocating economic programs, tough-on-crime policies, and social service–slashing proposals here. Optimism was now, literally, a thing of the past, deracinated and familiar.

All the existential dread was reduced to a simple question: Do you still believe in this country's great destiny? If you did, then all you needed to do was trust these leaders to lead us back to the future. And if you wanted to worry, then you could worry about those who were questioning our singular Western heritage and threatening to overwhelm our European American cultural core.

THE RAINBOW MOMENT

The emergence of a new America had been born of the brief civil rights consensus, and could be seen in two major demographic shifts.

The first had occurred with the advent of public school desegregation. In the year of the 1964 Civil Rights Act, researchers Gary Orfield and John Yun noted a mere 2 percent of Black students in the South attended majority white public schools. By 1970, the number was 33 percent, and the South had become "the nation's most integrated region for both Blacks and whites."[18] Through the 1980s, busing and consent decrees continued to diversify the schools.

In one generation, the nation had come a long way from "separate but equal." Racial desegregation in secondary education peaked in 1988, Reagan's last year in office. In the South alone, almost 44 percent of Black students now attended majority white public schools.[19] National trends mirrored these numbers. To be sure, the picture wasn't entirely rosy. Well over half of Black students were still attending majority-minority schools. After this moment, such segregation would intensify again.

The other powerful demographic shift had been initiated in a legislative break-through that no one wanted to claim. The 1965 Immigration and Nationality Act quietly reversed the nation's long-standing exclusion of non–Western European immigrants.

Immigration policy had long been based on a national origins quota system, a pro-gram aimed at restricting undesirable immigrants from Eastern and Southern Europe, Africa, and, most forcefully of all, Asia. In addition, Mexican and Native peoples of the Southwest, who were indigenous and not immigrant populations, faced waves of depor-tation terror. Pathways to citizenship for nonwhites were severely limited. Through seven presidencies, Democratic Congressman Emanuel Celler steadfastly argued that the national origins system was, in fact, racist.[20]

With the historic passage of the Civil Rights Act and Voting Rights Act, Celler's hope had finally found its moment. Buoyed by the civil rights consensus, he and Dem-ocratic senator Philip Hart sponsored a bill to sweep away national origins quotas. It passed both the House and the Senate with overwhelming majorities. By removing "the twin barriers of prejudice and privilege," Lyndon B. Johnson said when he signed the bill at the foot of the Statue of Liberty, the act "does repair a very deep and painful flaw in the fabric of American justice. It corrects a cruel and enduring wrong in the conduct of the American Nation."[21]

In the decades afterward, immigration from Mexico and from Asian and Central and South American countries rose sharply. Through the end of the 1950s, only a quar-ter of immigrants had come from Third World countries. After the 1960s, more than three-quarters did.[22] Anti-multiculturalists would come to liken the bill's passage to the fall of the Alamo. But by 1983, the demographic shifts were so tangible that they could encourage civil rights activist Jesse Jackson to begin his unlikely candidacy for the Dem-ocratic Party presidential nomination.

Jackson felt the Democrats were increasingly slouching to the right, accommo-dating Nixon's Southern strategy in their rush to court the shrinking population of white "Reagan Democrats." Instead he chose to barnstorm Black churches through the South with a message to both the grassroots and the Party: "Reagan won by the margin of our nonparticipation."[23] The path to the future, Jackson argued in his signature rhyming cadences, lay in expanding, not abandoning, the Democratic base. "My constituency," he told the 1984 Democratic National Convention, "is the desperate, the damned, the disinherited, the disrespected, and the despised."

For the next five years Jackson gave activists a wealth of inspirational images—he was a veritable meme machine. The Iowan small farmer, the Native American environmentalist, the immigrant, the disabled veteran, gays, lesbians, youths—all, Jackson said, were part of an American quilt, "many patches, many pieces, many colors, many sizes, all woven and held together by a common thread." The following year, AIDS activist Cleve Jones began the NAMES Project AIDS Memorial Quilt.

Jackson's presidential aspirations ended with his 1988 loss to Michael Dukakis. But he had helped fire a movement's imagination. He had incepted into the mainstream the prophetic images of the rainbow: the lapel button of the 1968 Third World Strike, the image of red, yellow, brown, black, and white fists coming together, echoed again in Romare Bearden's 1973 commissioned artwork for the city of Berkeley, with its four faces in white, brown, tan, and black.

"Our flag," Jackson had said in his 1984 speech, "is red, white, and blue, but our nation is a rainbow—red, yellow, brown, black, and white—and we're all precious in God's sight."[24]

PUSHING OVER THE MELTING POT

In 1908, at the peak of European immigration and amid successful efforts to shut down Asian immigration, the Russian Jewish immigrant and activist Israel Zangwill wrote and staged a play called *The Melting Pot*. It became one of the biggest Broadway plays of its day, and fixed the century's dominant American narrative around race and ethnicity in politics, pop culture, and sociology—the story of assimilation.

Zangwill's play is about a poor immigrant musician named David Quixano, who is prone to speaking and acting in exclamations. At one point, Quixano says to his Old World uncle, "I keep faith with America. I have faith America will keep faith with us." Then he starts praying to an American flag.

The play's message was just as unsubtle: in America, all the ethnic hatreds, blood ties, and cultural bonds that had defined the Old World would dissolve and give rise to a new kind of global superman. Quixano is a migrant survivor of a Russian pogrom. But he falls in love with Vera, the daughter of Russian Cossacks. "America is God's Crucible," he exclaims to her, "the great Melting-Pot where all the races of Europe are melting and re-forming!"

The couple splits for a moment when David learns that Vera's father, Baron Revendal, presided over the massacre that killed most of his family back in Russia. Yet in the end they reconcile, because, well, that's America. "Ah, Vera," Quixano sighs, "what is the glory of Rome and Jerusalem where all nations and races come to worship and look back, compared with the glory of America, where all races and nations come to labour and look forward!"

Zangwill understood that the immigrant's aggressive ambition was less threatening to white Americans when coupled with the promise that all that baggage of history and difference would be shed. Small wonder the metaphor remained so dominant for so long. But by the 1980s, the melting pot idea had run its course. There would no longer be just one way to be American.

Multiculturalism was about recognizing and representing how Black it was to be an American, how Latino, how Asian, how indigenous it was to be an American. Being American was a thousand narratives, not just one. Ishmael Reed and his friends Rudolfo Anaya, Shawn Wong, and Victor Hernández Cruz would write, "'Multiculturalism' is not a description of a category of American writing—it is a definition of all American writing."[25] They were writing about writing, as well as the history of writing, but they were also capturing the shape of a groundswell.

Through the decade, multiculturalists were founding art collectives, expanding alternative spaces, starting up journals, writing books. They were organizing street protests from the Bronx to Broadway to Sunset Boulevard against movies, plays, and TV shows they considered racist. They found platforms at universities, local and state agencies, and in the rapidly expanding network of community arts organizations. They were institutionalizing themselves. In the language of their activism, they were "building power," working toward "cultural equity."

In 1983, Alice Walker's *The Color Purple* won the Pulitzer Prize and the National Book Award. Soon the list of writers of color who won a Pulitzer or a National Book Award grew to include Toni Morrison, August Wilson, Gloria Naylor, and Maxine Hong Kingston. Suddenly battles broke out—often gendered, and waged with the intensity of sectarian infighting—over whose stories represented "the real" and "the fake." Reed's ugly public rift with Walker, as well as his friend Frank Chin's scabrous criticism of Kingston, seemed to indicate that multiculturalism had finally produced stakes—aesthetic, financial, personal—worth fighting over.

But even as they quarreled, the onrushing wave of young people of color made their claims feel more prescient, urgent, and viable. "The United States is unique in the world," Ishmael Reed wrote, "the world is here."[26] The browning young nation was the multiculturalists' validation. People had to start paying attention.

THE BACKLASH GOES TO WASHINGTON

Perhaps it was impossible to stop all those brown bodies from streaming into American life. But you could try to stop the ideas they were bringing in with them. You could try to stem their prodigious production of new images of America. You could try to stop them at the level of culture. And that is how a minor government agency—the National Endowment for the Arts—became the focus of the anti-multiculturalist backlash.

In 1989, George H. W. Bush was the new president, Lee Atwater was the new head of the Republican Party, and Communism was collapsing all across the Eastern bloc. By summer the intellectual Francis Fukuyama was declaring the "end of history," the final triumph of Western liberal democracy and capitalism. In this context, Bush appointed John Frohnmayer his chairperson of the National Endowment for the Arts. What was great for democracy over there might have been, in an odd way, spectacularly bad for Frohnmayer and even worse for American arts and culture.

The NEA had been established in 1965. President John F. Kennedy first outlined a rationale for a national cultural policy in a speech honoring the poet Robert Frost at Amherst College delivered a month before his assassination. He said:

> Our national strength matters, but the spirit which informs and controls
> our strength matters just as much.... The artist, however faithful to
> his personal vision of reality, becomes the last champion of the individual
> mind and sensibility against an intrusive and an officious state. The
> great artist is thus a solitary figure.... If art is to nourish the roots of our
> culture, society must set the artist free to follow his vision wherever it
> takes him. We must never forget that art is not a form of propaganda, it is
> a form of truth.[27]

The speech bore the imprint of Kennedy's close advisor, Arthur Schlesinger Jr., who saw American arts and culture in the context of global soft power. Supporting it was a way to show the world that the United States was not, he said, "a nation of money-grubbing materialists."[28] Communism reduced Soviet artists to the role of functionaries for state propaganda. In the United States, Kennedy said, "the highest duty of the writer, the composer, the artist is to remain true to himself and let the chips fall where they may."[29] Artistic freedom was proof of the vitality of democracy.

The NEA's charge had been influenced not only by the expansiveness of sixties liberalism but by the long shadow of the 1930s Cultural Front and the continuing threat of Second World Communism. Kennedy's revival of the romantic vision of the artist was twinned with a Cold War realpolitik. But with the fall of the Berlin Wall and the end of history came the end of the romance. The new enemy was within. Now cultural conservatives trained their sights on artists, and wrangling those high-plains drifters of the American imagination.

In the spring of 1989, the Methodist minister and religious conservative activist Donald Wildmon began a direct-mail crusade to end government funding for the arts. He had been angered over a NEA grant given to the artist Andres Serrano, a New Yorker of Afro-Cuban, Spanish, and Chinese descent, who had displayed a Cibachrome print of a luminous crucifix in a pool of his urine, a work that he called *Piss Christ*. Wildmon sent a letter to members of his American Family Association linking Serrano's print to Madonna's *Like A Prayer* video and director Martin Scorsese's *The Last Temptation of Christ*—all of it degenerate art that fostered an "anti-Christian bias." "Maybe, before the physical persecution of Christians begins," he wrote, "we will gain the courage to stand against such bigotry."[30]

Senators Alfonse D'Amato and Jesse Helms soon joined Wildmon in his NEA protest. Helms had been waiting for a moment like this. Fourteen years before, he had attacked the NEA for giving a grant to Erica Jong to write what became her best-selling feminist novel, *Fear of Flying*. To Helms, artists belonged with people of color and feminists, welfare recipients, and the poor—they were all despoilers of freedom.

Debates over public art and publicly funded art spread. Richard Serra's *Tilted Arc* was removed from Manhattan's Federal Plaza. A judge ordered that a David Avalos sculpture of an undocumented worker being frisked by a Border Patrol agent be taken down from the plaza of the San Diego federal courthouse, not far from the Immigration and Naturalization Services office.[31]

Not long after being appointed Reagan's chair of the National Endowment for the Humanities in 1986, Lynne Cheney denounced a public television series that her own agency had funded. *The Africans*, written by Kenyan American professor Ali Mazrui, had dared to discuss European colonization and exploitation, leading Cheney to call it an "anti-Western diatribe." She pulled $50,000 earmarked to publicize the series, explaining that her action was, in fact, "a defense of free speech."[32]

Defunding public culture proved good Republican politics—it brought together cultural conservatives and fiscal conservatives. In his very first budget to Congress, President Ronald Reagan recommended that the National Endowment for the Arts and the National Endowment for the Humanities budgets be slashed in half. For his part, the *New York Times* critic Hilton Kramer left the newspaper to launch the journal *The New Criterion*, with funding from the John M. Olin Foundation. Kramer immediately attacked the NEA and won, quickly bringing down its arts criticism program.[33]

All of this happened *before* Frohnmayer took over the NEA chairmanship. In 1989, his first year as chair, he faced the controversy over *Piss Christ* and further Wildmon-led attacks on the work of queer artist David Wojnarowicz. He received a letter signed by one hundred Congress members denouncing an NEA-funded Robert Mapplethorpe retrospective.[34] He faced Jesse Helms's proposal—known as the Helms Amendment—to establish new limits on NEA funding of art considered obscene or indecent, or denigrating of people based on their religion, race, creed, sex, handicap, age, or national origin. And he confronted a torrent of bills meant to defund or abolish the NEA, one of which was unambiguously entitled the "Privatization of Art Act."

By the winter, Congress had approved a diluted version of the Helms Amendment, and Frohnmayer had inserted what the theater producer Joseph Papp would angrily label the "loyalty oath" into NEA grant applications: grant-seekers had to pledge not to make obscene work.[35] Frohnmayer then revoked a $10,000 grant to Artists Space for its exhibition on the AIDS crisis, *Witnesses: Against Our Vanishing*, because the catalog included a Wojnarowicz essay critical of public figures, including Jesse Helms.

Frohnmayer's end came in 1992. The trigger was a poem by a young Black writer named Ramona Lofton, whose pen name was—in a nod to the stereotype of the Angry Black Woman—Sapphire.[36] She had published a poem in a small literary magazine called *the portable lower east side* in an issue entitled "Queer City" that had received a $5,000 NEA grant.

In "Wild Thing," Sapphire took on one of the most infamous cases of the day—the 1989 Central Park jogger rape, in which four black boys and a Latino boy were, as it turned out, wrongly accused. Fictionalizing one of these rapists, she gave voice to a mother-hating, whiteness-fetishizing, fatherless, hopeless boy. The poem concluded with the shock of the violent act, and the even bigger shock of the boy's apparently cold-blooded rage. But in a letter to members of Congress, Donald Wildmon fixated on these lines:

> I remember when
> Christ sucked my dick
> behind the pulpit,
> I was 6 years old
> he made me promise
> not to tell no one.

With these words, Sapphire had dared to give the boy-rapist some humanity—he too had been a victim of sexual abuse.. But in the same way that Bill Clinton would later choose to read Sister Souljah and Charlton Heston would Ice-T, Wildmon read Sapphire the way that he read the Bible—literally. He contended that the poet was glorifying violence against the white female jogger and portraying the Lord Jesus as a pedophile.[37] Even Frohnmayer had to blanch at Wildmon's philistine silliness. But he likely sealed his political fate when he said that the poem needed "to be read in its entirety in order to receive a fair appraisal."[38]

Days later, taking a cue from Helms and the far right, Republican presidential candidate Pat Buchanan's team lifted scenes of Marlon Riggs's groundbreaking NEA-funded film on Black queer life, *Tongues Untied*, for a television attack ad that claimed Bush supported pornography. They hoped to trump Bush's image of Willie Horton with the image of Riggs—Black, male, "criminal," and gay. In the New Hampshire Republican primary, Buchanan received a surprising 37 percent, finishing a strong second behind Bush. The White House quickly sought and received Frohnmayer's resignation.

An April 1990 poll showed 93 percent of Americans agreed with the statement, "Even if I find a particular piece of art objectionable, others have the right to view it." Sixty-eight percent supported federal funding of the arts.[39] But Frohnmayer had left a legacy of controversy and defunding that had touched major alternative art spaces and established institutions alike.

Lower down the food chain, hundreds of smaller organizations that funded artists of color faced the 1990s worried about their survival. Those who in 1979 had protested *The Nigger Drawings* exhibition at Artists Space could hardly have imagined how the right would adopt and deploy their protest tactics a decade later. The NEA's artist grants were doomed, and the agency became a perennial budget target.

The attack had been framed around questions of religion, obscenity, and taxes, but in practice it had been accomplished through the targeting of queers, women, and artists of color of the new avant-garde. The critic Michele Wallace, Faith Ringgold's daughter, wrote, "The clear goal of the conservative movement is to discredit progressive reform on all fronts and shore up a hopelessly obsolete 'white' patriarchal status quo against the tide of demographic changes in U.S. populations."[40]

The battle over the NEA effectively destroyed the argument for public culture. Almost alone among the wealthiest nations, and also many of the poorer ones, the United States had all but abandoned a commitment to its national arts. The production of culture was effectively ceded to those who could find the money to do it or those who could make a profit at it. It was a quiet but lasting victory for neoliberalism.

While the culture wars raged, George H. W. Bush had sent troops to the Gulf and Panama and raised taxes to deal with military-driven deficits. He was moving forward with the North American Free Trade Agreement amid a recession-ridden economy characterized by massive layoffs. Neoliberalism—which would strangle government, dismantle the welfare state, allow capital to flow across national borders, eliminate millions of jobs, exacerbate income inequality, and undo civil rights for corporate rights—could not be sold to the American electorate on its merits. Who would buy it?

Instead the culture wars offered a kind of shock doctrine—if you don't follow *us*, *they* will overrun your America.

THE END OF WESTERN CULTURE

The threat was perhaps most visible in higher education. In 1970, the United States had been 83 percent white. By 1990, whites had dropped to 76 percent and, more pointedly, made up only about two-thirds of all Americans under the age of eighteen.[41] With the rise of affirmative action, students of color were finally reaching critical mass on many university campuses. America's new identity crisis would break out amid the ceremonious greens and brick edifices of elite college quads.

In 1985, the University of California at Berkeley reported that for the first time in history its freshman class was less than half white. This tipping point would fire national debates over affirmative action and campus diversity through the new millennium. Both sides agreed: what was being taught to these young people was crucial—universities produced the nation's future.

Albert Camarillo—a Stanford history professor who, at UCLA in 1966 had been one of only forty-four Mexican American undergrads on campus, and, upon his arrival at the Farm in 1975, joined a small number of Mexican American faculty—said, "You had a substantial cohort of students of color on campus with white students and others who had grown up in segregated communities coming to Stanford for the first time to make diversity or multiculturalism work. It was difficult. They were ill-equipped. They didn't have language. There were a whole bunch of things that were percolating to blow up."

In these newly heterogeneous settings, routine personal interactions in close quarters—a dorm, a professor's office hours, a Greek fraternity party—could become fraught with live-wire tension. Drunk white revelers in blackface, slant eyes, or sombreros; scrawled insults of students of color and gays on dorm doors; race riots on crowded university avenues—the casual microaggressions that once might have gone unremarked before now sometimes paralyzed campuses. Across the country students of color began to report increasing incidents of hate violence. They organized to demand that the institutions respond with sensitivity programs, ethnic studies courses, staff-of-color hirings.

In California, where the demographic shifts were happening the fastest, insurgent demographics and ideas came together. In 1986, students in the University of California system succeeded in forcing the system to divest $3 billion in investments in South African apartheid. They then turned their efforts to focus on what they were calling "educational apartheid." They pointed to the invisibility of people of color in the curriculum and the educational pipeline; demanded course graduation requirements in the study of race, gender, sexuality, and identity; and called for programs to increase racial diversity at all levels of the educational system.

At Stanford University, where activists had registered voters for Jesse Jackson's 1984 presidential run and held a sit-in at the Hoover Institution in 1985 to demand a boycott of South African–made goods, a coalition of ethnic student organizations began to push for the replacement of a graduation requirement called Western Culture with a canon-expanding survey course called "Culture, Ideas and Values." Steve Phillips, a leader of the Stanford Black Student Union who was later elected student body president, argued that they were "unleashing the social change potential of the aspirations of people for equality and justice, particularly people whose cultures are denied and are excluded and are diminished."

And so lines were drawn. Phillips recalled a meeting with *Stanford Daily* news editors after he had helped lead a large number of students of color and white students in taking over the Main Quad. One of the editors expressed sympathy for President Don Kennedy. "Poor Don Kennedy?" he responded. "I'm thinking, 'Poor students who don't have their culture reflected in the curriculum and are not validated here [at Stanford].' Who do you empathize with?"

On January 15, 1987, the twentieth anniversary of the founding of the Black Student Union and what would have been Martin Luther King Jr.'s fifty-eighth birthday, Jackson visited the campus to speak to the students. "No one can be truly educated in this world limited to one language and obsessed with one race," Jackson told the students. "We must live in a real world."

Then they marched to the Faculty Senate meeting where students would deliver hundreds of petitions to members. Along the way the students chanted, "Hey hey ho ho, Western Cultures got to go!" They thought the cry was pretty clever—transgressive and hilarious. To traditionalists, it was evidence that the barbarians were taking over.

SAVING CIVILIZATION

Published just weeks later, 1987's most unlikely bestseller was a dense polemic by an obscure University of Chicago philosopher named Allan Bloom. Five years before, he had secured a small book contract based on a piece he had written for the conservative *National Review*. In it he had argued that, since the 1960s, the American student had become uninterested in the great questions of mankind, that the best now indeed lacked all convictions, and that universities that no longer valued the close study of the Great Books were inculcating an "easygoing American kind of nihilism."

"The palliation of beliefs culminates in pallid belief," he wrote, echoing both the aesthetic concerns of Hilton Kramer and the judicial concerns of strict constructionists. "Schools once produced citizens, or gentlemen, or believers; now they produce the unprejudiced."[42]

By the time Bloom's book-length argument, *The Closing of the American Mind,* was published, the nation was ready for its formalist foretelling of doom, even its detours into blanket denunciations of feminism, rock music, and affirmative action. American elite universities were slouching toward relativism and "relevance," Bloom argued. "The new American life-style," he wrote, "has become a Disneyland version of the Weimar Republic for the whole family."[43] But truth remained truth, context was nothing, and all cultures were not made equal. The openness of cultural relativism indicated the closing of the American mind.

The Stanford Black Student Union takes over the President's office to press for curricular reform, 1987. Photo by and courtesy of James Rucker.

Bloom's unapologetic elitism offered its readers a bracing shot of intolerance for tolerance. It ratified a suspicion that the price of allowing all these dark-skinned youths into elite institutions was nothing less than the ruin of American civilization. Civilization versus culture—that old conservative preoccupation that Ralph Ellison had so casually dismissed in the prologue to *Invisible Man*—was back. *The Closing of the American Mind* created its own ponderous genre—the end-of-civilization jeremiad set on the colorizing campus—and focused the expanding anti-multiculturalist backlash.

Bloom's rage had been born from a 1969 confrontation between the university and Third World student activists, in a moment that may have been as crucial to Bloom's intellectual formation as his studies with the influential conservative philosopher Leo Strauss. In April of that year, Bloom was a young assistant professor at Cornell University. At that point, a multi-year administrative effort to recruit Black students to this Ivy League school had created strong pockets of white resistance. On Parents' Weekend, a spring ritual especially beloved by alumni and their legacy admits, the antagonisms between Black students and those who opposed their presence on campus exploded.

After midnight on Friday the residents of a Black women's student co-op awoke to find a cross burning on their lawn. This precipitating event never made it into Bloom's recountings. Instead, he would begin by noting what happened next: at dawn a group of Black students marched to Willard Straight Hall and began occupying it. They said they wanted to call attention to the administration's ineffectuality at dealing with racism. They demanded the immediate establishment of an Africana Studies program.

Hours later, a white fraternity stormed the building trying to rout the occupiers. Fights broke out and the frat was repelled. Soon progressive white activists set up a support cordon around Straight Hall. But, unsatisfied and anxious, some of the occupiers decided to arm themselves. Police were called from neighboring counties, assembling down the hill in downtown Ithaca. Tense negotiations with the administration ensued. One police officer recalled thinking that a shootout "could have made Kent State and Jackson State look like the teddy bear's picnic."[44]

But in the end, university officials agreed to accelerate the development of an Africana center and to begin an Africana Studies program. Almost two days after the cross burning, the students left Straight Hall victoriously, some brandishing rifles and bandoliers. Photos were snapped, and headlines were written: "Universities Under the Gun." Bloom was enraged that the university administration and his faculty colleagues had capitulated to Negroes With Guns. He soon chose to leave Cornell.

Two decades later conservative scholars felt that things had become even worse. In 1988, a strong majority of Stanford's faculty Academic Council passed the expansive Culture, Ideas, and Values proposal to replace the Western Cultures graduation requirement. Faculty passage of similar requirements at Berkeley and the University of Wisconsin at Madison followed shortly. Diversity proposals around admissions and curricular reform were being taken up across the country.

Until that moment cult-cons had difficulty articulating their anger at the ways the world was changing around them. They often derided the multiculturalists as "academic Marxists." The term was wildly inaccurate—this motley bunch included post-Marxists, anti-Marxists, and the ideologically nonaligned. But now Bloom's book, the students' vulgar chant, and the spread of diversity requirements had given cult-cons the language for the backlash.

In November 1988, a group of three hundred met in New York City to form the National Association of Scholars. In the name of objectivity, scholarship, and merit, they called for a restoration of great Western tradition, vowing to confront affirmative action, diversity trainings, "tenured radicals," and their "oppression studies." "The barbarians are in our midst," thundered Penn history professor Alan C. Kors in his keynote. "We need to fight them a good long time. Show them you are not afraid, they crumble."[45]

THE FAITHLESS

Pat Buchanan captured the spirit of the growing backlash. He decried the "across-the-board assault on our Anglo-American heritage." He said, "The combined forces of open immigration and multiculturalism constitute a mortal threat to American Civilization."[46] To him, faith in Euro-American ideals was the basis of culture, which in turn was the very foundation upon which civilization rested. "When the faith dies, the culture dies, the civilization dies, the people die," Buchanan wrote. "That is the progression."[47]

But traditionalists did not come from only the right. Arthur Schlesinger Jr.—the Kennedy advisor, a supporter of civil rights and immigration reform, and a historian whose interest in the study of slavery had once marked him as a radical—said in a speech:

> The ideologues of multiculturalism would reject the historic American purposes of assimilation and integration. They would have our educational system reinforce, promote and perpetuate separate ethnic communities and do so at the expense of the idea of a common culture and a common national identity.[48]

In his sculpting of Kennedy's cultural policy, Schlesinger had redefined American nationalism. But his position on multiculturalism seemed to reveal a faith in his country that was both strikingly fragile and narrow. There could be no room for integration that was not assimilation, no concession that cultural change might or should move in more than one direction at once.

New York Times writer Richard Bernstein—returning from a frontline posting to Berkeley—wrote, "The plain and inescapable fact is that the derived Western European culture of American life produced the highest degree of prosperity in the conditions of the greatest freedom ever known on the planet Earth."[49] In challenging the standards that made America great, he wrote, multiculturalism "sanctions a cultivation of aggrievement, a constant claim of victimization, an excessive, fussy, self-pitying sort of wariness that induces others to spout pieties."[50]

In this, the white liberal establishment agreed with the right. To them, the civil rights movement had established integration's natural limit—*you've won the right to try to be us.* But now, everywhere, all those Others—the charter school teachers, corporate consultants, state college professors, urban school board members, first-generation college students, Afrocentrists, Ebonicists, and "reverse racists"—were, in their refusal of that aspiration, balkanizing America.

Bernstein compared multiculturalism to the moment the French Revolution turned from "the enlightened universalism of the Declaration of the Rights of Man and Citizen into the rule of the Committee of Public Safety and the Terror."[51] Multiculturalism, he wrote, was "nobility perverted."[52]

But a dollop of intellectual honesty required anyone to admit the persistence of racial discrimination and cultural inequity. Here was a new, particularly vexing kind of First World intellectual problem: if one just came out and said he was against inclusion, opportunity, and diversity, people might think he was a racist asshole. Bernstein admitted, "Nobody wants to appear to be against multiculturalism."[53] And this is how the word "multiculturalism" came to be associated with two weirder words designed both to evade and shut down debate—"identity politics" and "political correctness."

Charging someone with "identity politics" meant: there's all these problems in the world, like, say, the hole in the ozone layer, and all you want to talk about is *your own little oppression*. It meant that "race" was never about being white, "gender" was never about being male, and "sexuality" was never about being straight. Those were *your* problems. Whiteness was just the flavor the diverse frogs in the pot were melting toward. "Identity politics," as Kwame Anthony Appiah once quipped, "is what *other* people do."[54]

Charging someone with "political correctness" was like putting on white-guilt deodorant—*smells like freedom of expression!* If cultural openness was really the emerging orthodoxy, then bigotry could be a form of good old American contrariness, a necessary national self-corrective. But also, calling someone else PC meant never having apologize for being a racist. It was a phrase with as much power to end a conversation as the word "racist"; the restorationist's trump card.

All these new misdirections felt, well, hypersensitive. And these debates were really about what the novelist Paul Beatty would call in his perceptive novel, *The White-Boy Shuffle*, with equal parts sarcasm and sentiment, "the eternal war for civility."

What was the right place for people of color? "All of us appreciate a diversity of restaurants and food," Pat Buchanan wrote, "French, Chinese, Japanese, Italian, Mexican, Serb, Thai, and Greek, for example."[55] In response, multiculturalists could summon a line from Malcolm X: "I'm not going to sit at your table and watch you eat, with nothing on my plate, and call myself a diner."[56]

A CRISIS OF IDENTITY

Multiculturalism, Richard Bernstein wrote, had sown "considerable confusion about who, exactly, we are, how worthy we are, and whether we have any things in common."[57] But who was confused? Who doubted whose worth? As E. Nelson Bridwell's old Tonto joke in *Mad* magazine went, "What you mean 'we,' white man?" If Bloom had been clear about the entitlement and exclusivity of the (supposedly) civilized class, Bernstein had precisely captured the anxiety and agitation of the liberal elites. "Who Are We?" became the question of the moment.

For the Fourth of July weekend in 1991, those words were emblazoned across *Time* magazine's cover, over a Ruth Marten painting that updated *Spirit of '76*, Archibald Willard's famous 1875 painting of the Yankee Doodling fife-and-drum trio leading Revolutionary War patriots across the battlefield. Here in her revision the brown-vested, Washington-tressed white male drummer remained dead center. But now the other drummer was a kerchiefed conga-playing Black woman, the fife player a feather-wearing American Indian. A flag carrier in the rear appeared to be a Latino male, and an Asian woman followed.

Before multiculturalism, Paul Beatty had suggested, "White wasn't the textbook 'mixture of radiations from the visible spectrum'; it was the opposite. White was the expulsion of colors encumbered by self-awareness and pigment."[58] Now multiculturalism had revealed a whiteness newly burdened by self-awareness. The identity crisis at hand was less one of American civilization than of American whiteness.

In the riot-starting year of 1992, after his failed presidential run, Pat Buchanan stepped to the podium at the Republican National Convention to name the civil strife in American culture. "My friends, this election is about much more than who gets what. It is about who we are," he said. "There is a religious war going on in our country for the soul of America. It is a cultural war, as critical to the kind of nation we will one day be as was the Cold War itself."

He railed about "homosexual rights," "radical feminism," and "environmental extremism." And he closed with a story, likely apocryphal, set in the ashes of the Los Angeles riots, whose endless televised stream of images of fire and chaos seemed to evoke antebellum nightmares of some vast colored people's vengeance:

> Hours after the violence ended I visited the Army compound in south LA, where an officer of the 18th Cavalry, that had come to rescue the city, introduced me to two of his troopers. They could not have been twenty years old. He told them to recount their story.

They had come into LA late on the second day, and they walked up a dark street, where the mob had looted and burned every building but one, a convalescent home for the aged. The mob was heading in, to ransack and loot the apartments of the terrified old men and women. When the troopers arrived, M-16s at the ready, the mob threatened and cursed, but the mob retreated. It had met the one thing that could stop it: force, rooted in justice, backed by courage.[59]

Multiculturalism was the fetish of elites gone soft before the mobs—all those spineless university, corporate, and civic leaders caving before demographic change. In belligerent speeches and writings, Buchanan echoed Bloom's warning that the country was headed for a Weimar-style collapse. Only a proper show of force could stop it.

There was a dizzying sweep to the time—the proliferating armies, the counterrevolutionary edge, the sudden turns for the worse, bellicosity thickening the air. It was a great time to be making art.

→Opposite page: *Wee Pals* Sunday strip, February 4, 1973. Courtesy of Morrie Turner.

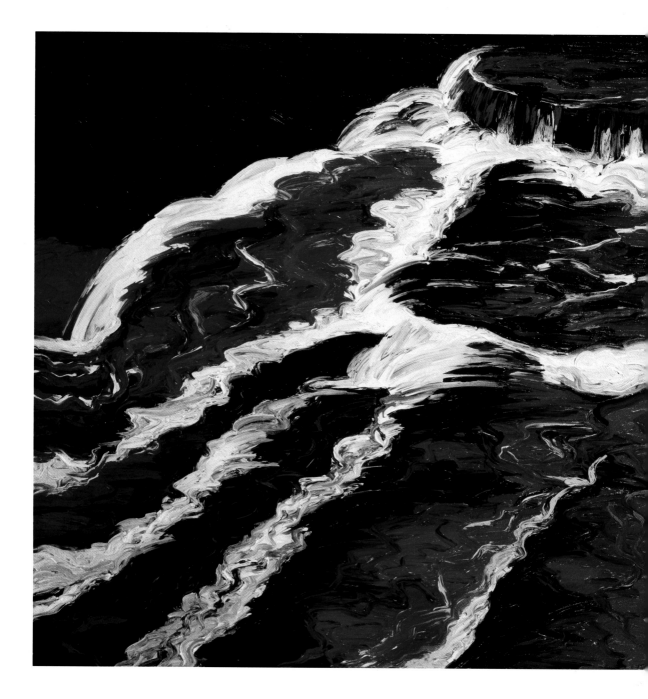

Who We Be

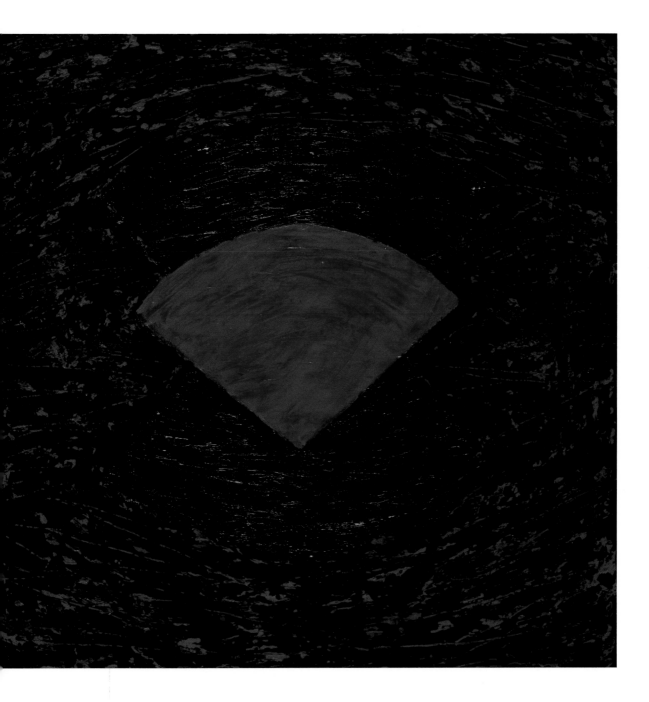

CHAPTER 7

UNITY AND RECONCILIATION

THE ERA OF IDENTITY

I see, you are seen; I desire, you satiate; I know, you are known;
I rule, you are ruled. "You" are the Other.
—Eunice Lipton, "Here Today, Gone Tomorrow? Some Plots for a Dismantling"

In a 1990 address, Modern Language Association president Catharine Stimpson argued multiculturalism offered "the necessary recognition that we cannot think of culture unless we think of many cultures at the same time."[1] It made little sense to think anymore of cultures as fixed and unchanging. That kind of thinking led to imperialist conceptions of identity that offered only a choice between civilization and barbarism. A prescripted life or a kind of death.

←Previous page: *The Abyss* by Kay WalkingStick. 1989. Acrylic, oil, and wax.
Diptych of paintings. Courtesy June Kelly Gallery.

In an influential 1985 essay, from an anthology he curated for a special issue of the literary journal *Critical Inquiry* on "Race, Writing and Difference," Henry Louis Gates Jr. reminded readers race was a biological fiction, spoken in figures of speech. "Who has seen a black or red person, a white, yellow, or brown? These terms are arbitrary constructs, not reports of reality," he wrote.

Yet if an artist of color wanted to express the fullness of his humanity, he might still find himself bound by his difference. "We accepted a false premise by assuming that racism would be destroyed once white racists became convinced we were human, too," Gates wrote. He retold the story of an early-twentieth-century Haitian writer named Edmond Laforest, who, "with inimitable, if fatal, flair for the grand gesture, stood upon a bridge, calmly tied a Larousse dictionary around his neck, then leapt to his death."[2]

But what of life? What other choice did an artist of color have but to try to make herself seen, make her story legible? People created, improvised their identity, often in stunning and hopeful ways. They sought commonality even as they asserted their uniqueness. Diversity and difference—not exclusion and domination—were the basic conditions of vital cultures.

In the early 1990s, two books—Lucy Lippard's *Mixed Blessings: New Art in a Multicultural America*, and an anthology issued from Marcia Tucker's New Museum of Contemporary Art entitled *Out There: Marginalization and Contemporary Cultures*—captured a bright urgent optimism. Cornel West's essay in the latter was received like a manifesto by a mass reaching criticality—both in numbers and theoretical sophistication. He wrote:

I would go so far as to claim that a new kind of cultural worker is in the making, associated with a new politics of difference.... Distinctive features of the new cultural politics of difference are to trash the monolithic and homogenous in the name of diversity, multiplicity, and heterogeneity; to reject the abstract, general, and universal in light of the concrete, specific, and particular; and to historicize, contextualize, and pluralize by highlighting the contingent, provisional, variable, tentative, shifting, and changing.[3]

THE BIG IDEA

And so in early 1989, the directors of three small museums in New York City began to talk about doing something that would be dizzying in its bigness, dazzling in its ambition: a joint exhibition that would capture the entire decade of the 1980s and frame the discussions for the art world of the 1990s, centered around the expansive, continuing project of *identity* itself.

The idea had come from the beautiful mind of Marcia Tucker. In 1977, after eight years as the first hired woman curator at the Whitney Museum of American Art, Tucker had left to form the New Museum of Contemporary Art. She wanted, she said years later, "to see what happens when you don't look at everything through white, male eyes."[4] Now Tucker approached two friends, Nilda Peraza, the director of the Museum of Contemporary Hispanic Art (MoCHA), and Kinshasha Holman Conwill, the director of the Studio Museum in Harlem, and the idea began taking shape.

It would be named *The Decade Show*. The show would simply, Holman Conwill said, "Let the art talk." A list of artists, breathtaking in its scale and diversity, would be hung at all three museums simultaneously. "What we really are doing, what we really need to pursue," Peraza said, "is working towards the creation of a very generous and open art environment in this country, one that will allow and accept artists from all backgrounds, without stereotyping and pigeonholing."[5]

In another time, the notion might have sounded bland, almost sentimental. But in the context of neocon attacks from the Beltway, a heated tug-of-war over the direction of the art world, and a social environment impacted by high-profile hate crimes, AIDS, and demands for truer representation, it sounded visionary.

The beginnings of the *The Decade Show* lay in the foundational networks of alternative arts spaces that had developed in communities of color for the better part of a century. Artists of color had built local and regional ecosystems of art production—not just places to make art, but places to show, buy, and discuss the work.

Take the arc of development for Asian American arts. In the early twentieth century, immigrant and second-generation artists mostly living on the West Coast like the painters Chiura Obata, Chang Shu-Chi, Hisako Hibi, Yun Gee, and Dong Kingman; the photographers Irene Poon, Hiromu Kira, and Toyo Miyatake; and the female proto−graphic novelist Miné Okubo had preceded even the term "Asian American." But they had set up schools and organized themselves into groups like the Chinese Revolutionary Artists' Club, where they mounted exhibitions and discussed how to create art that might avoid, as Gee put it, "Western appetites for orientalia."[6]

In the 1970s, nonprofit Asian American arts organization startups, including New York's Basement Workshop, San Francisco's Kearny Street Workshop, Los Angeles's Visual Communications, and Boston's Asian American Resource Workshop, gave a new generation places to explore the emerging notion of an Asian American identity.

Basement Workshop was a movement space, formed around an ideology of artists serving the people. But by the mid-1980s, art historian Alexandra Chang wrote, its leadership was destabilized by sectarian infighting and struggles between those focused on politics versus those focused on cultural production. In 1986 the Workshop closed. But by then the Asian American arts movement was broad and vital enough to survive the end of a single organization.

Invisibility remained the unfinished cultural agenda. By the end of the 1980s, national networks of artists, curators, scholars, policy makers, and educators, from Appalachians to Afrocentrists, had cohered, such as the national Association of American Cultures, and the Cultural Diversity Based on Cultural Grounding conferences organized by the Caribbean Cultural Center in New York City. They talked about "cultural equity"—expanding standards of aesthetic excellence, advancing "the cultural empowerment of our communities," and securing parity in representation in everything from exhibitions to decision-making positions.[7]

Such initiatives were often supported by the National Endowment for the Arts's Expansion Arts program, established in 1971 and reenergized after the *Nigger Drawings* protest, whose charge was to fund emerging arts organizations "deeply rooted in and reflective of culturally diverse, inner-city, rural, or tribal communities."[8] State and municipal arts funding for underrepresented groups grew, such as the San Francisco Arts Commission's innovative Cultural Equity Grants program. In 1992, the NEA published a broad national survey on 543 cultural centers of color, marking a moment of official recognition of the contributions that multiculturalists had made to the "unique cultural and artistic pluralism of the United States."[9]

The creative ecosystems that made up this national movement were producing large amounts of worthy art that the mainstream art-world market could not or would not absorb. So the new decade would open with ambitious identity shows. The largest was a survey exhibition called *Chicano Art: Resistance and Affirmation: An Interpretive Exhibition of the Chicano Art Movement, 1965–1985*, which opened in September 1990 in the Wight Gallery at the University of California at Los Angeles. Shorthanded as CARA—"face" in Spanish—the show included no fewer than 128 pieces and 54 mural images by 180 artists.

It had been a grassroots project of cultural empowerment and canonization, a people's art history and an art history-making act. CARA was curated and organized by a national advisory committee made up of dozens of artists, activists, and scholars, structured not unlike a political party, with a central decision-making body and regional organizing bodies to ensure democratic input.[10] It had taken seven years to assemble and toured for the next three years.

CARA meant to show the heroic telos of a Chicano art history inseparable from movement history. It began with one of the first pieces of Chicano art, Antonio Bernal's 1968 mural painted on a humble building used by El Teatro Campesino called El Centro Cultural in the farmlands outside Fresno. Bernal had painted a line of revolutionaries—from *indio* warriors through Chavez, Tijerina, Malcolm, and Martin—all turned to face an unseen opponent, armed and ready for battle. After Bernal's piece, grand murals would unfurl in San Diego's Barrio Logan and Los Angeles's Estrada Courts, up the coasts, across the Southwest, north to Chicago and Ann Arbor, and guilds and collectives and print workshops would fill the city streets with bright bursts of pride and protest.

CARA also gave installation space over for the more formal experimentations of urban collectives like the Royal Chicano Air Force, Los Four, and Asco. It attempted to forge a unity of an impossibly diverse group of artists, including the sweet South Texas family narratives of Carmen Lomas Garza; the fearless future-facing women of Yolanda Lopez; the starkly charged printmaking of Rupert Garcia, Malaquias Montoya, and Ester Hernández; and the spectacular sunset car crashes of Carlos Almaraz.

Timelines captured the march of history: the East Los Angeles High-School Blowouts, Alurista reading the "Epic Poem of *Aztlán*" and introducing *El Plan Espiritual de Aztlán* with Corky Gonzales at the first National Chicano Liberation Youth Conference in Denver, the founding of MEChA at a student conference at the University of California *El Plan de Santa Barbara* the following month, the Chicano Moratorium and the death of Rubén Salazar. Recognition and representation, CARA argued, were aesthetic, cultural, *and* political questions.

Large crowds would greet the show in its ten-city run, which included a stay at the National Museum of American Art in Washington, DC. As UCLA Chicano Studies professor Alicia Gaspar de Alba sifted one day through the documents that CARA had left behind, she found a handwritten note in one of the comment books from the show's stint at the Albuquerque Museum of Art. It read simply: "I loved this exhibit. It's like looking in a mirror. It's really seeing the heart of my people."[11]

Art critics seemed to have seen a different show. William Wilson's *Los Angeles Times* review scanned like an old anthropologist's field notes, full of half-digested ethnic notions. "CARA shows a complete sensibility," he wrote. "It's socially concerned, inbred, romantic, proud, nostalgic, ceremonial, masochistic, fetishistic and original. Where would the Anglos have been for fashion after World War II without the zoot suit?"

And more: "CARA's collective look becomes a simile of a stay-with-the-gang subculture. That works among the home folks but in a larger world, it's different—as proven by the growth of numerous artists here. Now they are in the Wight Gallery, which once housed a retrospective of Henri Matisse."[12]

That such street-primitive, "stay-with-the-gang subculture" had been allowed into the spaces where we housed the highest eternal accomplishments of our civilization caused not a little unease in art-world quarters. In the *Washington Times*, Eric Gibson dismissed the entire show as visual affirmative action, writing, "[I]t is simply another attempt to cater to and/or pacify some political interest group, all at the expense (as always) of any real aesthetic standards."[13]

RETURN TO JERICHO

By then art-world formalists, following the neoconservative intelligentsia, were mobilizing their own forces. In the *New Criterion*, Hilton Kramer extended the stakes of the campus culture wars back to the art world in an essay called "Studying the Arts and Humanities: What Can Be Done?" He concluded, "The defense of art must not … be looked upon as a luxury of civilization—to be indulged in and supported when all else is serene and unchallenged—but as the very essence of our civilization."[14]

The insurgent multicultural avant-gardes were a horrifying sign of chaos and misrule. If the formalists were reacting against the words "recognition" and "representation," they were also rallying around another word: "quality." The Q-word pronounced merit, order, universality, and timelessness. It was the opposite of that other Q-word: quotas. It summoned a time before the 1960s, before the barbarians started in with their comic strips and news clippings and defaced flags and stacked bricks and music videos and race riots and heathen animal rituals and vagina-shaped banquet tables, back when a picture was a picture and a drip was a revelation.

Here, too, was a clash of worldviews. For the formalist, everything anyone needed to know about art was within the frame. Art that was worth celebrating was beyond the grip of time. Its beauty was evident in its formal qualities of composition, technique, color, line, space, and the other components that made up its natural essence.

Everything else was irrelevant—history, context, and even the artist himself, with his distracting talk about inspiration and intent. Artists might pour into their work emotion, memory, meaning, and soul—but those were things of which the formalists were most suspicious. Concern for worldly matters, the things beyond the frame, might only reveal an artist who aspired to something that was less art than mere propaganda. "The purely plastic or abstract qualities of art are the only ones that count," Clement Greenberg famously wrote.[15]

Formalism was a language made for and by elites, a way through which art history would be recorded. It never aspired to be a way through which the masses might encounter and enjoy art. And although these critics would summon the full thrust of thousands of years of "civilization" on their side, their school of thought—not unlike that of the Western Civ traditionalists in the academy—had been ascendant only since the 1940s, the moment they had fled from Social Realism, seeking to establish the global hegemony of homegrown Abstract Expressionism by extolling its transcendence and purity.

Yet many American artists expressed an opposite point of view. "Everything is propaganda for what you believe in, actually, isn't it?" Dorothea Lange once told an interviewer. "The harder and the more deeply you believe in anything, the more in a sense you're a propagandist. Conviction, propaganda, faith."[16] Her words came to define Social Realism, and yet they seemed as applicable to Pollock as herself.

Writing in the light of the Harlem Renaissance, W. E. B. DuBois argued Black artists were finally shaking off post-bellum feelings of shame and inferiority. They were experiencing "stirrings of the beginning of a new appreciation of joy, of a new desire to create, of a new will to be." They had in their protean powers the ability to expand American ideas of Beauty, Truth, and Goodness. DuBois said:

The apostle of Beauty thus becomes the apostle of Truth and Right not by choice but by inner and outer compulsion. Free he is but his freedom is ever bounded by Truth and Justice; and slavery only dogs him when he is denied the right to tell the Truth or recognize an ideal of Justice.

Thus all Art is propaganda and ever must be, despite the wailing of the purists.[17]

But by the late 1960s, in his position as *New York Times* art critic, Kramer was deploying formalism to deny Black visual art any value. He reviewed Henri Ghent's 1968 show at the Studio Museum in Harlem, *Invisible Americans: Black Artists of the 1930s*, under the headline "Differences in Quality."[18]

He dismissed the work of these divergent artists as "mainly banal, academic, and incompetent. Some of it is plainly amateurish."[19] He wrote, "In matters of artistic standards, there is no 'justice' in the social sense. There are only the values which artists themselves have established through the practice of their art." Here was a closed circular logic. The title that accompanied Kramer's 1977 review of Dr. David Driskell's *Two Centuries of Black American Art* exhibition—a broad survey of 200 works by 63 artists spanning 1750 to 1950, including Robert Duncanson, Edmonia Lewis, Elizabeth Catlett, and Sargent Johnson—was even blunter: "Black Art or Merely Social History?"

"We," Kramer wrote, the first person plural a deliberate choice, "do not feel the presence in this exhibition of any stringent esthetic criteria in its selection."[20] Driskell's poor selection seemed to Kramer to reveal the inadequacy of a "Black esthetic." The notion of "Black art" had little to no value in describing timeless form. It was useful only as content, as "social documentary." Artists, Kramer argued, needed to be thought of solely in art-historical terms—as neo-primitivists or social realists, as modernists or abstractionists—not socio-historical terms. But if in the intervening decade he had learned a little about some Black artists, it was undoubtedly due in part to the same group exhibitions he felt bound to dismiss.

Formalism paralleled capitalist realism: let us act as if we had always recognized the greatness of artists we once (and still) objected to seeing. It restated the lie of colorblindness: I refused to see you before because of your color, and now that you have revealed my blindness, I see you *despite* your color.

For Black artists, this presented an untenable double bind. They were ignored as individual artists. But the group shows that presented them were never worthy of being seen. And even if they aspired to formalist standards of beauty, they might still be seen as just artists of color. What they put into the frame would not matter. They would still be judged for who they were outside that frame.

It was Laforest on the bridge. The absurdity chased itself in circles.

Small wonder that many heard in the invocation of "quality," "No Colored Allowed." In a famous essay memorializing Jean-Michel Basquiat's career as the "flyboy in the buttermilk," the cultural critic Greg Tate wrote:

> In every arena where we can point to Black underdevelopment or an absence of Black competitiveness there can logically be only two explanations: either Black folks aren't as smart as white boys or, racism. If the past twenty years of affirmative action have proven anything it's that whatever some white boy can do, any number of Black persons can do as good, or, given the hoops a Black person has to jump to get in the game, any number of times better. Sorry Mr. Charlie, but the visual arts are no different.[21]

Curators and artists of color such as Kinshasha Holman Conwill argued that those most ready to deploy the Q-word were the least qualified to judge the merits of art by artists of color. She recalled:

> I remember being on panels on the NEA where it would be some well-known white artist, and people would say 'We don't need to see the slides.' And I'd say, 'Oh yes we do, we're evaluating what's being presented to us, not who we know or who we like.' Same token, we would be looking at people of color and people would say, 'I haven't heard of these people' and I'm saying, 'The point is to review the material in front of you, you know?' … Like in criminal cases, [a person of color] didn't have a jury of one's peers.

In 1987, in conjunction with the opening of that year's Whitney Biennial, an anonymous feminist collective wearing gorilla masks opened a downtown conceptual show called *Guerrilla Girls Review the Whitney*. It was art as pure protest, the art of exclusion. The highlight of the show was a "Banana Report" in which they laid out the numerical facts of continuing invisibility of women and artists of color.

Soon a similar women-of-color group calling itself PESTS stepped up the attack on "art world apartheid."[22] If Spiral had once used aesthetics to combat invisibility, PESTS now had the language of cultural equity. Howardena Pindell conducted a study of underrepresentation in the art world, which she described as "a closed circle which links museums, galleries, auction houses, collectors, critics, and art magazines."[23]

In the 1987–88 *Art in America* annual, the group took out two full-page ads. The first featured a picture of a solitary table setting, as if for a banquet that had been suddenly canceled. In flowery italics, the setting card read, "The Following New York Galleries Are 100% White," and listed thirty-eight galleries, including the hottest galleries of the decade—Annina Nosei, Leo Castelli, and Metro Pictures. The second ad listed twenty-five more that were overwhelmingly white.[24]

These flyers from the anonymous group PESTS began appearing in 1988 at New York art-world gatherings.

PESTS's motto was, "We plan to bug the art world!" And just like the Guerrilla Girls, its hit-and-run tactics rocked the liberal art-world elite. On the exclusive streets of Soho and Chelsea, gallerists fretted over how to both contain these anonymous reputation-wreckers and sign up artists of color as quickly as they could.

ALL IDENTITY

By the summer of 1990, multiculturalism's time seemed to have arrived. The critic Maurice Berger asked the question that artists of color had been asking for decades: "Are art museums racist?"[25] *The Decade Show* would have to be a response, in Holman Conwill's words, "a Joshua move" to bring down the Jericho walls of art-world segregation.

The Decade Show's grand provocation was its subhead: "Frameworks of Identity." The 1980s had been a decade of excess, both commercial and intellectual. The early decade's art market boom had created—and destroyed—sizzling young artists and flashbang movements like Graffiti, Appropriation Art, Neo-Expressionism, and Neo-Geo as fast as the bubble economy could transact. As political reversal continued and the cultural turn began, the leftist avant-garde went bookish, French, and British, mostly, going high-cryptic with their deconstruction and post-everything theories.

If you had been an auction-drunk gallerist, you might have missed the rise of what Peraza called "parallel cultures" and "parallel aesthetics," and their reframing of "separate but equal." And if you had been a jargon-addled critic, you might have missed the distinctiveness of the insurgency that these parallel cultures and aesthetics signified.[26] "Frameworks of Identity" suggested a third way to view the moment—that form and content were inseparable; that the artists exploring questions of identity, many of whom had not already been anointed by the gallerists or the critics, had quietly made much of the best work of the 1980s; that the sheer volume of great unseen work might forcibly transform the art world.

Physically, it sprawled beyond the gates and across the great city—from the New Museum and the MoCHA spaces on lower Broadway to the Studio Museum's building on 125th Street. It would feature no fewer than 134 artists and four artist collectives, a list shaped in lively joint meetings between the staffs of the three museums. The culture wars had certainly expanded the category of Other. The curators shared a faith that some sort of new kind of unity might be pulled out of their grand massing of the Opposition.

Superstars of the decade—Basquiat, Prince, Holzer, Serrano—would be recast in a new light, away from the casino hazards of the auction block or the fluorescent inquisitions of government meeting rooms. Other artists, like Pindell, Ringgold, Robert Colescott, Mel Edwards, Adrian Piper, and Jimmie Durham, would demand rethinking. Long-deserving artists like Tomie Arai, Edgar Heap of Birds, Cecilia Vicuña, and Kay WalkingStick would finally step into the spotlight.

If Kramer had argued that identity art had nothing to say formally, the curatorial teams would prove him wrong. They would not organize work by race, gender, or sexuality, but by theme: the New Museum would house works on myth/spirituality/media and discourse/media; MoCHA on biography/autobiography, gender/sexuality; the Studio Museum on social practices/cultural criticism, history/memory/artifact.

Barbara Kruger's installation was uptown in Harlem, not far from where James Luna had put on a loincloth and lay down in a sandbox with random Indian rez "artifacts." Pat Ward Williams's reappropriated lynching photos were downtown at the New Museum near Cindy Sherman's photo of herself in a red bathrobe. Yong Soon Min's self-portraits, out of which the words "assimilated alien" or "objectified other" had been cut, were shown with Mary Kelly's photo of a dyke's leather jacket over the word "Menacé" at MoCHA.

Gran Fury's posters on the AIDS crisis filled the subway stations and lines. Alfredo Jaar's corrective animation piece—which included the words "This Is Not America's Flag" superimposed on an image of the U.S. flag and concluded with an image of the Western Hemisphere over the word America—took over a Times Square signboard.

Staffers quickly realized they would have to address a host of peculiar micro-encounters. Buses were organized to bring showgoers uptown, dropping off bewildered blue-hairs, blue-suits, and blue-bloods in pre-gentrified Harlem. David Wojnarowicz won over audiences of color with his passionate condemnation of politicians' silence on the AIDS crisis.

The Decade Show made the case that "parallel cultures" and "parallel aesthetics" actually described the shape of the new art world. Reflecting later on the show, Michael Brenson wrote, "One problem with the word 'quality' is that it suggests something finite at a time when the artistic possibilities and the ways of looking at art seem infinite. This decade is not devoid of aesthetic standards but exploding with them."[27]

THE MONSTER RISES

After *The Decade Show*, New York artists Ken Chu, Bing Lee, and Margo Machida began talking about what it might take to open an Asian American contemporary arts museum. These discussions did not result in a museum, but did evolve into the creation of a new Asian American artist network.

If the art collectives of the previous decade had been beset by debates over ideology and politics, this new network would give artists a chance to hit the reset button. Chang wrote, "[I]t was formed not as an outgrowth of Basement's political agendas, but rather as a reaction to its own perceived need for a community of artists, critics and arts admin-istrators to come together to focus on issues pertaining specifically to the art world."[28]

For veterans of the community arts world who had their eye on breaking down the doors to the art world, a network like this was strategic for artists. Yong Soon Min, who worked at the Asian American Arts Alliance while trying to advance her work at the same time, said, "There was hardly ever any presence or visibility of Asian Americans in [art-world] exhibitions. And also then, it became evident that maybe Asian Americans might get educational programs, but never in the galleries proper."

For a young artist like Byron Kim, the network offered something different. "Yong Soon Min, she would tell you that it was about activism, and you know, I would be lying if I told you that I thought it was about that from my point of view," he said. "For me it was purely a social thing."

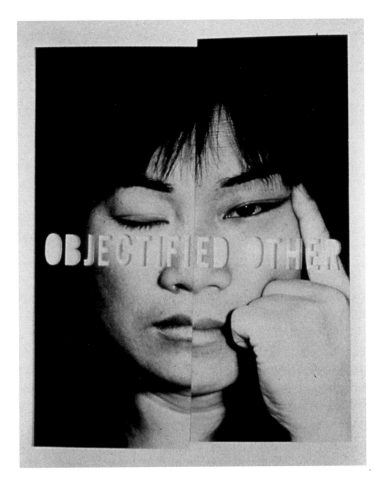

Make Me by Yong Soon Min. 1989. Photograph and printed text on paper.
Six panels, overall 96 × 120 in.

He could share his ideas, eat great cheap lunches on Tuesdays, and hang out with great artists like Martin Wong. "That guy could eat," Kim said. "He was this skinny guy." Since artists always showed up late, the group would move to the next cheap spot and eat again. "We'd have the three-lunch lunch," he said. To him the network was about feeding starving artists.

Unity and Reconciliation: The Era of Identity

For an aspiring curator like Karin Higa, it was a diverse group of the best and the brightest. "When things are not yet something, when they're evolving, as far as I'm concerned, is the time when it is the most exciting because it's filled with possibility, and the possibilities are endless because everyone has their own idea about what it might be," she said. "And [the group] embodied both the kind of possibility and the excitement of what banding together as a group of people interested in race and identity could mean and also its pitfalls."

The network would be a mainstream batteram, a conscious party, an act of strategic essentialism. They chose to name it after—who else?—Godzilla. Here was a monster created by atomic imperialism in the Pacific; he rampaged through movies in which, when Asian people spoke, the words that were heard weren't the ones coming out of their mouths; and he was super-famous on American TV. Higa would later write, "Nothing about Godzilla was authentically Asian."[29]

In the coming months the Godzilla Asian American Art Network would play an important role in the art world. But for now, it had become a locus of much artistic and intellectual activity. They put together "slide slams," where dozens of artists could show each other their work. They plotted on how to crash the art world.

And they debated whether there really was an Asian American aesthetic. Machida, Higa, and others argued that there was not; the community was just too diverse. A young Paul Pfeiffer, still a grad student, an ACT UP activist, and not yet the art-world star he would become, argued that there was, and that, given Asian American artists' lack of representation and misrepresentation, it was important to stand in support of that notion. In 1991 he spoke on a panel at Hunter College addressing this topic:

> When we speak of Euro-American aesthetics, there is room for diversity
> and a myriad of cultural influences, many of which come from Asia and
> other parts of the world. But suddenly when we speak of the possibility of
> an Asian American aesthetic, it must either be monolithic or not viable.
> Our diversity, our myriad of influences, and our history of cultural interac-
> tions are problematic only when discussing Asian American aesthetics...."[30]

For now the idea of identity in multiculturalism was sustained by the larger division of white/Other, inside/outside, mainstream/margin. But what would happen when artists began to *really* work both sides of the slash at once and those walls began to fall? In a sense, the art that fell under the heading of multiculturalism was already surpassing the idea itself, running headlong into something else, toward new unities and reconciliations, new conflicts and contradictions.

AFTER THE EITHER AND THE OR

Kay WalkingStick was the kind of artist for whom *The Decade Show* and the era of the identity show seemed to have been created. She had been creating challenging, beautiful, accomplished works that explored difficult questions of personal biography. And she had come from far outside of the closed circuit. Her life had been one of reconciliations.

WalkingStick was born in Syracuse, New York, in 1935 to a Cherokee father on a football scholarship to Dartmouth and a white mother from Syracuse. The two had met on a long train ride to Philadelphia. Kay was born as the youngest of five children and raised in a Presbyterian household, estranged from her father and her Indian background.

She learned to draw in church. "I was given paper and pencil in church to keep me quiet for the long sermons," she recalled. She took up art and was trained at a women's college in eastern Pennsylvania in the late 1950s, then settled down with her husband to start a family. "I painted at home in the kitchen," she said. "I made a lot of bad art for about ten years."

When her two children were older, she began showing her work at small galleries in New Jersey. She was making hard-edge figurative work, brightly colored outlines of nudes. In 1969, she had her first New York show at a place called the Cannabis Gallery. "I had a five-person show there, and five people showed up for the opening, including myself and my husband," she said.

She enrolled at Pratt Institute on a women's fellowship. The times were changing, and so was her art. "I had a husband, two kids, and a house in the suburbs," she said. "I was raised by two women who both worked, who believed that women had to learn how to take care of themselves and who told me every day I had to make something of myself. So I was always a feminist in a sense. But the American Indian Movement made me realize that I had to find out who I was as an Indian. I mean, I'm my father's daughter. I look like him. I'm big and muscular and all that. I'm probably like him in other ways that I don't know even."

She was drawn to the tragedies of Indian history, the stories of Chief Joseph and John Ridge. She was also experimenting with paint mixtures made of wax, ammonium carbonate, water, and pigment that gave her work dense, ambrosial surfaces. She was painting, layering, carving with her bare hands. The result was her Chief Joseph series, in which paired arcs and rectangles were cut out of thick dark backgrounds in ways that suggested, as the Pueblo/Latino writer Margaret Archuleta wrote, "a death chant, long, drawn out, and mournful."

After she had finished her graduate degree, her work came to the attention of the Flathead Salish painter Jaune Quick-to-See Smith, who was organizing Native artists around the country and doing shows. WalkingStick showed with Smith and was eager to meet other Indian artists. But her gallerist friends and former professors didn't like the idea.

"It was suggested to me that it was an unwise move because you don't want to appear too 'ethnic.' You don't want to look like a Santa Fe Indian. You don't want to look like you're doing kitsch," she recalled. "Which is, I think, pretty racist."

To be sure, WalkingStick had no desire to make what she termed "wish fulfillment for a white culture: art by the 'Vanishing American.'"[31] She had to admit they had a point. She thought, "How often did Robert Rauschenberg talk about his Indian heritage?"

For WalkingStick, identity was complicated. She said, "I really want to make it on what I'm doing in the studio. I really want to be seen as an American artist who's also a Native. I think that's the way most Native people prefer also."

But, she added, "If I'd wanted to not be Native, I could have. I always thought that this was what you do—you present yourself the way you really are. I am who I am. And that was what was important—to present myself as this biracial women who was part Cherokee, who identified as Cherokee.

"I just couldn't imagine not being who I was," she said. "Still can't."

In 1984, she was asked to do a painting for an exhibition entitled *Homage to the American Elm*. She told the curator, "I'm not Seneca and I don't do realism." But the curator knew she was some kind of Indian—couldn't hurt on grant applications, could it?—and asked her to take on the work anyway.

"I did a painting of the American elm with my hands just to see what it would look like, and I kind of liked it. So I put it next to an abstraction I was working on. I said, 'Aha!'" she recalled. "One was like a snapshot, a memory of an immediate thing, and the other had a lasting impression of the earth and its geology. And the whole thing kind of grew from there."

WalkingStick had arrived at her generative idea—juxtaposing texturally thick, minimalist abstractions with images of vast archetypal landscapes. She believed that people were hardwired to make distinctions and set up dualities—Self/Other, Order/Chaos, Nature/Culture, Form/Content. During the 1980s, such binaries had become politicized—White Male/Other, Formalist/Multicultural, Art/Kitsch, American/Un-American. For WalkingStick, the binaries plunged into the personal—White/Indian, Childhood/History, Land/Body, Tradition/Innovation, Ancient/Abstract. By exposing the process of building oppositions, she could allow viewers to form their own conclusions, reach their own accords.

The Decade Show had included two of her diptychs, *Canyon De Chelly*, a piece that she later destroyed, and *Loss*, one of a gorgeous, emotionally harrowing series of paintings, featuring primal shapes reminiscent of her Chief Joseph series paired with images of waterfalls and river rapids rendered largely in black, white, and scarlet. This series, which included paintings entitled *The Abyss* and *Grappling with Chaos*, described her emotional state. Her pride at being included in the show with artists she admired—Eric Fischl, James Luna, Howardena Pindell—was tempered by the grief she felt over the recent passing of her husband.

While *The Decade Show* secured a lot of press, WalkingStick noticed that much of the critical reception focused on the meaning of the show as opposed to the work of the artists. "I guess I, like a lot of other people, thought that something big would come of this, that we'd all be picked up by major galleries and have huge careers," she said. "And of course it didn't happen." In five years, she had gone from "don't be ethnic" to "you're just ethnic." Was that progress? Wasn't there another choice?

WalkingStick was moving into criticism and curation as well, helping to introduce the world to older and younger American Indian artists. Now that the door seemed to be opening for some, she had her eye on the next door. "Not to receive serious critical review is a kind of disempowerment," she wrote in an issue of *Art Journal* on "Recent Native American Art" that she coedited in 1992. "If there is no in-depth critical discussion of the value of the work that is included in these exhibitions, then multicultural exhibitions become just another way to segregate artists."[32]

In fact, very soon, the art of multiculturalism would receive intense scrutiny, but perhaps not the kind she or her peers had been seeking.

A security guard at Biennial of the Whitney Museum of American Art, 1993.
Photo courtesy of Daniel Joseph Martinez & Tilton Gallery.

CHAPTER 8

IMAGINE/ EVER WANTING/ TO BE

THE FALL OF MULTICULTURALISM

If art is made to belong, it seems to me that it is the poorer for it.
This is especially the case when art is made to belong to art itself.
—Paul Chan, "What Art Is and Where It Belongs"

In the pecking order of New York's great art museums, the Whitney Museum of American Art tailed the Met, the MOMA, and the Guggenheim in endowment, attendance, and prestige. But to the multiculturalists clamoring for representation in the galleries, the Upper East Side guardians casting a nervous eye on their gates, and the relentless media circling like coyotes, the Whitney was as appropriate a setting for a showdown as could be imagined.

The museum had been founded by Gertrude Vanderbilt Whitney to champion working American artists against European predominance. She had been a maverick—an accomplished sculptor and a strong supporter of women artists and young modernists, including Alexander Calder, Edward Hopper, Georgia O'Keeffe, Stuart Davis, and Yasuo Kuniyoshi. She opened the Museum in Greenwich Village in 1931 only after the Met refused her collection. Not long after, she held her first Whitney Annual, in order to showcase great artists dismissed in their own country.

After World War II, the rise of Abstract Expressionism—and the school of formalist criticism that accompanied it—came to define the highbrow side of American global cultural hegemony. In a sense, the Whitney's mission had been accomplished. But by the roaring eighties, all eyes around the world returned to the hothouse New York scene.

Even after the 1987 market crash, the Whitney felt like the most compelling space in town. Every leadership tussle, every curatorial shift, every gala opening was scrutinized and dissected. And the Whitney's new director, David A. Ross, cut the kind of stylish profile that generated lots of copy. What other museum could drive the arts, style, society, and gossip pages, all at the same time?

By then, Gertrude Whitney's Annual had long since become a Biennial. But the sweeping survey of contemporary American art remained the museum's signature event. It was a star-making, zeitgeist-defining machine that left no one—least of all, the formalists and the highbrows—remotely neutral. The art critic Steven Kaplan summed up the Upper East Side ritual:

> For three months every other Spring, this most prestigious and wealthy
> museum dedicated to the exhibition of American art serves up its
> version of the best and the brightest, raising the hackles of critics, the ire
> of excluded artists and galleries, and providing a sitting target for jibes,
> in-jokes, innuendo, and controversy.... It's downright unfashionable for
> any professional observer of the arts scene to approve wholeheartedly of
> the exhibition.[1]

The exhibition had also long been a recurring target for activists. Ten weeks before the 1970 Annual, Faith Ringgold, Lucy Lippard, Poppy Johnson, and Brenda Miller protested the lack of women's representation, demanding that half of the artists chosen be women, and half of the women be of color. They left tampons and cracked eggs in the galleries for the curators.

By the late 1980s, Guerrilla Girls and PESTS had revived the issue of representation with flyers, pamphlets, posters, and counter-exhibitions. The poet and critic John Yau wrote a much-discussed *Arts* magazine article pointing out that Jean-Michel Basquiat was the only artist of color invited to a Biennial that entire decade. "For the artist of color, the news is still the same," he wrote. "The past was horrible, the present is grim, and the future is bleak. The art world continues to admire its carefully cultivated brand of sensitivity. Advice: Break the mirror and drive the glass home."[2]

WHOSE MUSEUM?

In February 1991 David A. Ross plunged into the Whitney fishbowl. He was a flash of color—a quotable renegade, a devoted artist's advocate, and a mediagenic crowd-pleaser, seemingly cut from the mold of Gertrude Whitney herself. In fact Ross had grown up far from the WASPy Upper East Side, where careers in arts administration were like family inheritances. Instead he was the son of a dentist in the Long Island village of Malverne. Although little had been made of the fact, his appointment had been historic: Ross was the first Jewish American director of the Whitney.

His career had taken him through the Long Beach Museum, the University Art Museum in Berkeley, the music industry, and finally the Institute of Contemporary Art in Boston. It was not the kind of CV that comforted much of the art-world elite. The influential critic Robert Hughes once described Ross as "Pat Rileyesque," and he did not mean it as a compliment.[3]

Ross's career had begun with a generational confrontation. At Syracuse University, he had been a loud and proud '68er, growing his Jewfro long and marching against the war. Assigned by a newspaper to photograph the new director of the university's art museum, Ross grew impatient with waiting for his subject and started insulting the man. That man, a radical curator named James Harithas, was duly impressed, hired Ross on the spot, and gave his young apprentice a philosophy.

"The art museum is a social instrument," Harithas told Ross. "It is either used directly by the people who run it or used indirectly by the people who own it. Make your choice."

After the freedom of the ICA, Ross knew he'd find high intrigue awaiting at the Whitney. The 1980s bull market was over, and blood needed to be spilled. The previous director had been forced out amid loud accusations—duly reported in the mass media—that the museum had become too involved with downtown dealers. Now Ross had to forge a post-boom agenda for the high-profile museum. The Upper East Side whispered: could he conquer the Whitney or would it conquer him? For his first important exhibition, the 1993 Biennial, he went to the one person he could trust in a treacherous new environment, Elisabeth Sussman.

Since 1982, Sussman had been Ross's right hand at the ICA. "We decided in the beginning of David's term there that the best thing we could do for the place was to just inundate them with contemporary art," she said. "We had a limited budget and space but unlimited ambition." They had developed ties to the rising intelligentsia—Hebdige, Gilroy, and Jameson. They had showcased young stars—Koons, Simpson, Levine. When the Robert Mapplethorpe exhibition was axed from the Corcoran, Ross secured it for the ICA and appeared as a hero for artistic freedom.

After declining to step into Ross's job at the ICA, Sussman had moved to New York to join him. Sussman wore her outsiderness like a badge, too. "I'm in no one's pocket," she told *Art & Auction* magazine. "Leo Castelli virtually doesn't recognize me."[4]

One of Ross's first hires was Thelma Golden, the first African American curator ever hired at the Whitney and, still in her midtwenties, the youngest. Golden had not marked the passage of time by her high school levels, but by the springtime return of the Whitney Biennials. Her first was in 1981, and in the March before she graduated another opened. This class of 1983 had marked the changing of the guard. It included, for the first time, Cindy Sherman, David Salle, Jenny Holzer, Barbara Kruger, Keith Haring, and a Brooklyn-born twenty-two-year-old son of a Haitian father and a Puerto Rican mother named Jean-Michel Basquiat, whose singular example made everything seem possible.

Golden attended Smith College during the height of national campus ferment over multiculturalist revision of the canon. Upon commencement she hurried back to New York City to see the 1987 Biennial, and landed internships at the Studio Museum in Harlem, then the Whitney. She joined up with the curator Kellie Jones, who was turning the Jamaica Arts Center in Queens into a hub for contemporary Black art. In 1991, with the organization battered by NEA and arts funding cuts, Golden was laid off.

That was when David Ross hired her. She knew everyone, he would say, and did everything with "100 percent energy." He appointed her the director of the Whitney's Philip Morris branch near 42nd and Park. Sussman made Golden the first pick to her Biennial team, which would include continuing Whitney curators John Hanhardt and Lisa Phillips, new education director Connie Wolf, and for a short time, *October* magazine critic Benjamin Buchloh.

The Manhattan media rushed in to interview Golden, and she delivered with charm, style, and intelligence. Golden was as aware of the meaning of her appointment as Ross was of the Whitney's symbolism. She knew that expectations ran high from both the African American community and the art-world elite. In one breath the gatekeepers would note that she embodied the change multiculturalism promised and in the next they wondered if she was "qualified" for the job. Older African Americans in the art world publicly expressed pride in her appointment but privately wondered how she would represent "her community."[5]

All of this gave Golden a keen focus and made her impatient for a post-multicultural future. She could see the outlines of this future taking shape in the work of her contemporaries—artists like Glenn Ligon, Carrie Mae Weems, Lorna Simpson, Gary Simmons, and others who were making work informed by Conceptualism and the history of the

Black image. They were a new breed. They worked with rigor and hip-hop-size ambition but without apology.

Asked once in a public forum about the marginalization of Black art and artists, Golden admitted, "I'm extremely tired of (talking about) it, perhaps because in my very short career I have been called on to do it so much." Those sympathetic to her would say with mixture of admiration and concern that she had entered a minefield of high-stakes double-consciousness. But Thelma Golden was clear about where she stood, what she needed to do, and where she needed to take the art world.

"I'm a curator of color, at a major museum. So I exist as either friend or foe—depending on who you talk to, on which day, and depending on when you talk to me in the course of the day," she said.

"I feel that now we are in the fallout of an either/or, black/white, margin/center debate," she added. "Instead of looking at it as a position of schizophrenia, I look at it as one of power."[6]

THE TAKEOVER

The watchers of the Upper East Side eyed the new team on 75th and Madison with rising anxiety. Hilton Kramer immediately launched ad hominem attacks on Golden and Ross. He wrote that Golden was "a recent college graduate with no advanced degrees in the field, no record of scholarly publication, no experience in other major institutions and, at best, a spotty acquaintance with the art history of recent decades and a dim grasp of the ideas that have governed the whole span of art in this century.[7]

"Ross has never demonstrated that he has an understanding of art-as-art," wrote Kramer, who, like Ross, was also a Syracuse graduate and an art autodidact. "He's made it a vehicle for political correctness and multiculturalism."[8]

On the other hand, as soon as Ross and Sussman came on the job, they were confronted by the Godzilla Asian American Art Network. When the 1991 Whitney Biennial exhibition opened, members Margo Machida, Yong Soon Min, Byron Kim, Paul Pfeiffer, and Eugenie Tsai sent a letter to Ross, noting that the Whitney had failed to include Asians and Asian Americans in the Biennial and offering to open an "ongoing dialogue" with the museum. The letter stirred waves in the art world.

Although Ross had arrived only a month before the Biennial opened, too late to have been involved in most of the process, he agreed to meet with the group. When he did, he had to admit that Asian American artists had not been on his radar. Godzilla agreed to submit artist slides from its growing network to the Whitney staff. From that point forward, Ross's openness to emerging artists remained consistent.

"For better or worse," he said, "the museum needs to be seen as an active coconspirator with artists, and the museum needs to be willing to share the consequences for failure, and in fact, embrace failure as well as it embraces success."

If the artists were taking on identity, Ross was sympathetic. "I think the attitude was prevalent that if you accepted that art was political, you couldn't be serious about aesthetics. And if you accepted the politics of identity as a significant central issue, you were imposing it [on people]," he said, "as if somehow formalism doesn't have an ideological substructure."

Instead, he said, "There were other issues. There were other histories. It doesn't negate the histories that are written through the vocabulary of formalism at all. Why should it?"

Ross also felt that the role of the Biennial had changed. The expansion of the gallery system, including the rise of alternative spaces and nonprofit cultural organizations, was allowing many new artists to be seen. The Whitney's role was to make sense of it all. He said, "The job of the Biennial was to stake out a point of view that could generate a useful discussion about the state of the arts in America."

Outside the Whitney fishbowl, the world was splitting in two: Bush v. Saddam, Bush v. Clinton, Thomas v. Hill, the Moral Majority v. the AIDS generation, Euro-America v. Other America, the Far Right v. the art world, culminating in the Los Angeles riots, which pitted everyone against everyone. But in shows like *The Decade Show*, *Witnesses: Against Our Vanishing*, and Robert Mapplethorpe's *The Perfect Moment*, artists were rising to the occasion.

Art reflected a spirit of democratization, and this spirit had changed what could be seen as art. There had been no middle ground in the George Holliday video of the Los Angeles police beating Rodney King, a fact that the Biennial team acknowledged when film and video curator John Hanhardt proposed late in the process that it be included and everyone agreed.

Bolstered by the work of intellectuals like Cornel West, Michele Wallace, Gloria Anzaldúa, and Homi Bhabha, the team focused on the theme of borders. They were interested in artists who were crossing lines, who worked between and around fixed identities of race, gender, sexuality. They made a concerted effort to move past the top galleries and seek out emerging artists of color, women artists, and gay artists.

In the Biennial catalog, Thelma Golden laid out the curatorial mission and a preemptive strike against the critics in her essay, "What's White...?":

Artists in the nineties have begun to fully deconstruct the marginality-centrality paradigm. Marginality, in effect, becomes the norm while the center is increasingly undefinable and perhaps irrelevant. Although many may call this Biennial the "multicultural" or "politically correct"

Biennial, it should be read as a larger project which insists that decentralization and the embracing of the margins have become dominant.[9]

The performance artist and public intellectual Coco Fusco's essay, "Passionate Irreverence: The Cultural Politics of Identity" read like an artist's wartime statement. Conflict over identity and culture, Fusco wrote, seemed inescapable and interminable. "Behind each debate lingers fears and hopes about the image this country projects of itself to its people(s) and to the world," she wrote. "Culture in this country is a critical, if not the most crucial area of political struggle for identity."[10] She ticked off the media's central obsessions: *Who are we? Whose values? Whose museums and whose aesthetics? Whose icons? Whose image?* Multiculturalist artists might hold the answers.

Art & Auction's exhibition preview reported the final list of Biennial artists as if it were an affirmative action report, a progress index for those like the Guerrilla Girls, Godzilla, and PESTS who cared about the numbers, and a zero-sum anxiety trigger for those like *Time* critic Robert Hughes; *Newsweek* critic Peter Plagens; and *Art in America* contributing editor Eleanor Heartney, who pretended not to: 82 artists (excluding a record number of performance, film, video, and installation artists) up from 72 in 1991, white males down from 60% to 36%, women up from 34% to 41%, white females holding at 30%, men of color up from 6% to 23%, women of color up from 4% to 11%.[11] Even before the doors opened the 1993 Whitney Biennial marked a turning point. It would by far be the most diverse exhibition ever held in a major American museum.

Without having seen any of the art, critics began to position themselves. "Now, instead of being run by the market, the Whitney is being run by a kind of mild but moralizing political orthodoxy that above all wants to inscribe itself on the public consciousness as not having been on the wrong side," *Time*'s Hughes told *Art & Auction*. "You get this kind of Stalinism without Joe."[12] Years later, Elisabeth Sussman would admit that she had been ready for the cultural conservatives to line up against the show, but that she was not ready for the liberals to join them.

At that moment, she was most disheartened that two artists would not be in the show. David Wojnarowicz, the artist who had been attacked by Jesse Helms and Donald Wildmon and reacted with searing, beautiful work indicting the cult-cons for their cruelty toward gays and victims of AIDS, had finally succumbed in 1992 to the disease. Sussman felt Wojnarowicz was the ghost in the galleries. His presence was felt in a Nan Goldin portrait. The catalog cover was a close up of Kiki Smith and Wojnarowicz's powerful *Untitled* piece, in which they covered themselves in blood—blood as bond, community, and death.

For almost two years, Sussman had tried to get another David—David Hammons—into the Biennial. In his own mysterious ways he had eluded her. On opening night, February 24, 1993, Sussman found herself not inside the museum, but on the other side of

Madison Avenue. Charles Ray's fifty-foot-long toy fire truck was parked to the right of the entrance, cartoonishly unequipped to contain any fire inside. In the display window hung Pat Ward Williams's eight-feet-by-sixteen-feet photo mural of five relaxed young Black men gazing back behind the spray-painted words, "What You Lookn At." A huge crowd packed into the lobby.

Suddenly David Hammons appeared next to her. Together they watched the spectacle across the street unfold. Hammons laughed. He leaned toward Sussman and said, "I'm so glad I'm not in this show."

IN THE GALLERIES OF AMERICAN ART

When you stepped into the Whitney and paid your $6, you were handed one of six museum tags in one of six colors. The first five tags were: "I," "can't imagine," "ever wanting," "to be," and "white." The sixth included all of the words together. They had been designed by Daniel Joseph Martinez, a Los Angeles artist appearing in the Whitney for the first time.

Through the window and over the railing you could see a loud crowd gathering downstairs in the patio off the café. They massed around a gilded cage in which Coco Fusco and Guillermo Gómez-Peña had installed themselves. You promised to come back to see exactly what was going on.

At the next desk, you were handed another work of art—an audiotape recording assembled by Andrea Fraser from interviews with Ross and the curatorial team to accompany you on your Biennial tour.

If you thought of yourself as fairly informed about the art world, you saw familiar names as you browsed the program guide—Cindy Sherman, Chris Burden, Spike Lee—and some you did not recognize yet—Matthew Barney, Renee Green, Julie Taymor. You noted some had been in *The Decade Show*—Shu Lea Cheang, Guillermo Gómez-Peña, Jimmie Durham, James Luna. You might have also noticed Fred Wilson's name, the artist beginning to become known for his provocative recontextualizing of racially charged museum artifacts and artworks.

When you took in the well-heeled patrons gawking at Gómez-Peña and Fusco, frowned down again at Martinez's museum tag, then slipped on your headphones for Fraser's exhibition guide, you might have wondered if the Biennial curators had abdicated all of their authority to those smirky students of the school of Institutional Critique. If you were a professional art critic, perhaps you were very annoyed by now.

You walked down the stairs and joined the crowd by the gilded cage.

You saw the woman appearing in a leopard-skin top and grass skirt, her face painted green and yellow, sporting scuffy Converse lows and a spangled baseball cap turned sideways. She sat at a table, sometimes sewing "voodoo" dolls, sometimes reading a monograph on Christopher Columbus. You saw the man dressed in a feathered headdress, leopard skin *luchador* mask, and a fringy gold *naguilla*. You saw him lifting weights and pacing through the cage in freshly shined *banda* boots. You saw him cradling his boom box.

You could hear a young guard explaining that these "fine specimens" were previously undiscovered savages from an island in the Gulf of Mexico called Guatinau. They were members of the tribal elite who had chosen to tour the West in order to represent their culture.

You saw the spectators dropping money into a coin box, making their requests to the Guatinaui to perform. She danced a bounding two-step to a rap song. He told the epic story of their tour, in a high whine of gibberish dotted with words "Chicago," "Mexico," "Minnesota," and "America." Some spectators—instant experts—translated the Guatinaui into English for the benefit of other onlookers.

People took pictures. They fed the savages bananas. The guards explained that if they paid more they could see the man's genitals. Sometimes the man and the woman got bored and turned away from the crowd to watch a TV beaming images of happy natives dancing to a mambo on a distant tropical beach.

You heard the guard explain that this exhibit was part of a tradition started five centuries before by no less than Columbus himself. You saw displays of the geography and culture of Guatinau. You noticed both were wearing fashionable shades. You discovered a small wall card revealing the name of the piece—*The Couple in the Cage: Two Undiscovered Amerindians Visit the West*. You might have begun to suspect there was no such thing as an island called Guatinau. You might have been less sure that Columbus had *not* paraded Arawaks around the Portuguese court.

Perhaps you wondered as you turned away: Was this all a joke on you?

You got into the elevator, pressed play on the sound device, and heard Ross and the team welcoming you. "Buckle your seats," Ross genially warned as you ascended, "it's going to be a rough ride."[13]

IDENTITY ON PARADE

On the fourth floor, you walked up to Janine Antoni's *Gnaw* installation. It featured a 600-pound cube made of lard and a 600-pound cube of chocolate, a display of 150 lipstick tubes made from the lard she had chewed off the lard block and twenty-seven empty heart-shaped candy boxes made of the chocolate she had chewed off the chocolate block, minimalism reduced, reused, and recycled for a third-wave feminist party.

You wandered through video installations, past hotly flashing works by the Gulf Crisis TV Project, Not Channel Zero, and Sadie Benning, and a reading room stocked with books on cultural theory.

You came upon Pepón Osorio's *The Scene of the Crime (Whose Crime?)*, a dense installation of a Puerto Rican family's living room in which a bloodied body lay covered with a sheet. It was a klieg-lit set for a noir movie, an ethnographic diorama, a maximal family altar. Amid it all—the flamingo stickers on the mirrors, the porcelain black-skinned saints, the sports trophies, the framed pictures of the family, the wallpaper made of Latino celebrity tabloids and *El Diario*—you saw a welcome mat cut away to reveal a text so that it read,

> Welcome ... only if you can understand that it has taken years of pain to
> gather into our homes our most valuable possessions; but the greater pain
> is to see how in the movies others make fun of the way we live....

Perhaps you wondered what role you were playing here as you walked through the galleries: Were you a detective, a witness, a leering voyeur?

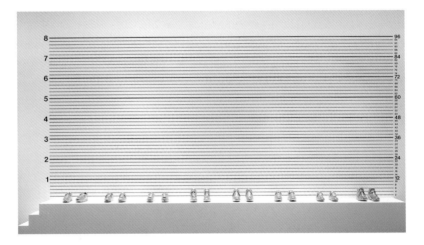

Lineup by Gary Simmons. 1993. Synthetic polymer on wood with gold-plated basketball shoes, 114 × 216 × 18 in. (289.6 × 548.6 × 45.7 cm). Whitney Museum of American Art, New York; purchase with funds from the Brown Foundation, Inc. 93.65a-p Photography by Jerry L. Thompson.

You saw Gary Simmons's *Wall of Eyes*, a fifteen-foot-long blackboard on which he had drawn dozens of cartoon eyes—evoking minstrel songs and Mel Blanc voices—then partially erased them as if in an agitated frenzy. You saw his other work—high-top sneakers aligned in front of a police station measuring wall, bodiless but gold-plated. Simmons called it what they called something like this in America, *Line-Up*. Golden called it "the inner-city equivalent of a casting call."[14] The British would have called it an "identity parade."

Going down a floor, you came upon Lorna Simpson's installation, *Hypothetical?*, which presented a grid of trumpet mouthpieces opposite a photo of a Black man's lips, accompanied by sounds of breathing—perhaps sighing, perhaps the exhale that had been waiting—and capped with a *Los Angeles Times* clipping that dated back to the riots: "Asked whether he would now be afraid to be a black man in Los Angeles if he were not the mayor, Mr. Bradley paused, then said, 'No, I would not be scared. I would be angry.'"[15]

You went into another room to find Glenn Ligon's *Notes on the Margin of the Black Book*. Framed erotic Robert Mapplethorpe photos of Black men were hung with text panels, words from Jesse Helms, Jack Walls, Essex Hemphill, Audre Lorde, and some guys at bars Ligon frequented, disorienting the discussion from the old binaries of art/obscenity and censorship/freedom.

There was Charles Ray's other sculpture, *Family Romance*, a model of a white nuclear family holding hands, naked and average, except that each individual—father, mother, young son, toddler girl—was the same height, a disturbing distortion that elicited Freudian distress and Golden's phrase, "the vertigo of displacement."

You entered a darkened corridor, triggering the appearance of a series of ghostly projections—a Black man, an Asian woman, a white man, an elderly woman who moved toward you, gestured welcomingly or menacingly, then turned back as you passed. This was Gary Hill's *Tall Ships*, and it begged a question worthy of Octavia Butler: Would you allow what you have changed to change you?

THE LAST TURN

On the second floor, you stumbled upon what looked like a number of pregnant bellies mounted in shades from dark to light like Faith Ringgold's *The American Spectrum*. They had been created when the artist filled a panel with various tints of flesh-colored latex and hot encaustic, then let gravity and drying do the rest. Were these meant to suggest something about the art of the Biennial itself, the birthing of something new?

The next wall featured more than two hundred ten-inch by eight-inch chips, each painted a color within the spectrum from pink to bister brown. They seemed to be arranged randomly, but the wall text revealed an alphabetic list of names. Each name, you realized, corresponded to a unique chip and tone.

These were Byron Kim's *Belly Paintings* and *Synecdoche*.

Kim had odd fascinations: abstraction, the color-field painter Ad Reinhardt, the minimalist Brice Marden, and Process Art, all interests that tilted toward the formal. The *Belly Paintings* had begun as an experiment when he was a young resident artist at Skowhegan. The idea of bodies—so hot in intellectual theory and multiculturalism—had been the furthest thing from his mind. He had been obsessing over process and rigor and materials and color.

But his friends were all calling them "belly paintings." This annoyed Kim.

"I thought it was trivializing," he recalled. "I was thinking, 'No! These are more tougher, and these are more theoretical.'"

Yet he reluctantly gave in to their interpretation. The next idea he had was even simpler. "If these are bellies," he said, "then I can make paintings of skin color." And he began a weird kind of portraiture, rendering his friends' skin colors on wood chips. He stacked those paintings against his Williamsburg studio wall.

That's where they sat until a friend, Paul Blood, came over to see Kim's belly paintings for a show he was curating. Blood was instead struck by the flesh paintings. He told Kim that if he made more, he could fill an exhibition wall with them and even mount them next to a work by rising star Kiki Smith. "Kiki Smith?" thought Kim. "OK then."

Kim began heading out to the Williamsburg library and McCarren Park and asking random people to pose. Then he would take their name, write it on the back of the chipboard, and proceed to mix up colors to match his subject's skin tone. In the next month he did a hundred of them. Blood hung them next to Smith's piece, and *Synecdoche* began its journey to the Biennial.

In an issue of Godzilla's newsletter Kim wrote an earnest manifesto with an ironic title, "An Attempt at Dogma." "'Synecdoche' as a whole will have the look of a huge, formalist painting," he wrote. "While I want these chips of brown and beige to push in and pull back and give visual pleasure, I also want them to have the mundane flicker of an art that is inclusive as a matter of fact."[16]

And there was your Biennial—a synecdoche, the part representing the whole, every manifesto a song, every inclusion an invitation, every breath a relief.

Or perhaps instead your Biennial was a mess of big vacuous pieces of "Oh Duh" white hating male dogma that was now mercifully almost over, except for those irritating museum tags clipped near your neck.

I CAN'T
IMAGINE
EVER WANTING
TO BE
WHITE

▲

*Museum Tags: Second Movement (Overture); or Overture con Claque
(Overture with Hired Audience Members)* by Daniel Joseph Martinez. 1993.
Courtesy of the artist and Roberts & Tilton Gallery.

When Daniel Joseph Martinez had been asked to participate in the Biennial, the tags had not been his first proposal. He had initially suggested projecting at night a Diogenes quote onto the Whitney's exterior: "In the Rich Man's House the Only Place to Spit Is in His Face." That was Martinez's style. Inside his head and outside the house was where he liked to work.

He had always been small, a wiry loner. He had learned to armor his gentle, idealistic core with an intensity that might melt rebar and bore through concrete. He had grown up in the Lennox section of Los Angeles, a barrio separated from the airport and the west-side beach suburbs of El Segundo and Westchester only by Interstate 405. To him, Lennox felt closer to Inglewood, the neighborhood of poor whites to the north, and to Watts, the neighborhood of poor Blacks to the east where he saw flames lighting up the skies the summer he was eight years old.

Martinez was the only child of Mexican Americans from the old mining town of Durango, Colorado. He felt that he had not chosen to be an artist—he had been born that way. Not long after the Watts riots Daniel threw his first art show. He hung his drawings and paintings on a fence in the alley behind the projects where he lived, and invited the neighborhood kids to come see them.

The exhibition came down the same day it went up. As he was giving his first artist talk, some young thugs came in, ripped the works off the walls and trashed them, then proceeded to kick his ass. If Martinez was going to survive as an artist, he needed to think hard.

Imagine / Ever Wanting / To Be: The Fall of Multiculturalism

He went back to them with a proposition. "Look," he said, "I'll make you guys a deal. I'm tired of getting hurt. And you guys are all a bunch of idiots; you do all this bullshit but then you all get caught. You get thrown in jail, someone else beats you up, someone gets shot. I wanna make sure I have complete protection. What I'll trade you for is my brains. You tell me what you wanna do and I'll figure it out for you."

With the partnership struck, he was never bothered again. "In fact," he recalled with a chuckle, "at that point, other people tried to buy me off 'cause I just happened to be good at thinking. And they were all a bunch of morons." By the time his family moved to the Aliso Village projects in the Boyle Heights neighborhood of East Los Angeles, he was confident he could handle himself.

Daniel had been the only one in his extended family to be born in a big city, the only one for whom Spanish was a second language. Although his father had never earned a college degree, he had become an aerospace engineer at Hughes Aircraft, designing machines of space exploration. All that young Daniel knew of his work was that when the big rocket launches came on television his father was never home but somewhere else—in Houston, perhaps, or someplace called Cape Canaveral.

By the late sixties, his father was depressed. While his white colleagues were climbing the ladder on his innovations, he had hit the glass ceiling. The daily sandpaper-chafe of racism in Los Angeles had become intolerable. "It psychologically broke him," Martinez said. "My dad was a proud man." His parents announced they were moving back to Durango. Soon the sixteen-year-old Daniel was living on his own.

The counselor at his Jesuit high school suggested that he apply to art schools, a notion he had never imagined. He put together his first portfolio, sent off applications, and was rejected by all of them. But he had not applied to CalArts. In an interview there, he impressed school officials, who offered him a full scholarship. When he enrolled he realized that he and an African American were the only students of color in the school. Later he understood what it meant to be the first kid from the projects of Lennox and East Los to come into the floating world of Valencia.

Martinez took classes led by the top conceptualists, was freed from slavish devotion to form, liberated by Asher's explorations of context and Baldessari's and Huebler's brainy wit. "The combination of my street experience with this new influx of extremely dense Eurocentric thinking about art—they are the elements that made the chemistry that made a lot of who I am," he said. "But it was a cold, harsh, alienating place. I felt a lot of animosity. And that 'How did I get into this school,' you know?"

In time he found his voice. He made a replica of an AK-47, painted it white, and mounted it upside down. On it he stenciled in army-style letters, "MARTINEZ, PATRON SAINT OF LOST CAUSES 73–74." He stretched a canvas and wrote in black three words: first "I," then right below, "HATE," and farther down with a slight tilt, "WHITE." The painting was part of a series that he called, "I hate everyone and everything; I am at war with the world." In studio crits, his classmates did not know what to say to him.

These two pieces would be among a small number from his youthful years to survive time's sundry disasters—earthquakes, floods, and fires. Martinez hung them above his mantel at his modest book-cluttered home in the Crenshaw district. He still got a kick out of them.

"It had nothing to do with race," he would say to guests. "I just hate white. Period." Then he would grin broadly and let out a long satisfied laugh.

POST-IDENTITY BEGINS

After leaving CalArts in the middle of a master's program and finding himself back in the neighborhood, Martinez heard of a group of unusual Mexican American artists who called themselves Asco.

Young veterans of the 1968 East Los Angeles High-School Blowouts, Asco had emerged on Whittier Boulevard. They decided to turn the popular low-rider cruising-strip—which had also been the setting for the 1970 police riots against the Chicano Moratorium—into a site of high-concept street theater. In *Walking Mural*, members dressed up as a Christmas tree and *La Virgen de Guadalupe in Black*. Another, in the words of one of the leaders, Harry Gamboa Jr., appeared as "a mural that had become bored with its environment and left."[17] Then they marched down the boulevard to defy the city's prohibition of Mexican American Christmas parades and to criticize the stagnation of the Chicano art movement. Here was a group that got the absurdity of it all.

From Whittier Boulevard they went downtown to announce themselves on Wilshire Boulevard. In 1972, they were in the Los Angeles County Museum of Art wondering why there were no Chicano artists on display. When Gamboa confronted a museum curator with the question, he was told that Chicanos did not make art, they formed gangs and wrote graffiti. That night the group returned to tag the entrances with their names. These were *placas*, yes, but also the biggest wall labels ever. They called the piece *Spray Paint LACMA*. They crowned their achievement by declaring that they had "momentarily transformed the museum itself into the first conceptual work of Chicano art to be exhibited at LACMA."[18]

Asco stood against both the racists and the nationalists. They took their name from the reaction they heard from both: *me da asco* (it disgusts me). "Asco saw identity as less a question of form and content—that is, a proper name—and more one about the context for speaking and being heard," wrote Chicano art scholar Chon Noriega.[19]

Daniel Martinez had missed the Chicano Movement, whose formative events had taken place before he was in his teens. He had also missed the Chicano art explosion. He had returned from Valencia feeling that identity might be a trap. "Identity was necessary because we didn't exist," he said. "As soon as identity was established, that's the same moment it needed to be rejected." He felt that the members of Asco shared his ambivalence, so he joined up.

Asco was the cool center of the East Los alternative scene, punk *pachuc@s* in black leather and lipstick and shiny New Wave suits who owned the night. No mythic Aztlán icons here. Instead, they made drawings, murals, mixed-media installations, stills for fake and actual movies, "experimental telenovelas," plays, events, and "nonevents."[20] And then suddenly Asco was no longer, imploding in a series of bitter public fights.

Now Martinez rejected the iconography, philosophy, and methodology of Chicano art as nostalgic and essentialist. Still, he shared the belief that every human act was political, form and content were inextricable, that art could create a language for something that did not yet exist, and this language needed not to be whispered but screamed.

"The idea of masterpieces was a joke. Who would want to make a masterpiece in this day and age?" he said. "It seemed to me that the most viable thing, the most exciting thing to be doing as an artist was to be experimenting like a scientist: mixing everything up, moving around, changing content, asking different questions, hybrids of forms, mutations."

He sought art that could resist easy consumption, ally itself with the underdog and outcast and of color, impose itself on the environment, and sweep everyone up in its intervention.

WORK PLEASURE RIOT

By the 1990s, Martinez settled into practicing what was being called "new public art," the often explosive result of two colliding trends: intensifying culture-war polarization between arts administrators and their political patrons, and city leaders' need to soften the displacing impact of urban redevelopment with new art commissions. In cities where the liberal elites bankrolled both gentrification and the arts, public art could crack open the contradictions, offer the possibility the futurist Filippo Tommaso Marinetti had celebrated of massing "great crowds excited by work, by pleasure, and by riot."[21]

In 1991, long before Rudy Giuliani inserted the term into national discourse, Martinez titled a Seattle Arts Commission–funded work *Quality of Life* and ignited an uproar. At the height of holiday season, he hung 150 banners on streetlamps in the downtown retail-shopping district. On one side, a banner might read like a bank ad—"Do you have a trust fund, savings account, or a credit card?"—on the other, like a personal crisis— "Choose one: Do you buy food, pay rent, or buy shoes for the kids?" Business leaders protested, asked how anyone could consider this art, fretted that guilt was a poor lubricant for commerce.

In San Francisco, Martinez and his collaborators, the artist Renée Petropoulos and the architect Roger F. White, entered a city competition for a work that would cap the expansion of the Moscone Center, whose construction had flattened blocks of tenements, dispersed a working-class immigrant Filipino American community, and left behind the Yerba Buena cultural district, a complex of gleaming shopping malls and museums. In presentation after presentation, city leaders assured the finalist teams, "This is going to be a wonderful neighborhood."

Martinez, Petropoulos, and White proposed four thirty-six-foot-high steel signs that would straddle Howard Street: "This," "Isa," "Nice," "Neighborhood." At night, on the signs facing Chinatown, Chinese characters repeating the message would light up. Those facing in the other direction, toward the Mission, would flash the message in Spanish. By giving the city leaders exactly what they wanted, the three won the competition. But powerful local newspaper columnist Herb Caen, who perfectly understood the anger and irony the artists had embedded in the work, began attacking the proposal. The project was permanently tabled.

Martinez moved next to Chicago, to team with Sculpture Chicago's curator Mary Jane Jacob on a project they called Culture in Action. The University of Illinois at Chicago was dismantling a Greek-style agora in the center of its campus. The outdoor theater had failed its modernist mission as a commons. Students feared walking through there at night.

Martinez arranged for the agora's granite remains to be moved to a muddy public space called the Maxwell Street Market that served on weekends as a community farmer's market and that the University had recently purchased and fenced in with chicken wire. The agora's ruins were reborn as a new granite floor for the market. Martinez did not tear down the fences, but he replaced University signage with placards commemorating the city's radical labor history. He then helped organize a day of carnival marches that took thousands of community members from the Maxwell Market to two other neighborhoods, one Black and the other Mexican, bringing an afternoon of joy to the segregated city.

Here was a different kind of appropriation art, played out on a grand physical and historical scale. In an artist statement he sent to the Whitney, he proclaimed:

I Am Interested in a Mode of Experimental Behavior Linked to the Conditions of Urban Society.

I Am Interested in Exploring the Possibilities of Disorder.

I Am Based in Los Angeles and Working on the Western Front of the Great North American Culture Wars.[22]

BETWEEN THE PAST AND THE FUTURE

When 1992 broke out, Coco Fusco and Guillermo Gómez-Peña were caging themselves against the backdrop of celebrations for the five hundredth anniversary of Christopher Columbus's "discovery" of America. They would soon bring their performance to the Whitney. Multiculturalism had hit an inflection point. It had also hit a cleaving point.

In her Biennial essay, Fusco had argued that "the postmodern fascination with the exchange of cultural property and with completely deracinated identity can seem for many people of color less like emancipation and more like intensified alienation."[23] Against such an everything-is-everything sensibility, Fusco favorably namechecked Gayatri Spivak's idea of "strategic essentialism."

Put another way, multiculturalism itself was strategic. Perhaps it did limit the expression of identities to what the philosopher David Hollinger would term the "ethno-racial pentagon" of white, Black, Latino, Asian, and Native American identities. Perhaps it might also reduce radical diversity to what Fusco called "exotic entertainment for the dominant culture." But multiculturalism also did the important work of validating the histories of those who were marginalized, staking their claims against the ruling class for the sharing of power.

Fusco argued that multiculturalism allowed identities to change and evolve. She also concluded that in order to transform America, artists needed to:

> look back to histories that have circulated mainly in marginalized communities … Although American society has defined progress as a focus on the future, we must now return to the past in order to place ourselves in that history and understand how we got to where we are. As we try to grasp at crucial parallels, and tease new stories out of them, new alternative chronicles surface; these are the latest examples of how collective memories, those storehouses of identity, once activated, become power sites of cultural resistance.[24]

In this sense, Fusco and Gómez-Peña's Biennial piece, *The Couple in the Cage*, was not an attempt to break the mirror—as John Yau had once suggested—but to make a mirror, one that forced people to *see* race and *see how they saw* it, too. Here are all of your ugly, stupid, imperialist stereotypes on steroids, Fusco and Gómez-Peña were saying: we should all be laughing *and* crying.

But Fusco and Gómez-Peña would admit later that they had not anticipated how many people would do neither. Some had accepted their Guatinaui guano as God's truth. Some were grandly entertained. And many critics simply distanced themselves from the politics, if not their own projected fantasies.

"I had thought about what I was probably supposed to be thinking, and in fact what I was thinking," wrote *Artforum* contributing editor Jan Avgikos. "I mean, I can't stand there and suddenly realize that cultural genocide is a horrible thing, or that native societies have been raped X number of times, or that when ethnic artists play with stereotypes the results are automatically instructive."

The Undiscovered Amerindians: 'Oh Please!' Begged the Gentleman at the Whitney Biennial
by Coco Fusco. 2012. Intaglio, engraving, and drypoint etching on paper.
Courtesy of Alexander Gray Associates.

"What I did think about," she concluded, "was how beautiful Fusco's scantily clad body was—which is probably what just about everyone else was thinking too."[25] Strip away multiculturalism's radicalism, and what was left were the imperial amusements and unseemly desires.

But Martinez would not be laughing at Fusco and Gómez-Peña's caged-bird follies either. To him, the piece offered confirmed that ideas like Chicanismo and Latinidad were taking minorities back, against the current, in a fruitless search for an unrecoverable past. He thought of himself as an anti-essentialist, working in the present tense. But it was the future that he really desired.

At the end of April 1992, the skies over Los Angeles again filled with flames, and urban disorder was no longer a possibility. Martinez's Biennial moment waited just beyond the fiery horizon.

THE SPEED OF SOUND, AND ALL THE NOISE AFTERWARD

Martinez had an operatic title for the museum tags: *Museum Tags: Second Movement (overture); or, Overture con Claque (Overture with Hired Audience Members)*. The little tags were a compression of everything he had been thinking about. Perhaps they also compressed everything else his fellow insurgents had been thinking about.

To the traditionalists fearful of Golden's contention that the center was giving way to the margins, the tags might have seemed like mere antiassimilationist chest-thumping. But Martinez was tapping into a debate that dated back long before "Black Is Beautiful" buttons.

In the June 1926 issue of *The Nation*, at the height of the Harlem Renaissance, George Schuyler argued that the notion of cultural difference and a separate and unique "Negro art" merely flattered racists and patronized Blacks. Langston Hughes had replied:

> [T]o my mind, it is the duty of the younger Negro artist, if he accepts any duties at all from outsiders, to change through the force of his art that old whispering "I want to be white," hidden in the aspirations of his people, to "Why should I want to be white? I am a Negro—and beautiful!"[26]

Hughes would further unpack these ideas in two of his most famous poems, "Let America Be America Again" and "I, Too." In the latter, the poem's protagonist dreams of the day he is no longer sent back to eat his meal in the kitchen when guests arrive, but offered a seat at the dinner table. He concludes:

> They'll see how beautiful I am
> And be ashamed—
> I, too, am America.[27]

Martinez was not dwelling on this history. He thought of the tags as tiny codes, pressed into tinplate-steel. What did it mean for a young urban white boy to wear a tag that read "White" when he was growing up in a culture less white than ever? What might it say for anyone to wear a tag that said "To Be" or "Imagine"?

The tags were Saussurian signifiers floating through the galleries, orchestrating operatic movements of big ideas and personalities. They opened up to endless interpretations, unforeseen interactions and reactions. When some of the security guards—the overwhelming majority of whom were of color—chose to wear one, two or several tags at once, a minor management-labor kerfuffle over uniform protocol broke out in which Martinez and the curatorial staff had to intervene. The tags democratized the museum a little. At the end of the day, everyone in the museum could go home with the tag—a work of art transacted for $6 or a work shift. They could collect them like baseball cards or Basquiat drawings.

The tags had elegance and symmetry—subversions within subversions, loops within loops of meaning. Martinez mused, "We know art affects people, but it affects ten people at a time, maybe. It's a very slow burn. And I was interested in testing. This was a test, an experiment, right? How could I speed that up? Could I just like, slam!" He clapped one hand forward off the other. "Like, salt flats! I wanna break the speed of sound."

"And it was just absolutely perfect."

He had been warned not to do them. As the Biennial had neared, big New York galleries were calling, wanting to represent Martinez. At the prestigious Venice Biennale, he was showing beautiful paintings of white oil on black velvet depicting the arrests of the Red Brigade and tagged with Situationist phrases. A big Cornell University commission was coming up. Over a decade after leaving CalArts he had become one of the hottest names in the art world. But when Martinez showed his ideas for the tags, gallerists were aghast. These things were alienating and noncommercial. They weren't beautiful. They weren't pleasurable. They would stop his career in its tracks. He told them he could not be passive.

Martinez's tags began the Whitney Biennial and ended it. They summarized everything that people loved or hated about the show. They were the arrival of new messages from new voices, representations of an increasingly complex world. Or they were an artless one-liner delivered at the expense of the art-world elite.

One critic called the tags "hostile," another "a ritual of humiliation," two more called them "racist"—representative of a show that had been as delightful as a hive of buzzing hornets, as deep as twelve syllables, as disposable as a museum tag.[28] Critics asked David A. Ross how he would have felt if a Black Muslim artist from Crown Heights had done tags that read, "I can't imagine ever wanting to be Jewish."[29] Arthur Danto wrote, "I can't imagine ever wanting to have had anything to do with the 1993 Biennial."[30]

Imagine / Ever Wanting / To Be: The Fall of Multiculturalism

THE RESTORATION

And so one of the most diverse major exhibitions in the history of American art became the most critically detested show in the history of American art. The two facts were not unconnected.

The 1993 Biennial was "The Biennial that Had Gone Too Far," "The Patronizing Biennial, brought to you by the Therapeutic Museum,"[31] "a showcase for political correctness," "a theme park of the oppressed," "the most disturbing show in living memory," "one extended exhibitionistic frenzy of victimization and self-pity," and "the most alienating, depressing, horrifying show I have ever seen."[32]

The show was about "Victim Chic," "Mope Art," "sound bite art," "grievance art." It was about "multicultural anger ... at the European-American White Male," and had "the cordite aroma of cultural reparations."[33] One pundit declared the show to be "a cultural war to destabilize and break the mainstream."[34]

Then Hilton Kramer weighed in, with dyspeptic disgust and a raw woundedness. "There is no point in 'reviewing' the carloads of junk that David Ross' apparatchiks have accumulated for the current exhibition as if it had anything to do with art," he wrote. "He has brought the Whitney down to his own cultural level, which is that of a comfortably situated middle-class voyeur with a prurient interest in the fantasy life of the underclass."[35]

Kramer conceded that identity was the point of the 1993 Biennial. Perhaps, unlike the white liberal art critics who had taken such offense, he had come to view the work of the insurgents less as slurs than as facts. For in the end, it was not really about them, nor was it about petit bourgeois Ross and his staff of degenerates. It was about those who had betrayed the institution, and by extension, their class, their race, and the nation itself, those who had sponsored this travesty—the old white wealth of the Whitney's board of trustees. In his *New York Observer* review he was both bilious and defeated:

> Don't they understand—if only just a little bit—that this whole exhibition is,
> in effect, a death sentence on everything they are, everything they own,
> and everything they hope to pass on to their nearest and dearest? Don't
> they understand that this Biennial is filled to overflowing with a rabid hatred
> for everything they have achieved in life? Are they really so stupid that they
> don't understand that they are the targets in this assault on our society?
> Or are they so mired in liberal guilt for the vast wealth that they command
> that they are willing to collaborate in their own destruction?[36]

In the fall Daniel J. Martinez went to Cornell University and built a big black asterisk in the middle of the Arts Quad, not far from Willard Straight Hall. He called it *The Castle Is Burning*. It was the twenty-fifth anniversary of the student riots in Paris, and Martinez meant for the asterisk—emblazoned with the Diogenes quote and other provocative ones like "No Player Must Be Greater Than the Game Itself"—to be a barricade, an interruption in the daily flow of business.

Students apparently understood Martinez's intent better than many of the university administrators. The piece was quickly vandalized with swastikas and graffiti that read, "Bean Eaters Go Home," "Kill the Illegals," and "White Power."

Faced with official indifference, Latino students decided that they had to protect the piece, and they formed a human cordon around it, just as progressive white students had encircled the Black occupiers of Straight Hall twenty-four years before. Then the students spontaneously marched on the administration building, and occupied it for four days, demanding that the school add Latino faculty, history courses, and resources.

Martinez sent the student protestors a fax. "When Surrounded by Dangers, Fear None of Them. When without Resources, Depend on Resourcefulness," it read, quoting Guy Debord's favorite Sun Tzu quote. "When Surprised, Take the Enemy by Surprise." Cornell University soon agreed to establish a Latino Living Center dedicated to the study of Latino culture.

Martinez felt 1993 had been a banner year. In Venice and Chicago, at the Whitney and Cornell, he had excited crowds with work, pleasure, and riots. Surely the art world would open its doors to him now. Then in the first week of 1994, *Newsweek* featured Martinez in a list of actors, writers, musicians, and artists to watch, alongside the likes of Gwyneth Paltrow, Joshua Redman, and Laura Esquivel. Martinez's heart dropped.

"As soon as that came out," he said, "I immediately knew it was over."

The commissions stopped. His phone calls to galleries and curators went unreturned. Martinez had been eclipsed by his little museum tags. "It framed me as the angriest artist in the United States," he said. "After the '93 Biennial, people just thought I was a raging lunatic. Nobody would touch me."

For nearly a decade after, Martinez felt as if he had been blacklisted by the art world. When he looked around, it seemed a lot of others had been, too. For the generation of artists who would follow, the lesson had been learned—say what you want, but you might be punished.

"'93 was the last shot of the war," Martinez said. "We lost right at the moment we thought we were winning."

Thelma Golden was searching for a third way beyond the multiculturalists' call for positive representation and the reductive formalism of the "quality" cabal. If difference happened between perception and appearance, if race happened when people were seeing but not really seeing, how could a Black curator make people aware of the Ellisonian dilemma?

Golden threw her energies into her first major exhibition at the Whitney, an epic, transgressive show called *Black Male*. But many in the Black community rose against the show. Rodney King, criminalization, hypersexuality—these were reminders of the shackles, Golden's critics said, not the redemption that they had fought for. "We as black people cannot look to the Whitney to represent us," wrote Ronda R. Penrice.[37]

In 1995, the Guerrilla Girls printed flyers and posters that read "Traditional Values and Quality Return to the Whitey Museum," misspelling intended. In the 1995 Biennial, the flyer pointed out, white males were back up to 55.5% from 36.4%, white females down to 27.7% from 29.5%, males of color down to 11.1% from 22.8%, females of color down to 5.5% from 11.4%.

Multiculturalism would continue—as a magazine cover, a marketing plan, a human resources agenda, a presidential commission, an educational curriculum, and much more yet. Beyond 75th and Madison, there was a mainstream to conquer.

But oh multiculturalism—where was your sting, where was your victory?

The Los Angeles riots seemed to expose all of Benetton's multiculti platitudes. With its "race" issue, the *Colors* staff gamely tried to do something honest in an inherently dishonest situation.

CHAPTER 9

ALL THE COLORS IN THE WORLD

THE MAINSTREAMING OF MULTICULTURALISM

Everywhere everything gets more and more like everything else as the
world's preference structure is relentlessly homogenized.
—Theodore Levitt, "The Globalization of Markets"

In 1984, an Italian clothing company began marketing itself with pictures of children of all races wearing its gumball-colored polos, berets, canvas sneakers, and white shorts. They held bright balloons. They smiled, frowned, stared. They picked their noses. Against empty white backgrounds their varied skin tones pulsed with ambrosial luster. They were the children of Benetton and they seemed to come from another world, which in a sense they had. No other world like this could be seen except through the lens of the Milan-based photographer Oliviero Toscani.

Toscani's patron was the Treviso-born clothing magnate Luciano Benetton, who had over the course of two decades built his family business into the largest Italian fashion firm. Benetton had been opening shops in the United States since 1979 without much note until a blue-and-white rugby shirt caught on with Ivy League preppies in the fall semester of 1982. Then sales went vertical and store openings accelerated. Luciano believed his company—structured on franchising, subcontracting, and outsourcing—was perfectly set up for the Global Century. All it needed was a new image.

Toscani had a casual bush of hair and a rakish beard, a hunter's aim and a huckster's charm. In the sixties, he had gone to King's Road to capture the Swinging London scene. During the Warhol years, he was in the East Village shooting the flamboyant regulars of Max's Kansas City. He went on to work for *Vogue*, *Elle*, Chanel, and Fiorucci, making fantastically erotic pictures hawking furniture and clothes. He did an ad for a line called Jesus Jeans that pissed off the Vatican. The art featured his then-fiancée Donna Jordan's lubricious ass exploding out of her denim shorts. The copy read, "Chi Mi Ama Mi Segua"—"Who Loves Me Follows Me."

Behind the wit and magnetism Toscani was a man of serious and conflicting convictions. He had spent his childhood in darkrooms, at murder scenes, and at newspaper desks. He had been an assistant to his father, Fedele, a famed wartime photojournalist and photo agency head who at the age of thirty-six had captured the defining image of Mussolini's corpse hung upside down before the crowds in Milan's Piazzale Loreto.

If his father had made pictures of toil, grit, and conflict, Toscani was attracted to portrait photography and its parvenu cousin, fashion photography: the frank Southern mystery of Disfarmer, the expansive humanism of August Sander, and most of all, the beauty and distinction of Richard Avedon. When Benetton approached Oliviero Toscani to make his images, the photographer was reaching that midcareer moment when one begins contemplating his legacy.

In interviews Toscani described himself as "a total anarchist" and "a radical libertarian." He claimed affinity for the provocations of Debord and the Situationists. He called his fashion shoots "a kind of reportage," his photos "sociopolitical documents."[1] But if advertising offered the highest profile of the industrial arts, Toscani would use it. "I think it is immoral how much money has been thrown out the window to say, 'Coke is better than Pepsi,'" Toscani told the *New York Times*. "With this money, you can do something much more intelligent, much more broadening."[2]

He was Michelangelo, and Benetton was his de'Medici. "I take as an example the Renaissance painters," he would say. "Just a few of them believed in God, but if you wanted to be a painter you had to paint churches. That was the only place where your art was published. Big multinationals are the modern churches."[3]

So in 1984, when multiculturalism was the idea whose time had come, Toscani pitched Benetton on a concept even bigger than sex: "All the Colors in the World." Somehow the United States remained indifferent to its gorgeous diversity, its bounty of beauty. But to Toscani, the connection was clear. In Giuliana Benetton's vibrant fabric palette, the clothing might became a metaphor for diversity and Old World idealism might meet its modern dream of America.

Perhaps Toscani could not have imagined how perfectly oppositional this notion was in the context of American race politics. President Reagan's image-maker Hal Riney's Morning in America was even whiter than Bill Backer's "Friendly Feelings" for Coke had been. In the neocons' soft utopia of imperialist nostalgia, consumerism was strength, compassion was weakness, and diversity was the threat beyond the frame.

As Benetton tried to gain a foothold in the United States, it was taking a big risk by choosing sides in the gathering culture wars. But in the end the children of Benetton were not angry, unquenched orphans ready to riot. They were the bright heralds of the coming "We Are the World" moment. Once, American capitalists had gone to an Italian hillside to teach the world to sing. Thirteen years later, Italian capitalists with a new "global vision," as they called it, went to America to help colorize the United States itself.

BRANDING MULTICULTURALISM

At that moment, the prophets of globalization were pressing American businesses to expand into new markets, not to fear difference but to tame it. In "The Globalization of Markets," an influential article published in 1983, Harvard Business School marketing professor Theodore Levitt argued that technology had made the earth flat. The new global business would standardize its product as much as possible, using technology to lower its production costs and communications to align its far-flung customers.

The best brand "will never assume that the customer is a king who knows his own issues."[4] Instead it "sells the same things in the same way everywhere," he wrote. "The products and methods of the industrialized world play a single tune for all the world, and all the world eagerly dances to it."[5]

There was an odd resonance between the arguments of multiculturalism's critics and Levitt's assertion: pluralism was not the way to address proliferating, bewildering diversity. The success of the new global corporation was no longer based on respecting and adapting to "entrenched differences within and between nations."[6] Instead, he wrote, "The same countries that ask the world to recognize and respect the individuality of their cultures insist on the wholesale transfer to them of modern goods, services, and technology." Globalization, in other words, was simply a way of making multiculturalism serve a corporate monoculture.

One afternoon, a committee of UNESCO officials who were considering giving Toscani a prize visited his Paris studio. He had gathered twenty-five kids for a photo shoot for the children's catalog. They were, he recalled, "of all colors, from very light blond to very dark black." As Toscani took a break to speak to his visitors, the children began playing with each other. An impressed diplomat mused, "Well, here are the United Colors of Benetton."

Toscani's communications strategy was balanced precisely on the tension between difference and homogenization. "All the Colors in the World" seemed to connect to the claims of the U.S. multiculturalist avant-garde: against "colorblind" conformity, imperialist nostalgia, and state violence, diversity was radical. Benetton could embrace difference even as it clothed everyone in the same bright sweaters. Difference was the means and homogenization was the end.

Between 1986 and 1993, the Benetton Group—including brands like Sisley, Nordica, and Killer Loop—expanded from 3,200 stores in 57 countries to 7,000 in more than 100 countries.[7] The company went public in Italy, Germany, and the United States. It became the world's single biggest consumer of wool. Its sales topped $2 billion.

Lifestyle and identity, national emergings and global longings—all had finally come together. By 1989 the green logo of "United Colors of Benetton" had become the company's brand. Its transformation from family-run village shop to worldwide sign of racial unity was complete.

THE WHITE SPACE

More than any other culture industry, fashion is ruled by the calendar of novelty. There is always a new season to be designed, debated, distributed, sold, and discounted. So it was that Irving Penn and Richard Avedon came to remove their subjects from time and place, photographing them before blank white backgrounds. Emptiness endowed the subjects with timelessness and distinction. "White space is extravagance," design critic Keith Robertson once wrote. "Clutter has come to represent working class (just as white space identifies high class)."[8]

From his earliest days Toscani had followed Penn, Avedon, and other fashion photograph pioneers. At Max's Kansas City, for instance, he had shot the club's outlandish regulars against the white wall in the club's stairway.[9] With this blank canvas, he could isolate, foreground, and transport them. "It's like pulling them from their space into my space," Toscani said. "It's a philosophical choice, an aesthetic choice."

Against the emptiness Giuliana Benetton's pastels and primaries glowed. So did the spectrum of skin tones. Toscani could be heard loudly objecting to the Claudia Schiffer standard of beauty as "extreme" and "Aryan." Instead he brought in African, Asian, and biracial models. It was as if Toscani had moved Riney and Reagan's figurative whiteness to the background. For people of color, the shock of the new was accompanied by the shock of recognition. Non-whiteness was suddenly, shockingly sexy. In Toscani's world the very borders of desire had shifted.

Toscani's white background was the screen for a new global economy and the bright children of Benetton were the flickering projection of a colorized ideal. Hung outside Benetton's storefronts on crowded streets around the world, Toscani's photos beckoned consumers. Inside the white-walled stores consumers were separated from the time-kept tyranny of production. After the end of history, here you were—out of both the Old World and the New, at home in the bright heaven of heavens, you alongside everyone everywhere, inside the market. All that was left was to buy something to cover one's Edenic nakedness back in the fuss and rumble of Babel's real streets.

The multiculturalists had valorized people's struggles and hopes, but fashion photography was about a utopian eternal Now. Toscani felt that this act of decontextualization could be useful for promoting peace, love, and understanding. In most of his early photos, young models of different backgrounds wrapped their arms around each other. He might have an Orthodox Jewish boy and a Palestinian boy posing, each with a hand on a small globe and an arm around the other.

Ad from the "United Colors of Benetton" campaign by Oliviero Toscani. 1985.

Toscani shot two Black toddlers—one wearing a Stars and Stripes sweater and holding an American flag, preparing to kiss another holding a Russian flag and wearing a Communist red sweater. Toscani's human subjects—for they were being sold as much as the clothes—lost almost everything about them that made them different. The clothing was the only context.

Out in the hot crowded world, critics from the left found such images at best naive and at worst exploitative. Critics from the right sought to ban them. The ad of the Black toddlers was censored in the United States; its opponents cited the Flag Protection Act of 1968. It would be the first of many controversies that Toscani and Benetton would face.

TOSCANI IN AMERICA

The photographer in Toscani wanted to make Benetton look cutting-edge and consumer-ready. But the provocateur in Toscani raged against a monoculture in which all goods were the same, and the affluence that made it possible for First World consumers to own enough goods for three lifetimes. He held extravagant contradiction in a way any Whitmanite or Marxist could admire.

Advertising agencies were simply "product pushers," Toscani said. "Ad people spend all that time brainstorming and thinking down to their customers."[10] Lifestyle advertising plagued consumers with guilt and insecurity, made them physically and existentially bulimic, forced them to retreat into an imaginary world. "The advertising industry has corrupted society," he argued. "It persuades people that they are respected for what they consume, that they are only worth what they possess."[11]

It was not that Toscani was anticapitalist. "A market is where people meet and love each other, make war, peace. The market is the world. So I think of ways to adjust to affect the market," he would say. "I'm a man of the market."

But as the apparel industry rushed to imitate his images, he increasingly positioned himself as antifashion, an enemy of advertising itself. Indeed Toscani insisted he was not making ads, he was making art. He was not promoting products, he was promoting social awareness. He vowed to make a new kind of realism, one that would confront its viewers and shock them out of their complacency. In a Benetton manifesto, he wrote, "I think that attempting to actively engage the public is more exciting than simply trying to convince them our product is better than others."[12]

Ad from the "United Contrasts of Benetton" campaign by Oliviero Toscani. 1989.

So in 1989, he began to transition beyond pretty pictures. For a new campaign called the "United Contrasts of Benetton," he employed a William Klein–style focus on visual contrast to explore racially charged content. He photographed a Black man and a white man in Benetton denims and coal miner's helmets laughing together. The Black man pointed to the blond man's face and skin, which had been colored with coal in a kind of blackface.

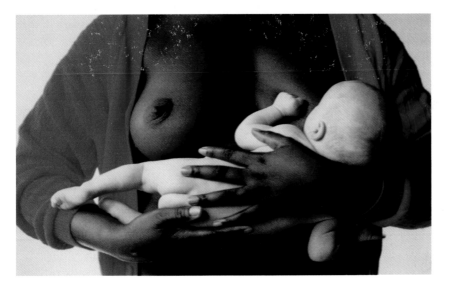

The wet nurse ad from the "United Contrasts of Benetton" campaign by Oliviero Toscani. 1989.

Two other images brought Toscani and Benetton their first racial controversy. In the first, a Black woman naked under her red sweater cradled a white baby who suckled on her breast. In the second, two hands, one white and the other Black, were handcuffed together. The photos won art prizes in France, Austria, Denmark, Italy, and the Netherlands. But in the United States many African Americans recoiled. The first seemed to be presenting a modish nursing Mammy; the second, yet another Black man destined for prison.

Clarence O. Smith, president and cofounder of *Essence* magazine, met with Benetton's American buying agency, J. Walter Thompson, to let them know he was not interested in running the wet-nurse ad. "For the most part, we applaud the effort Benetton makes in seeking to present different ethnic groups with an unusual and positive sensitivity," Smith later explained carefully to the media. "But we thought they erred in this execution, and were not aware of what the connotation would be to Americans. It conjures up images of a time when Black people were highly subservient to whites."[13]

The handcuffs ad from the "United Contrasts of Benetton" campaign by Oliviero Toscani. 1989.

The handcuff ad eventually ran in *Rolling Stone*, *GQ*, *Seventeen*, and *Glamour*, but not without loud protests from the NAACP, the Urban League, and others. "Is that brotherhood?" Black ad agency UniWorld director Byron Lewis asked of the image. "What are they trying to sell—handcuffs?"[14]

Toscani responded that he was asking viewers to confront their prejudice. For the handcuff ad, he alluded to Brecht's famous quote about the ethics of the bank robber and the banker: Who is more at fault here, he wanted to ask, the prisoner or the jailer? Who was to say which hand belonged to the jailer and the prisoner? The interpretations, he argued, said more about the interpreter than the artist.

And yet perhaps he was happy to discover that the photos had produced this kind of reaction. The reaction confirmed that the ads had transcended a merely transactional mode of advertising. They had a truth to them that the rest of advertising did not. That, to Toscani, was the real meaning of diversity: images that transgressed conformity.

Controversy was the price of championing diversity against conformity. Indeed it was, he said, "a sign of generosity," his personal gift to consumers. "A lot of people don't want to move their point of view, they don't want to be disturbed by new vision, by a different vision," he said. "People don't like diversity. So every time you offer diversity, you get into trouble."[15]

In 1990, he returned for a do-over. He shot a Black chef and a white chef holding a loaf of bread, flour wiped across both their faces; a Black toddler and a white toddler sitting on bright potties, the Black boy smiling and touching the white boy's face; a white hand passing a race baton to a Black one (a note on the end of South African apartheid); a Black infant's hand held in a white adult's.

There were shots of a Black baby sleeping in a blanket of white teddy bears, a white wolf licking a black sheep, and finally, a set of look-alike test tubes of blood labeled

Who We Be

after world leaders: "George," "Nelson," "Margaret," "Jiang," "Yasser," and "Fidel." The images brought the desired protests—Milan's church authorities banned a billboard of the innocuous shot of the toddlers on their potties as offensive to the Sunday faithful. But they must have felt unchallenging.

In 1991, a photo of a blond toddler, her hair tightly curled, and a Black boy in an embrace provided the last race protest over a United Colors of Benetton ad. Toscani had shaped the boy's hair into devil's horns. He said later that he had wanted to ask: could one really look at these toddlers and deem one more angelic than the other? But to some African Americans, it looked like "Shirley Temple and Buckwheat," another example of "age-old cultural stereotypes."[16]

The children's ad from the 1991 United Colors of Benetton campaign by Oliviero Toscani that sparked the last major protest from organizations of color.

Such images failed the positivity test. And when Toscani attempted to infuse them with significance they toppled over from the burden of history. The same racial innocence that had brought Toscani to America in the first place was doing him in now. In turn, Toscani seemed to have become bored with this conversation.

Benetton's sales had reached the height of penetration into the American market. Sales were peaking at over $2.1 billion. Perhaps just as important, his aesthetic had taken hold. In 1989, the radical art collective Gran Fury, which had designed the "SILENCE=DEATH" banners for the AIDS activist group ACT UP, parodied Toscani's look for twelve-foot-long ads on the sides of city buses in New York, San Francisco, Chicago, and Washington, DC. Against a white background, three handsome young multiculti couples—two of them same-sex—locked lips over copy that read, "Kissing Doesn't Cause Kill: Greed and Indifference Do." Gran Fury's ad became a signature moment in "subvertising," the guerrilla design practice of turning ads against themselves and advancing anticonsumerist aims.

When they were producing it, Gran Fury's members had gleefully called it their "Benetton ad."[17] Yet when the ad was chosen—reappropriated—to illustrate the editorial/manifesto of Benetton's new magazine, *Colors*, difficult questions arose: Should the collective extract a price from the corporation? Did that mean they had sold out?

On the other hand, now that Toscani had helped bring multiculturalism inside the market, he could leave it to the catalog. There seemed little more controversy left to wring—it had lost its concussive novelty. He needed new taboos to smash, a new aesthetic to forge.

THE SHOCK CYCLE

As the Gulf War begin, Toscani released an ad featuring a photo of tombstones in a soldier's cemetery. A series featuring multicolored condoms spoke to the AIDS crisis while poking at the Christian right. A nun kissing a priest targeted Catholic sexual edicts. A striking shot of a screaming mucus-covered newborn suggested that Toscani was readying himself for a new era.

Central to this new phase would be a new collaborator, the renegade designer Tibor Kalman. Born in Hungary, Kalman's family had fled the Communist advance and brought him to the United States. There he had been a '68er, joining the NYU chapter of Students for a Democratic Society. He left to cut sugarcane in Cuba with the Venceremos Brigade and returned to the East Coast to organize factory workers. But he soon decided to leave the revolution. He went to work for Leonard Riggio, a bookseller who would eventually buy a store called Barnes & Noble. Kalman talked his way into becoming the house designer for the burgeoning empire.

By the early 1980s, Kalman had opened his own firm, M&Co., and gained the confidence of the downtown creative scene—Warhol on the one end, David Byrne and Brian Eno on the other. He had secured a rep as a bomb-thrower at staid design industry conferences and functions. "99% of design is about selling stuff. And I believe that in order to sell stuff, you can't really tell the truth," Kalman would say. "Graphic designers have become the liars for corporations, just in the way that I think accountants are liars, and I think that lawyers are liars."

The old standards aggravated Kalman. "I mistrust design and I mistrust style and I mistrust form," he said. "Good communications begins with content. It begins with an idea, as opposed to a look."[22] He called himself an anti-designer, an "un-designer." He said his method was purely about "fucking things up." He was partly color-blind.

Kalman's redesigns for *Artforum* and *Interview* magazines brought him to the attention of Toscani. "I didn't particularly like the things he did with M&Co. What I really liked about Tibor was his brains," Toscani said of Kalman. "We were like brothers. You know, like, 'Tibor, you are an asshole.' 'Well, Oliviero, you are a piece of shit.'"

In charisma, creativity, and contradiction, Kalman was every bit Toscani's equal. He once angrily wrote, "Corporations have become the sole arbiters of cultural ideas and taste in America." But he also advised designers to find themselves "lunatics" with lots of dough: "Treat them well and use their money to change the world."[19]

Kalman entrusted a young journalist named Karrie Jacobs, an art and design critic for the *New York Times* and *Metropolis* magazine and a graduate of the iconoclastic Left Coast college Evergreen State, to write and edit his public speeches in that signature tone, equal parts irony and earnestness. After Toscani and Kalman met she quickly assumed a much bigger role in their evolving ideas.

"The two of them had a lot in common," she recalled. "Both of them are gifted in thinking in one-liners, very concise little ideas that get under people's skin even though they seem simplistic beyond belief."

One of the first things Toscani and Kalman did together was to collect and sort through thousands of news photos from the Sygma and Magnum agencies. "Tibor and Toscani were sitting around in Tibor's office and they called me in and asked me to react to a pile of photos," Jacobs recalled. "I went through the pile and said which I thought were too horrifying. The ones that come to mind are the guy dying of AIDS and the car blown up, someone in Italy being assassinated. Those are the ones that I said, 'Those are absolutely 'no way.'" Toscani and Kalman thanked her, then used in Benetton's 1992 campaign, "The Shock of Reality," many of the photos she had rejected.

Gone were the fashion photo conventions, the white backgrounds, the colorful clothes. Toscani was returning to his teen years as a runner for his father's photo agency. He was delivering photos of a dead mafioso; an African soldier holding a human shinbone; a Bosnian soldier's bloodied clothes; Albanian refugees clambering onto an overcrowded ship bound for Italy; and most controversial of all, the dying AIDS patient David Kirby in a hand-colored, retouched *Pietà*-like scene. Then he was slapping the United Colors of Benetton logo onto them. Appropriation art had become appropriation advertising. Reality had fallen in lockstep with what visual culture scholar Nicholas Mirzoeff would call, after Debord and Baudrillard, the "parade of copies."[20]

Toscani argued that he was waking people up. "You can see a news photo of the fighting in Sarajevo, and it's in context; it conforms to your expectations. Shocking violence in the news is normal," he said. "But when you take the same photo out of the news and put a Benetton logo on it, people pause and reflect on their position on the problem. When they can't come to terms with it, they get mad at us."[21]

And American advertisers got very mad. "This is desperate advertising," the American marketing giant Jerry Della Femina told *Advertising Age*. "The object of advertising is to get people to feel better about the product you're selling. This stuff insults the intelligence."[22]

But underwritten by the one of the world's biggest knitwear companies, Toscani had recreated capitalist realism, remade it for an era of disbelief in government and capital. And the shock cycle of ad → protest → company response → earned media → big sales continued to turn.

DIVERSITY IS GOOD

In advertising terms, print was archaic. All the good money was going to television. But Toscani went to Luciano Benetton and told him that doing an in-house magazine would put the company back in control of its communications strategy. It need no longer be at the mercy of traditional magazines that might choose to block their ads, or buying agencies that might lose their spine. Plus a house magazine could properly contextualize the company's values. It would be called—what else?—*Colors*.

Jacobs said, "Tibor called me on a Saturday and said, 'Hey, we're these two big guys wearing sweaters sitting around talking, come join us.' And so I went over to M&Co.'s office on a Saturday afternoon and sat around Tibor's office with Tibor and Toscani for a long time talking about what this magazine could be."

"They were talking about doing a magazine that was going to be really global and optimistic and upbeat and happy and I kept on saying, 'But, but, but there's this war going on.' I remember I made the obvious point about 'I don't want to do a magazine about sweaters' and Toscani went, 'No, no! This will not be a magazine about sweaters.'"

"We talked about the spirit of the magazine. About optimism and being global and how cool it was that Benetton had all these stores everywhere so there would be this distribution network," Jacobs recalled. "But I don't remember anyone saying, 'Oh yes, this is going to be the standard-bearer for the notion of multiculturalism.' We were not thinking in those terms. It was about Toscani wanting a place where his ideas could flow freely and be uncensored and Tibor wanting very badly to be the editor of a magazine and me wanting to do something that was lucrative and fun."

Colors was nothing if not ambitious. Beginning in late 1991 it would be published semiannually in no fewer than five bilingual editions: English and Italian, German, Spanish, French, or Japanese. The budget would be $3 million. The print run would be an astounding 800,000 copies—in Kalman and Jacobs's environmentally correct metrics, 6,000 trees. It would be distributed on newsstands. And in its stores, it would be packaged with the seasonal catalogs.

As for content, Toscani had one rule: "I don't want a magazine made with news and celebrities." Instead the magazine would look bold and loose like an after-hours freestyle design project and read like a series of tightly edited, jargon-free, impossibly hip cultural-studies assignments.

The first issue's cover featured Toscani's photo of a wailing, just-delivered baby girl against his trademark blank background. Bilingual cover lines radiated around her. The image recalled Toscani's fascination with the innocence of babes—it was an image pulled from a previous United Colors campaign—and heralded the arrival of the "rest of the world" beyond the old monoculture where diversity, affluence, and style converged in a knowing, colorized, consumer-friendly white space.

Colors would reveal the world's cool young tribes to each other. It featured activist groups of gay police officers and black models and abundant white space. It celebrated avatars of hybridity, groups Kalman and Jacobs called "cultural transvestites": Polish cowboys, Japanese hip-hoppers.

"The idea is a simple one," Jacobs wrote in the first issue's editorial-cum-manifesto, "Diversity is good."

In that statement of purpose, Jacobs tried to encapsulate the ideals she, Kalman, and Toscani had crystallized through hours of endless argument. *Colors*—and by extension, Benetton—would favor a forward-thinking grassroots authenticity, new-gen cultural relativism and "we're all connected" techno-optimism that would become voguish in the coming Internet age. If identity was the future of capitalism, that future was here.

But there remained a central contradiction. In sunny chatty prose, the voice that defined *Colors*'s early years, Jacobs wrote, "We think that positive change mostly comes from the bottom and percolates upward," and that "your culture (whoever you are) is as important as our culture (whoever we are)." But how could it live up to those claims especially with the smart, worldly audience of young people it wanted to attract?

Jacobs admitted, "We were sort of wrestling with what is our position in the world, and 'How can we be taken seriously if we're being financed by this sweater manufacturer?'" She thought hard about how *Colors* could "do something honest in a situation that was inherently dishonest."

Finally, she chose to give her post-Watergate, post-Marxist Evergreen skepticism a ride. She wrote, "What happens when corporations use imagery to make statements about social and political issues? Well you can't trust those statements any more than you can trust the statements of politicians." She pushed further, challenging readers to challenge Benetton on the gap between its own imagery and actions: "What does the company actually do to promote racial equality? Do their hiring practices match their image?"

But her editorial ended on an ambivalent note: "[W]e feel a little funny about being global. It makes us feel like we're McDonald's, and we're not. We don't want to sell our culture to you. We want you to tell us about your culture."

She didn't—because, really, she couldn't—challenge her readers to ask why they should.

HOW YA LIKE ME NOW?

Out in the real streets, Rodney King was getting the hope beaten out of him. In Congress, the culture wars were exacting their casualties. In retail and advertising, companies were losing their retail margins with suddenly brand-indifferent baby boomers, who had given up tastemaking for nesting; and struggling to understand a new generation, who were more diverse, tribal, and resistant to the old pitches than ever. Then the Los Angeles riots broke out.

The second issue of *Colors* hit the stands in that burning spring of 1992. Its cover featured one of the images that had shocked Jacobs: a recent news photo of hundreds of Albanian refugees fleeing ethnic violence, clambering by rope aboard a rusting, severely overcrowded ship bound for Bari, Italy. Kalman and Jacobs had come up with cover lines about immigration's transformational impact on "un mundo Viejo," the Old World, saying it brought "new music," "new food," "new romantic possibilities," and "new excuses for parades."

But while the text offered consumption and celebration, the image bespoke pressure and panic. Globalization had accelerated the forces of change. Neoliberalism, the state ideology that accompanied globalization, was about the flight of capital and the state from the spaces of the living. For those wired into the new world, globalization did mean connection. For others, it meant displacement and uprootings of people on a previously unimaginable scale. The *Colors* dialectic was trying to nimbly balance the cheery optimism of global flows with evidence of the profound, widening divide.

The staff felt caught between its ideals—uniting the world—and its audience—the elite youth of the connected class. Through its first three issues it was unsure of what it wanted to say and to whom it was speaking. "[B]ecause this magazine is produced by people from about 30 different countries, published in five bilingual editions, and distributed globally, we're not sure anymore which culture is ours," Jacobs wrote in the third issue's editorial. "We have cultural vertigo. We feel dizzy."

But when the Los Angeles riots broke out on April 29, 1992, just as they were putting the third issue to bed, Jacobs believed that they suddenly had a focus. Was it possible to be honest about the way people saw race and the problem of racism in a publishing situation that was inherently dishonest? "I think this thing started out cynical," Karrie Jacobs recalled, "and by the fourth issue we began believing in what we were doing."

As she would later write in that issue's editorial, "If there's one topic *Colors* was destined to address, it's racism and the devastation caused by racism."

In Milan, Toscani was preparing an installation opening for the same Venice Biennale that had included Daniel J. Martinez. His piece would be hung in a former church. It was fifty-six close-up photos of people's genitals—the source of all this gorgeous, restless diversity. In Manhattan, Jacobs and Kalman were discussing ideas for the new issue.

"This was the process. He and I would have a meeting and then he'd go off and hang with Toscani for some period of time and then he would come back from Italy looking tanned and healthy," Jacobs recalled. "And he'd come back and say, 'Well, Toscani and I have an idea! We should do an issue about race,' and we'd say, 'Oh, what a good idea!'" From here forward, each issue of *Colors* would have a single thematic focus.

In early 1993, as the Whitney Biennial opened, *Colors*'s fourth issue hit the stands.

The cover featured a Black woman and a white man standing naked and slightly—and oh so sexily—insolent against Toscani's white background, as if they, too, weren't at all sure about this experiment. They were covered only by the printed words "RACE Attitude Lies Truth Power First Dates and Sex." Over the white man's feet, in smaller print, were the words: "We're looking for trouble."

Jacobs and her staff found themselves in the middle of a broad soul-searching debate. The questions had started with "How many races are there?" They ended up at, "What is race anyway?" At the outset of her time at *Colors* she had asked readers to hold Benetton accountable around the question of diversity. Now circumstances had pushed the envelope further. Could a radical critique of imperialism and racial discrimination be advanced in a magazine financed by a sweater manufacturer?

Jacobs wrote in her editorial, "[I]t occurred to us that while the physical differences between peoples and individuals are real—all we had to do was look at [staffers] Amma, Soyeun and Catalina—the monoliths called races are a purposeful invention, once used to make Europe's slavery and colonial conquests seem moral and inevitable."

A *Do the Right Thing*–inspired feature depicted smiling faces identified by the ethnic insults used against them and the victimizers who used them ("'TUNDRA NIGGER'; who: Inuit; from: Alaska; by: white Alaskans. 'HAIRY WHITE BARBARIAN'; who: Nordics, etc.; from: anyplace but Japan; by: Japanese"). Kalman and Jacobs stared at a headshot of an African man for a long time, and debated whether they should put the word "nigger" with it. To do so would admit and implicate them in a deep history and context.

"Maybe that's what it should say," Jacobs said later. "But the idea of publishing a magazine, in fact, published by this billionaire, that was read by young people every-where, in which we were trumpeting the word 'nigger' in big type just seemed ultimately to be wrong. And I think it would've made the piece stronger, but who are we to be dis-seminating that word? What would it mean?"

In what she thought of as the issue's coup de grâce, Jacobs pulled together two infographic spreads, the first headlined, "Here's where the people live," illustrating the size of countries by population. "Here's where the money lives," read the next, this time proportioning nations by wealth.

"In this issue of *Colors*, we've outlined the physical differences between the earth's peoples. But to be honest," the spread read, "we don't think racism has anything to do with skin, hair, or eyes. Those features just provide easy targets. Racism is about money and power."

But Jacobs's spread would produce nothing like the reactions to Kalman's. First there was an article entitled "How to Change Your Race," jabbing lightly at *Cosmo* and *Glamour* in developing the theme of race and desire as social constructs, examining how Chinese, whites, and Blacks used plastic surgery to alter themselves. Across the bottom of the page, a half-Black, half–Native American model was made up as a dark-skinned African, a white woman, and an Asian woman. If appearance was so mutable, what did that say about our perceptions of difference?

But that was just the appetizer. Kalman and Toscani assembled pages of ravishing nude male and female Latino, Black, and Asian hotties. Small captions were inserted alongside their faces and appropriate body parts: "What would it be like to have sex with someone of a different race?" "Will they want to do it with their socks on?" "Will we be embarrassed by the things they cry out in the heat of passion?" The message: racism could be resolved, per MC Busy Bee, with sex and more sex. Jacobs mused, "We should have somehow put all that dense (race and wealth) information next to the naked people."

Finally Kalman conceived a spread he called, "How Ya Like Me Now?" which would be, he had written, a "series of retouched photos changing [the] race of some well-known internationals." With primitive and expensive proto-Photoshop software, design-ers executed the photos and the feature appeared under a new title: "What If?" Arnold Schwarzenegger got short dreads and a Wesley Snipes tan. Pope John Paul II turned Jap-anese. Spike Lee was wiggerized. A skin-lightened, blond, and blue-eyed Michael Jackson looked like, well, Michael Jackson. Queen Elizabeth became a Jamaican browning.

Jacobs was annoyed that so much time had been spent on such a thin idea. "To me it seemed like the dumbest gimmick," she said. "And for better or worse, it's the thing that this issue is remembered for."

Kalman had been inspired by no less a provocateur than David Hammons, who had expressed his anger at the tragedy of Jesse Jackson's defeat in the 1988 Democratic primaries by mounting a blond whiteface metal cut-out painting of Jackson across from the notably colorless National Portrait Gallery, tagged with Kool Moe Dee's line "How Ya Like Me Now?" At the time local Black activists had toppled the installation and destroyed it. Now Kalman had reappropriated the idea for a kind of an update of Toscani's United Contrasts campaign.

The Black Queen Elizabeth, from Tibor Kalman's "How Ya Like Me Now?" spread: "People are upset, and that's the way change happens."

"The idea was that if you could separate the person from their race you could then figure out how you feel about the race versus the person," Kalman said in media interviews. "So when you look at the Black Queen, you think, 'Does she dance better? Is Buckingham Palace playing cool Caribbean music at its receptions? Does the Black Schwarzenegger look stronger than the white Schwarzenegger?' And as you explore these questions you become conscious of your own racism."[23]

The resulting controversy only reaffirmed his point. On both sides of the Atlantic, tabloids exploded. "The Pekinese Pope," scoffed the *Daily Express*. "The African Queen," blared the *Daily Mirror*. One angry royalist wrote to the *Toronto Star*, "It's disgusting. I have nothing against the Blacks, but if we had wanted a Black Queen we would have had one."[24] Kalman just said to Katie Couric, shrugging, "I mean people are upset, and that's the way change happens."

Forget data points, history, money, power. Of course race was a construct. And if race, like beauty, was only skin deep, then racism, like ugliness, was just a personal problem to be confessed and corrected. Perhaps this was all the depth that the moment could bear. Was it all that any American race conversation could ever bear?

Jacobs's editorial would be her last. She had found her disagreements with Kalman increasingly unworkable. After the race issue closed, she left. Many years later, when she returned to the magazine, she wondered whether she had been naive. Back then she and Kalman had juxtaposed a photo of Blacks in Atlanta beating a white man after the policeman in the Rodney King case had been acquitted against a photo of neo-Nazis threatening a Southeast Asian family on a German subway. Next to this she had written:

> We wish we could step into these pictures and say politely, 'Hey you guys listen: the differences between peoples and between individuals are humanity's most valuable resources.'
>
> We wish that sort of thing worked.
>
> 'Hey guys,' we'd say, 'imagine a world in which everyone looks, talks, and thinks exactly like you. Everything, absolutely everything—sex, movies, fashion, football matches—would be boring.' Yeah, we know. Those would be our last words.
>
> But listen: we said this is in the very first issue of *Colors* and, unlike Machiavelli, we need to repeat ourselves: Diversity is good.

IDENTITY'S IDENTITY CRISIS

A decade before Oliviero Toscani and Luciano Benetton began their collaboration, Susan Sontag had described the image world in which they would be working. Our desire for images was endless, she wrote. We had all become "image-junkies." "As we make images and consume them we need still more images; and still more," she wrote.

"Images consume reality."[25]

She wrote, "A capitalist society requires a culture based on images. It needs to furnish vast amounts of entertainment in order to stimulate buying and anesthetize the injuries of class, race, and sex."

From this hunger, she argued, a new ideology would rise: "Social change is replaced by a change in images. Freedom to consume a plurality of images and goods is equated with freedom itself." This cycle was iterative, she concluded, "The narrowing of free political choice to free economic consumption requires the unlimited production and consumption of images."[26]

A decade after Toscani and Benetton had been working together, not long after Kalman had come aboard, the company had trashed the cardinal rule of advertising—make the buyer feel good. But Benetton seemed to aspire to social significance, and so it found itself alone in the marketing vanguard. An unusual *Advertising Age* survey was commissioned in 1992, finding that more than 80 percent of U.S. ad industry employees believed Benetton's approach was ineffectual.[27]

At first the dramatically shifting demographics of the North American market had vindicated their instincts. Canadian researchers found that while executives believed they might lose 1 in 5 consumers if they ran ads that included minorities, only 4 percent of consumers were actually turned off. Moreover, 46 percent of consumers of color and 21 percent of all consumers said they were more likely to buy the product if ads featured people of color.[28] Benetton had pursued consumerism's last frontier with more passion than perhaps any other postmodern conglomerate.

But advertising's moment is always in the eyeblink, in the languid decisiveness of a dream state, the place that Baudrillard once called the "instantaneous and instantaneously forgotten."[29] Benetton's success had changed the image world. Toscani had had the right instincts about that moment as well. He knew the image world needed new images. Perhaps instinctively he understood that if capitalism were to triumph, even reality would have to fall before it.

But his new capitalist realism—in which nothing, not war or racism or misery or oppression, would escape capital's panoptic eye; in which the masses would be mobilized to transform the world through the marketplace—threatened to collapse under its contradictions. Toscani had argued that if you saw misery and oppression and war in an ad, you would be forced to confront it. But what happened when the buying season ended? When the apocalypse itself became a trend, the moment of social possibility was over, too. It's hard to get worked up over anything disposable.

Toscani labored on, earnestly. As Gran Fury and ACT UP were dissolving in the midnineties, he began using Benetton ads to talk about AIDS. He and Luciano Benetton organized a campaign on hunger, a clothing donation program for the Third World. But by 1995 there were only 120 stores left in the United States, down from a peak of 750 during the mid-1980s.[30] As Benetton's profits and stock price slid, Toscani became the scapegoat. In Germany, angry storeowners filed a class-action lawsuit against the company claiming his ads were hurting their businesses.

Kalman, who had shuttered his company and moved to Italy to work more closely with Toscani, contracted terminal non-Hodgkins lymphoma and left *Colors* at the end of 1995 with issue eleven, a beautiful *Koyaanisqatsi*-style issue of pure wordless imagery. He passed away in 1999. Toscani's own tenure at the clothing company would come to an end a year later. The final offense: a ninety-six-page insert placed in *Talk* magazine and Benetton stores. Its subject: twenty-six death-row inmates. Toscani had made the politically unforgivable mistake of trying to humanize and individualize the incarcerated men.

Near the end of his time at the company, Toscani had returned to shooting photos of diverse children against white backgrounds. They had appeared alongside excerpts from the Universal Declaration of Human Rights. They offended no one. They felt nostalgic. The emerging global hip-hop generation—the image of which all marketers were trying to capture—was both edgier and more optimistic than the children of Benetton had been. The United Colors now signified the diversity that signified nothing.

Naomi Klein, who had spent her college years absorbed in the antiracist and feminist movements, wrote in *No Logo*,

> [F]or many of the activists who had, at one point not so long ago, believed that better media representation would make for a more just world, one thing became abundantly clear: identity politics weren't fighting the system, or even subverting it. When it came to the vast new industry of corporate branding, they were feeding it.
>
> The crowning of sexual and racial diversity as the new superstars of advertising and pop culture has understandably created a sort of Identity Crisis.
>
> Why, in other words, were our ideas about political rebellion so deeply non-threatening to the smooth flow of business as usual?[31]

If advertising had been desegregated (in its content, at any rate, because the ad industry itself remained overwhelmingly white), if it had made diversity sexy, smart, and aspirational, if the image world had been colorized, then what exactly had been won?

Back in 1993, after Jacobs had struggled with the question and decided to leave *Colors*, Kalman had thought hard about it. His half-answer read like a confession: "Instead of accusing Benetton of trying to sell sweaters with images of human suffering, think of their advertising as an exercise in challenging assumptions and raising issues: a media experiment sponsored by a clothing company," he wrote. Here was where usually Toscani ended his analysis. But Kalman, the former '68er, the former Marxist, somehow felt compelled to go further.

"We should value anything that encourages us not to believe in both pictures and the media," the anti-designer said, exposing capitalist realism on its own terms. "After all, the media are subject to manipulation by the government, police, and business. I'd be lying if I did not say that media is subject to manipulation by Benetton, too. So to be responsible, those of us who work in the media have to tell people not to believe us. In the final analysis, it is the only honest course open to us."[32]

In the nineties, capitalism had at long last embraced its future in identity and diversity. But had it been only a temperature-controlled reverie, something that melted into air once one, jolted awake by the humid pavement rush of the masses, was back out on the hot, flat, crowded streets?

After the L.A. riots, amalgamation by algorithim—the face of "Eve," November 18, 1993.

CHAPTER 10

WE ARE ALL MULTICULTURALISTS NOW

VISIONS OF ONE AMERICA

> Must I strive toward colorlessness?
> —Ralph Ellison, *Invisible Man*

In November 1993—twenty months after multiracial looters had filled Los Angeles streets with shopping carts full of shoes, diapers, soft drinks, and stereos; even fewer since the Whitney Biennial had closed and Tibor Kalman's "What If?" spread ran in *Colors*—*Time* magazine featured a computer-generated photo of a coyly attractive, brown-haired, brown-eyed golden lady. This product of amalgamation by algorithm looked uncannily like future CNN "race expert" Soledad O'Brien.

The Golden Lady's appearance was a breach into mass consciousness of the long-repressed eugenicist nightmare/liberal fantasy—seen in Stanley Kramer's *Guess Who's Coming to Dinner* or John Sayles's *Lone Star* or Warren Beatty's *Bulworth*—a nation united through miscegenation. Just thirty-five years before, a few years before Barack

Obama was born, the Gallup Poll had found 96 percent of white Americans opposed interracial marriage.[1] She was the belated projection of triumph over the old order. But she could only have been born into a world busily disappearing race into the marketplace. Maybe that was the reason for her silent Mona Lisa smile.

For those who thought the riots had been a malign virus or a system failure, Kalman's art prank and this New Face of America might have appeared as a kind of a rebuild. It was all very Baudrillard in Disneyland: history as tragedy, then as farce, finally the farce making history. But for American-led globalization to work, this is exactly what it needed to do: absorb the world's markets into itself. What was the alternative? More fires?

As the decade moved forward, multiculturalism began to look less like an insurgency and more like a fait accompli. In the rush to reconstruct America, conservatives became racially liberal; liberals became racially conservative; and through it all, colorization accelerated the creation of new images, new visions of one America. Words could barely keep up.

Difference was quickly deradicalized. With the image of this new American über-mestiza—the digital sum of what *Time* had termed the "World's First Multicultural Society" and Paul Beatty in his post-Black bildungsroman *The White Boy Shuffle* had called "the monochrome utopia"—America seemed to have acceded to its ethnically ambiguous future. Emphasis on "ambiguous." It might not be the past of cultural hierarchy that the traditionalists had defended. But it also might not be the future of cultural equity that the multiculturalists had imagined.

ONE MARKET FROM MANY:
GIVE ME YOUR HUNGRY SEGMENTS

Multiculturalism-as-arts insurrection had run into the buzz saw of elite disdain and was in retreat. Multiculturalism-as-public-discourse would lurch forward and back. But multiculturalism-as-consumer lifestyle only just begun its insinuation at the micro level: colorized Barbies, "ethnic cosmetics," a sudden efflorescence of flesh-colored crayons.

There was another name for this phenomenon: market segmentation. After the 1980s, national advertising was less about reaching the mass market than about absorbing all of the as-yet-unincorporated niche markets. Capital had long seen itself, in the words of pioneering adman Albert Lasker, as "making a homogenous people out of a nation of immigrants."[2] Benetton-style globalization extended this logic horizontally; it was about putting all the world's diversity into the same sweaters. Market segmentation shared the same imperial aspirations, but its logic was vertical. It was about changing the sweaters slightly for each of the different slivers along the entire spectrum.

The term "market segmentation" was coined by scholar Wendell Smith in 1956. Its first blockbuster success came four years later in the Pepsi Generation ads. Pepsi had shown that smart segmenting could turn a whole industry to its advantage, and that lifestyle appeals could create a more loyal consumer. A decade later, the consumer data revolution had begun in places like Palo Alto's Stanford Research Institute and Alexandria, Virginia's Claritas corporation where data miners sliced and diced the flow of information into market segments.

Claritas's "clusters" approach, for instance, explicitly tied geography to identity, offering forty different neighborhood descriptions with funny names. It could tell you that dieters tended to live in the places they called "Furs & Station Wagons," "God's Country," "Urban Gold Coast," "Young Suburbia," and "Blue-Collar Nursery."[3] It could tell you that in the "Furs & Station Wagons" zip codes, they read *Fortune*; and in the "Blue-Collar Nursery" codes, they read *Lakeland Boating*.

In other words, each segment demanded its own lifestyle, serviced with its own cart of goods. Identity could be eventually reduced to an algorithm finding the sum of all one bought. In this way, identity could be separated from fears and hopes, histories and yearnings, even ethics and values, and could simply be assigned *a value*.

Out of many markets, one. Here was a vision of one America as 100 percent sold-in, a summing of the differences. "Capitalism seamlessly occupies the horizons of the thinkable," wrote Mark Fisher, even the idea of the nation.[4]

This logic might have seemed elementary to anyone whose purchasing power was respected. And yet it would still take decades before people of color became demographically correct to American business, before capital would learn to speak their language, try their dances, and copy their styles in order to help them part with their disposable income. For a long time one size would have to fit all.

RECOGNITION, IDENTIFICATION, AND INVITATION

Scholars and publishers began studying the Black market seriously in the 1930s. As the national market expanded, a small number of large companies like Pepsi, Coke, and Sears became regular ad buyers in the Black radio and magazine industries. Yet for the most part people of color were still stigmatized as poor, ghettoized, and brand-indifferent, too insignificant a market to trifle with.

Market research on Blacks grew again in the 1960s, driven by the political and moral triumphs of the civil rights movement, which had in turn been catalyzed largely by strikes and demonstrations of Black buying power—bus boycotts and counter sit-ins. But experts seemed to find very little to be excited about.

Business scholars first tried to distinguish the Black market from those of, as one study put it, other "lower-income, lower-educated, and geographically concentrated group(s)."[5] In a 1961 study, Henry Allen Bullock argued that all consumers purchased things in order to have the security of "belonging," but that Blacks and whites had very different motivations. He bulleted his two main points:

- Negroes want group identification; whites, feeling that they already have this, want group distinction.
- More specifically, Negroes want to be identified with the general American society and all its peoples, while whites want to remain generally acceptable but particularly exclusive.[6]

Bullock illustrated his point by pointing to how Southern whites and Blacks that he interviewed completed the sentence "If I could change the world, I would...." The list of whites' most frequent replies included:

- "Make it so that people would not park in front of my driveway."
- "Stop the neighbors' children from cutting across my lawn."
- "Destroy the United Nations."
- "Change the Supreme Court."

But Blacks said:

- "Make all people the same."
- "Establish brotherhood."
- "Do away with war."
- "Break down segregation."[7]

To Bullock, consumption was key in helping Blacks overcome a sense of inferiority and attain a sense of security. On the other hand, moving the needle on white anger with the desegregationist Warren Court—an opinion apparently so banal that it appeared equivalent to stopping the neighborhood kids from crossing one's lawn—was far beyond the scope of an advertiser. So Bullock's central research question was tailored accordingly: "How can advertisers win Negro identification while avoiding white alienation?"[8] Bullock called his solution "integrated advertising"—companies only needed to carve out one smartly designed campaign for all of America.

In a later study, published the year after the passage of the Voting Rights Act, white researchers found that Black men liked Scotch whiskey because it made them feel rich. On the other hand, they learned that department store shopping made Black women anxious. In their view, the Negro problem was wholly one of assimilation.

"Negroes as a group have accepted the values of the majority white middle-class culture, but are at a disadvantage in acquiring the goods which represent some of these values," the authors Raymond Bauer, Scott Cunningham, and Lawrence Wortzel wrote. "In other words, the basic dilemma of Negroes is whether to strive against odds to attain these middle-class values (and the goods which come with them), or to give in and live without most of them."[9]

This kind of scholarship caused a frustrated Black public relations pioneer named D. Parke Gibson to publish a book-long pitch, *The $30 Billion Negro*. What the Negro wanted in the marketplace, he wrote, was the same thing he wanted in American society: "recognition, identification, and invitation."[10]

Writing not long after the assassination of Dr. Martin Luther King Jr., Gibson argued for a cold realism around race, free of assimilationist illusions. "There is little likelihood that in the near future the Negro community in the United States will be absorbed into the white community," wrote Gibson, "and this is the basis upon which business and industrial management will have to operate in the sale of goods and services to this expanding market segment."[11]

If the state couldn't legislate tolerance, Gibson seemed to be saying, perhaps the market could at least respect difference. But how much difference would the market be able to take?

DIVERSITY VERSUS NARROWCASTING

Market segmentation had been born of the information age and it would find its broadest expression with the rise of cable television. For decades, under pressure from the Big Three broadcast networks and movie theaters, the FCC resisted attempts to expand and commercialize cable. Instead cable thrived largely in rural areas, mountainous areas, and small towns where over-the-air signals didn't reach.

By 1970, both media activists and big business were pushing for the development of cable. Progressive visionary Ralph Lee Smith called for a "Wired Nation" connected by an "electronic highway," in which all necessary and desired information would immediately be accessible, and democracy's foundations would thereby be strengthened. Smith believed cable TV could diversify the media to better reflect the needs of invisible populations.[12] It was potentially a medium with a "global village" message—a counterbalance to mind-dulling mass media, a space for increased minority ownership, a potential wonderland of arts, educational, and local programming. Cable could liberate a diversity of communities and identities. One civil rights leader called it "the last communications frontier for the oppressed."[13]

People of color remained among the most invisible of all. One study of the twelve most popular magazines in the country from the years 1946, 1956, and 1965 found that Blacks appeared in fewer than four ads for every thousand pages.[14] On television, Blacks made up less than 1 percent of speaking roles in commercials. On TV programs, they fared little better—3 percent in speaking roles and 8 percent in nonspeaking roles.[15] By 1970, fewer than thirty Blacks were employed in the entire advertising industry, and most of those were in what scholar Dorothy Cohen called "show positions"—public relations, special markets, community outreach.[16] Other racial groups did not even register.

For its part, big business had become enamored of the potential of "narrowcasting." Being able to reach a collection of market segments could be a much more efficient way of exploiting unserved or underserved populations, instead of always having to appeal to mass markets. One adman celebrated the possibilities of this "new media" in a speech at the American Enterprise Institute: "For the past three decades, we have oriented ourselves to communicating to the *most mass*; we now possess the capability to concentrate on the *least waste*, to speak to smaller segments of our population, one group at a time."[17]

Beginning in 1972, the FCC began to remove many of its cable television regulations, but in the process, they obliterated Smith's vision of a system rooted in the decentralized sweat equity of local communities. A different kind of revolution had begun. Ted Turner became the first cable television mogul, transforming a tiny UHF station in Atlanta—so rundown it could only broadcast in black-and-white—into the first cable "superstation," WTBS. He told advertisers he would deliver them quality viewers from the suburbs and exurbs, bragging, "We're not wired to the ghettos."[18]

COLORIZING TELEVISION

In 1976, Robert Johnson was a young congressional staffer handling communications for Walter Fauntroy, the leader of the Congressional Black Caucus. Johnson was excited about the potential of cable television. He recalled, "[I]t became clear to me that programming could be segmented and targeted to different audiences, and so it didn't take a big leap from that to say, 'Wow, wait a minute, that's what we're already doing in the Black community with print.'"[19]

He told Fauntroy about the possibilities of a Black television network. Fauntroy understood Johnson to be describing a channel that would increase Black education and civic engagement. So he gave his blessing to Johnson to hit the revolving door and become a lobbyist for the National Cable Television Association (whose original name had been the National *Community* Television Council). "There was this idea that cable would create the kind of diversity that the broadcast networks never had. Someone was going to do it," Johnson said. "Why not me?"[20]

At the NCTA, Johnson's task was to push Congress to further loosen restrictions on cable and support business opportunities for his clients. In 1979 he took one of them, Ken Silverman, to secure Congressman Claude Pepper's backing for a movie channel for senior citizens. On the cab ride over, Silverman read Johnson his business plan—the demographics of the elderly, their buying habits, their viewing patterns. Johnson told Silverman of his idea about a network for Blacks. He asked if he could adapt Silverman's business plan. Silverman handed it to him. Soon after, Johnson secured a $15,000 bank loan and quit his job. On August 8, 1979, he announced the creation of Black Entertainment Television.

In return for a small stake, Johnson secured $500,000 in startup capital from a conservative named John Malone, a NCTA board member building a cable empire called Tele-Communications, Inc. Malone controlled the physical wires that operators needed to plug into. But he realized that cable's future was in creating content niche markets. In time, through his Liberty Media company and other companies, Malone held stakes in a broad array of media properties. Johnson's Black Entertainment Television was his first bet, the first in the building of a media empire.

At their peak at the end of the 1970s, the three major networks together reached more than 90 percent of all American households, half the entire population.[21] But things were changing. Johnson made two arguments to advertisers: Blacks watched much more television than Whites; and the Black population was growing at twice the rate of whites. They largely fell on deaf ears. "I remember walking out of some advertising agency almost in tears trying to sell this product," he said.[22] Yet he was still able to launch on January 25, 1980 with two hours of Friday night programming and ads from Anheuser-Busch, *Time*, Champale, Pepsi, Sears, and Kellogg. By 1986, he had turned his first profit.

Johnson had been very late to the game of developing the Black market. In the late 1960s, after civil rights legislation had passed and policies such as affirmative action had begun to create a new Black bourgeoisie, a number of Black-owned boutique ad agencies had sprung up to try to fill the expected business of corporate clients who wanted to reach new customers of color. But by 1975, most of these agencies had disappeared.

Forget Gary Becker's Nobel Prize–winning argument on the supposed inefficiencies of discrimination. Forget even Robert Downey Sr.'s outrageous film *Putney Swope* about a Black nationalist who takes over a white ad agency and brings down the wrath of the U.S. government. Black agencies would never be considered for general-market—read: "white"—accounts. So mainstream agencies stepped in to poach the talent and the accounts the Black agencies had nurtured; it was capitalist realism's answer to integration. One agency head told advertising historian Jason Chambers, "You can't survive on ethnic business, and yet they won't accept you on your merits as an advertising agency."[23] The ad industry would enter into the twenty-first century one of the least racially integrated industries in America.[24]

With cable's rise, advertisers finally began to adapt to media fragmentation. In 1990, the University of Georgia's Selig Center estimated the combined buying power of nonwhites at $455 billion.[25] The same demographic shifts that had unleashed the culture wars were also huge business opportunities. By being a decade behind the visionaries of Black advertising, Johnson was right on time.

JUST PAINT IT BLACK

Johnson would never become known as an innovative programmer. "I didn't see the connection between huge expenses in programming and advertisers stepping up their ad rates," he admitted.[26] Instead the network launched on a mix of music videos it received for free, coverage of Black collegiate football games for which it paid as little as $1000 to the competing schools, and old movies and television series it had purchased.[27]

It was not until 1988 that Johnson made his first significant investment in original programming. But during the 1990s, as the hip-hop industry expanded, Johnson moved back to the cheaper content. In 1991, 42 percent of programming was music videos. In 2000, 70 percent of it was. Music programming accounted for 80 percent of BET's annual cash flow.[28] "We don't need to reinvent the wheel," he told his staffers, "we just need to paint it black."[29]

Johnson's indifference to content sparked rounds of protest from the Black community. They bemoaned the network as, at best, a squandered opportunity to uplift the race and, at worst, a 24–7 minstrel show. In 1997, Lydia Cole, BET's vice president for programming, famously told a music industry conference audience that she did not let her own daughters watch the channel. By the turn of the millennium, Aaron McGruder's frontal attack on Johnson and the network in his strip *The Boondocks* was finding broad agreement. "BET is the only thing that black people have on television and it's gotten to the point that you don't want to come home and turn it on," radio host Tom Joyner told Pulley. "I've been inside Bob's office and he doesn't even have it on in there."[30]

"We were the only Black network," protested Johnson. "So we became the burden carrier for the Black community, with all of its desires about what we should do." At once he dismissed cable operators who wanted quality, Black intellectuals and middle-class viewers who wanted social redemption, and Black artists who wanted a more open door. "So, what we basically said is, 'We can't solve everybody's desires for BET. We have to run the business according to what we believe.' And for me that was rooted in having to be focused on running this as a business, a profit maximization business."[31]

Johnson had secured his niche, controlled his market segment. That was all that needed doing. Globalization's dream of multiculturalism was about absorbing all previously underserved markets into itself. It could be agnostic or naive about questions of content and representation. It simply believed that nothing—no expression, movement, or identity—should exist outside of it. When, just after the turn of the millennium, Viacom was completing its butterfly collection of narrowcasted networks—Nickelodeon for kids, MTV for youths, the History Channel for retirees, Spike for straight young men, Logo for LGBTs—they bought BET from Johnson for $3 billion.

From the Montgomery Bus Boycott in 1954, African Americans had harnessed their power as consumers as a means to win broader rights as citizens. A half century later, many wondered if consumerism marked the actual end of the movement. Given African Americans' "distinctive history of propertylessness and material deprivation," the Black British thinker Paul Gilroy worried that the energies once devoted to winning status as free subjects were now mainly being directed to the collection of status objects. He wrote that African Americans may have begun to "conceive *culture itself* as a form of property which is held as compensation for low status and heavily restricted access to both rights and wealth," a tragic move that accommodated "the diminution of citizenship" and "the privatisation of their culture."[32]

FINALLY READY FOR PRIMETIME

As for corporations, the demographer Peter Francese wrote, "The trick is to find a faster-growing segment before everyone else does or build market share faster than anyone else."[33] This is exactly what Fox TV tried to do in mobilizing new audiences. Launched in 1986 as "the fourth network," Fox hit its stride at the end of the decade by concluding, just as Pepsi and Nike once had, that the future lay in the market segments populated by youth and communities of color. Their early programming hits were *The Simpsons*, *Married with Children*, and *21 Jump Street*. When in 1990 Fox added *In Living Color* to its lineup, it was poised to make a run at changing broadcast TV. Keenen Ivory Wayans, the star and creator of *In Living Color*, said, "They wanted to be the rebel network."[34]

Wayans had a hip-hop attitude about the show: he didn't want just a Black audience, he wanted it all. When network head Barry Diller insisted Wayans get the approval of the NAACP and Urban League before airing it, Wayans refused, asking if Jackie Mason had ever had to clear his sitcoms with B'Nai B'rith. Instead *In Living Color* advance tapes gained such a buzz among industry insiders that, when no organization protested, Diller put it on the air.

It became a blockbuster hit, bringing characters like Ugly Wanda, Oswald Bates, Men on Film, Vera DeMilo, and Homey D. Clown into family rooms across the country. In "Ted Turner's Very Colorized Classics," the cast clowned Turner's controversial appetite for adding color to black-and-white films on his cable movie networks. Here the films stayed in black-and-white but the characters were of color. Tommy Davidson's Stevie Wonder stole the scene in "Casablanca" with a melismatic version of "As Time Goes By." Wayans and Davidson mocked Nixon/Reagan racial stereotypes in a version of Charlie Chaplin's *The Kid*, the classic silent that had featured Chaplin and Jackie Coogan eking out a living through low-level street scams. In the colorized version, Wayans and David-son played welfare cheats, fleecing the government for AFDC checks, walking a fine line between stereotype and satire.

In Living Color introduced the Wayans family, Jamie Foxx, and David Alan Grier to mass audiences. "The Fly Girls" included Jennifer Lopez from the Bronx, Carrie Ann Inaba from Honolulu, and Rosie Perez from Brooklyn. Jim Carrey was one of only two whites in the cast. Fox had one other wildly popular show featuring a disproportionately high number of people of color on-screen—a ride-along reality show called *COPS*. Stumbling forward, staggering back.

Still, the first half of the 1990s looked to many like a golden age for Black televi-sion. In 1993, Fox's lineup boasted no fewer than six shows starring predominantly Black casts: *In Living Color*, *Martin*, *Roc*, *Living Single*, *Sinbad*, and *Townsend Television*. Media scholar George Gerbner found that a Fox show was twice as likely to feature an African American as any other network's show.[35] Perhaps invisibility itself was fading to Black, especially for Black men.

Here was recognition, identification, and invitation. And audiences of color responded, in a way that assimilation-minded sociologists and general-market-focused broadcasters never would have predicted. Nielsen had been tracking Black household watching preferences against all households and found there was no crossover between the two. Blacks' favorites were *The Fresh Prince of Bel-Air*, *Roc*, *In Living Color*, and *Martin*. Whites watched *Roseanne*, *60 Minutes*, *Murphy Brown*, and *Coach*.[36] Rather than program its own Black shows against NBC's *A Different World* and *Fresh Prince*, Fox coun-terprogrammed its Thursday night against NBC's "Must-See TV" of the famous *Friends* and *Seinfeld* sitcoms, and the barely integrated ensemble drama *E.R.*

Fox didn't care about total numbers. They cared about what their shares were for 18-to-34s and Blacks. Network vice president of research Andrew Fessel said, "We have meetings and don't even look at the household figures. Demos are really the key to us."[37] One station in Augusta, Georgia, reportedly drew a stunning 52 rating for *Martin*—more than half of *all* households with TVs in the town.[38] Thursday night was beginning to look like Sunday morning—the most segregated hours of the week.

Then in 1994 Fox suddenly canceled four of its Black-produced shows: *In Living Color*, *Roc*, *South Central*, and *Sinbad*. Jesse Jackson and the Congressional Black Caucus threatened boycotts. Congressman Ed Towns accused Fox of "disrespect and apparent contempt."[39] What had changed? Rupert Murdoch had just purchased NFL rights for $1.6 billion. Fox had grown big enough, media critic and scholar Kristal Brent Zook argued, to stop playing in the niches and move back to the Big White Middle. "Fox cited poor ratings in canceling the shows, but it wasn't Black faces or producers that did the programs in," Zook wrote, "it was Black *complexity*."[40]

Black-produced shows did not immediately disappear from broadcast TV. In 1996, WB and UPN launched with former Fox programming execs at the helm, and offered shows such as *The Jamie Foxx Show* and *Moesha*. Fox still had the number-one Black show, *Living Single*, as well as *Martin* and *New York Undercover*. But its main focus shifted to shows like *Ally McBeal*, in which the feminism was in regression and the women of color played the Black-You-Go-Girlfriend and the New-Class Dragon Lady.

When the 1999 season was introduced, *none* of the twenty-six new sitcoms from the top four networks featured a person of color lead. TV scholar Darnell Hunt found that people of color were most underrepresented at NBC and Fox, the two networks that had for a decade been the most-watched among Black audiences. "They build themselves up with Black audiences," Judith McCreary, the former producer of *New York Undercover*, told Zook. "Then once they're established, they dump us."[41]

The decade had begun with such color-consciousness, with such celebration at exposing racialized codes, with such gleeful crashing of barriers to representation. And now it was ending like this.

WHAT GOOD WERE EYES TO ME?

By the early 1990s, affirmative action had transformed the complexion of colleges and universities across the country. Yet it remained a dividing line. Blacks, Chicanos, Latinos, Filipinos, Southeast Asians, and American Indians remained underrepresented. But polls showed that up to 80 percent of whites opposed preferences for minorities.[42]

In 1993, conservative governor Pete Wilson appointed his old friend, Ward Connerly—a government consultant of Black, white, and American Indian descent who had grown up in the largely Black Del Paso Heights section of Sacramento—to a seat on the University of California Board of Regents. Connerly would help set policy for the most racially diverse public university system in the nation.

"I know I would not be on the Board of Regents were it not for the fact that Pete Wilson wanted to, quote, 'diversify' that board," Connerly admitted in an interview years later. "*That* is affirmative action."[43]

But Connerly was happy to become the spokesperson for the new colorblindness, using his appointment to lead a push for the elimination of affirmative action. A quarter-century before, Richard Nixon called for an end to white guilt and "the veil of hypocrisy." Now here was a Black man who called his work to undo civil rights–era programs an "equal rights movement," while saying he intended to "advance civil rights" and "equal opportunity."

Amid the culture wars, conservatives had been experimenting with new language around race. Conservative of color Dinesh D'Souza staked an extreme position: anti-racism was an "intellectually bankrupt" agenda, and Blacks and other people of color were not victims of racism, but practitioners of dangerous dysfunctional cultures that brought them to ruin.

"[B]lack cultural pathology has contributed to a new form of discrimination: rational discrimination," he wrote. "Rational discrimination is based on accurate group generalizations that may nevertheless be unfair to particular members of a group."[44] D'Souza had not only appropriated Democratic politician Daniel Patrick Moynihan's LBJ-era language of cultural pathology but had found an odd resonance with the Black nationalist Louis Farrakhan's calls to self-improvement.

But other conservatives gave up defending white privilege in explicitly racialized terms. Instead they tried to follow Nixon's directive to "devise a system that recognizes [Blacks are the problem] while appearing not to." The Southern-strategy alignment still depended on appealing not only to the angry heirs to the Wallace legacy but to the suburbanizing whites who were heirs to the Goldwater legacy. During the 1980s, Black thinkers like Shelby Steele, Black Reagan officials like Clarence Pendleton, and white ones like William Bradford Reynolds began arguing for "colorblindness" in government contracting and public education.

Connerly had drawn his language from them. He leaned especially hard on exactly one line from Martin Luther King Jr.'s "I Have a Dream" speech—by now canonized in post-multiculti elementary school classrooms everywhere—"that my four little children will one day live in a nation where they will not be judged by the color of their skin, but the content of their character."

Historian Daniel Rodgers noted that among the lines Connerly and his fellow conservatives left on the cutting floor were King's praise for the "[Black movement's] marvelous new militancy" and his condemnation of "the sweltering heat of oppression."[45] Instead, this selective forgetting was simply the flip side of imperialist nostalgia, a denial of the inequalities of the present that complemented a denial of inequalities past.

Despite massive protests on all of its campuses, the conservative-leaning Board of Regents voted 14–10 in July 1995 to end affirmative action in the University. When the ban took effect in 1998, Black and Latino enrollments dropped by at least half at the most competitive campuses. "We still have to be a place of opportunity for all," said UC Berkeley chancellor Robert M. Berdahl, "but the law is constraining us very, very substantially."[46] Despite the ban's repeal in 2001, it would take over a decade for enrollments of underrepresented students to return to pre-ban levels. By then Connerly had succeeded in winning bans on state-administered affirmative action programs through referendum votes in California and Washington. He went on to sponsor similar efforts in Florida, Michigan, Colorado, Nebraska, Missouri, and Oklahoma.

Those in Michigan, Nebraska, and Oklahoma passed. Legislatures in Florida and New Hampshire passed more limited bans. (Similar laws in Texas and Georgia were ruled unconstitutional by state courts.) As late as 2010, Arizona voters approved their own anti–affirmative action referendum, the same year their legislature and governor passed the notorious anti-immigrant bill, SB 1070.

With these victories the grand conservative project of racial restoration begun under Nixon moved closer to completion. More than three decades into the Southern strategy, conservatives had figured out how to successfully deconstruct the language, music, and visuality of the Civil Rights consensus. Prominent white liberals were eager to be the proof.

ONE-NATION LIBERALISM: SUBTRACTING THE DIFFERENCE

In 1997, *Mother Jones* magazine devoted an issue to "rethinking race." In it, cofounder and editor-in-chief Jeffrey Klein and writer Michael Lind blamed the left's demise on its support for affirmative action and immigration.[47] The politically correct move now was to swing back to the Big White Middle, a constituency that they argued was more united by its disdain for a "rainbow liberalism" that benefited Blacks, Latinos, and Asian Americans than anything else.

In "The End of the Rainbow," Lind slammed "the multicultural right" led by country-club Republicans "who rail against 'class war' while finding many kind things to say about high immigration (which is good for business) and even affirmative action (which makes corporate America look more diverse to a diverse public)."[48] He argued that this kind of politics not only divided whites, they presaged an all-out racial battle royale.

"As the percentage of whites diminishes [in states like California and Texas]," he wrote, "blacks and Hispanics and Asians will likely turn on one another, with representatives of each category demanding a 'fair share' of political offices, jobs, and opportunities for higher education."

It was a peculiar, faithless charge, reminiscent of the kind made by the anti-multiculturalist liberals of the early 1990s. Lind seemed unable to believe that communities of color might be as invested as white liberals were in the project of making America. Conservative forgetting had found its soul mate in liberal fatigue.

Instead Lind proposed a "one-nation liberalism," a return to a New Deal–style era agenda of economic uplift. He did not note that the housing and infrastructure-building policies of the oft-touted golden age of Roosevelt liberalism were far from color-blind and, in fact, had often been premised on exclusion and segregation. How might a new New Deal address the long-term effects of racialized poverty, ghettoization, and educational segregation left by the old one? He did not say.

But electoral politics is about addition, not subtraction. How would a new coalition that distanced itself from communities of color still hold them? Lind turned to pop culture for the answer. Americans, he argued, might forge a "common identity" through the "disproportionately Black vernacular culture shared by American whites and blacks alike." He elaborated on this essentially Schlesingerian view:

> That common national culture is Judeo-Christian, not Black Muslim; its
> holidays are Thanksgiving and Christmas and the Fourth of July, not Yul or
> Kwanza [sic]; its common institutions include sports and the military; its
> mythic homeland is not Europe or Africa, but North America; and it can
> find symbols in vernacular-culture heroes like Elvis Presley, the mixed-race,
> white/Cherokee prole who sang like a black man.[49]

Yet Chuck D's line about dead Elvis was already eight years old. Lind insisted, "The radical transformation of American culture by the influx of new immigrants is unlikely." But even Pat Buchanan had learned how to order Mexican and Thai food.

Lind could not imagine a nation that might be "all of the above." Progressives unacknowledged by the men of *Mother Jones* were discussing the notion of "intersectionality," an idea developed by Black feminist Kimberlé Crenshaw and elaborated on by a new school of critical race theorists, to talk about how different oppressions operated simultaneously. But the message was hopeful: race, gender, sexual, and class identities produced opportunities for new vital coalitions to be born.

Lind still lived in a black-and-white world. A decade after Lee Atwater had renewed the Southern strategy and won, the anti-multicultural left was lurching into reverse, going back to the future, waxing nostalgic for that time before race complicated it all, and abandoning the Democratic Party's most loyal constituencies.

Meanwhile the intellectual right swung forward. The same year that Lind's screed appeared, neocon Nathan Glazer—whose book *Affirmative Discrimination* had been an inspiration for Ward Connerly—quietly changed his mind. He had been asked to participate in a controversial revision of the New York public school social studies curriculum and become "impressed" by the "strength of multiculturalism, the apparent inevitability of multiculturalism."[50]

In a book called *We Are All Multiculturalists Now*, he wrote,

> When I say multiculturalism has won, and that "we are all multiculturalists now," I mean that we all now accept a greater degree of attention to minorities and women and their role in American history and social studies and literature classes in schools. Those few who want to return American education in which the various subcultures were ignored, and in which America was presented as the peak and end-product of civilization, cannot expect to make any progress in the schools.[51]

A year later, Federal Reserve Board chief Alan Greenspan appeared before Jesse Jackson's PUSH Coalition. Greenspan described a new Wall Street consensus when he said, "Discrimination is patently immoral, but it is now increasingly being seen as unprofitable." When *Grutter v. Bollinger*, an affirmative action case involving the University of Michigan Law School, came before the Supreme Court, the U.S. Army, MTV Networks, General Motors, and other Fortune 500 companies filed amicus curiae briefs in defense of affirmative action. Although the Republican Party opposed affirmative action in its platform, it played its own representational game, becoming the party of Clarence Thomas, Colin Powell, and Condoleezza Rice.

Multiculturalism now looked like what the scholar Vijay Prashad called an "ideology from above." It was now merely "diversity," and diversity was a cliché, an evasion. The fears of the anti-multicultural left and right had been misplaced. The state had hardly given way to a vast multicultural uprising. It had given way to a capitalism furiously reorganizing itself for a global, browning, urban world.

The right remained as divided about this development as the left. The leadership of the Republican Party—among them, Atwater's protégé Karl Rove and Harvard Law School graduate Ken Mehlman—knew the census numbers well. In that sense, they, too, were multiculturalists now. And yet Republicans remained, even in D'Souza's words, "the de facto party of whites."

On July 31, 2000, the first night of the Republican National Convention, Colin Powell stepped before the Party in the evening's showcase address to deliver a ringing endorsement of affirmative action. His words bounced off the ceiling of the First Union Center and dissipated into air. The arena audience's tepid applause, cued by the maverickhatted Texas delegation, suited and booted in blue denim and cowboy leather and seated dead center, was simply reflexive.

After George W. Bush's acceptance speech on Thursday night, when the balloons came down and the Bushes had left the stage, Chaka Khan came out to sing "I Feel for You" and Brian McKnight followed with "One." But if the Republican brass had hoped this closing-night programming would bookend its commitment to diversity, the Texans and the rest of the rank-and-file were already voting loudly with their feet.

CLINTON'S ONE AMERICA

Alone perhaps among his cadre of Democratic centrists, President Bill Clinton seemed, at least intuitively, to grasp the implications of colorization. Long before the madness of the Monica Lewinsky scandal and the travesty of Florida, he had told those close to him that he hoped to leave his singular legacy around race. He had come into office in no small part because of the Rodney King riots. He had blamed Republicans for causing racial division by neglecting urban policy and poor people of color.[52] But he, too, had played culture war politics, using a deliberate misquote of the rapper-activist Sister Souljah to mobilize white voters. Like Lee Atwater, Clinton was a Southern politician who could work both sides of the color and generation lines.

The president was in his fourth year of office, and his domestic agenda had already done its damage. He had pushed through welfare reform, a dubious achievement of upward income distribution that had eluded both Nixon and Reagan. He had advanced policing and criminal justice policies that had fueled the massive growth of what Angela Davis would call the "punishment industry," the permanent feature of which would be racial disparities in arrests, sentencing, and incarceration. His agenda had so nakedly pandered to the archetypal Southern-strategy white voter that his efforts to address demographic and cultural change felt like another act of triangulation, utopian, unempirical, underthought.

Now as Clinton began his second term, the reporter John Harris wrote, he had become passionate about leading "a sustained one-year campaign of discussions, travel, study, and finally recommendations about the challenges of diversity."[53] He would choose a campus at the University of California, in the state where the Gettysburgs of the culture wars had been fought, to inaugurate his project of reconciliation.[54]

In June 1997, Clinton gave his race speech in commencement exercises at the University of California at San Diego, a university set at the southwestern edge of the continent like a city on the hill, its face turned to the western destiny of the Pacific, all the colors of future rippling before him in cerulean caps and gowns.

He spoke of growing up in the South, and his grandfather's grace in teaching him that segregation was wrong. "But those who say we cannot transform the problem of prejudice into the promise of unity forget how far we have come," he said, "and I cannot believe they have ever seen a crowd like you." The young graduates burst into applause.

The day before, Clinton had signed Executive Order 13050 creating the President's Advisory Board on Race to "advise the President on matters involving race and racial reconciliation." Clinton argued that perhaps now—five years after the Los Angeles riots, in a time of a strengthening economy and relative domestic peace—the United States might be ready to have what he called a "constructive national dialogue to confront and work through challenging issues that surround race."

There was an urgent business reason. Clinton said, "With just a twentieth of the world's population, but a fifth of the world's income, we in America simply have to sell to the other 95 percent of the world's consumers just to maintain our standard of living. Because we are drawn from every culture on earth, we are uniquely positioned to do it.

"The best example of successful affirmative action is our military," he added. "So much for the argument that excellence and diversity do not go hand in hand."

There was a moral obligation, too, for the president who had stumbled in responses to ethnic wars in Rwanda, Somalia, Bosnia, and Herzegovina. He now needed to restate American exceptionalism in his own words. "Beyond commerce," he said, "the diverse backgrounds and talents of our citizens can help America to light the globe, showing nations deeply divided by race, religion, and tribe that there is a better way."

Now he was recasting Rodney King's question—"Can we all get along?"—by asking, "Can we become one America in the twenty-first century?" He said, "We must be honest with each other. We have talked at each other and about each other for a long time. It's high time we all began talking with each other.

"What do I really hope we will achieve as a country?" Clinton asked. "If we do nothing more than talk, it will be interesting but it won't be enough. If we do nothing more than proposed disconnected acts of policy, it would be helpful, but it won't be enough. But if ten years from now people can look back and see that this year of honest dialogue and concerted action helped to lift the heavy burden of race from our children's future, we will have given a precious gift to America."[55]

This, Clinton concluded to the students in La Jolla, was "the unfinished work of our time, to lift the burden of race and redeem the promise of America." And so he left his advisory board chair, the esteemed Black historian John Hope Franklin, and the panel members to the work of drawing the nation into a final cathartic conversation on race.

Over the next 15 months the One America commission toured the country, logging dozens of public forums and hundreds more events. The board debated the relative legacies of anti-Black racism and the emerging forms that targeted Latinos and Asian Americans. They heard from workers, students, ministers, veterans, business owners, race experts, American Indians (who had not been represented on the board), affirmative action opponents, and not a few white hecklers.

A staff of thirty-five compiled long lists of programs, leaders, and organizations representing "best practices." They put together downloadable info kits for civic groups that wanted to hold their own dialogue sessions. They drew up a list of "Ten Things Every American Should Do to Promote Racial Reconcilation." But what did it all add up to?

The scholar Claire Jean Kim argued that Clinton's advisory board compared unfavorably to Gunnar Myrdal's 1944 report *An American Dilemma* and the 1968 Kerner Commission report on urban disorders because, unlike those landmark reports, it refused to press the government on racial justice or equality.[56] This kind of racial reconciliation, Kim said, devolved the burden of change from the nation's institutions to its communities and individuals.

Early on in the project, advisor Christopher Edley of the Harvard Civil Rights Project had warned that it was doomed: "The problem is that [a bold Marshall Plan–style agenda] would be dead on arrival because we don't have the moral or political consensus to take those steps."[57] And in the end, the board did not turn in anything resembling a unified agenda. Their final product was a thicket of recommendations, without order or priority, presented as if it were an overstuffed folder of random clippings and incomplete thoughts scribbled on Post-its.

Between the convening of the panel and its final report, a politics inclined toward a moral call had been displaced by a politics of moral panic. On September 18, 1998, the day that President Clinton was to receive the findings of the One America board, the House Judiciary Committee voted to release the findings of Independent Counsel Kenneth Starr in the strange Monica Lewinsky affair. Whatever remained of a national conversation on race and reconciliation would be sidelined by the unseemly details of an extramarital relationship—the sly smiles, furtive trysts, and a single stained blue dress—between the president and the young intern.

On Martin Luther King Jr. Day in 2001, President Clinton submitted his last message to Congress, "The Unfinished Work of Building One America." In it he rehashed the highlights of his UCSD speech, and presented the recommendations of the advisory board as a long incoherent list of unimplemented policy proposals. That was how the Clinton's great conversation on race ended, not with purgation but procedure, not with reconciliation but exhaustion.

And now, as Paul Beatty had put it, everything and nothing was multicultural. It was the air everyone breathed. It was the mercury promise of freedom for all always slipping away.

"Humor In Hue" from *Black World*, April 1971. Courtesy of Morrie Turner.

We only see what we look at.
To look is an act of choice.

—John Berger

PART THREE

THE
COLORIZATION
OF
AMERICA

1993—2012

After Identity, What? by Hank Willis Thomas. 2012. Aluminum letters on wood and inkjet print. Courtesy of the artist and Jack Shainman Gallery, New York.

CHAPTER 11

I AM I BE

IDENTITY IN POST TIME

But if I have to choose between
I choose me
—Erykah Badu, "Me," *New Amerykah Part One: (4th World War)*

There was a joke that was everywhere at the turn of the millennium. It had started long before, among high-school friends, back when the saying was, "It's a Black thing, you wouldn't understand." But this post–"Black thing" thing was much smaller than that, even more impenetrable, a sub-tribal sign.

The joke had begun with a group of Black guys at a diverse high school in West Philly. It first surfaced in a two-and-a-half minute film short Stone had made with some of those same friends, called *True*.

It opens with a shot of Stone lying on the couch watching a football game. The cordless rings and it's his friend Paul, lying on his own couch watching a kung-fu flick.

"'Sup with you?"
"Nuttin' man, just chillin'."
"True, true."

The other characters don't do much either: Dookie draws comic book characters, Fred picks up the phone and buzzes his friend Porto Rock into the apartment. The dialogue amounts to maybe a dozen words, the most meaningful of which is simply "Wazzzaaaaauuuuuup?!" When each says it, he stretches out the "aaauuuuuuuuh," wags his tongue, bobs his head, improvises his own stupid faces in his own way.

By the end, Paul has changed the channel to the game, and he and Charles watch together, still having a non-conversation conversation.

"So what's goin' on, B?"
"Chillin'. 'Sup with you?"
"Nuttin man, just chillin'."

And that was it—a group of Black men at rest, not called upon to perform, just being who they be. The short was like what an anthropologist might call "thick description," what a psychologist might call "the opposite of microaggression," what a comedian might call great material. Years later, when director/actor Charles Stone III's "Whassup?" commercial for Budweiser debuted in the 2000 Super Bowl, it seemed that millions were let in on the joke, too.

Multiculturalism had allowed artists of color to toy with the possibility of no longer having to play a role already scripted for them. After multiculturalism, they might move beyond the aesthetics of uplift and respectability, be freed from the burden of representing positivity or confirming oppression. They could aspire just to *be*. They might still choose to represent identity, race, difference, and inequality. But they wanted to consider it a choice.

"Individuality," wrote the philosopher Kwame Anthony Appiah wrote in his 2005 post-multiculturalism book *The Ethics of Identity*, "is not so much a state to be achieved as a mode of life to be pursued."[1]

Stone had been a music-video director, making videos like A Tribe Called Quest's *Bonita Applebum* and the Roots's *What They Do* that had slyly subverted Black male stereotypes. By the late 1990s the industry was changing. This short was Stone's bid for new work. He knew he had something good, so he took his time. He spent two years writing it, and one more to shoot and finish the edit. He debuted *True* at a music video short festival in the summer of 1999.

An Irish-born-and-raised copywriter at agency DDB Chicago named Vinny Warren spotted *True* at a festival and brought it to Budweiser. Stone had worried about how the ad would play in the real world. "When people do it and do it badly, it's like some old Blaxploitation shit, like straight-up minstrel," he said.

True required context and specificity to work. Saying "Wazzzaaaaauuuuuup?!" to each other was an act of recognition. I *see* you. You and I are together in this moment. The ad had to be made by a Black director featuring an all-Black cast. Stone knew there would still be objections that his concept was "niche market." Warren's Irishness, his foreign-ness, Stone felt, allowed him to understand the nuances and see the big picture.

They still needed to pitch the concept to all the confused marketers, casting agents, and execs. In those sessions, Stone decided to describe it in gendered terms. "Look, it's really simple. It's men holding hands through the phone," he would tell them. "It talks about that wonderful nothingness that men do that is actually quite complicated."

One day DDB execs told Stone they wanted to try out a "multicultural" cast. By this, they meant that they wanted to try white actors. Maybe it was progress that whites could now see themselves in the "multicultural" thing. But wasn't that still kind of missing the point?

On the last day of casting, Stone and Warren asked to bring back four of the five actors from the original *True* cast, just to compare them to the "multicultural" cast. Stone recalled, "Sure enough, they were like, 'What are we doing? We should just stay with the original cast.'"

And so Stone turned up the lighting, put bottles of Bud in each character's hands, and further slashed an already haiku-length script into what would become the commercial called "Whassup?" At the end the word "true" rested over a Budweiser logo. Six months later, he and his homies were partying in Cannes after receiving the Grand Prix, the global ad industry's top award.

Fred Thomas—Stone's old buddy turned international star—told a British reporter, "It was strictly our thing. Strictly our clique. It never went all over Philadelphia. Now the whole world is part of our clique."[2] One of the Cannes judges agreed, "It's not just an ad campaign, it's a movement."[3] Who in the history of advertising could have predicted that a sixty-second spot featuring a group of bored Black males would become the first globally viral ad of the millennium?

The joke among friends had become a joke shared around the world. But what was the world seeing?

THE CULTURAL POLITICS OF DIFFERENCE, AND THEIR DISCONTENTS

Some years before, amid the heated campus debates over multiculturalism, the white Canadian philosopher Charles Taylor had written an influential piece entitled "The Politics of Recognition." He wrote, "Nonrecognition or misrecognition can inflict harm, can be a form of oppression, imprisoning someone in a false, distorted, and reduced mode of being."[4] In a society dedicated to equal dignity, he argued, it was reasonable for marginalized minorities to expect equal access to having their stories told, their books read, their cultures respected. "It is only arrogance, or some analogous moral failing, that can deprive us of this," he wrote.[5]

But he also argued that minorities did not have the right to demand that their cultures be deemed equally worthy. If that demand was granted, he argued, one ethnocentrism would replace another. Some sort of aesthetic judgment needed to prevail or else, he wrote, "[T]he politics of difference can end up making everyone the same."[6]

Taylor's argument almost sounded naive to a young generation raised on Frederick Douglass's maxim that power would concede nothing without demand. Who was this "us" he was referring to anyway? Stone and his hip-hop-gen peers had approached the culture industry as insurgents. They were not wrong.

Not long after Cannes, the execs told Stone they wanted to expand the *Whassup?* concept. They would do it with Italian mobsters, Star Wars characters, squawking parrots, and weird extraterrestrials. Stone, who had already cut fifteen spots and was preparing to direct *Drumline*, was insulted. It was as if they were saying, "Everyday Black guys, talking parrots, weird extraterrestrials—they're *all* funny to *us!*"

Both Taylor and the hip-hop-gen insurgents were right. Difference was not only in danger of becoming Benettonized, it was in danger of being stretched to the horizon, leaving all the old inequity and inequality in place. "Whassup?" was being restored from a new kind of joke—one that let everyone in—back to the old kind—enjoyed by the majority at the expense of the minority. Change the joke and revert the yoke.

Not long afterward Dave Chappelle would have a similar revelation while working on his own set for his own wildly successful breakthrough comedy show. His success had brought him a $50 million contract from Comedy Central. But he began to worry about the price of that success.

The breaking point came when he shot a skit in blackface. The scenario was of a public incident of awkward Blackness in a colorized world. Chappelle-the-star is seated in first class, being asked by the airline stewardess if he wants fish or fried chicken for dinner. Suddenly Chappelle-the-blackface-pixie is tap-dancing and cane-stomping across the headrest, crying, "Hooooo-wee! I just heard the magic word—chicken." Chappelle-the-man-of-color frowns and orders fish, hoping to avoid looking like a stereotype.

The skit captured the micro-pressures of the post-multicultural moment. If the world had indeed become colorblind, history's burden might truly feel pixie-size. But it had not, and the only consolation was irony borne of acute self-consciousness. The problem of invisibility had been replaced by the problem of visibility—what did you see when you looked in the mirror? What did *they* see?

As Chappelle acted out his part in blackface, a white crew member laughed in a way that terrified him. What if all of them weren't laughing *with* him, he wondered, but *at* him? What if it had been that way *the whole time*? Suddenly he felt guilty, he later told Oprah Winfrey, "socially irresponsible."

He fled the show and his family into a surreptitious pilgrimage to Africa. In the aftermath, he would blame the network, his coworkers, himself. "I feel like they got me in touch with my inner coon," he concluded, that empty third-person plural indicating both phantasmal conspiracy and despairing confusion.[7] The burden of representation had ripped the swagger from him.

You might tag that wall. You might kick down that door. You might even pull off an Ali shock-the-world upset. But were you prepared for what came next? Where would you draw the line? Even if you had been compensated very well, better than anyone who had come before, had you really changed the game? In the face of such questions Chappelle had torpedoed his own brilliant career.

By comparison, Stone was lucky. "The truth about *True* is that these are real dudes and a lot of the ideas are still grounded in a reality," he said. "So I ended up pulling myself out as the director and as the character."

Artists often apprehend something genuine about the world long before the language coheres enough to allow change to sweep through it. But what if what we needed to have was a conversation about race and history and equity in the new millennium? What would we say to each other after "Whassup?"

A JOKE THAT GOT SERIOUS

In the late 1990s Thelma Golden and Glenn Ligon had their own joke. Not really a funny ha-ha kind of joke, more like the kind that made you smile and say "True," shared between two friends who had made careers of defying others' expectations and denying the names with which others wanted to bind them, a joke between two who, in that sense, were something like escape artists.

No one understands the power of fetters better than the Houdinis who try to convince an audience that they can be slipped. The illusion lies in presenting escape as inevitable. Success lies in convincing the audience that in some small way reality itself has been changed. Sometimes a magician *is* able to break through, enabling a kind of mass unshackling. But most mornings they simply wake up to confront the restraints of the everyday and the work of creating their next fictions. That is the life of a creator.

The joke began like this. After two spectacular performances in the 1993 Whitney Biennial and the 1994 *Black Male* exhibition, both before the age of thirty, Thelma Golden found herself at the top of the art world but in a tenuous position. "[The critique of multiculturalism] really changed the discourse among visual artists," the curator Lydia Yee said. "Artists also were concerned about being labeled as a Black artist, as a woman artist, as an artist who deals with AIDS."[8] What was true for those artists was true for her, too.

By 1998, her embattled boss David Ross was leaving the Whitney for dot-com-booming San Francisco to run the Museum of Modern Art there. The nasty backlash against the uprising of the early 1990s was settling in and soon she and Elisabeth Sussman had both resigned from their curatorial positions at the Whitney. Their departures felt like the end of an era. To the formalists it was like the last emptying out of a particularly noxious, entropic party.

At the turn of the millennium Golden reemerged uptown, as the deputy director of the Studio Museum in Harlem. The generation of artists of color she had introduced to the world—including Lorna Simpson, Carrie Mae Weems, Gary Simmons, and Ligon—were all entering rich periods of creativity and rising quickly in the art world. It was time for Golden to turn her attention to the next generation of artists. "Post-Basquiat and post-Biggie," she would call them, and in fact most of them were also post-conceptualist and post-MFA.

Golden and Ligon had come from different backgrounds. She was the granddaughter of Afro-Caribbean immigrants and the daughter of an insurance broker and a civic leader who grew up in the Black middle-class neighborhood of St. Alban's in Queens. He was the son of an autoworker and a nurse's aide who grew up in the Forest Houses projects in the South Bronx.

But each had been one of precious few Black faces at their white, progressive schools in Manhattan. Both had matriculated from elite East Coast liberal arts colleges, she from Smith, and he from Wesleyan. They came of age at a time when Basquiat was becoming a superstar, Black galleries were on the rise, and campuses were exploding in protests for diversity in the faculty, the student body, and the canon. They entered the art world as its doors were being forced open to artists of color for the first time since the late 1960s.

Some older Black artists and curators would charge that Ligon's and Golden's—and by extension, an entire generation's—subsequent success appeared to be rootless. The suggestion was that they had bypassed "the community" on their way in to the white museums and galleries. These accusations rankled and bored Ligon and Golden. Both had interned at the Studio Museum in Harlem and worked under legendary Black curators. They knew their Black history and their Black art history. They also both had resolutely future-oriented personalities. "Every generation has the thing that they react against," Ligon said. "We were a different generation than the people who had picketed MOMA or the Met."

Working within, instead of outside, the white art-world elite, Ligon and Golden knew their rise meant accepting that they were delivering a kind of performance. "[It was] as if identity was this thing that artists of color had the most immediate access to. There's the bucket and you just dip into it. There's your content. Throw it on the canvas," Ligon recalled. They both resolved not to take the easy way out.

Golden's *Black Male* exhibition was anchored by Ligon's Richard Pryor text paintings. To Ligon, Pryor had been as incisive as anyone in the Black intelligentsia. The comedian was, he said, "'ha-ha' funny, but … also scary."[9] In the paintings, Ligon reproduced some of Pryor's lines, like the one from his "Cocaine" bit that went: "Niggers be holding them dicks too.… White people go 'Why you guys hold your things?' Say 'You done took everything else motherfucker.'"

Pryor's comedy was conceptual from jump. His jokes started with what people saw, but they ended up really being about what people *thought* they saw and what they thought *about* what they saw. So the paintings often shocked many white audiences silent. But they bitterly divided Black audiences. Was it proper for the N-word and cultural stereotypes to be displayed in a place that some artists of color were still calling the Whitey Museum?

Ligon recalled the heated discussions the paintings catalyzed:

"Don't you like Richard Pryor?"
"I love him at home, on my stereo, not on the walls of this museum. Where are the portraits of Frederick Douglass that we were expecting?"

Negotiating identity between the formalists who wanted their art colorblind and multiculturalists who wanted their art uplifting had been the burden of Golden's and Ligon's generation.

But toward the end of the 1990s, during the half-decade after the Biennial and *Black Male*, something had changed. The emerging generation of artists—people like Mark S. Bradford, Julie Mehretu, Sanford Biggers, Nadine Robinson, Kori Newkirk—seemed less encumbered by those vexing questions and the debts due their forebears. Crossing over gave them no angst. So one day when Golden was talking to Ligon about all of these new magicians, he said to her: "Oh yeah, those are your *post-Black* children."

That was where the joke started. "Post–*Black Art*" was what they meant at first. "Post-Black" was the intimate shorthand, the most inside of inside jokes. It may have captured their ambivalence about their positions in the worlds they straddled—the joys, the bothers, the troubles, the transcendence. It also compressed a vast body of shared knowledge, something that outsiders—that is to say, most of the known art world—had never bothered to learn: the artist biographies, works, values, and positions within the sprawling century-old debate over Black art.

Among the moments still lost: George Schuyler mocking his friend Langston Hughes's call for artists to uplift the race, calling the whole idea of Negro Art a "hokum";[10] Alain Locke's retort to W. E. B. Dubois's argument that all art was propaganda: "My chief objection to propaganda, apart from its besetting sin of monotony and disproportion, is that it perpetuates the position of group inferiority even in crying out against it";[11] Bay Area painter Raymond Saunders's 1967 pamphlet "Black Is a Color," opposing the Black Arts movement with these words:

Art projects beyond race and color; beyond America. It is universal, and Americans—black, white or whatever—have no exclusive rights on it....[12]

Certainly the American Black artist is in a unique position to express certain aspects of the current American scene, both negative and positive, but if he restricts himself to these alone, he may risk becoming a mere cypher, a walking protest, a politically prescribed stereotype, negating his own mystery, and allowing himself to be shuffled off into an arid overall mystique.[13]

Saunders had concluded, "Can't we get clear of these degrading limitations, and recognize the wider reality of art, where color is the means and not the end?"[14] At the end of the twentieth century—when invisibility was no longer the central issue for African Americans—such contrarian notions sounded less and less like treason.

When the portrait artist Kehinde Wiley was once asked if he was making Black art, he answered, "I think one of the primary goals of what we defined as 'Black art' in the 1960s had to do with presenting the ills of society to the world. That Black art was concerned with correctives," he said. "The fact that [my] paintings of Black men can occupy an uncontested space in the art world is important and transgressive. But that is, in my view, only a starting point. The areas with which I am more engaged in have to do with a more personal toying with the possibilities of easel painting."[15]

Golden's curatorial work had liberated him to come out as a formalist. To him, she was interested in asking two questions: "'Why do we always have to talk about race when we talk about people of color creating beautiful stuff?' and 'Is it ever possible to create an authentic moment without referencing race first?'"[16] When the writer Touré asked Kara Walker to define Post-Black in a word, she responded, "Individualism."[17]

For Golden, Post-Black felt institutionally right. "Let us say," she told *Bomb* magazine's Betty Sussler, almost as if she were addressing her board at the Studio Museum, "that as an institution we were now willing to exist at a place where we could talk about the complexity of Black creation and the politics behind it through multiple voices and through multiple strands." And it felt personally right. "[Post-Black] wasn't a kind of art, it wasn't a particular way of making work. It was a stance, an attitude, a vibe, a feeling," she said.[18]

But how would the art world respond? After the early 1990s, it had closed itself to discussions about racial identity, even as it was increasingly open to gender and queer identities. It had also closed itself to discussions about equity and representation, even though the numbers were as bad as they had ever been. Golden was faced with a two-ended trap. She needed to force the question of identity and the reputation of her uptown museum into the center of the discussion.

The Post-Black idea cleared space for young Black artists to express themselves. Color could be the means *and* the end. Or color could simply be the means *or* the end. But it also meant to expose the new artists, make them legible to the mainstream art world. It had to help a new generation escape the old traps.

And so the idea of Post-Black—as opposed to "Post-Blackness," which would come later, when the joke had gotten far away from two friends and the whole world was more confused than amused—became a generative idea. Soon there would be talk of "Post-Latino," "Post-Chicano," "Post–Asian American," "Post-Native," "post-identity," and most controversially of all, "post-racial." Perhaps the elders weren't yet ready to embrace this development. But maybe the key to fostering the radical diversity that they had demanded for a quarter-century might be found here.

THE RUINS OF THE CULTURE WARS

The twentieth century had begun with the morphology of race, the notion that difference was biological and unchangeable. But the Post Time of the millennium was about the morphology of racism, the ways that structures were shifting to maintain inequity along color lines.

From the early 1990s young artists of color had more access to the mainstream. They appeared on the horizon as the exceptional—the exceedingly well-pedigreed—and the exceptions—negations of the angry old race-men and race-women. But in their MFA programs and beyond racial identity had simply become "passé." As in—fine, race is a construct. So what? *Next.*

It was a casual kind of violence.

The novelist Zadie Smith told a story. When she had been a precociously well-read and opinionated fourteen-year-old, her mother brought her a copy of Zora Neale Hurston's *Their Eyes Were Watching God.* She was not interested. The young girl did not yet know the backstory, though if she had she may have been even less interested.

It was the late 1980s and Hurston's works had long been unavailable. In previous eras of integration and uplift her books had fallen out of print, her reputation out of favor. Perhaps she was too ribald, too comfortable in her own skin to suit the tastes of those times. In her piece "How It Feels to Be Colored Me," Hurston had written, "Sometimes, I feel discriminated against, but it does not make me angry. It merely astonishes me. How can any deny themselves the pleasure of my company? It's beyond me."

But now, at the same time hip-hop heads were moving as far as they could from crossover Motown nostalgia, sampling P-Funk and the Meters from out-of-print records secured at used record stores or spirited from family collections, Hurston's work was undergoing a revival. What George Clinton and Co.'s psychedelic disquisitions on race and democracy and the Uptown Rulers's deconstructed architectures of space and rhythm signified to hip-hop heads, Ms. Hurston's aphoristic folk wisdom and earthy language were for a generation of writers and critics trying to make a canon of their own.

Yet Smith's mother may as well have been handing her daughter a plate of broccoli. Zadie had already declared herself partial to Nabokov and Keats, indifferent to Morrison and Rhys. If anyone was going to resist Ms. Hurston's company it would be this girl. "I wanted to be an objective aesthete and not a sentimental fool," Smith wrote. "I disliked the idea of 'identifying' with the fiction I read: I wanted to like Hurston because she represented 'good writing,' not because she represented me."[19]

After not a little prodding Smith cracked open *Their Eyes Were Watching God*, finishing it in a single reading. And she wept. Smith wrote, "At 14 I couldn't find words (or words I liked) for the marvelous feeling of recognition that came with these characters who had my hair, my eyes, my skin, even the ancestors of the rhythm of my speech."[20]

One of the things multiculturalists had won for their daughters was the privilege of taste and judgment. When her mother had pressed a copy of *Their Eyes Were Watching God* into her hands, Zadie Smith could be skeptical of her mother's claims of its greatness. That she did not find it wanting was evidence that her mother's generation had been right.

"Fact is, I am a Black woman (I think this was the point my mother was trying to make) and a sliver of this book goes straight in to my soul, I suspect, for that reason," she wrote years later. "Those aspects of *Their Eyes Were Watching God* that plumb so profoundly the ancient build-up of cultural residue that is, for convenience sake, called 'Blackness' … are the parts that my own 'Blackness,' as far as it goes, cannot help but respond to personally."

Yet in writing of this awakening decades later, Smith was uncomfortably aware that in championing *Their Eyes Were Watching God* she risked sounding like her Black mother and her mother's Black friends "talking about a Black book." She still needed to justify her pleasure. It was very Post-Black to be more self-conscious than enraged that the modifier Black could still signify "something less than." For all the talk about white guilt and identity fatigue, the traumas and ruins of the culture wars remained.

RAISE YOUR FLAG

In 1988, about the time that Zadie was discovering Zora, twenty years after Ernest Withers shot the famous photo of a line of striking Black workers in Memphis raising placards that read "I *Am* a Man," Glenn Ligon made a painting that mimicked the sign in thick black and white strokes. This was the work that shot him to fame. It had, the art critic Darby English wrote, fused "three ostensibly irreconcilable representational modes—the formalist painting, the political statement, and the private question—into something fraught but whole."[21] In this way, Ligon and his contemporaries forged the kind of practice that would be taken up by the Post Generation.

The private question was the thing. What did it mean that a placard calling for union recognition of nameless sanitation workers gathering on a Memphis street had been transformed into a text painting by a gay Black man to hang in a white New York gallery? There were layers here—history, masculinity, class, generation, movements, legacies. Ligon seemed to want to create the work less to find an answer than to ask questions that opened into more questions.

Another of Ligon's early oil stick paintings, hung prominently in the 1991 Whitney Biennial, featured one of Hurston's money lines from "How It Feels to Be Colored Me": "I feel most colored when I am thrown against a sharp white background." In retrospect, the painting seemed to form a dialogue with Daniel J. Martinez's 1993 Biennial tags. It also seemed to reverse polarities on its viewers, the way Faith Ringgold had reversed chiaroscuro. "When do you feel most white?" was a question that would gain steam in the new millennium.

But Ligon's work—and those of many of his colleagues—also positioned itself against previous art movements. Against realism, the work took a sharp conceptual turn. Irony replaced ardor. Doubt replaced dogma. Ambivalence replaced moral drama. When the pieces caused anguished debates in the galleries among Black crowds, they had done their work. They were unromantic, antiessentialist, irreducible.

Yet they carried within them their own kind of hope. Responding to Charles Taylor, the philosopher Kwame Anthony Appiah had written, "If I had to choose between the world of the closet and the world of gay liberation, or between the world of *Uncle Tom's Cabin* and Black Power, I would, of course, choose in each case the latter. But I would not like to have to choose. I would like other options."[22]

Writing "as someone who counts in America as a gay Black man," Appiah closed on a note of optimism. If some had been concerned that identity politics might leave society wracked on the shoals of either-or dichotomies, Appiah wrote, "[I]t is equally important to bear in mind that a politics of identity can be counted on to transform the identities on whose behalf it ostensibly labors."[23]

In 1996, Ligon unveiled large unstretched wall-size canvases onto which he had silkscreened newsprint-like images from the Million Man March. He had been inspired by a debate between Isaac Julien and Essex Hemphill about whether Black gay men should participate in or protest the march, and come away with an overwhelming ambivalence.

Hands captured an image of hundreds of palms and fists and peace signs raised into the black air, as if in praise and affirmation. In *We're Black and Strong*, there were shadows of the crowd's heads and fists against a towering white sign that had featured those words. The sign flew like a "flag of representation," as the curator Franklin Sirmans put it, but Ligon had removed the text.[24] So now it stood taut in the wind, wordless, a tabula rasa for the new writing of history—or maybe the writing of nothing at all.

Glenn Ligon, *We're Black and Strong (I)*, 1996. Silkscreen ink and gesso on unstretched canvas.

NO WORDS, PART 2

The fruit of Thelma Golden and Glenn Ligon's Post-Black discussions was a 2001 exhibition at the Studio Museum in Harlem called *Freestyle*, which featured twenty-eight young Black artists.

On a personal level, it marked Golden's return to uptown, the place to which her paternal grandparents had immigrated, and to the museum, where she had first interned in 1987 during the multiculturalism era, a space that itself had been inaugurated in 1968 by partisans of the Black Arts movement. Her curatorial question was simple: after the twentieth century, after Colescott and Hammons and Piper, after the crossovers of multiculturalism and hip-hop, after Ligon and Weems and Simpson, what kind of art would Black artists make?

Los Angeles–based artist Kori Newkirk was experimenting with form, making abstract curtains with hair beads and wall-size paintings with pomade. But it was a self-portrait called *Channel 9* that magnetized Golden. Newkirk had taken a photo of himself standing at the end of a graffitied alleyway in front of a silver metal riot gate. His hands were behind his back, and he was dressed in a bright red tee over a white tee and blue jeans. He had pixilated his face as if he were a brand logo in a music video or a criminal suspect on the evening news.

With this digital masking the image exploded in potential meanings. Was this a televised image of a gang member? An unfairly profiled Black man? A photographer's test-shot of a stand-in? A guy who photo-bombed a picture of a riot gate? Was this a denial, an erasure, a private joke? Newkirk's work startled Golden. She later told him, "I realized that [the self-portrait] intrigued and unnerved me because I didn't have a vocabulary to describe it."[25]

She would have similar revelations throughout the process. Dave McKenzie's videos *Edward and Me* and *Kevin and Me* showed him performing dances and movements in a Middle American town in Maine, at a supermarket entrance and on a footbridge. He began by acting out movie scenes—as Ed Norton in *Fight Club* or Kevin Spacey in *The Usual Suspects*—then, as if possessed by the spirit, rolled, shook, hand-sprung, and tap-danced as white passers-by gaped or ignored him.

Then it was over. He replaced his glasses and walked on. He later said he made the videos because he "lacked the words to say what needed to be said."[26] He seemed to embody the moment: here I am, in America, inside the break, doing my thing without words.

The title *Freestyle* was a direct nod to the hip-hop cipher, that freedom space in time where the MC or b-boy/girl, Golden wrote, "finds the groove and goes all out in a relentless and unbridled expression of the self." "Freestyle" was a generational neologism. It seemed to acknowledge ideas like "freedom song" and "freedom struggle."

But this cipher was not Raymond Saunders's feared "mere cypher," that reduced the artist to an empty vessel for words and ideology. This cipher released the artist, freeing him from the constraints and oppositions of the past, firing the flame of creation, bestowing him with that inchoate, ephemeral feeling of fullness just before meaning cohered.

"Post-Black," Golden concluded, naming the moment after *that* moment, "was the new Black."

Golden's gambit was risky. *Freestyle* was first about being, loudly and proudly, an all-Black show at a historically Black institution at a time when both things were unhip in the art world. It was about whether a show of young Blacks could be seen as something other than a show about the state of Blackness. And it was a concession to mainstream critics who felt artists of color were not overly concerned with formal quality. As an identity parade, it was both an act of defiance and a strategic retreat, the least likely path to victory.

But, opening five months before 9/11 amid a period of art-world conservatism, the show felt like An Event. *Vibe* magazine did a five-page spread, treating the artists as they would have rising rap stars. The *New York Times* critic Holland Cotter wrote, "Ms. Golden may have located a paradigm shift in contemporary art. She didn't engineer the shift, and she is by no means the first to detect it. But she gave it a name, which is what often snaps an amorphous, floating-around-out-there idea into focus and ends up bringing about change."[27]

In the galleries, crowds gathered around six seven-hundred-watt soundclash-size twelve-inch woofers boxed and branded in red-white-and-blue. This was *Americana*, the work of Nadine Robinson, a Jamaican American artist. Her family and friends were in the rap and dancehall industry. She also loved the intellectual rigor of the minimalists, and found in the designed space of the dance an analogue to Ryman and Reinhardt's experimental paintings. For her, culture was embedded in form, roots with quality. Bass, as much as race, was in your face.

Pumping through *Americana*'s stacked woofers was audio of Dr. Martin Luther King Jr.'s "I Have a Dream" speech. But Robinson replaced the sound of applause with the sound of laughter. She turned a block-party mood bone-chilling. Robinson was mocking the way movements for representation had created false hopes. But she was also reprehending the way anti-diversity demagogues had turned King's words against him. She was questioning the value of all the old words.

In Newkirk's pomade painting of a diving police helicopter, Mark Bradford's epic perm-paper constructions, Kira Lynn Harris's photos of her flickering light walls, David Huffman's Afrofuturist space travelers, Julie Mehretu's deconstructed architectural flows, Sanford Biggers's turntablized fatlace-draped Buddhas, and Adler Guerrier's placeless travelscapes, the new energy pushed out as if freedom no longer felt finite.

CAN YOU SEE ME?

The implications of *Freestyle*—and Golden's subsequent exhibitions *Frequency* (2006) and *Flow* (2008)—were immediate. By the mid-2000s Asian American and Chicano curators had assembled their own presentations.

In September 2006, Melissa Chiu, Karin Higa, and Susette Min's *One Way or Another: Asian American Art Now* opened at New York's Asia Society featuring seventeen young artists born between 1966 and 1980. The exhibition would open during the Asia Society's fiftieth anniversary and twelve years after curator/critic Margo Machida's groundbreaking 1994 *Asia/America* exhibition show there. But what began as a simple Asian American generational survey became an extended inquiry into the changing condition of marginality, and even the viability of the identity show itself.

A divide appeared. In *One Way or Another*'s catalog essays, Machida, Higa, and famed Asian American journalist Helen Zia contextualized the rise of Asian American identity and art history. Underrepresentation and invisibility framed their narrative. But some of the young artists appearing in *One Way or Another* had already shown at major museums. Many had not come up through the ranks of Asian arts organizations. Some did not feel attached to being called Asian American artists.

Invisibility was met with irony or absurdity. Indigo Som's *Mostly Mississippi* photos of Chinese restaurants paid tribute to eateries as pervasive and unseen as kudzu, behind whose fading signs and crumbly facades labored working-class Asian America. In her *Human Advertisement* videos, Xavier Cha danced around dressed as a pink fingernail in front of a nail salon, or a shrimp in front of a sushi bar, as if to scream, "Consume this!"

Ala Ebtekar—whose installation *Elemental* placed boom boxes decorated like Persian miniatures and fresh-out-of-the-box Adidas sneakers with Tehran-textiled fatlaces into a minimalist mock-up of a centuries-old Iranian tea house—told the journalist Cynthia Houng, "We may be speaking in a third language, unlike the older generation, which tended to place a hierarchy upon the cultures and to place them into confrontation with each other."[28]

Jean Shin's *Unraveling* took hundreds of sweaters donated by artists and community activists and used the yarn to trace the social network of affiliations. Her work was a map of institutional Asian America, the process of collective identity-making that Asian Americanists called "panethnicity." Glenn Kaino's *Graft* stitched taxidermy models of a salmon made from the skin of a shark, and a pig with the skin of a cow. Was it hopeful or unnatural for one to try to change the skin they were in?

As a display of radical diversity, the show became, Karin Higa said, "an anti-identity identity show." "The whole point was heterogeneity," she said. "What could you glean from the Asian American experience from looking at this show? Well, what you could glean from it is, 'Wow, you can't really fix it 'cause it's all over the place.'"

At a time when, as Bronx Museum curator Lydia Yee noted, it was as easy as it had ever been for mainstream curators to "end up with a show of all white males," the curators were sure that exposure for the artists was enough of a reason to have mounted the show.[29] Still, Chiu said, she felt that the Asia Society might never do another exhibition of this kind again. "As a curatorial thematic, it feels very forced to do," she said. "I feel it would be forcing something onto artists that is not really coming out of the work." But without such shows, how might non-Black artists of color be seen and recognized?

Laurel Nakadate shot sad and funny movies with lonely white men she had just met. With a circle of her finger she might command an overweight, bespectacled man stripped to his BVDs—with the sad look of a character in a Dan Clowes comic—to do a slow twirl. Then she, also down to her bra and panties, might reciprocate the gesture.

These movies would be discussed in the art world in terms of postfeminist sexuality, not her mixed-race identity. But in an interview with the *One Way* curators, Nakadate returned to intersectionality. She was a *yonsei*, and her father had been born in a World War II internment camp. While making the videos, she realized she had been working with what she called "a trace" of memory.

"At first I thought [these movies were] about girlishness and going out and finding lives to try on but then I remembered finding out that my great-grandmother was a war bride. These women had photos taken of them before they left—a photograph of them with the strange men they had just married," she recalled. "I then realized that these were the same kind of pictures that I was making. It struck me that I was making these pictures that I had never seen."[30]

Susette Min's catalog essay was entitled "The Last Asian American Exhibition in the Whole World," an allusion to Suzan-Lori Parks's multiculti-era play *The Death of the Last Black Man in the Whole World*. Multiculturalism, she wrote, had long been reduced to "a Band-Aid solution," "just a 'trend' that has now fallen out of fashion."[31] "To unmoor from race is alluring," Min added. "Were this truly a post-multicultural world could we really see Asian American art with fresh and untainted eyes?"[32]

THE EVIDENCE OF PHANTOMS

In that sense, these post-identity shows could not escape the questions multiculturalism had raised. Presence, diversity, transformation—all of those seemingly obsolete concerns had yet endured.

By the turn of the millennium, half of Los Angeles County's population was Latino. In 2004, the Los Angeles County Museum of Art and the UCLA Chicano Studies Research Center announced a five-year initiative led by the Center's director Chon Noriega to create exhibitions, publications, and art purchases for LACMA. The exhibitions would include a retrospective of Chicano paintings from the comedian/celebrity Cheech Marin's collection and a new survey called *Remix: Today's Chicano Art*, featuring artists working in painting, sculpture, installation, conceptual, video, and performance art. As Noriega's team proceeded with *Remix*, they, too, began to focus on a new generation of artists.

They realized first that they would need to reckon with the legacy of the massive 1990 CARA exhibition. CARA had been full of prophets, heralds, seers, and documentarists, most of them proudly, politically, explicitly Chicano. But what did it mean now to be a Chicano artist?

To Noriega and fellow curators Rita Gonzalez and Howard N. Fox, this new generation was "populated with tricksters, shape-shifters, doppelgangers, ventriloquists, and personas—real presences, but ones known primarily by indirect, oblique, or camouflaged presentation."[33] They were doing work that chose "conceptual over representative approaches, and articulate[d] social absence rather than cultural essence."[34]

What's more, the thirty-one young artists they chose, all MFA'd up, called themselves all kinds of things besides Chicano—Post-Chicano, part Chicano, Mexicano, not Chicano but Pocho, not Chicano but Latino, not Chicano but half-Latino and passing, or none of the above. How could the curators square the legacy of the Chicano movement with all of this new energy?

Asco founder Harry Gamboa Jr. had long written of the way Chicanos constituted a "phantom culture" in the United States.[35] One night Gonzalez made the connection. Each of these works of art was a "phantom sighting," evidence of people still unseen, caught in that liminal space between invisibility and materiality. So the exhibition would be called *Phantom Sightings*. But this still did not solve the problem of what to name the artists. How did you name what wasn't there?

Gonzalez approached Daniel J. Martinez to seek his input. Since the 1993 Whitney Biennial, Martinez had poured his energies into making uncompromising work and mentoring a new generation of artists and curators in Southern California, including Mark Bradford, Ruben Ochoa, and Eungie Joo. He taught at the University of California at Irvine, and with Glenn Kaino he opened the influential Deep River gallery in downtown Los Angeles.

When Rita Gonzalez and Ken Gonzales-Day had organized a discussion among artists and curators to talk "post-identity," Martinez showed up and told the gathering, "I feel like we're in this record that's skipping and we can never get out of it." To him, the facts of underrepresentation were separate from questions of aesthetics, and *Freestyle* marked a promising strategy for desegregation. "Post-Black was a lure. It was a trick. It was a sleight of hand. There was no such thing as Post-Black," he said. "It might be all-Black, but she picked talented people that happened to be Black."

Martinez suggested that everyone think of Chicano identity in a truly antiessentialist way. "If you explode that idea, the playing field's left wide open," he said. He proposed that they take LACMA's money and give it to underrepresented artists of all races, genders, and sexualities. "Call them all Chicanos," he said. "You would come up with brand-spanking-new work that shows that there's an actual possibility of a change and a shift in the culture."

"They all laughed at me," he said.

But now one pressing question—how could one do a Chicano show that wasn't about Chicanos?—gave way to another that seemed more distressing—what kind of strategy for recognition and advancement dismantled any structure for recognition and advancement? "Without a name and a context," Chon Noriega asked in his catalog essay, "how can this work be seen, let alone integrated into the art world and our national visual culture?"[36]

So the show's subtitle—"Art after the Chicano Movement"—would prove more provocative than the title itself. By shifting from identity to chronology, the show would elide the need to name the artists, construct an untenable identity, and stake political claims or histories. But it would also confuse art-world supporters and critics and leave a lot of Chicano elders' hearts cold.

CONCEPTUALISM WITH DIFFERENCE

The first image in *Phantom Sightings* was a photo of Asco's *Spray Paint LACMA* from 1972, with Patssi Valdez looking punk-rock vivacious in bright red lipstick, red sleeveless blouse, and rhinestone jeans, standing on the museum footbridge that had been adorned with the names of her Asco *camaradas*: "Herrón Gamboa GRONKIE."[37] Here was LACMA, at the institutional direction of Chicanos, validating an image of Chicanos protesting LACMA for the exclusion of Chicanos from LACMA. The image felt, at the same time, like the raised flag and the flowers on the coffin of an alternative art history.

Phantom Sightings began with disappearances, erasures, and traces. Ken Gonzales-Day's Erased Lynching and Hang Trees series were based on his research of lynchings of Mexican Americans. He digitally expunged the victims of lynching photo postcards, leaving just the crowds dressed in their Sunday finest and posing for the camera, chatty and celebratory, the initial subject of their interest—in his final race performance—removed from history.

Ruben Ochoa installed paintings onto freeway walls that made them look like they had been cut out. His work pointed to Judy Baca and SPARC's monumental *Great Wall of Los Angeles* and Willie Herron's mural, *The Wall that Cracked Open*. But instead of the people in all their struggle, rage, and glory, Ochoa put up trompe l'oeil landscapes, revealing how walls had grown where people and neighborhoods were being disappeared.

Yet clandestine movements still gathered. In *The Breaks*, Juan Capistran b-boyed on what looked like Carl Andre's floor piece, *Equivalent VIII*. In *Los Angeles/White Riot*, he put a white X on a five-foot canvas—drawing together the connections between mid-nineties Malcolm X baseball caps, the band X's song about white flight (whose album cover evoked a KKK burning cross), the Clash's tribute to the Notting Hill carnival Black uprisings, Malevich's art theories, and Ryman's white paintings.

ASCO, *Spray Paint LACMA*. 1972. © Harry Gamboa

Artists addressed how NAFTA had ensured free flows of capital while border militarization blocked flows of bodies. Margarita Cabrera had grown up in the El Paso/Juarez area, where exploited women workers in *maquiladoras* pumped out the low-priced apparel and consumer goods that filled suburban homes north of the border. She sewed a vinyl replica of a Volkswagen Bug, a German car mass-produced in Mexico, leaving loose threads dangling to remind viewers of her labor. Her puffy cacti for *Agave* were made of Border Patrol uniforms—a nod to the treacherous daily struggle played out between migrants and feds, and the fact that the ranks of ICE agents were increasingly being filled by young brown men and women who otherwise faced poor job prospects.

Photographer Delilah Montoya shot panoramas of abandoned high-desert camps along the migrant trail—the relentless stretches of dirt and creosote, the water jugs, the torn clothes, and all they had left behind. Julio Cesar Morales's ink-and-watercolor works depicted methods undocumented immigrants had used to cross the border—a man kneeling inside of a car seat, a four-year-old girl tucked into a PowerPuff Girl piñata, bodies conforming uncomfortably to the forms of North American constructs.

Phantom Sightings had opened almost exactly two years after millions—not solely Latino, but Asian, African, and European immigrants and their supporters—had taken to the streets across the country to demand immigration reform. Those demonstrations had led to the biggest congressional effort in a generation and impacted the presidential campaign between Barack Obama and John McCain. It was a moment, Rita Gonzalez said, when people were saying, "We are not invisible. We are not a phantom culture. We are the majority. We demand the stakes."

The Breaks by Juan Capistran. 2001. Courtesy of the artist.

THE END OF IDENTITY?

Yet if the culture was shifting, the language still lagged. Old binaries—the political versus the aesthetic, the real versus the fake, assimilation versus authenticity—framed the show for even *Phantom Sightings*'s most sympathetic critics. Art critic Natalie Haddad wrote in *Frieze*, "Does an unmarked Chicano identity equal a whitened one?"[38] Reyes Rodriguez, the owner of downtown gallery Tropico de Nopal gallery, challenged the museum, the artists, and the curators, telling Agustin Gurza of the *Los Angeles Times*:

The inherited plight and struggle and history of the Chicano art movement is not one you can toy with, not without expecting any sort of questioning…. Do we just keep quiet and allow LACMA to declare that Chicano art is dead? What does that really mean? That you want to be more European or more a part of, let's call it the Anglo world, or whatever it is that validates you? Is that really success?[39]

After the show closed, Rodriguez and *Phantom Sightings* artist Sandra de la Loza presided over an intense discussion of just these issues at the gallery. The curators were invited to sit and watch.

New York Times critic Ken Johnson was even less sympathetic. His review led with the question: "Is it time to retire the identity-based group show?" His answer—an unqualified yes. The notion, he wrote, was "a bureaucratic artifact as much as a curatorial one."

"Artists of many different backgrounds and sexual orientations have been assimilated into the art world," Johnson wrote. "It becomes readily apparent that the artists are not unified by any single style or conceptual approach…. Are they doing something unusual that the art world needs to catch up on? Not those in this show. Is it news that they are creatively diverse as American artists in general? It should not be."[40]

Johnson's job was to ask whether the show had succeeded or failed. But asking whether all identity shows should be eliminated was a different question altogether. "Those are the kinds of questions that don't get asked about other shows," Karin Higa said. "[Critics] don't even realize the kind of expectations they ask of race-based shows."

Johnson's dis was part of a maddening continuity. In an earlier generation critics had dismissed artists of color by calling their work "identity art." Now that a new generation of artists of color was "post-identity," critics were still uninterested in the questions of race they were raising. The world had been colorized, but the art world remained colorblind.

Phantom Sightings artist Eamon Ore-Giron mused, "People say multiculturalism is dead and we're like, 'OK, when's the Post-White show?'"[41]

POST-IDENTITY, THE MARKET VERSION

Out in the hot, flat, crowded streets, marketers and advertisers were taking identity much more seriously than much of the art-world elite. Multiculturalism had reaffirmed to big capital the centrality of identity and culture in the new global world. Advertisers all had the same research, but research only answered yesterday's questions. Now that everyone knew the demographics, what was next? For the young generation in the target sights, the question was now: How did it feel to no longer be a problem, but just another stick of gum for lifestyle capitalism to chew up?

To some it was liberating. In 2005, John Lee, a former professional skateboarder from New Zealand, and his partner Jiae Kim, a designer from Cupertino, poured their house savings into *Theme* magazine, a hip experiment whose goal was to capture "the global tipping point that is Asian influence … people and movements that are inciting cultural evolution." Tibor Kalman, Philip-Lorca diCorcia, and Mike Disfarmer were their influences. Nam June Paik, Nikki Lee, and Wieden+Kennedy's creative director, a pioneering Chinese American named John C. Jay, were their subjects.

But Lee and Kim would tell anyone who asked that *Theme* was *not* an Asian American magazine. "Ethnicity is a business. A big business, I guess," said Lee, whose magazine supplemented the work of their boutique marketing company, the Theme Agency. "And there's that smell of desperation."

To them, multicultural market segmentation had simply reinforced stereotypes based in being less than white. Too many Asian American–branded projects betrayed a sense of inferiority. Kim said, "I want to be part of people doing great stuff—people with confidence, poise, and something to say." Equality meant expecting more. In the new style vanguard, personal and cultural evolution was a hopeful process.

Identity was still the present and future of capitalism. And if productivity had been the central question of the industrial era, creativity would be the fetish of the postindustrial era. By the turn of the millennium, business magazine covers—most seemingly descended from *Colors*—looked more diverse than the companies they covered, and every issue promised to unlock the keys to creativity the way women's magazines promised to unlock the keys to desirability. It was no longer about harvesting the recognition of identity but monetizing the creation of identity.

In 1999, the year protestors clashed with police outside the World Trade Organization meetings in Seattle, Nike began an experiment called "NIKEiD." The idea was simple—consumer customization—and it had come from the streets. Long before brands even considered them worthy of their attention, long before anyone had heard of "the long tail," generations of hip-hop kids in neighborhoods abandoned by capital and the state had been making their own shirts, stenciling their own crew jackets, and painting their Air Force Ones. NIKEiD wanted in. It would allow consumers to design their own shoes based on Nike templates.

Individualized shoes were inherently scarce products. When Nike offered celebrity-designed shoes, they found they had stumbled upon a new market segment. The limited-edition shoe created a global cult of mostly young male sneakerheads, the most fanatical of whom could demonstrate indifference to extreme weather and personal grooming in pursuit of shoes they might never wear, but would put under a glass case. Why not make the limited edition available to everyone?

On a sunny Portland day over a decade later, before a crowd of industrial designers, Nike vice president of global design John Hoke III, the company's creative leader, stood before a projection of a slide that read:

B2B   B2C   B2ME   ME2U

He was giving a primer on the history of American business.

When American advertising and marketing emerged from the crucible of the Industrial Revolution, he explained, its primary purpose was to help sell goods from businesses to other businesses—B2B. Then, as the twentieth century proceeded, the industry matured into the task of selling products directly to consumers—B2C. Brand-building eventually led businesses toward segmentation and embracing identity. Now the Information Revolution allowed sales to be customized to individual consumers. In the B2ME era we were now living in, Amazon knew your tastes better than your spouse.

What was coming next, Hoke said, would radicalize creativity. It would unleash the power of design to the masses, who would transform business as we knew it. "Creativity is the purest of human endeavors. Creativity is the ultimate act of optimism," he said. Capitalist realism was transforming into something else—a kind of capitalist romanticism.

Hoke described Nike's experimental iD storefront at 255 Elizabeth Street in Manhattan's Soho district. There, he said, consumers could design their own sportswear lines using Nike's parts and pieces. The first run would have a global, post-multicultural slant: baseball-themed gear with graphics and letters that celebrated sport traditions from Cuba, the Dominican Republic, Japan, and Puerto Rico. Back in the hot crowded streets, consumers could then encourage friends and others to buy their designed "lines": ME2U.

In this "conceptual retail destination," the labor of production was invisible, a phantom act. Our labor no longer defined us. Consumption was the highest form of empowerment. Curating was a higher form of consumption. In this sense the act of creating oneself might be transacted. In capitalist romanticism, being radical was simply a matter of resources and taste.

The NIKEiD concept seemed awfully thin. But where else could they go? After consumerism incorporated formerly ignored markets of youths and minorities, after it shortened the process of mainstream adoption of subcultural stylistic uprisings to blink-time, the only place left to go was inside—to the heart of identity formation. There was no guarantee that this idea could succeed. But Nike was focusing on taming renegade creativity, the realest real thing, at its source. Imagination, the wellspring of identity and culture, was the last space left to privatize.

PRICELESS

This is where the Post Generation found itself in the new millennium, working at the confluence of surging tides—white elites still begrudging their inclusion, older generations doubting their commitment to the race, corporations anticipating their next step.

Kehinde Wiley offered epic high-definition portraits of young Black men, often queer, in the romantic easel-painting style. The pictures were about surface and concept at the same time. They flipped the context of traditional portraiture by depicting nonelite males in classical poses against ornamental, sometimes culturally specific textures that dipped and swung into the foreground. They were perfectly post-millennial hip-hop: low and high, visceral and intellectualized, glossy and flat, garish and beautiful, streetwise and aspirational, Renaissance and Harlem. Wiley's portraits were power moves: the Black male as object of fascination, awe, and desire.

They were also about a different kind of capitalist romanticism, made possible by the new global circulation of identity in the brand economy. In 2006 he began a series entitled The World Stage, in which he depicted men of color from Senegal, Nigeria, China, India, Brazil, and Israel, countries he chose after reading a Goldman Sachs paper on the world economy of the new millennium. If, as Charles Stone had discovered, multiculturalism was now about whiteness, Wiley offered American Blackness as a stand-in for global non-whiteness.

Not unlike Jay-Z, with whom he was often compared, Wiley managed an easy flow between capital and art. He picked up commissions for Nike, VH1, Puma, Infiniti, and other consumer-goods companies. His division of labor even mimicked flows of global capital. Wiley did the intellectual, top-level work—scouting models, taking reference photos, laying out the paintings, working on the main subject and the foreground. Then he outsourced the completion of the intricate background patterns to studios of painters in China, Brazil, and India.

"These paintings are high-priced, luxury goods for wealthy consumers. I'm opening up studios in different cities, and the price of this painting would save their entire village, much less their individual lives," Wiley admitted. "How do we interface the market economy with the fact that these objects are rude in their very existence? We don't. I create something that means something to me, to the world, and try to do my best. I can't fix everything."[42]

In Vancouver, the Canadian Aboriginal (Dunne-za First Nations) artist Brian Jungen created an alternative to Wiley's work in a series called Prototype for a New Understanding. He ripped apart red, white, and black Air Jordans and refashioned the parts into stunning pieces resembling "authentic" Northwest Coast First Nations crow, orca, and warrior masks—authentic, that is, in the white imagination. As critic Cuauhtémoc Medina joked, Jungen was working in a time-honored Native tradition: "If they want masks, why not sell them their own reflection?"[43]

He constructed blankets from basketball jerseys, aviaries from IKEA magazine files, totem poles from golf bags, sharks and crocodiles from suitcases, whale skeletons from plastic deck chairs, and walk-through turtle carapaces from recycling bins. His process of retooling the products of consumerist excess seemed to summon the postcapitalist utopia of *The Communist Manifesto* or *Adbusters*. But Jungen said he had been inspired by the long tradition of Native bricolage, which he called "a counter-logic to colonialists."[44]

He did drawings of little wood signs pointing away from each other, as if inspired by Kay WalkingStick's dialectical diptychs. *First Person* and *Third World* read the opposing signs in one, *First Nation* and *Second Nature* in another. Jungen's art suggested post-identity could play wildly in a hall of mirrors.

Between Wiley's readiness to play the game and Jungen's refusal, Hank Willis Thomas attempted to stake out a position of principled engagement, informed by personal tragedy. He created a series of photo images he called Branded—featuring the Nike swoosh burned onto Black men's bodies. He had been devastated by the senseless murder of his cousin, Songha Willis, a charismatic scholar-athlete, "the guy who was good at everything." Songha was the kind of person who could talk stickup kids stepping to him about his Air Jordans back down into some sense. Yet in the end, he had been shot for his gold chain outside a nightclub while prone on the ground.

At Songha's funeral Hank had taken a picture of his mourning family. On the photo he superimposed this text:

3-piece suit: $250
new socks: $2
9mm pistol: $80
gold chain: $400
bullet: ¢60

Picking the perfect casket for your son:
Priceless.

Then he affixed the MasterCard logo.

Hank went on to subvert other ads. A vodka bottle became a slave ship in *Absolut Power*. The Air Jordan logo was roped up and affixed to a tree in *Hang Time Circa 1923*. He replaced the basketball in one of the logos with a gun pointed at another. "Logos are our generation's hieroglyphs," Willis Thomas said. He wanted to appropriate them and the images they came with "to talk about things that advertising doesn't responsibly talk about."

These works became part of a series he called *Pitch Blackness*, a title that captured contradictory themes: his dark mood after Songha's murder, the intense stoking of desire behind an advertising pitch, the slavery-old notion of the Black body as property, and the role of the artist of color—from Betye Saar's armed Aunt Jemima to Ellen Gallagher's altered Black magazine ads to Michael Ray Charles's fake promo posters for minstrels gone mad—in attacking consumerism's pacification of identity.

By the end of the decade, in Unbranded: Reflections in Black by Corporate America 1968–2008, Willis Thomas was presenting the ad art of Black Cool, largely made by white designers, meant to elicit consent from minorities who lacked positive representation. But he stripped the art of their copy, leaving only images that haunted a complicated Post Time.

Here was a 1969 ad of a man posing shirtless like Jack Johnson, flexing his chest and arms, wearing plaid slacks. The words Willis Thomas had erased were "Slack Power." Another ad featured a white man holding a white-bread baloney sandwich staring covetously at a smiling Black man's sloppy joe. It was from 1970, two years into the Southern strategy, the start of the desegregation and affirmative action era.

A 1978 ad featured Joe Frazier, not long after his "Thrilla in Manila" victory, leaning over a table, one fist raised like it was a Black Power salute, the other around a glass of milk. Syrup, a bowl of margarine, and stack of pancakes sit before him. He is wearing a feminine blue bonnet, completely demasculinized.

"Race is the most successful advertising campaign of all time," Willis Thomas said. "We navigate our worlds around it. That's what's so fascinating to me."

THE LAST WORD AND THE FIRST

In 1993, the same year Glenn Ligon and Byron Kim had been reaching new heights of recognition through the Whitney Biennial, the two friends collaborated on a series they called Black and White. The pieces mimicked Kim's grand Synecdoche. Version 1 was a set of thirty-two chipboards mounted in a grid; the sixteen "black" pieces were hung to the left, the sixteen "white" boards to the right. The black pieces referred back to Ad Reinhardt's black paintings. The variations in tone and intensity were subtle—Black was black was black was black. But the "white" pieces were ivory, beige, pink, tan, and a range of different shades.

Kim had been especially ambivalent about the reception of works like Synecdoche and Black and White. "I got pegged as 'the skin guy' for a number of years," he said. For him the process was as important as the product. "When I look at it from my point of view, it's about meeting all these people and then engaging with them in this very idiosyncratic way," he said. "So the list of names is dear to me."

By the turn of the millennium, as discussions around post-identity began to swirl, Kim had finally come to terms with *Synecdoche*'s success. "I made something and people saw it in a different way and I accepted that," he said.[45] He had moved on. Now he was exploring the poetics of painting in works inspired by the glaze of Korean pots or the day and night skies, especially the infinite varieties of blue. When might color, as Raymond Saunders had asked, just be color?

Glenn Ligon was now making neon light sculptures. He had been inspired by David Hammons's 2002 piece, *Concerto in Black and Blue*, a piece so powerful it had changed even Black art criticism through Darby English's influential *How to See a Work of Art in Total Darkness*. Viewers of the work wandered through a darkened room armed with blue flashlights they could flick on and off. Beyond color, Hammons was moving toward playing with light, the source of sight itself.

Ligon's most famous light sculptures would feature a single word, the last word and the first, where the conversation ended and where it needed to begin: "America." He painted the front surfaces of the letters black so that the light—which fluctuated slowly in intensity—could only be thrown backward against the wall. As the pieces were being readied for his triumphant midcareer show at the Whitney in 2011, Ligon joked that critics would continue to read the piece too literally.

"Black America," he groaned, "blah blah blah."

Before the 2008 presidential election, Ligon had been pondering a national paradox: even as the United States was waging wars in Iraq and Afghanistan, even as the market was on the verge of complete collapse, American optimism seemed sky-high. How could this be? One day, he came across a newspaper picture of a child in Afghanistan standing amid the bombed ruins of his home, his family dead in the rubble, calling on America to live up to its democratic ideals.

"America just bombed your house, but there's still this belief in democratic ideas and America as this shining light and this beacon," said Ligon. "That's where the piece came from—light that is blacked out. It's there and it's not there."

The other inspiration, he added, came from a well-worn epigraph, a set of very old words: "It was the best of times, it was the worst of times."

The border at Nogales, with Mexico at left and Arizona, right. Photo by B+ for mochilla.com.

CHAPTER 12

DEMOGRAPHOBIA

RACIAL FEARS AND COLORIZED FUTURES

Mi vida va prohibida
Dice la autoridad
—Manu Chao, *Clandestino*

At the turn of the millennium, the economy was booming. Eminem—the white rapper from the other side of the Detroit tracks—and Shaggy—the Jamaican American immigrant who claimed both Kingston and Brooklyn—topped the pop charts. The culture wars seemed a memory, and the 2000 Census was a revelation.

Non-Hispanic whites had dropped to 69 percent of the U.S. population. Since 1980, the nonwhite population had grown at eleven times the rate of whites. Hispanic and Asian and Pacific Islander numbers had doubled. The key number was thirty-nine. It was the median age of non-Hispanic whites, and the percentage of those under twenty-five who were nonwhite. By 2050, demographers projected, the United States would be a "majority minority."

As their elders had fought over identity, this generation of youths was being raised on *Aladdin* and *In Living Color*, Tupac and Biggie. A national survey of youth's racial attitudes, jointly designed in 1999 by students and professors at Hamilton College for the polling firm Zogby, found large pluralities of young Blacks and whites supported diversity curricula, desegregated schools, and equal opportunity programs and policies.

But at the same time they expressed a deep pessimism. More than three-quarters described race relations in America as "fair" or "poor." A majority agreed with the statement, "It's OK if the races are basically separate from one another as long as everyone has equal opportunities." Fifty-five percent believed that the United States was "somewhat unlikely" or "very unlikely" to elect a Black president in the near future. Fifty-four percent of young Blacks, compared to 22 percent of whites, chose "very unlikely."[1]

The ebbing of the culture wars and the rise of state and corporate multiculturalism had changed everything and nothing. Young people seemed to have decided that diversity *was* good. But yet another American generation could not begin to discuss how to live together. Just as their elders once had difficulty imagining a post-segregated nation, they could not imagine a future after the culture wars.

THE NEW CITY

Then the September 11, 2001 attacks happened. Suddenly it seemed, Louis Menand wrote, as if "the divisions animating the so-called 'culture wars' ran less deep than the cultural warriors supposed … [T]he cultural pluralism that had once seemed threatening became, overnight, an all but official attribute of national identity. Inclusiveness turned out to be a flag around which Americans could rally. It was what most distinguished *us* from *them*."[2] Angela Davis called it "multicultural nationalism."

Black-white relations changed in strange ways. In Brooklyn's Fort Greene Park, a group of Black teens took a break from tossing around a football to talk to two reporters. They slouched in a cooling dusk, relaxed and carefree. They explained that since 9/11, the city looked and felt different, as if suddenly a new racial geography had appeared.

Miqueo Rawell-Patterson, a slim seventeen-year-old from Far Rockaway, said, "Ever since the bombing happened, people [in the neighborhood] have gotten agitated to a higher level than what anybody ever dreamed. The Arabs around my house just closed shop and moved on. I don't know where they've gone."

Louis Johnson, an eighteen-year-old from East New York, added that, in the past, "Police would probably racially profile everyone that's here. But now it seems like they don't really bother us. They stop everyone that has Middle Eastern features." He and his friends wondered aloud if the women in hijabs on the subway trains or the shopkeepers on their corner might be terrorists. "I thought of myself as Black before, but now I feel like I'm more American than ever," he said.

Culture had new uses. From the Hollywood Blacklist to the gangsta rap hearings, opposition to the entertainment industry had launched many conservatives' careers. But after 9/11, Karl Rove met with more than forty TV and film industry leaders, including heads from Paramount, Viacom, the Academy of Television Arts & Sciences, and the Motion Picture Association of America to discuss seven administration-approved themes. Rove avoided the word "propaganda." "The word I like is 'advocacy,'" one attendee said.

The big hit of the TV season, *24*, featured a white federal agent charged with protecting a Black presidential candidate from being assassinated by terrorists. Brown-skinned Muslim terrorists lived among us, even got engaged to blond Americans. When the show began airing torture scenarios it may have even influenced the abuses in late 2003 and early 2004 in the Abu Ghraib prison.[3]

Soon the nation would be plunged into one war, then two, catalyzed to catastrophic action by images of factories of weapons of mass destruction not actually seen but imagined. From intelligence images to real damages—hundreds of thousands dead, bodies physically and psychologically destroyed, human rights abuses accumulated, cities ruined, cultures looted. And, as it turned out, even the new inclusiveness was only flag-deep.

Against the backdrop of these wars George W. Bush officially outlawed domestic racial profiling. But he made a gaping exception for the broad purposes of fighting terrorism. Hate crimes against brown immigrants of Muslim, Arab, and South Asian backgrounds soared—over two thousand were reported in the five months after 9/11 alone. Mass roundups, secret detentions, and deportations began, sometimes depopulating entire neighborhoods of immigrants. "Everybody was seen like suspects," Pakistani American journalist Mohsin Zaheer told Tram Nguyen.[4]

The new homeland security complex sprawled. To the vast criminal databases that had been created for the purposes of containing urban youths of color were now added immigrant and refugee shopkeepers, seamstresses, students, and laborers. All could now be suspects, Nguyen wrote, labeled alongside gang members, drug and human smugglers, and actual terrorists as "clandestine transnational actors."[5] To the state the main thing immigrants shared with criminals was the quality of being otherwise unseen.

WHO ARE WE, REVISITED

In 2004, Harvard political scientist Samuel P. Huntington published his last book, *Who Are We? The Challenges to America's National Identity*. He had become famous for a previous book, *The Clash of Civilizations and the Remaking of World Order*, in which he argued that the world's coming conflicts would best be understood as a battle between Western and Islamic cultures. In *Who Are We?* he brought the clash of civilizations home. At stake now, he argued, was nothing less than national identity.

Huntington's work echoed the work of an early-twentieth-century Harvard-trained historian named Lothrop Stoddard who had published a bluntly titled and widely read book called *The Rising Tide of Color against White World-Supremacy*. Stoddard's book had included color-coded maps revealing that, everywhere, colored men were closing in on the white homelands of the West. "Colored migration," Stoddard wrote, "is a universal peril, menacing every part of the white world."[6]

Stoddard himself was elaborating an anxiety that President Theodore Roosevelt, former imperialist Rough Rider and *Melting Pot* playwright Israel Zangwill's most famous fan, had first made a national obsession—that declining white women's fertility rates would lead to what he called "race suicide." A century later, Huntington and his media counterpart Pat Buchanan were reviving parts of this strange thesis. The other side of imperialist nostalgia was Darwinian eclipse.

Huntington argued that the rise of Mexican Americans—who, through immigration and high fertility, were "establishing beachheads" across the Southwest—threatened to unravel a core national culture rooted in Christianity, Protestant values, the English language, British government, and European art and humanities. Huntington bemoaned the intergenerational retention of Spanish, which he saw as a refusal to assimilate. No matter that the overwhelming evidence pointed to immigrants' widespread adaptation of English. The mere prospect of bilingualism and biculturalism was threat enough.

Huntington was annoyed that Mexican Americans chose to "celebrate their Hispanic and Mexican past." It reflected that they were "contemptuous of American culture."[7] Most stunningly he misread a 1992 survey that had asked first- and second-generation Mexican American children what they called themselves. With alarm, he noted that most did not choose "American."

Huntington was probably unfamiliar with the work of his Harvard colleague Mahzarin R. Banaji, whose study with Thierry Devos on implicit bias and racial stereotype among young people was published several months after *Who Are We?* Banaji and Devos found that youths of *all* backgrounds tended to identify "American" as "white."[8] Yet to Huntington here was another sign pointing toward the potential rise of a Mexican-dominated breakaway state. In a line that would be quoted by white racialists for years to come, Huntington wrote, "Demographically, socially, and culturally, the *reconquista* (reconquest) of the Southwest United States by Mexican immigrants is well underway."

To Huntington, culture war was eternal. "No other immigrant group in U.S. history has asserted or could assert a historical claim to U.S. territory," he wrote in an article, evoking nothing less than the Alamo. "Mexicans do not forget these events. Quite understandably, they feel they have special rights in these territories." If the United States was not careful, he warned, it could end up like, God help us, Miami, where, he wrote, "the Anglos came to realize … 'My God, this is what it's like to be in the minority.'"[9]

Huntington's book, Menand wrote, was "about as blunt a work of identity politics as you are likely to find."[10]

A LOST AND DYING WORLD

These politics began at the intersection of race and generation, where looming minoritization appeared like the specter of defeat. The scholar H. Samy Alim had a term for this paranoid state of mind: "demographobia," which he defined as "the irrational fear of changing demographics." He added, "It is also apparently the only consistent aspect of Republican ideology."

Non-white births in the United States would soon exceed white births.[11] Yet the most politically influential American demographic, the post–World War II generation known as the Baby Boom, remained four-fifths white. Demographer William Frey named the divide "the cultural generation gap."

The cultural and political implications were huge. Political scientist Ron Brownstein wrote, "Over time, the major focus in this struggle is likely to be the tension between an aging white population that appears increasingly resistant to taxes and dubious of public spending, and a minority population that overwhelmingly views government education, health, and social-welfare programs as the best ladder of opportunity for its children."[12]

Frey measured the cultural generation gap by simply subtracting the proportion of white children in a state from the proportion of white seniors. In Arizona, the state with the widest gap, 83 percent of seniors were white and only 43 percent of children were. The next five gap states were Nevada (34% gap), California (33%), Texas (32%), New Mexico (31%), and Florida (29%). For close watchers on the left and right, all of these states were like barometers in tornado season.

For a quarter-century, California had been the bleeding edge of the cultural generation gap. The 1978 passage of Proposition 13—ten years after the triumph of Nixon's Southern strategy and two before the Reagan Revolution—defined cultural generation gap politics. This anti–property tax initiative effectively revoked the Golden State's expansive postwar social contract, an act of civic white flight.

Next, the culture wars moved to California's rapidly browning universities. In the 1990s they climaxed with the passage of ballot initiatives that banned affirmative action, bilingual education, and social services to undocumented immigrants, while fueling massive prison expansion. During these years, when a politics of abandonment were transforming into a politics of containment, there had been irrational exuberance among the state's Republicans. Party leaders often spoke of creating a permanent majority.

But by the new millennium, California had gone blue. Before most of the other gap states, its population of voting-age people of color had reached critical mass. The ongoing backlash drove them to the polls and helped forge a new cultural consensus with young and middle-class white voters, defined by technology, urbanism, and diversity, and leaning left.

In other states, politicos continued to exploit the cultural generation gap the way that Lee Atwater and the right had exploited Willie Horton. In the spring of 2010 the Republican-dominated Texas Board of Education voted to revise history, government, and economics textbooks for its five million students, 60 percent of whom were now of color. Two decades before, a multiculturalist challenge to California's history standards had influenced textbook writing and adoptions nationally. The Texas board was attempting a kind of restoration.

In the new textbooks, Moses would be credited with influencing the Founding Fathers. Slavery would be downplayed. Confederate leaders would be more closely studied. The Seneca Falls Convention that had inspired the women's suffrage movement and a court decision that barred segregation of Mexican American students in Texas public schools would be erased. Accounts of Martin Luther King Jr.'s nonviolence were required to be "balanced" by accounts of the Black Panther Party's stand on revolutionary violence. Latina board member Mary Helen Berlanga dryly noted that the board had not voted to require discussions of the Ku Klux Klan or the U.S. Army's role in the Indian Wars.

The main thrust of the revisions was to emphasize a "biblical worldview." Conservative board member Cynthia Dunbar had laid out the guiding vision of restoration that would be adopted by the board. "We as a nation," she had written in a 2008 book *One Nation Under God*, "were intended by God to be a light set on a hill to serve as a beacon of hope and Christian charity to a lost and dying world."[13]

NATION AS BORDERLAND

In Arizona, the cultural generation gap between white elderly and browning young post-boomers yawned the widest. The state seemed due for a Huntingtonian reckoning.

Self-styled "Minutemen"—often elderly snowbird couples in floppy sunhats and angry middle-aged survivalists in surplus-store camo, loaded with water bottles, suntan lotion, and armed to the teeth, gathered themselves in the high desert to defend their border. Day after day they sat forlornly in pickup truck beds and picnic chairs, looking through their binoculars at empty scrubland to detect something, anything to confirm that their country was being overrun. They looked in vain.

The real problem was in Phoenix, at the capital. For decades, huge government subsidies and unsustainable development-fueled growth had made Arizona a boom state. But the state of Barry Goldwater and John McCain had also long been an anti-tax, small-government state. By 2010, the real-estate collapse and the state's slash-and-burn austerity plunged it further and faster than the rest. Educational spending was slashed. Quality of life plunged. It joined Mississippi as the poorest in the nation. As longtime observer of state politics Jeff Biggers put it in his book, *State Out of the Union*, Arizona was a "failed state."

Enter a backbench Republican governor named Jan Brewer—who had been known largely for a blundering campaign to jail record-store owners for selling "obscene" rap and rock albums, and who, by virtue of being the secretary of state at the right time, had become governor when Democrat Janet Napolitano became President Obama's director of Homeland Security.

In early 2010, Brewer found herself in a three-way dead heat in her upcoming primary. Then a white borderland rancher named Robert Krentz saw a person on his land whom he thought was a crossing immigrant in need of aid. He radioed his brother and went to see about the person. He never came back. He was found in his truck, shot to death. The murderer was never found.

In an anguished statement Krentz's family called on the president to deploy military to the border to protect U.S. citizens from the drug cartel wars in Mexico. But though authorities believed the killer was likely a drug smuggler, Brewer quickly reframed the issue of border violence as an immigration issue.[14]

For years Arizona Tea Party head Russell Pearce had been floating a bill written for him by representatives of the conservative business lobbying group, the American Legislative Exchange Council (ALEC). The bill required anyone merely suspected of being an undocumented immigrant to produce papers proving their citizenship. It authorized state police to make warrantless arrests of anyone believed to be an undocumented immigrant. It criminalized undocumented immigrants looking for work. It all but legalized racial profiling and family separation. This so-called Show Me Your Papers bill was so extreme it had never gained traction. But after Krentz's death Jan Brewer went all-in on Pearce's bill, now called SB 1070.

In the mid-1960s, Barry Goldwater had cited states' rights to oppose federal troop deployment to the South to enforce desegregation plans. Now drawing on the Krentz family's call for troops on the border, Brewer not only decried President Obama's federal inaction around border security, she cited it to justify Arizona's right to supersede national law. The politics of the Southern strategy had been finally vacated of logic, leaving only ideology and fear.

"It started to dawn on me that this president and his liberal allies in Congress don't really understand what America is all about and what our fundamental principles are," Brewer would write. "It was then I knew that we were in a war."[15]

Her press statements shifted from the details of economic anguish and budget cuts to body counts and faceless hordes—allegedly beheaded white ranchers whose bones were bleaching in the heat, "illegal trespassers" who were mostly "drug mules," a full-scale invasion that amounted to unceasing "terrorist attacks." The images were apocalyptic and Stoddard-worthy. When she signed SB 1070 into law on April 23, 2010, she became a national figure. In November she was elected by a landslide to serve her first full term.

But Brewer's war—and her subsequent political success—had been secured only by fabricated images of terror. A Department of Homeland Security report found that the number of undocumented immigrants living in the United States had actually dropped from a peak in 2007 from 11.8 million to 10.8 million.[16] The sheriff of the county in which Krentz had died said he had not seen any increase in desert killings, or any headless bodies, for that matter. Even the issue of border violence had been overplayed. The *Arizona Republic*'s Dennis Wagner found that crime had been flat in the county for a decade, and, even at the peak, undocumented immigrants had only ever been implicated in 4 percent of violent crimes.

Wagner wrote, "In fact, according to the Border Patrol, Krentz is the only American murdered by a suspected illegal immigrant in at least a decade within the agency's Tucson sector, the busiest smuggling route among the Border Patrol's nine coverage regions along the U.S.-Mexico border." The crisis, journalist Jeff Biggers said, had been manufactured, nationally and locally.

"This is a media-created event," Pima County sheriff Clarence Dupnik told Wagner. "I hear politicians on TV saying the border has gotten worse. Well, the fact of the matter is that the border has never been more secure."[17]

Long before Brewer declared war on immigrants, right-wingers and prison companies had seen a post-9/11 growth opportunity. As immigration policies effectively became antiterrorism policies, the prison-industrial complex and the national security complex merged into a vast homeland security complex. In 1994, there were 5,000 immigration detention beds nationally. By 2011, the year the anti-immigrant business went vertical, there were 40,000.[18] Nearly 400,000 immigrants were deported, a record number.[19] Immigrant detention reached record costs, milking taxpayers of $1.8 billion a year.[20]

By 2010, there were ten Border Patrol agents for every border mile between Arizona and Sonora. Over half of *all* federal prosecutions were immigration-related, more cases than the FBI, DEA, and ATF *combined*.[21] In 2012, the United States spent $18 billion on immigration enforcement, about $4 billion more than the total spent on criminal enforcement.[22] Immigration was the primary feeder for the federal prison-industrial complex, and the main engine of the federal justice system itself.

Private prison companies had bankrolled ALEC, Brewer, Pearce, and most of SB 1070's sponsors. Ideologues, incarceration companies, and their lobbyists all knew the real question was not whether the feds had ignored immigration. It was: How could corporations and failing states like Arizona get in on some of the action?

OF BOOKS AND BARS

Arizona, as Democratic congressman Raúl Grijalva put it, was becoming "a petri dish" for an anti-immigrant, anti-youth experiment. Maricopa County sheriff Joe Arpaio had turned his jail into a "Tent City" of petty criminals and undocumented immigrants, filling it through workplace raids conducted by a posse of thousands of deputized volunteer vigilantes whom he would outfit with assault weapons. Other bills that the far right had tried to advance for years were dusted off, including proposals to curtail immigrant rights cannibalized from California's Proposition 187, which had been ruled unconstitutional by that state's Supreme Court.

In the renewed culture wars there was again a close link between containing bodies and containing ideas. "How long will it be before we will be just like Mexico?" Russell Pearce had written in the lead-up to the vote on SB 1070. "We have already lost our history since it is no longer taught in our schools."

Two weeks after Brewer signed SB 1070, she signed HB 2281, a bill meant to eliminate Tucson Unified School District's vital Mexican American Studies program. In a district in which almost one in three of every students was Mexican American, the program had a record of excellent curricular design and student performance. On average, the 6,000 students served by the program—over one in ten were not Latino—scored higher on achievement tests and graduated at higher rates than their counterparts.[23]

But under the guise of having students "be taught to treat and value each other as individuals and not be taught to resent or hate other races or classes of people," HB 2281 gave the state board of education or the superintendent broad powers to shut down Ethnic Studies and other such courses. State politicians, with the backing of conservative judges, soon forced Mexican American Studies into dissolution and fired nationally recognized, award-winning teachers.

The school district removed hundreds of books from the shelves, including Rodolfo Acuña's *Occupied America: A History of Chicanos,* Richard Delgado and Jean Stefancic's *Critical Race Theory*, Sandra Cisneros's *The House on Mango Street*, Paulo Freire's *Pedagogy of the Oppressed*, and Elizabeth Martinez's *500 Years of Chicano History: In Pictures*. Literature teacher Curtis Acosta, who taught Shakespeare's *The Tempest*, was told by officials not to teach the book any longer. One saddened TUSD board member, Adelita Grijalva, told Biggers, "We're banning books in this district, not even anything controversial. We're banning *pictures*."[24]

A loud multiracial student movement greeted these developments. They organized their parents and peers. They disrupted board meetings, chaining themselves to the chairs in the council chambers. They mounted street protests and set up spaces to study their histories. They knew that Tucson was a possible vector of national battles to come. "We want an educational system, not just in Arizona, but beyond, where many cultures fit in," said Leilani Clark, a student organizer with UNIDOS, the scrappy group of young activists at the heart of the fight.[25]

With a few exceptions the new front lines broke out where the largest percentages of young people of color lived, along an arc stretching from the Atlantic through the South and Southwest to the Pacific. Prison growth was exploding the fastest in cultural generation gap states like Arizona, Texas, Florida, and New Mexico.[26] Texas, Georgia, and Arizona had the largest populations in private prisons. By the end of 2011, SB 1070 copycat laws had passed from Utah to Indiana to Alabama, Georgia, and South Carolina.

Brown and Proud/Todos Somos Arizona by Melanie Cervantes of Dignidad Rebelde. 2011.

The gap states began in Florida, leaped across the Gulf to the Texas coastline, and swung up into California.[27] In between were the states that African Americans had long called the "Black Belt," stretching through the former Confederacy from Virginia down through the Carolinas around to Louisiana. Nixon and his advisors had once seen this region as the foundation of the Southern strategy and a Republican majority. Front lines of wars past were those of the present.

Who We Be

Rice University sociologist Stephen Klineberg told Ron Brownstein, "The future of America is in this question: Will the baby boomers recognize that they have a responsibility and a personal stake in ensuring that this generation of largely Latino and African American kids are prepared to succeed?"[28]

THIS AIN'T NO PARTY

But there was another potential future, one welling up from the dusty streets and the far corners of the Internet, advanced not by top-down, divide-and-conquer elites, but by the multitude—potentially, a new cultural majority. It believed, as Michael Hardt and Antonio Negri had written, "Empire can only isolate, divide, and segregate."[29] Its energy was youthful, self-organizing, and inclusive. It had appeared in the streets in 1999 in Seattle. It became the multitude in the streets against the wars.

This generation had been disaffected by politics, particularly the electoral kind. Ever since Bill Clinton's 1992 election turned out a record number of young people to vote, civic engagement among under-thirties plunged to new lows each election season. The Democratic president had, with welfare reform, pushed thousands into subsistence-level conditions, and presided over unprecedented growth in the incarceration of youths of color, not the substance of hope. Young people weren't apathetic. They were militantly skeptical.

"During our lifetime, the political system hasn't often shown and proved it can be a viable force for change," said James Bernard, former editor of *The Source,* who had become executive director of the National Hip Hop Civic Engagement Project in 2004. "That's what we're working against."

The fact that "hip-hop" could be juxtaposed with "civic engagement" was a sign of something new. The concerns were political: militarism abroad and at home, profiling and incarceration and deportation, educational opportunity, health care, media justice, environmental justice, poverty, and inequality. But culture was the force through which the multitude was gathering.

In a 2009 *Atlantic* article entitled "The End of White America?," Hua Hsu wrote:

> As a purely demographic matter ... the "white America" that Lothrop
> Stoddard believed in so fervently may cease to exist in 2040, 2050, or 2060,
> or later still. But where the culture is concerned, it's already all but finished.
> Instead of the long-standing model of assimilation toward a common
> center, the culture is being remade in the image of white America's multi-
> ethnic, multicolored heirs.[30]

He added, "[E]very child born in the United States from here on out will belong to the first post-white generation."[31]

Hip-hop activism, in particular, had become a refuge for true believers of cultural change. During the 1980s, the hip-hop arts movement had drawn in multiculturalist renegades like filmmaker Carmen Ashhurst, who went to work for Russell Simmons because, she said, "Getting control of our images was my idea of what I would be doing in the movement." By 2000, when the rap industry was peaking with ninety million albums sold, the idealists were no longer in the industry. They were in local collectives and youth-focused nonprofits.

They felt, as the spoken-word poet Jerry Quickley said, that "99 percent of what is foisted on us as 'hip-hop culture' is produced by less than 1 percent of the artists involved in the culture—those who have massive commercial support." But they still trusted in the power of hip-hop as a grassroots movement to make social change. What if, they asked, we could leverage the cultural power of hip-hop into political power?

So in 2003, young visionaries—including author Bakari Kitwana, organizer Angela Woodson, community leader Ras Baraka, future Green Party vice presidential candidate Rosa Clemente—began to map out what they called a National Hip-Hop Political Convention. Inspired by the 1972 National Black Political Assembly, out of which a generation of new Black elected officials had emerged, they could connect strong local networks from the San Francisco Bay Area to the Twin Cities to Atlanta to New York. Delegates would qualify by registering fifty people to vote, and would fashion the hip-hop generation's first national political agenda. On Tupac Shakur's birthday in 2004, the convention opened in Newark to 6,000 attendees, including some 400 delegates from 25 states and 10 countries.

In the hallways outside crowded workshops, radio personalities and rappers like Jim Jones mingled with basketball jersey–sporting b-boys, headwrapped sisters with baby carriages, Discman-carrying high school students, and iPod-wearing businessmen. All week in Newark, freestyle ciphers spilled out onto the sidewalks. Thousands attended the free all-night park jams, featuring performers like dead prez, Doug E. Fresh and Slick Rick, Wyclef Jean, and Busta Rhymes. Organizer Ras Baraka noted, "This Convention is not a construct of the Republican or Democratic Party." He received loud applause.

The convention ended chaotically, with a patience-testing general assembly platform vote that dissipated in the gathering dusk. But the impact of the event rippled. That fall, the Hip-Hop Civic Engagement Project, Sean P-Diddy Combs's Citizen Change, and Russell Simmons's Hip-Hop Summit Action Network registered hundreds of thousands of new young voters of color across the United States.

On Election Day, more than four million new voters under the age of thirty showed up, the biggest youth surge since the voting age had been lowered to eighteen. Over half of them were African American or Latino, precisely the group that the journalist Farai

Chideya had called "the most discouraged voters." Turnout rates for youths of color even exceeded that of whites.

In Milwaukee, the newly formed organization Campaign Against Violence returned from Newark to register and turn out enough first-time young people of color to swing Wisconsin back in favor of Democratic candidate John Kerry. They soon parlayed this effort into blocking the passage of an anti-loitering ordinance. In Ohio young activists forced Congress to hold hearings over voting irregularities.

By the turn of the decade, half the of children under the age of three would be of color—a fact that already seemed equally banal and convulsive.[32] Demographobia had led to the return of the culture wars. But the same changes that had raised so many irrational fears might also carry the new hopes of an emerging population into the mainstream. This time the stage would be national.

Original art of *Wee Pals* strip, published November 19, 1979. Courtesy of Morrie Turner.

Demographobia: Racial Fears and Colorized Futures

Obama Unity by Marlena Buczek Smith. 2008. Courtesy the artist and Creative Action Network.

CHAPTER 13

THE WAVE

THE HOPE OF A
NEW CULTURAL MAJORITY

We thought this was an election with one big macrotrend—change....
Or so we hoped.

—David Plouffe, *The Audacity To Win*

Colorization was in the streets. After the turn of the millennium, millions were marching, protesting the wars or demanding immigration reform. The signs were everywhere: hand-size stickers, wheatpaste posters, "liberated" billboards, spray-painted murals or stencils covering urban surfaces of gray.

Graffiti, hip-hop and skateboard street marketing, guerrilla postering, and subvertising had long been DIY things. The 2000s became the decade of street art in part because the kids raised on these movements had reached critical mass. But what would they have to say?

Shepard Fairey, the biggest American street artist of all, had grown up during the early 1980s in Charleston, South Carolina, a mischievous skateboarder in a Clash T-shirt he had hand-stenciled, zipping through town on a board he had customized with handmade stickers of punk bands and skate companies.

When he arrived at the Rhode Island School of Design, he underwent a minor identity crisis. He had always stuck out in Charleston. How could he make his mark here among classrooms full of creative, competitive kids eager to enter their names in the annals of art history? Perhaps by avoiding the question entirely.

Fairey's inspiration came from the street. He began photographing stickers he saw, and designing T-shirts for the skate shop he worked at in Providence. When he went with his class to New York City on a museum-hopping field trip, he didn't care about the art he saw in the galleries. He was mesmerized by the graf tags on the way.

"From outside the city going in, there was a number of tags and it became more frequent, larger, more daring as you went into the city," Fairey told the street artist and curator Aaron Rose. "People were taking great risks to do these works that they would be doing anonymously other than the nom de guerre of the piece itself, and that inspired me."[1]

Back at the skate shop, he showed his boss how to make stenciled stickers using a picture of French pro wrestler Andre the Giant. His boss gave up in frustration. But Fairey, who had joked to his boss that Andre would accumulate crew bigger than the shop's, needed to finish the punch line. His finished stickers read "Andre the Giant Has a Posse," and on the back, baseball card–style, listed his weight and height: 7' 4", 520 lb.

Fairey got such a laugh that he printed more at the local copy store, then even more, and spent the rest of the summer on a one-person bombing mission, covering Providence with "Andre the Giant" stickers like a NYC tagger. Soon the local alt-weekly offered a reward to anyone who could identify the perpetrator behind the sticker. Fairey was giddy. He decided to seek, he said, "world domination through stickers."[2]

Posters, T-shirts, and skate-mag ads quickly followed. Then he defaced a political billboard trumpeting the return bid of the infamous Providence politician Buddy Cianci, a former mayor whose first term in office had ended when he pled guilty to beating and torturing a building contractor. Fairey replaced Cianci's face with Andre's, altered the billboard text to read "*Andre* never stopped caring about Providence" and affixed a sign reading "Join the Posse." Suddenly the small town was abuzz with conspiracy theories. Fairey realized people thought he had made some kind of agitprop.

FUN-ISM

His private joke had gone public in a big way. Over the next seven years, he made over a million stickers. He started selling T-shirts and posters through his own company. Inspired by *They Live*, John Carpenter's 1988 antiauthoritarianism/anticonsumerism horror flick, he called it Obey.

He cast the logo in the stark Barbara Kruger red, white, and black. Andre the Giant's newly stylized face—reportedly reworked to dodge a lawsuit from the sports company who owned the trademark—appeared above the word "Obey" or "Giant."[3] The real Andre the Giant died in 1993, but by then, thanks to Fairey, he was known more as a meme than as a wrestler.

In the nineties, no one went bigger than Fairey. Through his tireless labor, his wheatpasted posters suddenly seemed ubiquitous, not just on the buildings, billboards, water towers, and highways of the east, but all around the world. He was on more streets than the most up taggers. He was winning more impressions than big corporations armed with street teams and marketing budgets.

He told Rose:

> When I was in school and people said to me, "You know what, this Andre the Giant thing, I read your manifesto about phenomenology, it's well-written, I think if you expanded upon that you could get a grant, and you could continue to pursue this project." What I said was, "This project is about connecting with people who are not already familiar with the fine art world, or even the conceptual art world, and maybe even the politics of graffiti."... I'm just making my work democratic.[4]

Fairey didn't aspire to be a fine artist, he wanted to be a known artist. Perhaps all his talk about democracy and McLuhan and Heidegger and the rest was ex post facto left-brain justification for the insane adrenaline rush of getting up along the city skyline after midnight.

He had contracts with Pepsi, Honda, Dewar's, and Sprite. He was selling a lot of Obey gear. He was being seen. It was all fun. That was what distinguished this as-yet-unnamed street art from art-school art. It wasn't about formalism. It was about fun-ism. If shit was fun that was reason enough to do it. If it was risky and controversial, it would probably be even more fun.

Fairey was attracted to radical art the way some DJs were to Eastern Bloc psych-rock 45s. He sampled poster art from Cuba, Mexico, and China; the work of American social realists, Russian Constructivists, and German Expressionists; the designs of Black Panthers and the American Third World movement.

But then he stripped the images of their political content and dropped in the words "Obey" or "Giant." He would put Fidel Castro, fist raised, in bold strokes of red, yellow, orange, and black, above a tagline like "Power to the Posse." After he did Lenin, Che, and Mao, he did Nixon, Saddam Hussein, and Ming the Merciless the same way just for kicks. Some called his posters Orwellian, some Warholian. Others saluted them as effective branding. Fairey called them "a Rorschach test," and he had everyone taking it.[5]

That meant, of course, that he was also amassing haters. There were angry municipalities and businesses, police and anti-graffiti ideologues. There were art critics who laughed off Fairey's claims that he was trying to undermine authoritarianism and advertising. (One called Obey Giant "Hello Kitty with pretensions."[6]) Those types didn't seem to bother him. But then there was the community of artists and activists with whose early support he had built his rep and who were now questioning his very intentions.

Some called Fairey a culture vulture. In a Web broadside, artist Mark Vallen revealed Fairey's sources, putting originals side-by-side with the Obey posters to show how they had been emptied of meaning. Fairey was not a real artist, Vallen charged, just a plagiarist trafficking in radical chic. "I am outraged that anyone could make a career out of the consistent, secretive and wholesale copying of other people's artworks," Vallen wrote.[7]

To others, appropriation was just a technique and not the problem. Stencilist and printmaker Josh MacPhee, who had with the artist Favianna Rodriguez coproduced *Reproduce & Revolt*, a highly popular clip-art book, asked, "Does Fairey have less right to the social imaginary of revolution than the rest of us?"

Artists, he wrote, "had reached the terrible point that what is important to us is trying to rip our identity from the jaws of Fairey (capitalism), rather than fighting capitalism itself. Fairey is simply an obvious visual example of the process that goes on around us each and every day. Is there any image we can create that isn't going to be immediately absorbed by advertising, and thus capitalism?"

MacPhee wrote, "His work will only be successful (at more than making money) when he cites his source materials and tries to cut through the amnesiac haze of our society instead of adding to it. When a Fairey wheatpaste on the street becomes not an advertisement for his clothing site but a site for arguing over how we fight and struggle in this world today, I'll be the first one to send people out to look at it and argue about it."[8]

At an exhibition opening in Los Angeles, Pacifica Radio journalist Aura Bogado confronted him over a poster in which he had altered Alberto Korda's famous portrait of Che by replacing the icon's face with Andre the Giant's. Fairey replied that he wasn't commenting on Che, but on the fact that Korda's picture had become a cliché. His work, he seemed to be arguing, was post-Post.

"Many of these so-called 'radicals' have adopted the politically correct doctrine that says white people have no right to try to relate to, or comment on, other cultures," he retorted to her and his critics in *Tokion* magazine. "I use figures in my work who I feel are used and abused as symbols, but without telling the viewer how to feel about them."[9] Bogado replied that she was not making a point about *white* appropriation but about *mis*appropriation. "I will write now what I said then: your work disrespects icons of color," she wrote. "That is what I remember about our conversation, I was trying (and obviously failed) to explain the way in which you culturally appropriate the images of icons of color, like Che and others, for capitalist gain."[10]

Fairey defended himself by declaring himself apolitical. "There is no specific political affiliation behind what I do, only the philosophy 'question everything,' which is why I can use Jesse Jackson and Joseph Stalin in the same body of work," he wrote. "As disconcerting as the word 'Obey' may be, when not attached to any further command, it poses no threat beyond forcing viewers to face their feelings about obedience."[11]

This sounded evasive. Up until then, Fairey had been less a provocateur than an artist who admired the style of provocation. But to what end? Most street artists were too busy having fun to think about such a question. And now he had to.

WHAT YOU GOT TO SAY?

While the politicians chased tail and posed for the cameras, graffiti, capitalist realism, and postmodernism had given Fairey the tools to play in the field of radical histories, to clown the business of icon-making while making money off it, and to be received as an artist who might have something to say. Now his work was taking a turn that belied his own public words.

Fairey was making the largest works of his career. In his wall installations, he simulated the natural decay of the wheatpasted city wall surface the way that New Urbanist-influenced developers mimicked old Gothic, Craftsman, or Classical styles. He tore away posters to reveal layers of images and ideas. He textured backgrounds with Asian and Arabic floral designs or the filigrees found on paper money. Sometimes he printed his images on collaged paper dense with even more images, headlines, signifiers. He seemed to be reaching for a new language.

He offered a pensive image of Malcolm X, a series of Arab and Asian women he called "Peace Women," and most compellingly, remixes of Al Rockoff's Vietnam War–era images in a series called "Duality of Humanity" (which he credited as a collaboration with the photographer). In the series—a clear critique of the Iraq war—Fairey slightly muted his bold Kruger palette, using deep reds, tans, and grays to contrast innocence and war.

The mischief-maker had hit middle age, gotten married, and had kids. His wife and girls figured prominently in some of the peace images. Perhaps it was time to be serious about the world, and to be taken seriously.

But many pieces felt visually crammed. The texts were *too explicit* about what the viewer was supposed to feel. It was as if Fairey wanted to obscure his sources more and at the same time be clearer about what he meant. But was he any clearer about what he meant? "Obey with Caution," read a poster in which a woman threw her head back, grimaced, shut her eyes, and covered her ears. "Blind Acceptance Can Be Dangerous." After almost two decades, what did he really want to say?

Then along came Barack Obama.

VISUALIZING HOPE

A youth wave had coalesced around the Democratic senator who had introduced himself at the 2004 national convention by saying, "Let's face it, my presence on this stage is pretty unlikely." By all standards, and in ways pundits and opponents would never let him forget, Barack Obama's story was at odds with that of all the nation's leaders who had come before.

Born of a mother from heartland Kansas and a father from colonized Kenya, the biracial boy—which in America meant he was Black—had spent his childhood in Jakarta with an Indonesian stepfather and his teen years in Honolulu, Hawai'i; his college years searching for his true self with dalliances in student protests against apartheid and for faculty and student diversity; and had landed in the South Side of Chicago as a community organizer working the same deindustrialized streets that Saul Alinsky had.

Obama seemed to embody reconciliation. "There's not a liberal America and a conservative America; there's the United States of America," Obama had said in that defining speech. "There's not a Black America and white America and Latino America and Asian America. There's the United States of America."

When he announced his candidacy on a bitterly cold February 2007 day in Springfield, Illinois, he seemed a curiosity, if not a long shot. But by the end of the year, Obama had not only appeared on the cover of *Time*, but *Vibe*, *GQ*, and *Esquire*. He was, as DJ Kool Herc would have put it, the people's choice.

Yosi Sergant had grown up a Westside Jewish American b-boy, club kid, and graf writer who had gotten his first taste of peace activism at the University of Jerusalem on the eve of the Rabin assassination. A decade later, he was a self-described "couch activist" going nowhere in his tastemaker gig. After seeing Obama's convention speech he decided to quit selling booze and cars, and volunteered for the campaign.

But, Sergant said, the campaign was interested only in landing newspaper endorsements. He said, "That to me is not how you win the hearts and minds of youth." Instead Sergant thought it would be better to engage street artists in reaching their audiences. When the campaign opened an office in Los Angeles in late 2007, Sergant brought his old friend Augustine Kofie to execute a six-panel graffiti mural.

In October at a nightclub party Sergant threw, Fairey mentioned how intrigued he was by Obama. "Why haven't you done anything?" Sergant asked. Fairey had doubts about his own effectiveness. "I wasn't sure if my support would help Obama or brand him as fringe, since I'm a street artist who's been arrested fifteen times," he said. But he joked with Sergant about getting the campaign to enlist him in designing an official poster. Sergant went to the campaign staff. Weeks later, as the high-stakes primary showdown with Hillary Clinton on February 5 neared, the consensus came back—don't bother waiting for an official OK, but go ahead.

Fairey had done "Vote" posters in 2000 and 2004, less out of excitement for Al Gore or John Kerry or electoral politics than a duty to register his dislike of Bush. But Obama was different—an antiwar candidate sounding a politics of hope and a theme of unity. Inspired, Fairey decided he wanted to put together a poster for Obama as well. But this one would have to be different, something worthy of the candidate and his message.

Fairey wanted to make an image that was Korda-esque, something that would convey, he later wrote, Obama's "idealism, vision, and his contemplative nature."[12] Through a Google search, he found an AP photo that had been taken by self-described "wire guy" Mannie Garcia at an unremarkable April 27, 2006 presser on Darfur hosted by Sam Brownback and Obama at the Washington, DC Press Club.[13] Garcia had actually been sent to capture George Clooney, and snapped 275 shots at the event.[14] This one featured Obama sitting at a table listening to Brownback, as Clooney leaned forward to Obama's right.

Fairey's eye may have been initially drawn by the fact that Obama's head was perfectly framed by an American flag and a light blue scrim. But he also liked the direction of Obama's gaze and the way the light cast shadows on his face. Fairey cropped the photo and tilted it slightly to the right. Now the candidate looked wise, open, even prophetic.

Working quickly, he hand-cut his illustration into Rubylith, the screen-printing film in which he did much of his work, making four layers for each of the colors—navy blue, bright red, and two shades of light blue. Then he scanned the layers and made the final composition on the computer.[15] The darkest shadows in the photo had been converted to the navy hue, the flag removed, and the background reduced to powder blue on the left and red on the right.

He wanted, he later wrote, to "convey the idea of blue and red states, Democrats and Republicans, who are frequently in opposition, converging." Fairey had encapsulated what would become the themes of Obama's candidacy—discernment, unity, vision. He had colorized a Black-and-white man into red, white, and blue.

The next day, on January 25, eleven days before Super Tuesday, Fairey posted this first image on his Web site. He had replaced the Obama campaign logo with his Obey star, and added text across the bottom: "Progress." Paying out of his own pocket, he made arrangements to make 3,700 copies—350 to sell, 350 for the street, and 3,000 offset posters for campaigners. He offered the image on his Obey Web site for download, and five days later he began shipping the poster.

Sergant and other staffers and volunteers were excited. But they came back to Fairey with a suggestion for a critical change. From the campaign's point of view, Sergant said, "progress" sounded loaded, but "'hope' summarized the essence of the campaign." Fairey wasn't sure. "At first I thought maybe 'hope' was too much about thought and not enough about action," he recalled. "But then I realized that without optimism people won't act, so hope is the first step."[16]

The Wave: The Hope of a New Cultural Majority

Fairey took out the Obey logo, changed the tag from "progress" to "hope," and altered the print run to feature the new image. As he worked, his wife was due any minute with their second daughter. Super Tuesday was only five days away, and a major rally at UCLA featuring Oprah Winfrey and Caroline Kennedy was scheduled for Sunday morning. On his Web site, Fairey posted the redesigned Obama HOPE image. Then he gave Sergant some printed posters to take down to Pauley Pavilion.

"I literally ran up and down, looking for where the cameras were. And I placed them behind Oprah's head," said Sergant. "All over the TV there were the HOPE posters behind Oprah and Caroline Kennedy. Front page of every newspaper the next day were the posters behind Oprah and Stevie Wonder." By Monday night, the image had gone viral.

Fairey's first campaign on Andre the Giant had been a fluke, an inside joke. But this HOPE campaign had meaning, as if all of his work had crystallized in this singular moment. He later wrote,

> A lot of people thought it was ironic that I made an image directly supporting something, since I've encouraged people for years through my Obey campaign to question the visuals they're confronted with and look at things more cautiously, but with the HOPE portrait I was very sincerely making propaganda to support Obama. I still encourage people to question everything, but irony is frequently a way to be noncommittal with views. Once you've examined things, it's important to actually have a point of view that you're willing to stand behind.[17]

After the Super Tuesday primary, Shepard Fairey took the money he made from the limited-edition poster sales and plowed all of it into making more to be distributed to organizers across the country. He later estimated he had made about three hundred thousand posters and five hundred thousand stickers, the foundation for the largest grassroots street art mobilization in history.

Fairey referred Sergant to Matt Revelli, the San Francisco Bay Area–based owner of a group of galleries and clothing, music, and furniture shops called Upper Playground, and the editor in chief of *Juxtapoz* magazine. Revelli's $10 million business catered to the street art crowd, the kind unlikely to be found haunting Chelsea galleries. It reached the vibrant, lucrative youth underground where graffiti, tattooing, design, illustration, comics, and erotica came together.

Revelli picked up the poster-selling business and both he and Sergant began asking street artists like El Mac, David Choe, the Date Farmers, and Morning Breath to make their own images. The projects generated perhaps a quarter of a million dollars, which went back into more production. Through commissions and contests, they vastly expanded the volume of images and content generated. Street teams and fans did the rest, blanketing the country with stickers and posters. The team also focused on purchasing billboards in areas they thought might be strategic to the campaign.

Yet the operation had no formal connection to or coordination with the Obama campaign. They were working on passion and pots of coffee. "There was no one to get approval from. We were able to move with lightning speed," Revelli said. "There was a certain freedom too because it financed itself."

By the time the Democratic convention had come to Denver in the late summer—where Fairey's HOPE image was everywhere, not just on authorized or commissioned posters and building-size banners, but on bootleg T-shirts, buttons, and coffee mugs—the hottest party was the opening of the Manifest Hope pop-up gallery that the group had set up to accommodate the results of a national contest cosponsored by MoveOn .org, for which they had received more than a thousand entries.

Irony, fun-ism, the outlaw impulse—all this was growing into something else. "I'm a populist. I'm trying to reach as many people as possible," Fairey told National Portrait Gallery curator Wendy Wick-Reaves when it bought the poster for the collection. "I love the concept in fine art of making a masterpiece—something that will endure. But I also understand how short the attention span of most consumers is and that you really need to work with the metabolism of consumer culture a lot of times to make something relevant within the zeitgeist."[18]

The street artists had created a process that was driven not from the top down but from self-organized groups working up: street artists and graffitists steeped in the aesthetics of Maileresque self-advertising; entrepreneurial tastemakers working giant steps ahead of the brand marketers; DIY activists with guerrilla strategy and network power. Colorization meant in part the maturation of insurgent cultural energies.

AFTER MOBY

Perhaps it was finally time for colorization to hit mainstream national politics. In the late 1960s, Nixon advisor Kevin Phillips had famously predicted a Republican realignment, rooted in the cultural politics of racial reaction. But by the turn of the millennium, political scientist Ruy Teixeira and journalist John Judis were arguing that the demographic and political tide had finally turned toward an "emerging Democratic majority." People of color, women, young people, and professional white voters, they argued, could form the basis of a new left-leaning coalition.

Maybe all of this was nonsense—like old predictions of a permanent Republican majority. At any rate, most Democrats were far from ready to accept Teixeira and Judis's argument. The Southern strategy loomed large over Clinton's New Democrat agenda.

What Cornell Belcher, a pollster who closely studied racial attitudes, called "the culture war realignment" had been so thorough that even Jimmy Carter and Bill Clinton had worked within its framework.

So-called centrism in the 1990s was about catering to the perceived needs of the ficklest white voters. These politics were rooted in a post-'68 critique of the party. New Democrats argued that Nixon had triumphed and the Republicans stayed ascendant because the party was pandering to its loud minorities: Blacks, women, antiwar liberals, and so on. To win, the party needed to escape "identity politics."

That was the theory. In practice, New Democrats were able to secure their agenda only through an increasingly unsustainable kind of identity politics, one that required the periodic *Pequod* hunt for the elusive undecided white voter. It was the political equivalent of losing the forest to count the trees. It was also a good reason for many Democrats to care so little about electoral politics. But through the late 2000s, it also amounted to the commonsense wisdom around electoral strategy.

Primaries were about gaining momentum first in nearly all-white early-vote states like Iowa and New Hampshire. General elections were about honing in on the smallest groups of "swing voters" in a very narrow set of "swing states"—usually aging Rust Belt states where union power had been decimated, like Ohio and Pennsylvania, or gap states that had not yet tipped, like Florida or Nevada. But in the gap states, where Black, Brown, and youth populations were considered part of "the base," most of the attention and resources went to the white exurbs. And in Rust Belt states, focus turned to "independent" white voters who might be attracted by repackaged conservative ideas and messages.

Clinton's pollster and strategist, Mark Penn, was a genius at applied market segmentation research and the master of this strategy. His book was called *Microtrends: The Small Forces behind Tomorrow's Big Changes*. His job was to find demographic slices of undecided-but-likely-to-vote whites. He had in fact been the Christopher Columbus of soccer moms. His strategy was to bombard these niche voters with strong-on-crime or end-welfare-now messages until they voted blue.

Penn was capable of poetry, as long as it was poll-tested. He had given Clinton what would become one of the president's most famous phrases, "building a bridge to the twenty-first century," after a sample of likely voters gave it the nod. When Penn took over Hillary Clinton's presidential campaign in 2007, he wrote a memo to her about Barack Obama's liabilities. In this instance he had probably not tested his ideas:

> All of these articles about [Obama's] boyhood in Indonesia and his life in Hawaii are geared towards showing his background is diverse, multicultural and putting that in a new light.

Save it for 2050.

It also exposes a very strong weakness for him—his roots to basic American values and culture [sic] are at best limited. I cannot imagine electing a president during a time of war who is not at his center fundamentally American in his thinking and in his values.[19]

During the summer of 2008, as Obama was bodysurfing at Sandy Beach in Hawai'i, ABC pundit Cokie Roberts echoed Penn's Ahab wisdom, saying Obama's home vacation to that "foreign" place made him seem "a little bit more exotic than he perhaps would want to come across."

But days later, new census projections were released. They asserted that the United States might become majority-minority by 2042, eight years earlier than previously expected. The Brookings Institution followed with an estimate that under-thirties would reach that point in 2028, a single generation. Even the term "majority-minority" seemed stupid now. If *everyone* was a minority, then what did the word even mean anymore?

One other development made it the perfect time to test a new theory of the party. In 2004, the Atwater protégé Karl Rove had engineered George W. Bush's narrow reelection by tossing out the conventional wisdom that elections were won by appealing to the Big White Middle. Pre- and postelection polls had found Republicans were more fired up about reelecting Bush than Democrats were about electing John Kerry.[20] So instead, the Bush campaign won by turning out their base, the Great White Right, thus introducing a new term into the political lexicon—"the enthusiasm gap."

By 2006 Democratic National Committee chair Howard Dean was taking a page from Rove, unveiling a so-called fifty-state strategy that stirred anger among small-thinking New Democrats but put organizers and infrastructure in every state. That year the Democrats succeeded in winning back Congress. Now Obama's state-to-state primary battle with Clinton had forced him to adopt a fifty-state strategy as well. When Clinton focused on white and Latino voters, Obama moved outside to bring in Black and young voters and build an enthusiasm gap. He prevailed.

In the general election, Obama's fundraising prowess could keep local organizations well-oiled and allow him to concentrate on swing states. But as the campaign staff looked at the map they realized that they could be competitive in many more states than just the traditional battlegrounds of Ohio, Pennsylvania, and Florida. Blacks, youths, and "creative class"–types had put Bush states like North Carolina and Virginia into play. Latinos and independents might help flip Colorado, Florida, New Mexico, and Nevada. As Teixeira and Judis had predicted, demographic and economic shifts had indeed changed the game.

When the general election season opened, an innovative Web infrastructure had already brought in two million grassroots donors and allowed seven million potential volunteers to organize themselves into what Obama strategist David Plouffe called his "persuasion army." These tools would prove important. The surge of rising interest in the candidate—after such a punishing and divisive primary—also suggested that something deeper might be at work.

Perhaps the most surprising development of 2008 was the emergence of a small but incalculably influential group within the Obama persuasion army, one that didn't even think of itself as partisan or even as a group—the street artists.

THE OCEAN MOVES

In politics, the artist had long been the romantic outsider of Kennedy's rhetoric, or the committed cultural worker of Mao's. But now it seemed that the artist was something else, a seer working in the future imaginary, capturing and gifting people with glimpses of possibility. The artist became key to an extraordinary cultural moment, when something abyssal and indefinable turned and the whole sea seemed to move.

Fairey's image of hope had inspired thousands more. Once the picture of Obama had been transformed into red, white, and blue, it could be reimagined by tens of thousands of artists in full color, a field of blossoming dreams reaching toward the horizon.

Ron English made a series of oil paintings in which Lincoln morphed into Obama, history as redemption song. El Mac applied his trademark calligraphic strokes—influenced by French graphic novelist Moebius and indigenous tattoo arts—to create an Obama who looked resolute and canny, ready for the world. Jon-Paul Bail made screen-print shirts and posters portraying the candidate, his hair braided, earring blinging, and smiling behind gold fronts, over the words: "Barack Obama: Clean."

Other pictures seemed even less tied to the moment of the election. Wheatpaste legend Robbie Conal pictured a smiling Obama with the words: "Climate Change." The multicolored silhouettes of Marlena Buczek Smith's "Unity" and the stretching, clasping brown and orange hands of Karla Mickens's "Yes We Did" called back to 1968, summoning the Third World Liberation Front and the Situationists of the Paris Spring. Amy Martin's HOPE poster featured a young mother lifting her daughter to catch butterflies.

The idea of creating images of Obama itself had gone viral. In Providence, recent RISD graduates Aaron Perry-Zucker and Adam Meyer had set up a Design for Obama Web site. Quickly, hundreds of images were uploaded, offered free by the artists for anyone to print out and use. Obama's image was now connected to all kinds of histories, emotions, even to public policy ideas that the official campaign had never vetted. Art was overspilling the bounds of a mere election.

By the summer of 2008, John McCain's campaign was surprised to find it was being forced not just to deal with the man himself, but the image of the man. They put out ads juxtaposing photos of him with those of Britney Spears and Paris Hilton. They called him "the biggest celebrity in the world," said his supporters were just "fans fawning over The One."[21] They had missed the point. As Angela Davis put it, Obama's visage had become "a canvas onto which many of us are painting our desires and our dreams and our hopes."[22]

As the fall began, a wave grew. Across the country, in big cities and small towns, an ocean of images was pouring forth. They were in windows, on telephone poles, at busy intersections, on people's clothing and bodies. His likeness had unleashed one of the strongest currents of popular art-making since Franklin Delano Roosevelt had funded the Works Progress Administration and the Farm Security Administration art programs.

These pictures were not uniform and they were not random. They could not have bloomed as they did without a mass audience eager to see and affirm them. As the stock market plunged, the images seemed to circulate at an even swifter pace. The art campaigns had tapped something even deeper than the traditional political campaigns.

They were pictures of a new cultural majority, the proliferating projections of a colorized America. The multicultural avant-gardes of decades past had said they were not just about changing representation but changing America—lifting but not forsaking its burdens of history, encompassing the broadness of its present, staking a trust for the future. That was what they had meant by a radical diversity.

In these images were new hopes—that a new majority might forge the first consensus about race and nation since the civil rights movement had led to the passage of legislation around voting rights, immigration, and discrimination; that it might be built on the values of inclusion, opportunity, and diversity, and be bound together with the values of responsibility, reciprocity, and sustainability; that the nation might be able to harmonize diverse modes of expressing Americanness.

TWO SCENES

I

A year and a half after the climax of the 2008 Democratic National Convention in Denver's Mile High Stadium, the entertainer sat back and thought. He was trying to evoke the feelings he felt that evening—soaring joys that had come from deep wells of pain.

William "will.i.am" Adams had begun that storied evening backstage a mess, emotional and weeping. He looked into the mirror. He was seeing the public housing projects where he was raised—the two-story Estrada Courts in the Boyle Heights neighborhood of East Los Angeles—where a 1978 mural by Congreso de Artistas Chicanos en Aztlán featured Che pointing like Uncle Sam straight at the young fathers and mothers pushing strollers and the kids kicking soccer balls, saying, "We Are NOT a Minority!!"

He was seeing his homies—Lalo, Coque, Joselito, Lil' Georgie; the Mexican and Filipino guys he was bused away from in the morning to schools on the Westside. He was seeing his mother and the uncle who raised him, his grandmother and his grandmother's grandma, a Mississippi slave.

"My brother's in prison. My homeboy's in jail for life. It just hit me like, *Wow*, we just some guys from the neighborhood. I was supposed to be written off," he said. "No bitch tears. Those were the hardest tears ever. Hot lava tears."

Then Will was onstage, before eighty-four thousand in the stands and millions more at their televisions, standing alongside John Legend and the Agape Choir on the world's biggest stage to perform "Yes We Can"—a song that had never entered any charts but that the audiences already knew the words to, because they were Obama's. When the song was done, Will looked out across the crowd, people of all faiths, colors, and generations gathering in rapt anticipation as the sun set over the snow-capped Rockies, and bit his lip to keep from crying again.

Back in his studio he came up with a chorus for the new song he was writing. "I got a feeling," he sang to himself, "that tonight's gonna be a good night."

II

As the campaign built to its November climax, Charles Stone III decided to reunite his "Whassup?" friends for a new video.

He opens this one with a shot of himself sitting on a plastic chair in the apartment. His hair has grayed. He looks wan and tired. He has the classifieds in hand and moving boxes are scattered through an empty room. He watches McCain give his acceptance speech at the Republican convention and shakes his head. The wonder years are over.

He gets a call from Paul—who has shaven his Afro, his bald head now sitting beneath sand goggles and a combat helmet. Paul is calling from a payphone next to a rubble-strewn house. Helicopters kick up dust.

"Whassup B?"
"Nuttin'. Lost my home. Looking for a job. Whassup with you?"
"Still in Iraq. Watching my ass."
"True. True."

Fred walks in and drops a box. His neck is in a wrap, his arm in a cast. He needs painkillers. Really, he needs health insurance. Where's Dookie? Staring at the screen of his laptop watching his stocks tumble. He gets up on a chair and prepares to hang himself. Maurice buzzes from outside. He is screaming, getting blown away by the force of the hurricane raging outside. The "Whassaaaaaaaaaa's" have become cries of pain. Dookie's rope rips out the ceiling plaster and he tumbles to the floor.

"So, whassup B?"

Stone looks at the TV, as Barack and Michelle face the convention crowd, tickertape and confetti raining down. He smiles.

"Change, that's whassup. Change."
The screen goes black. "True," it says.
"Change," it says. "Vote."

MINORITY'S END

Obama's candidacy had advanced on images of hope and reconciliation. And then, after a summer of seesawing polls, the housing bubble popped and global markets began to unravel under the weight of their moral hazards. Suddenly there was a shared crisis.

The wave broke on November 4, 2008, giving Obama a record-breaking 69 million votes, 365 electoral votes, 28 states—including three, sociologist Douglas Massey noted, of the former Confederacy.

Under-forty-fives overwhelmingly voted for Obama. And, continuing the turnaround begun in 2004, young people, Latinos, Asian Americans, and gays voted for Obama at or above 2–1 margins.[23] Almost every African American voter chose Obama. Young Blacks, in particular, registered both the highest increase in youth turnout since 2000 (almost 20 percent) and the highest rate of any racial youth group ever recorded (58 percent).[24]

Over-sixty-five-year-olds went overwhelmingly for McCain. Baby boomers split down the middle.[25] White voters went for McCain by 55 percent to Obama's 43 percent. Their enthusiasm was decidedly low; their turnout rate actually declined.[26] Only young whites gave Obama their vote, joining the new cultural majority.[27]

Change had come. But exactly what kind? The incoming tide of racial change had once driven white pundits into panic and hysteria. But were those fears dissipating like a threatening line on the ocean's horizon that merely washes into the sand?

Obama had presented himself to whites as conciliatory. In his famous race speech in March he had refused to "disown" either his former Reverend Jeremiah Wright or his white grandmother. "Let us be our brother's keeper, Scripture tells us. Let us be our sister's keeper," he said. "Let us find that common stake that we all have in one another, and let our politics reflect that spirit as well."

The social psychologist Claude Steele wrote, "In [Obama's] example, identity wasn't a source of balkanization and threat; it was a source of wisdom about the challenges of a complex and diverse society that ultimately made him the most suitable person to lead such a society. To the surprise of all, perhaps, it was his stress on identity, not his suppression of it, that made him a symbol of hope."[28]

Andrew Sullivan, as the young editor of the *New Republic* in the mid-1990s, had instigated a famous culture-war battle by championing Charles Murray and Richard Herrnstein's dubious, neo-eugenicist "Bell Curve" theory that suggested Blacks and Latinos were less intelligent than whites and more susceptible to crime, poverty, illegitimacy, and unemployment. But now Sullivan was recanting, in a way.

At the end of 2007, in a cover story for the *Atlantic* called "Goodbye to All That: Why Obama Matters," Sullivan praised Obama for representing "both an affirmation of identity politics and a commitment to carving a unique personal identity out of the race, geography, and class he inherited." He argued that Obama might be the bridge to the twenty-first century that Hillary's husband had talked about. Sullivan wrote:

> At its best, the Obama candidacy is about ending a war—not so much the war in Iraq ... but the war within America that has prevailed since Vietnam and that shows dangerous signs of intensifying, a nonviolent civil war that has crippled America at the very time the world needs it most. It is a war about war—and about culture and about religion and about race. And in that war, Obama—and Obama alone—offers the possibility of a truce.[29]

Pundits like Sullivan were especially invested in Obama's racial symbolism. He would be their redemption—proof that the past was past, that we were all post-racial now.

But if the election had made clear that no one could postpone thinking about colorization until 2050, it also revealed again a cultural polarization. Pollster Cornell Belcher told the reporter Marc Ambinder that even white voters most concerned about the economy voted for Obama in much smaller numbers than they had for Bill Clinton in 1992—a nearly 20 percent difference. He said, "You can't look at that swath of hard-red counties that actually grew even redder and say that we are post-racial."[30]

Perhaps, as journalist Ann Friedman put it, all politics were identity politics—all politics emerged from that space between appearance and perception.[31] And maybe, in fact, most of what politics had to say in this moment was about who we *were* rather than who we could be.

Hua Hsu concluded, "This moment was not the end of white America; it was not the end of anything. It was a bridge and we crossed it." He asked the question that still seemed unanswerable: "What will the new mainstream of America look like, and what ideas or values might it rally around?"[32]

Perhaps that task was wholly beyond politics, and the answers would have to emerge from the culture—where the clash between colorization and restoration would rage again.

From *Staying Cool*, published 1974. Courtesy of Morrie Turner.

The Racial Dot Map of Tucson, Arizona, based on 2010 Census data reveals both racial integration and continuing segregation. Blue dots represent whites, green dots represent African Americans, red dots represent Asian Americans, yellow dots represent Latinos, and brown dots represent Native Americans/Multiracial/Other populations. Image Copyright, 2013, Weldon Cooper Center for Public Service, Rector and Visitors of the University of Virginia (Dustin A. Cable, creator).

CHAPTER 14

DIS/UNION

THE PARADOX OF THE POST-RACIAL MOMENT

Screw Diversity, Celebrate Excellence
—A post-millennial bumper sticker

Race was an inescapable text of Obama's triumph.

In an extraordinary concession speech, Senator John McCain turned his Arizona crowd's boos at the mention of Obama's name to applause when he said, "A century ago, President Theodore Roosevelt's invitation of Booker T. Washington to dine at the White House was taken as an outrage in many quarters. America today is a world away from the cruel and frightful bigotry of that time. There is no better evidence of this than the election of an African American to the presidency."

How far had we come? Polls taken shortly after Obama's inauguration found a striking new optimism around race relations. Harvard sociologists Lawrence Bobo and Alicia Simmons asked whether Americans believed Blacks had achieved racial equality. More than four in five whites believed they had or would soon. A much smaller plurality— 53 percent—of Blacks agreed, but this majority seemed significant.[1]

A few months later, University of Chicago political scientist Cathy Cohen asked the same question of young people aged fifteen to twenty-five. Seventy-eight percent of young whites believed Blacks had achieved racial equality or would soon. A similar proportion of Latinos agreed. Black youths mirrored their elders' more cautious hope.

Cohen also asked the youths if they felt racism was still a major problem. Here the break was clearer. Sixty-eight percent of Black youths and 58 percent of Latinos said yes. But 67 percent of whites said no.[2] The new generation—more culturally desegregated than any previous American one—was already showing the same divides over questions of race as their elders.

Other divides seemed to be emerging. Smaller numbers of each group believed Latinos had achieved or would soon achieve racial equality. When youths were asked if they felt like "full and equal citizens," 69 percent of whites and 55 percent of Blacks answered yes. But only 39 percent of Latinos felt the same way. Perhaps the 2007 collapse of congressional immigration reform efforts had made them pessimistic.

Still Obama's victory seemed to point toward a new conversation about race. Majorities of whites, Blacks, and Latinos told the Gallup Poll both before the election and again in the fall of 2009 that they believed an open, honest discussion might improve race relations.[3]

But how would that discussion begin? And where would it go? Nothing captured the optimism and confusion of the moment more than the word most often used to describe it—"post-racial."

THE NEW CONFUSION

The most successful ad campaign of 2009 starred Isaiah Mustafa, a strikingly handsome Black man, in a set of commercials for Old Spice shower body wash called "The Man Your Man Could Smell Like."

Studies had shown that women made 70 percent of all body wash purchases, so Mustafa, acting as "The Old Spice Guy," began his ads with a hearty "Hello ladies!" In a deep, almost Shakespearean baritone, he pattered on about how attractive he was. He began the ad wearing only a towel and—through set changes that took him quickly from the shower to a yacht to a white horse—he remained half-naked.

The ad went stupendously viral. Its runaway Internet popularity caused the corporate giant Procter & Gamble to commission 185 more video clips featuring the Old Spice Guy responding directly to tweets, posts, and e-mails from fans. The videos garnered hundreds of millions of YouTube views. In all of them Mustafa appeared shirtless.

Katie Abrahamson, a spokesperson for Wieden+Kennedy, the same agency that pioneered the Spike Lee/Michael Jordan ads for Nike in 1988, denied that Mustafa was cast based on his race. "The truth of the matter is, Isaiah was one of hundreds who auditioned for the spot in a standard casting-call and was simply the best performance and overall best fit for the creative idea—it had nothing to do with the color of his skin," she said. "The challenge was finding someone who would appeal to both genders."

But did the ad execs really believe that? The witty, de-Ebonicized, confident, but far from *threateningly* confident Old Spice Guy looked like he had ridden his white horse right out of David Ligare's painting *Areta*. He recalled no one so much as Obama himself, who when the paparazzi captured him in some pre-inauguration bodysurfing at Sandy Beach in Hawai'i, appeared shirtless on a news tabloid cover above the headline: "FIT FOR OFFICE: Buff Bam Is Hawaii Hunk."[4]

Advertising met politics when the Old Spice Guy took to YouTube to answer a question from the television host and former Democratic advisor George Stephanopoulos. How, Stephanopoulos wondered, could President Obama stop losing women voters? The Old Spice Guy advised Obama to "henceforth only be seen in a towel" and to begin his State of the Union addresses with "Hello ladies!" If the going got tough, just remind them of "his presidential ab-boards."

Not so long before, an image of a shirtless Black man might have caused race riots. One of the most indelible images of the American Century had been the mutilated body of Emmett Till, a Black boy brutally tortured and murdered in 1955 by two white men in Mississippi for allegedly whistling at a white girl. Till's mother insisted on an open-casket funeral—"I wanted the world to see what they did to my baby," she said—and the shocking photographs of Till sparked the nascent civil rights movement.

Could we now canter away from that history, with its fecund, corrosive brew of desire and debasement, love and theft? The comedian Stephen Colbert explored this question in a riotous ongoing gag. One night he told Samuel L. Jackson, "I don't see race. I'm not a racist."

Caught by surprise, Jackson blurted, "Yes, you do!"

"No, I don't see race. Are you a Black man?" Colbert asked. "Are you an African American? Because as I said, I took King's lesson to heart. I don't see the color of anyone's skin, I only see the content of their character."

"Really?!!"

"Yeah."

"Awesome. Unfortunately I don't have that luxury."[5]

On the night after Obama's inauguration, Colbert delivered a monologue that perfectly captured white post-PC, post-racial confusion:

You know, I noticed something interesting this afternoon. The inauguration of Barack Obama seemed to mean something special to African Americans. Even more interesting, it seemed to mean something to *me,* too.

But I never empathize with people who are not like me. So the reaction I had to Barack Obama's inauguration must logically mean that I am a Black man.

I had no idea! Because I don't see race. People tell me I'm white and I believe them because I dance with my thumbs out. But now I know I'm Black. Which is great, because there really ought to be more of us in late night.[6]

Perhaps race comedy was one of the few places in which truths might be told, where an honest conversation might still be started. The late Black comic Patrice O'Neal had a bit where he said that being onstage was the one place where "I can say anything I goddamn want racially. And white people have to sit there and take it. 'I am evil, yes.'"[7]

Colbert's "Don't See Race" bits revealed a freshly nuanced sympathy for the devil: high-wire individualized absurdity to combat high-stakes social absurdity. They exploded two myths—that the mere act of seeing and acknowledging difference made one a racist, and that race was a problem for everyone else but whites to deal with. The jokes worked because of another strange idea prevalent in the era of post-multiculturalism—that whites as a group could never be culturally cool.

Hua Hsu called this phenomenon the "flight from whiteness"—the eagerness, especially among young whites raised under multiculturalism, to "divest themselves from their whiteness entirely."[8] Hsu cited the success of Christian Lander's blog Stuff White People Like, a relentlessly hip skewering of white hipsterism. But all of these myths still depended on the old idea that whiteness was the unspoken universal.

And so there would be the confusion that drove McCain's followers first to boo Obama then to cheer him in the chill of the Arizona desert night. There would be the mad pendulum swing between colorblindness and hyperawareness, between the silence and the crazy talk. There would be the new confusion of the moment, only perhaps it was just another version of the old.

UNDONE

Sometimes when people used the term "post-racial" they were speaking about the ways that identity and pop culture seemed more fluid and permeable and less "white" and therefore cooler than ever. But to many, the term "post-racial" signified less about how to face the future than about how to address the past.

For some, it signaled a desire for an end to the politics of Black consciousness. Pundits like Juan Williams and Matt Bai hoped that a new generation of politicians of color—including men like Newark mayor Cory Booker and Los Angeles mayor Antonio Villaraigosa—might douse the old fires of Black and Brown Power, give them relief from diversity fatigue, and replace "political correctness" with a deracinated rhetoric of class.

In this narrative, "post-racial" signified not only an American sense of transcendence, a victory of will over history, but as Gary Younge put it, "a repudiation" of claims for equality.[9] It signified a *return* to whiteness.

Back in 2007 when Obama began his presidential run, Ward Connerly had praised him as a "post-racial candidate" and made a great show of sending in a campaign donation.[10] But not long after, he and other Black neoconservatives like Shelby Steele were criticizing him for supporting policies like affirmative action.[11] When Obama was "not Black enough," he had been attractive. Now he was not post-racial enough.

To others "post-racial" signified an end to white comfort. A post-racial America, the conservative activist Lawrence Auster wrote, meant "a post-white America, an America transformed by the symbolic removal of whiteness as the country's explicit or implicit historic and majority identity.... Post-racial America is an America in which whites, as whites, go silent forever."[12] Pat Buchanan called white America "an endangered species," as if it had entered the final spiral of Theodore Roosevelt's "race suicide."[13] And because whites were in their "demographic winter," the nation had entered—all clashing, cringe-worthy metaphors intended—"the Indian summer of our civilization."[14]

The implication was clear: defend your birthright, fight for your future. As Obama began his presidency, the right did not wait long to launch ferocious cultural attacks. Media crusaders Andrew Breitbart and Glenn Beck trained their sniper focus on newly appointed, culturally savvy Obama administration officials like NEA communications director Yosi Sergant and environmental advisor Van Jones and won their resignations. The sad episode of Department of Agriculture appointee Shirley Sherrod's resignation seemed collateral damage.

As image of the Obama Joker went viral, his face was no longer the screen on which to project desires, dreams, and hopes but the sum of all fears. Obama was no longer just the product of miscegenation, no longer just Black. He was now also a Muslim, a socialist, an illegal alien, a demon of disorder. He was all things Other.

When an Internet video surfaced of a white student being beaten up by a group of Black students in a dispute over school-bus seats, Rush Limbaugh told his audience of millions, "It's Obama's America, is it not? ... You put your kids on a school bus, you expect safety but in Obama's America the white kids now get beat up with the black kids cheering, "Yay, right on, right on, right on, right on."[15]

Had we all really just crossed the bridge together? For years good-willed people had believed in a conceit—perhaps it was multiculturalism's core conceit—that if more people of color, women, and gays were represented, that if they could tell their stories and the stories were heard, then empathy would follow, and equity, too. A new kind of cultural politics that lifted everyone together could emerge.

But by the summer of the Tea Party's rise, at the midpoint of Obama's first term, that kind of cultural politics seemed as distant as ever. All optimism was gone. When the

Gallup Poll asked Americans how they felt Obama's presidency had changed race relations, 64 percent said either nothing changed or things had gotten worse.[16] Instead there was the fog of the renewed culture war. "Post-racial" did not point to a new consensus on race, but the seeming impossibility of one.

THE SILENCE SPEAKS LOUDLY

In each generation, race is rearticulated and reconstructed. A quarter-century since conservatives had remade national politics with the idea that colorblindness and colormuteness were the only appropriate ways, individually and politically, to deal with race, the idea had become orthodox for many liberals, too. Being blind and silent had insinuated itself down to the personal level.

In a broad 2007 study of almost 19,000 subjects, a team of scholars from Vanderbilt University found that 75 percent of white parents never or almost never discussed race or ethnicity with their children.[17] Some of the parents didn't think it was a big deal. Others genuinely did not know how to talk about race so they avoided talking about it altogether. Many of those parents—Po Bronson and Ashley Merryman, the coauthors of *NurtureShock,* found—believed teaching their children not to see race *was* the proper way to teach them how not to be bigoted or racist.

"[T]he habit of ignoring race is understood to be a graceful, even generous, liberal gesture," Toni Morrison said in 1990, when the culture wars were raging and conservative dogma was quietly hardening into new rules for civil conduct. "[E]very well-bred instinct argues *against noticing* and forecloses adult discourse."[18]

The new common sense was: if bad people had used race to divide and debase, that is to say, if they had used race to be *racist*, then good people would be polite to never acknowledge race at all. It was better not to say anything than to risk being seen as a racist. Nothing was worse than being called a racist.

In the post-racial moment there was a "watching you watching me" meta-absurdity. No theory better explained it than education psychologist Claude Steele's idea of "stereotype threat." Steele had stumbled onto the idea when he tried to explain why high-achieving Black students still underperformed in college, decades after programs designed to help them had been put in place. He found that when they were reminded that, as a race, society *expected* them to fail, they underachieved. The same happened with women in mathematics. In integrated environments, Steele argued, the threat of confirming a negative group stereotype could place extreme stress on individuals and cause them to fail.

Steele then tried a different experiment. He asked whites to lead a topical discussion with a group of random people they did not know. He then asked them to situate the chairs for their guests. In actuality Steele and his researchers were not interested in the discussion but in where their discussion leaders placed the chairs. For most topics, they chose to move the chairs close to their own, suggesting that they wanted to encourage trust and intimacy with their subjects. But when they were told that the topic was racial profiling and their guests would be Black, they pushed the chairs much farther away than they normally would have. Steele theorized that the white subjects were afraid to be seen as racist. Stereotype threat had led them to distance themselves from their Black discussants.

After multiculturalism, we knew what *not* to say to each other, but not what *to say*. Multiculturalism had given us protocols and scripts. When these were exhausted, we were lost. We did not know how to improvise a new way.

If Steele had been interested in individual distancing, sociologists Eduardo Bonilla-Silva and Tyrone Forman were interested in social distance. They interviewed and surveyed white college students on their racial attitudes, then compared the answers. In their written surveys, white students showed support for affirmative action and interracial marriage. But in interviews, many of them contradicted their answers, using indirection, displacement, or claims of ignorance.[19] Racialized issues were too uncomfortable to talk about candidly and directly.

"Evasion," Toni Morrison had also said, "has fostered another, substitute language in which the issues are encoded, foreclosing open debate."[20]

Being colormute was safer. Po Bronson and his wife had chosen to send their child to a culturally diverse preschool in San Francisco. But one day he was mortified to find his young child happily pointing out Black people on the street. "That guy comes from Africa!" the boy said. He had just completed his preschool lesson on diversity and difference, and was pleased to have new words to talk about what he was seeing.

Bronson listened in as his son and his white pals discussed their friends' skin colors as "brown." Not knowing what to call their own color, they spoke of friends who had "skin like ours." Then he heard one of the boys tell his son, "Parents don't like us to talk about our skin, so don't let them hear you."[21]

Bronson realized that the children were simply trying to find language to discuss identity and diversity. But their good liberal parents—conditioned by stereotype threat—were instead trying to teach them to be colormute. "Avoidance," Steele wrote, "becomes the simplest solution."[22] If difference itself could not be named, how could anyone begin a conversation about what really needed to change?

Silence and evasion, distance and avoidance. Forman called it "racial apathy." Bonilla-Silva called it "colorblind racism." The writer and activist Tim Wise called it "post-racial liberalism." Stanford law professor Richard Thompson Ford called it "post-racism," arguing that it did not "signify 'the end' of racism, or even necessarily the beginning of the end.... It means the 'next stage' of racism."[23] If the word "post-racial" was intellectually inadequate, these scholars were devising oldish new names for a new-old problem.

LOOK AT YOU FOOLIN' YOU

There was a paradox at the heart of the "post-racial" moment. While our images showed a mostly optimistic nation moving toward cultural desegregation and racial equality, our modes of living together reflected distancing and blindness, rancor and silence; our politics bespoke deep pessimism and a desire for disengagement; and our social indexes revealed increasing social resegregation and racial inequality.

How did Americans value diversity and integration? Over the course of four decades, the Gallup Poll had asked whites, "Would you move if great numbers of Blacks moved into your neighborhood?" In 1958, 79% said they would. In 1997, 75% said they would not.[24] A month after Obama's victory, a report from the Pew Research Center showed that almost two in three Americans—including 52% of Republicans, 60% of whites, 83% of Blacks, and 76% of eighteen-to-twenty-nine-year-olds—said that they preferred to live in a community made up of people who were a mix of different races.[25] The numbers were similar for religious, political, and socioeconomic diversity.

Fully 68 percent of those making $100,000 or more a year—a much larger proportion than every other income bracket—said they preferred to live in a community with a mix of economic classes. But when Stanford professors Sean F. Reardon and Kendra Bischoff examined the data from 1970 to 2009, they found that not only had residential segregation by income soared, the wealthy had segregated themselves the fastest.[26]

Large majorities told pollsters they wanted integrated schools and diversity in education. Pundits and politicians would often trot out such polls as cause for optimism. But in light of the actual social facts, the survey data looked less like a consensus for cultural equity than evidence that multiculturalism had made some better primed to answer the questions "correctly."

In this colorized generation, public schools were resegregating at a dramatic rate. By 2010, 80% of Latinos and 74% of Blacks attended majority nonwhite schools. Around 40% of Blacks and Latinos in public schools attended hypersegregated schools in which more than 90% of the students were nonwhite. Blacks and Latinos were also twice as likely to attend a school predominantly serving low-income students than white or Asian students. White students were the most racially isolated of all—the average white student attended a school that was 75% white.[27]

Resegregation did not escape even the rapidly diversifying suburbs or the most liberal strongholds. From city to exurb, the San Francisco Bay Area—one of the nation's most diverse regions, the birthplace of the multiculturalism movement, and the site of Berkeley's national model public school desegregation program—also boasted California's highest rates of white isolation. Although white students made up only 28 percent of the Bay Area's student-age population, 65 percent of them attended majority white schools.[28] Those schools were eight times less likely than predominantly nonwhite ones to be deemed "high-problem" schools.[29]

After 1968, busing, court orders, and district plans had helped to integrate the schools from the Deep South to the Northwest. In turn, school desegregation climbed sharply and peaked in the late 1980s.[30] But then anti-integrationists began to accumulate victories in the courts and the legislatures. During the 1990s, while multiculturalists were winning the battle to change school curriculum and staffing, they were losing the battle to desegregate the next generation of public school students. By the new millennium, the same Southern school systems that had made the most progress toward integration were the fastest to resegregate. Progress had always been fragile.

ESCAPE FROM EVERYWHERE

Public school resegregation was tied closely to housing resegregation. Housing was, the Georgetown law professor Sheryll Cashin wrote, "the realm in which we have experienced the fewest integration gains." She added, "When it comes to integration, housing is also the realm in which Americans most seem to agree that separation is acceptable."[31] To be sure, times *had* changed since the period of white flight from the chocolate cities. The romance of the city was back. A Manhattan Institute study by Edward Glaeser and Jacob Vigdor titled "The End of the Segregated Century" found that "American cities are now more integrated than they've been since 1910." Segregation in the metro areas they studied had dropped by almost half from its peak in 1970, with a notably accelerated drop during the 2000s. But had they simply taken a snapshot of the moment before displacement and gentrification sealed a new era of segregation?

The weight of history was on segregation's side. Expansive New Deal policies gave working-class and middle-class white homeowners a fresh start in home ownership and wealth building, leading toward the suburban boom of the mid-twentieth century. In essence, they had been granted mobility. But these same policies locked out people of color, who were often bound by racial covenants, zoning laws, and racial steering to urban neighborhoods "redlined" as too risky for lenders.[32] Postwar highway building then tore through those neighborhoods and sped their decline.

By the 1990s, federal housing policies were focused on creating mixed-income communities. Efforts to destroy substandard housing projects and build less dense developments with fewer affordable housing units were often necessary and noble. But without any efforts to grow or replace the below-market housing stock, gentrification was inevitable. A host of declining neighborhoods—like the Mission District in San Francisco; U Street in Washington, DC; Wicker Park in Chicago; Fort Greene in Brooklyn—became newly desirable. Young professionals and families streamed back into the cities.

Fleeing the suburban for "the urban"—that key marketing construct around which colorization in the 1990s had turned—reflected an embrace of multiculturalism. But for longtime residents the impact could be bittersweet. Redevelopment resulted in the mass disappearing of families of color. With gentrification, those who stayed suddenly had supermarkets, cafés, restaurants, bike shops that they never had before, along with expensive boutiques and real estate agencies. But many also experienced what Columbia professor of psychiatry and public health Mindy Thompson Fullilove labeled "root shock," the trauma of loss coupled with the threat of displacement.

As the suburbs depopulated, they grew browner and became potential flashpoints. When George Zimmerman shot Trayvon Martin in cold blood, a killing that evoked the murders of Michael Griffith in Howard Beach and Yusuf Hawkins in Bensonhurst more than two decades before, it happened in Sanford, Florida, a declining node within the Orlando sprawl, inside of the kind of gated community that had once symbolized protection from non-whiteness and gun violence.

White flight continued in a new vein, too. Thousands of carpetbaggers were steering their SUVs toward the Palinesque "real America" paradise of small-town Pleasantvilles, gated eighteen-hole idylls, or sizzling boomtown exurbs. Author Rich Benjamin noted that the fastest growing white communities in the 2000s—places like Idaho's Coeur d'Alene, Utah's St. George, and Georgia's Forsyth County—were already overwhelmingly white. He called them "whitopias."

Amid demographic change, the new exodus was now driven by a sense of cultural estrangement. It was a flight *into* whiteness. Freedom was a highway-run away from immigrants, gangbangers, and the urban ruins, toward bigger houses, better schools, open spaces, leisure, and pleasure.

Whitopian developers almost always evoked the mythos of the frontier. But now the imperialist logic of penetration had been replaced by the apocalyptic logic of evacuation. Whitopias marked the end-vectors of tipping-point politics—soon to become Tea Party politics—the culmination of complete civic disengagement. Even a real belief in American exceptionalism seemed exhausted. Heaven on earth was not to be found in the city on a hill after all. The torch of freedom burned on in a shelter—tax-free, guilt-free, carefree—distant from the lost and dying world.

Perhaps it was premature to declare the end of the segregated century.

THE POINT OF COLLAPSE

If the 2000s had meant gentrification for urban communities of color, suburbanites of color began the millennium buoyed by rising affluence. In 2002, President George W. Bush announced his "Blueprint for the American Dream" to "close the minority home-ownership gap." His goal was to create 5.5 million homeowners of color by the end of the decade. He wanted to lead families of color into what he called "the ownership society."

The key to his plan was an expansion in lending. At the center was the subprime loan, in which lenders charged higher interest rates than the Fed prime rate. The loans had been designed for borrowers with lower-than-average credit scores. When they were repackaged with adjustable-rate mortgages (ARMs), subprimes became a potent lure for new borrowers. During the boom of the 2000s, in fact, they would be packaged and sold for many with strong credit scores.

ARM loans started with low teaser interest rates that would increase dramatically above prime as the loan aged. Short-term interest-only or minimum-payment options were also offered to borrowers who wanted to reduce their monthly bills. There's always tomorrow, lenders told them, to refinance, to pay down your principal, to take care of business. But when the time came, monthly bills spiked. If a borrower fell behind, there would be the cascading set of penalty fees. The subprime loan—an extremely high-cost loan; a trap, really—became the prototypical product of the Era of Debt.

Big lenders quickly redesigned their entire mortgage loan businesses around them. Loan officers received bigger bonuses if they steered prime-worthy borrowers to subprimes, because the banks made more money on the interest rate and fees. "[A]s a company, Wells Fargo pushed the subprime loans, because it was their goal to have the subprime division pay for the fixed costs of the whole company," said Elizabeth Jacobson, a former subprime loan officer who turned whistle-blower.[33] In 2003, just 8 percent of all loan originations were subprime. By 2005, 20 percent of loans were. Interest-only and payment-option loans increased tenfold.[34]

Bush's Blueprint allowed predatory lenders to see Blacks, Latinos, and Asian Americans as key growth market segments for subprimes.[35] For a century the housing industry had been built on a foundation of racial inequality, abetted by racial covenants, racial steering, zoning laws, and redlining. Only the covenants had been ruled illegal. Steering, zoning, and redlining had continued apace.[36] But now these old neighborhoods, along with the suburbs and exurbs to which Blacks, Asian Americans, and Latinos were being steered, were potential gold mines for "reverse redlining."

Lenders like Wells Fargo, SunTrust, and Bank of America's mortgage lending subsidiary Countrywide Financial—all of whom would soon be paying out hundreds of millions in civil rights lawsuit settlements to distressed cities and foreclosed homeowners—were particularly aggressive. According to sworn testimonies from former Wells Fargo bank officials, the bank's marketing department sold what some of its white loan officers called "ghetto loans" by hiring new employees of color to seed local Black churches with finder's fees for every loan secured, and to print up culturally correct flyers in every language including "African American."[37]

When Princeton policy analyst Jacob Rugh and sociologist Douglas Massey sifted through the wreckage of the collapse, poring over data from the largest 100 metro areas, they did not find that borrowers of color were significantly less creditworthy than whites. Instead, they wrote, the government had failed to enforce civil rights laws against predatory lending.[38] The result: by 2006, at the peak of the housing market, 54 percent of all Black, 47 percent of all Latino, and only 18 percent of white mortgage holders were under subprime loans.[39]

Flush with campaign contributions from lenders, the Bush administration then went to work at deregulating the banking industry. *New York Times* writers Jo Becker, Sheryl Gay Stolberg, and Stephen Labaton wrote that they "brandished a chain saw over a 9,000-page pile of regulations as they promised to ease burdens on the industry," bringing down the legal firewall between retail banks and investment banks in the process.[40]

Now banks could make money coming and going. The retail side generated subprime loans as fast as they could. The investment side bundled them up into new investment products for premium investors and cashed in a second time.

These products, called mortgage-backed securities, bundled high-risk subprime loans, but were sold to credulous investors as low-risk, high-return. Credit rating agencies certified this rapidly expanding poison pool of products as high-grade. Companies like AIG made an additional killing by selling so-called credit default swaps, worthless guarantees against the toxic mortgage-based securities.[41] In this New Gilded Age, it seemed as if gravity itself could be defied.

Suddenly moral hazard—the strange term invented to describe the moment capitalism broke free from the restraint of ethics, when transactions were no longer bound by risk, and players had a criminal incentive to take the money and run—loomed as a threat to the entire system. But as long as housing prices—steroided by speculative dollars—continued to climb, few sounded alarms.

From the Clinton through the Bush years, home-ownership rates soared. This was great politics, especially for Republicans like Bush and Rove eager to win the hearts of voters of color. By 2006, the administration could claim credit for historic home-ownership rates for Latinos (49.7%), Blacks (48.4%) and Asian Americans (60.8%), and for closing the racial home-ownership gap by 3% for Latinos and 5% for Asian Americans.

"No one wanted to stop that bubble," Bush economic advisor Lawrence B. Lindsey told the *New York Times*. "It would have conflicted with the president's own policies."[42]

But Bush's boom was balanced precariously on two dubious notions: that, without regulation, businesses would avoid moral hazard and manage risk wisely; and that housing prices would never come down. As early as 2005, urban and suburban communities of color in Cleveland, Chicago, Philadelphia, and Atlanta became ground zero for the foreclosure crisis. By the end of 2006 prices began to slip and housing inventories increased. Within the next year, subprime foreclosures doubled.[43] The collapse had begun. Households of color tragically and predictably led the national plunge.

Bush had aimed for 5.5 million new homeowners of color by the end of the decade. When 2010 arrived, the Center for Responsible Lending estimated that no fewer than 735,000 African American households and 1.1 million Latino households had lost or were in imminent danger of losing their homes to foreclosure.[44] What's more, studies showed that the subprime market had been 59 percent refinance or home improvement loans.[45] The foreclosure crisis was taking down long-time homeowners.

Before the Great Recession, the racial wealth gap had been so wide that economists estimated if progress continued at the same rate, by 2042 Latino household net worth would be 25% that of whites, Black net worth just 19%.[46] Afterward those projections looked hopelessly optimistic. Between 2005 and 2009, white household median net worth dropped by 16%. But it dropped by 53% for Blacks, 54% for Asians, and 66% for Latinos. The median Asian household was now worth 69% of a white household, the Latino household 6%, and the Black household just 5%.[47]

Back in the bright summer of 2002, President George W. Bush had brought the media into the modest new home of an African American police officer in Atlanta named Darrin West. The officer had been the beneficiary of Bush's down-payment program, which, along with a subprime loan, brought him to the instant in which cameras flashed and the president shook his hand. By the time McCain was giving his concession speech, the bank had repossessed West's home.[48]

Neighborhoods that President Bush had touted as beacons of his Ownership Society—from North Philadelphia to North Little Rock—were now dotted with "For Sale" signs. The crisis spread from communities of color across the map like a contagion.

The Great Recession was a rupture that might bring a kind of cultural leveling, not only dispersing anxiety like a toxic cloud rising over all, but firing the masses to gather, to occupy, to imagine together. It might also do the opposite.

When President Obama announced a $275 billion mortgage modification plan—a modest proposal dwarfed by the $700 billion bank bailout—the Tea Party was born. In a February 2009 rant on CNBC Rick Santelli delivered from the floor of the Chicago Mercantile Exchange, he expressed fury at the Obama mortgage proposal. Should government "subsidize these losers' mortgages," he asked, or should it "reward people who can *carry* the water instead of *drink* the water?"

Then he pointed to a cheering crowd of traders behind him—all white men—and shouted, "*This* is America!"

THE NEW HOSTILITIES

As the winds of December brought 2009 to a close, the political pollster Cornell Belcher sat for an interview in his Washington, DC, office. He had spent a good part of the past few years polling voters' attitudes on race, often self-funding the research because he had "questions about race that, frankly, none of the campaigns or institutions that I work for would fund."

Belcher was from Norfolk, Virginia, born to a classically Democratic household—the youngest son of a cement finisher and a factory worker, union, middle-class, African American. He had come of age during the high-water mark of desegregation. He recalled his neighborhood and schools being "probably fifty-fifty" Black and white. "It wasn't till late in elementary school where me and my friend Shawn, who was also Black, we were down at the waterfront literally skipping rocks, and someone drove past and called us 'Niggers' that it was like, 'Wow,'" he said. "You never really thought about it."

Forty years before, Kevin Phillips had helped Nixon understand the importance of the Southern white voter to a new Republican coalition. It was now Belcher's job to help his party—first Howard Dean, then Barack Obama—understand the importance of the emerging multiracial electorate to a new Democratic coalition. "I think there's a *moral* imperative to diversity, but quite frankly, in the cold hard world, it's a *strategic* imperative to diversity," he said. "We know this is a country that's increasingly becoming more diverse. Marketers get it. People selling sneakers get it. People selling Coca-Cola get it. But from a political standpoint, we haven't really got it."

In his work, Belcher had come to the same conclusion Phillips once had: voters tended to vote for the candidate they thought best shared their values. Through the 2000s, voters believed Republicans shared their values. But in 2008, Belcher said that Democrats exposed the gap between Republicans' stated values and real actions: "We hammered Republicans on jobs and the economy and on health care, and drove up a huge advantage." What resulted, he said, was "a realignment. Suddenly there's nothing the matter with Kansas because Democrats are winning in Kansas."

But Belcher, whose intellectual hero was W. E. B. DuBois, also realized that the values argument was double-edged. It had allowed the Republicans to reframe the debate for nearly five decades. The most vexing question facing this Democratic realignment, Belcher believed, had to do with the white voter and what Belcher called "racial aversion." How, Belcher wondered, might racial aversion impact candidates of color or campaigns around issues that had been racialized?

Even before Obama had been elected, Belcher had concluded that "a Black man can't become president of the United States of America. A unique, inspiring, intelligent individual who also happens to be Black can be. And to understand the difference is awfully important. It's about individuating you or your candidate." Obama became a viable candidate, Belcher believed, because he had undergone a "Michael Jordanification," "which means I don't have to carry around all the baggage of my racial stereotype."

But how true was that, really? And did it mean that a Black president could not engage in a politics that pointed toward cultural equity, racial justice, and real integration? Belcher paused for a long moment. Finally he said, "I've been looking at numbers. It is a pickle because you always have to walk a very fine line in order not to trigger an appearance of tribalism."

By the summer of 2012, another polarizing election was ahead and Obama appeared on the wrong end of the enthusiasm gap. The president had won majorities in Congress, but he had miscalculated on stimulus proposals and on healthcare reform. If some had hoped that he might address foreclosures, immigration, prison sentencing, and the racial wealth gap, their disillusionment was now complete.

"As a country we're increasingly diverse, we have tremendous white anxiety and we have a racial polarization in our structures, our schools, our housing, in our lives. Where is the leadership?" asked John A. Powell, then director of the Kirwan Institute for the Study of Race and Ethnicity at Ohio State University. "We will have a multiracial future. Is it Arizona? Is it Texas?"

The writer Ta-Nehisi Coates evoked the lost promise of the 2008 election. He wrote, "Obama's primary triumphs in predominantly white states gave rise to rumors of a new peace, one many Blacks were anxious to achieve."[49] Hope had been more than symbolism. It was the possibility of being able to move past what Sheryll Cashin had described as "integration exhaustion." It was being able to ask, with Cashin, "Is segregation an inherently natural consequence of human nature?" And it was being able to answer along with her, "I think not."[50] But now Coates noted that although Obama's election "was alleged to demonstrate a triumph of integration," the reality had fallen very short of the hope.

"The irony of Barack Obama is this," Coates wrote, "he has become the most successful black politician in American history by avoiding the radioactive racial issues of yesteryear, by being 'clean' (as Joe Biden once labeled him)—and yet his indelible blackness irradiates everything he touches," he wrote.

How far had we come since DuBois and Ellison? In the spring of 2011, in order to quell a media furor created by disbelievers of his Honolulu birth, the president had been forced to show the world his long-form birth certificate, as if he, too, were an immigrant stopped by Arizona police. To some he would always be what the historian Ron Takaki had once called "the perpetual foreigner," "a stranger from a different shore."

Here was what Coates called "integration's great limitation—that acceptance depends not just on being twice as good but half as Black. And even then, full acceptance is withheld."[51] Coates pointed to the research of University of Pennsylvania political scientist Daniel Gillon, who had "found that in his first two years as president, Obama talked less about race than any other Democratic president since 1961."[52] The most powerful Black man in the world had been rendered all but colormute. Now the president seemed not just the new face of neoliberalism but of the modern racial state, a tragically constrained figure presiding over a government that limited claims to racial justice and reinforced structures of exclusion.

Americans of all backgrounds, Cornell Belcher argued, shared certain nationally defining values: freedom, fairness, opportunity, equality. "However, this is the problem with equality," he said. "In certain groups, it triggers a conversation that goes like this: '*They're* trying to get equality, which means *I'm* losing something.'"

"You have to be very careful about triggering this fear of 'us versus them,'" he said. "I can't answer [the question], 'How do you address this issue of inequality without having the race part of the discussion?' *That* is what's not easily reconciled now in our politics."

From *Getting It All Together*, published 1972. Courtesy of Morrie Turner.

Dis/Union: The Paradox of the Post-Racial Moment   **289**

April 4th, 1968 by Nikkolas Smith. 2013. Courtesy the artist and Creative Action Network.

CHAPTER 15

WHO WE BE

DEBT, COMMUNITY, AND COLORIZATION

We are caught in an inescapable network of mutuality,
tied in a single garment of destiny.
—Martin Luther King Jr., "Letter from a Birmingham Jail"

Can We Dream Together?
—Dream Defenders slogan

In the March 1957, fifteen months after the start of the Montgomery Bus Boycott, five after the Atlanta airport episode, Martin Luther King Jr. was among those invited to witness Kwame Nkrumah declare Ghana's independence from Great Britain.

King was impressed that Nkrumah had chosen not to wear to the ceremonies fine garments suggestive of new royalty, but instead appeared in his old prison cap and coat. After Nkrumah's speech, King heard the children and elderly in the crowd crying, "Freedom! Freedom!" It reminded him of a spiritual he loved: "Free at last! Free at last! Great Thank God almighty, I'm free at last!"

The next day he saw Nkrumah dancing with the Queen of England's representative, the Duchess of Kent. "Isn't this something?" King remarked to a friend. "Here is the once-serf, once-slave, now dancing with the lord on an equal plane." To him, the scene contained a lesson on nonviolence.

"The aftermath of nonviolence is the creation of beloved community. The aftermath of nonviolence is redemption. The aftermath of nonviolence is reconciliation," he continued. "The aftermath of violence, however, are emptiness and bitterness."[1] True democracy was not just about representation and transformation, it was about forging diverse communities rooted in equality and mutuality. Every democracy needed to habitually ask its subjects anew: What do we owe to each other?

When King gave his "I Have a Dream" speech in 1963, he argued, "[W]e've come to our nation's capital to cash a check." In the Constitution and the Declaration of Independence, America had created "a promissory note ... that all men, yes, Black men as well as white men, would be guaranteed the 'unalienable Rights' of 'Life, Liberty, and the Pursuit of Happiness.'"[2] The nation itself was, the intellectual David Graeber wrote, "a moral debtor ... freedom [was] something literally owed to the nation."[3]

In *Debt: The First 5,000 Years,* published during the germinating summer between the appearance of the *indignados* in Madrid's public square and the Occupiers on Wall Street, Graeber offered a rethinking of the idea of indebtedness. King's call for America to redeem its promise exemplified the thrust of anticolonial, anti-imperialist, and identity liberation movements to address what Graeber called "the crisis of inclusion."

But by the late 1970s, a new era had begun. As wages began to stagnate dramatically in relation to productivity, popular movements shifted from claiming the rights of national citizenship to claiming access to capitalism. Neoliberalism meant the financialization of everything, including notions of credit and debt, resistance and freedom.

If one could only ask the question of what we owed each other in the context of endless war or unbridled capitalism, what would be the answer? We might owe each other protection against enemies, real or conjured. We might owe each other lower tax bills. We might owe some the reduction of restraints on doing business. But this would leave us a much narrower notion of freedom than the one King had proposed.

As it turned out, for much of the half-century following King's speech, Americans chose to answer the question of what we owed each other in those narrower terms. Addressing national debt pertained less to the discharging of a social obligation, such as reducing inequality, but to the paying down of an economic obligation caused by government spending. In 1980 President Reagan ran on the platform of addressing the latter, especially when that spending was going to social safety-net programs. During the twelve years he and President George H. W. Bush led the country, the federal deficit increased at the fastest rate in history, through a combination of tax cuts and huge increases in military spending.

To be sure, the national debt was not at all like personal debt. The U.S. government was never in danger of foreclosure. Indeed the postwar debt had played a central role in the long boom, and expanding tax revenues had rendered national debt irrelevant as an economic and political problem. Yet extremist free market ideology prevailed.

Graeber wrote,

> Financial imperatives constantly try to reduce us all, despite ourselves, to the equivalent of pillagers, eyeing the world simply for what can be turned into money—and then tell us that it's only those who are willing to see the world as pillagers who deserve access to the resources required to pursue anything in life *other* than money. It introduces moral perversions on almost every level.[3]

Capitalism aspired not only to be the law, but morality, too. Freedom meant being free even from responsibility or empathy. All values would bow before economic value. Redemption would be redefined. Consumption would set the terms of the social. Creditors ruled everything around us. Debtors—a category that included almost everyone— were parasites. Capital and the state debased fundamental human relations.

Politics could be reduced to a depersonalized transaction concerned less with forging equality but finding equivalence, the right price. We might come together only to the tasks of increasing the military budget, reducing the national debt, and cutting taxes, the better to be able to spend time and money on ourselves. But beyond these moments of exchange, we would owe each other nothing. Graeber wrote, "[I]t's sociality itself that's treated as abusive, criminal, demonic."[5]

King's "I Have a Dream" speech had been turned inside out. Graeber wrote, "[W]hereas the first postwar age was about collective claims on the nation's debt to its humblest citizens, the need for those who have made false promises to redeem themselves, now those same humble citizens are taught to think of themselves as sinners, seeking some kind of purely individual redemption to have the right to any sort of moral relations with other human beings at all."[6]

Financial indebtedness narrowed notions of citizenship. It fostered cynicism and isolation. Graeber wrote, "In fact, it could be well said that the last thirty years have seen the construction of a vast bureaucratic apparatus for the creation and maintenance of hopelessness, a machine designed, first and foremost, to destroy any sense of possible alternative futures."[7]

Perhaps we really had entered what Rich Nichols, the manager/philosopher of the hip-hop band the Roots, had called the "post-hope era." In the wake of the bank and corporate bailouts and the Tea Party revolt against even minimal foreclosure relief, hopelessness had even swallowed the colorized image of Obama, which had so inspired the young, dispossessed, and marginalized. Judith Halberstam seemed to capture the moment in a book called *The Queer Art of Failure*, which began, "We are all used to having our dreams crushed, our hopes smashed, our illusions shattered, but what comes after hope?"

In this context, Graeber ventured that the global economic collapse might mark the beginning of a new era of popular movements. The problem would be one of imagination:

> [T]here seems to have been a profound contradiction between the political imperative of establishing capitalism as the only possible way to manage anything, and capitalism's own unacknowledged need to limit its future horizons, lest speculation, predictably, go haywire. Once it did, and the whole machine imploded, we were left in the strange situation of not being able to even imagine any other way that things might be arranged.[9]

A bitter old radical joke, attributed to Jameson and refined by Žižek, had begun to recirculate in certain circles—that it was easier to imagine the end of the world than to imagine the end of capitalism. Indeed it was easier to imagine the end of the world than the end of racism, the possibility of people learning to get along. Hollywood's dream machine had already begun milking the end-of-days genre, characterized by the $200 million film *2012*. In such dreams things could only end badly.

A FLASH OF INSIGHT

For over two decades, a collective of creative folks in Vancouver and Berkeley, led by an Estonian immigrant to Canada named Kalle Lasn and a biracial postgrad named Micah White, had been plugging away in a far corner of the revolution. Along with their crew of culture jammers, they had been distilling subversive ideas about consumerism, prisons, environmental collapse, global financial crisis, and global insurrection. Their main provocation was a bimonthly magazine called *Adbusters*, featuring these ideas in short essays and pithy pull quotes alongside well-designed images and witty fake ads.

We lived in the era of the image. Culture was the battlefield. In his manifesto, White wrote:

> We live in a world where a constellation of cognitive illusions—that infinite growth can be sustained on a finite planet, that consumerism can make us happy, that corporations are persons—are dragging us into an ecological apocalypse. These cognitive illusions won't disappear because they've been proven false—they must be overcome at a deeper level. We need something other than rationality, statistics, scientific thought ... we need

something more, even, than what has passed for activism thus far.
We must spark an epiphany, a worldwide flash of insight that renders our
blind spots visible once and for all.[10]

Both Lasn and White seemed to think of change in almost mystical ways. Lasn once said that his experience as a young war refugee had taught him, "World wars, revolutions— from time to time, big things actually happen. When the moment is right, all it takes is a spark."[11]

By the summer of 2011, the wars, the recession, and the breathtaking uprisings of the Arab Spring in Tunisia, Egypt, Libya, Yemen, and Syria; the Spanish *indignados*; the unionists in Madison, Wisconsin; the *aganaktismenoi* in Athens, Greece; and the students in California and Chile had made the Adbusters collective restless. In a July blog post, they addressed their network of "90,000 redeemers, rebels and radicals," asking them, "Are you ready for a Tahrir moment?"

They cited Spanish political scientist Raimundo Viejo, speaking about the large *acampada* that had taken over Madrid, Barcelona, and dozens of other Spanish cities that June:

> The antiglobalization movement was the first step on the road. Back then
> our model was to attack the system like a pack of wolves. There was an
> alpha male, a wolf who led the pack, and those who followed behind. Now
> the model has evolved. Today we are one big swarm of people.[12]

In their magazine they included a poster of a ballerina delicately balanced en pointe on Wall Street's bellicose bronze *Charging Bull* sculpture, while in the background masked protestors surged through a tear-gas fog. The poster had just four lines:

WHAT IS OUR ONE DEMAND?
#OCCUPYWALLSTREET
SEPTEMBER 17TH.
BRING TENT.

Within days, the meme had spread across the net and excited activists and artists. On September 17, after months of meetings, more than a thousand protestors showed up at Bowling Green Park to find that New York police had already barricaded the *Charging Bull* sculpture. Instead they moved up the street to their backup target, an open expanse of concrete, planters, and polished stone tables called Zuccotti Park. It was a public space owned by Brookfield Properties and therefore, the organizers knew, not subject to curfew restrictions. Zuccotti's symbolism seemed even more conceptually rich—originally the park had been named Liberty Plaza, but was renamed for the corporation's chair.

That night their encampment became the occupation seen around the world. Within a month an encampment of hundreds had multiplied into hundreds of encampments dotting the globe. At the movement's peak the sun would never set on Occupiers.

A grand revelation had preceded Occupy. After the 2008 market collapse, governments had facilitated the bailout or repudiation of billions in bank and corporate debt while allowing the debt of common people to be pursued with an almost moralistic fervor by many of those same banks and corporations. Now, as the new slogan went, *here came everybody*. Suddenly everywhere were rabbles of student debtors; invisible artists; foreclosed homeowners; collegiate freethinkers; everyday laborers of the material and immaterial; the unemployed and the underemployed; the displaced and the homeless; the silenced of every flag, religion, and identity.

The Occupy movement did not begin from the old protest politics. It began as a cultural move, a call to the imagination. It was not about locating hope in a symbol but in each other, a notion embodied in a simple slogan designed by David Graeber and others: "We Are the 99 Percent." It was not a top-down, centralized process. It was about coming together horizontally to retake space, reestablish the commons, discuss the undiscussed, and hammer out a new understanding of community.

By design Occupy was not led by a vanguard, but by direct democracy. Decisions were made in—some complained, frustrating and interminable—General Assembly meetings, with extensive protocols to allow for minority voices and to build consensus. As another popular slogan went, "This Is a Process Not a Protest." Listening and commitment were the minimum of what we owed each other.

But identity and race became one of the first issues Occupy Wall Streeters had to address. They had begun with a language of denial. Their September 17 declaration began:

Representing ourselves, we bring this call for revolution.

We want freedom for all, without regards for identity, because we are all people, and because no other reason should be needed.[13]

Debate over these lines immediately took up heated discussions in the General Assembly. First, what about that word itself: "occupation"? In an influential blog post called "An Open Letter to the Occupy Wall Street Activists," Nishnaabe teacher JohnPaul Montano gently raised the historic meaning of occupation for indigenous Americans. "I believe your hearts are in the right place," he wrote. "It just seems to me that you're unknowingly doing the same thing to us that all the colonizers before you have done: you want to do stuff on our land without asking our permission."[14]

Why, some ask, why wasn't the Occupy movement linking with working-class movements, such as those led by immigrants in nearby Chinatown, or the anti-foreclosure movements in largely Black and Latino urban neighborhoods? If we were building a community, some argued, we owed it to each other to recognize each other's struggles.

We also owed it to each other to see each other in their fullness. Many of those who had joined the encampments had come from people of color, women's, and GLBTQIA movements. If this was a people's uprising, why should people be denied the right to name themselves, to present themselves as they wished to be seen?

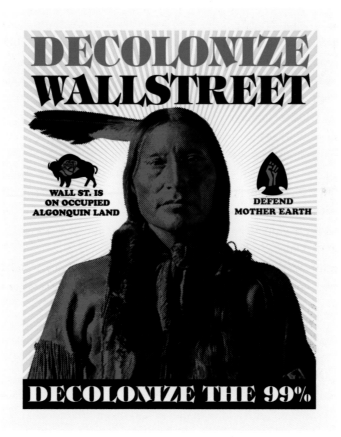

Decolonize Wall Street by Ernesto Yerena, Ricardo Lopez, and Orlando Arenas. 2011.

By the evening of September 29, the General Assembly had unanimously approved a "Declaration of the Occupation of New York City" brought on behalf of "one people, united," and noting the fact of "inequality and discrimination in the workplace based on age, the color of one's skin, sex, gender identity, and sexual orientation." Printmakers

Ernesto Yerena and the Dignidad Rebelde collective made and circulated posters that read, "Decolonize Wall Street," which soon appeared around the country. A Tumblr blog called We Are the 99 Percent revealed a rainbow of thousands articulating the crisis of debt and inequality through their stories of anxiety, sorrow, shame, and rage.

Stories were the raw material from which empathy, community, and democracy were molded. They were gifts that bound the giver and receiver in a virtuous cycle of values. The intellectual Ronald Takaki had once said, "In the telling and retelling of our stories we create a community of memory."[15] For Takaki each story was a musical note that found harmony with others, joining together to create what Lincoln called in his first Inaugural Address "mystic chords of memory" in "the chorus of the Union." But of course these new sounds, sights, and stories also easily traversed national borders, sparking explosions around the world. Occupy became something of a global image and story machine, pushing toward a new imagination.

For the second time in three years, a creative explosion had accompanied a social uprising, as artists, designers, and printmakers organized themselves into collectives and working groups. Theater and carnival-like parties filled the streets. Pop-up printmaking shops and open-source design and art Web sites proliferated.

As the winter approached, Occupy's critics, including many sympathizers, became impatient with the movement's apparent disinterest in forging a "list of demands." Increasingly the critics' language—"Just tell us what you want!"—sounded like that of an abusive relationship. Occupiers suspected that what lurked behind the demand for demands was dismissal or reversion. When asked, "What do you want?" many began answering, "Everything."

The claim sounded audacious as long as the physical encampments hummed along, but naive when, as the cold drew in, impatient local governments began routing them and dispersing the gathered into the windy night. In the end Occupy certainly was better at process than protest, symbolism than strategy. It was best at stirring the busy cacophony of democracy, the noise of waking collective dreamtime.

The most poignant new ritual was the mic check—an artful solution to restrictions on amplified sound. When speakers needed to speak, they shouted their words in brief bursts to the circle around them, who then would repeat the words so that the next ring could hear them, and on until all the gathered had heard. The process favored elegant, accessible thinking. It allowed for immediate feedback. It released the generative power of a hip-hop cipher's call-and-response. The mic check was a wave of ideas rippling outward in all directions, an echo heard around the world.

When Angela Davis stood for her mic check in Zuccotti Park in October, she said:

> We challenge language. We transform language. We remain aware of all the resonances of the language we use....

We must be aware when we say "Occupy Wall Street" that this country was founded on the genocidal occupation of indigenous lands. We must be aware when we say "Occupy Wall Street" or "Occupy Washington Square" that occupations in other countries are violent and brutal....

At the same time transform the meaning of "occupation." We turn "occupation" into something that is beautiful, something that brings community together. Something that calls for love and happiness and hope.[16]

NO COUNTRY FOR THE WEAK

As the 2012 election neared, an enshrouding sense of dread was descending. The Occupy encampments were gone. The birther controversy would not die. As billions in corporate money poured into shadowy super PACs the nation girded for what Mike Davis would call "the most racially polarized presidential election in American history."[17]

Obama's Republican opponent, Mitt Romney, had been born into wealth and political power. He vowed to undo Wall Street reform. He would privatize FEMA disaster services because government debt needed to be cut. He declared himself the mortal enemy of bad debtors. In the America of Romney's speeches, families were rewarded for their hard work, in which they saved and got ahead, in which they could in old age look proudly back on their work and say, "We built that."

But Romney was not a builder. He had grown his family fortune by playing shell games with debt. At his private equity investment firm, Bain Capital, Romney borrowed heavily to acquire existing companies, journalist Matt Taibbi wrote, "then [extracted] million-dollar fees from those same companies, in exchange for the generous service of telling them who needs to be fired in order to finance the debt payments he saddled them with in the first place."[18]

He was a perfectly cynical candidate for the age of precarity. Underneath his mask of imperialist nostalgia was a culture warrior's mindset. He saw the nation as divided between winners like himself and losers, whom he termed "the 47 percent," the half of Americans "who are dependent upon government, who believe that they are victims, who believe the government has a responsibility to care for them, who believe that they are entitled to health care, to food, to housing, to you-name-it."[19]

In Romney's America, the winners had discarded any pretense of honor. They owed the losers nothing. His answer to the immigration issue was, he said, "self-deportation, which is: people decide they can do better by going home because they can't find work here because they don't have legal documentation to allow them to work here."

Polls showed Republican enthusiasm, fueled by Tea Party reaction, ran much higher than Democratic.[20] But as strategists stared at the changing map, they fretted about the math. In 1963, two months after the March on Washington, New York Republican Jacob Javits had tried to stop the Southern strategy before it started. He passionately pleaded with his party to stop defending segregation. "I am not for possible short-term gain at the risk of extinction," he said. "I am, in short, for basing Republican strategy on the South's future, not its past."[21] Javits was wrong in one sense—that "short-term gain" had lasted a half-century. But perhaps his future had finally arrived. After nearly a half century, the politics of the Southern strategy no longer added up. Republicans could only succeed through subtraction.

So not long after the 2010 elections swept in a new class of Tea Party freshman and state-level conservatives, Republicans loudly began challenging "voter fraud," launching what the Brennan Center for Justice called "the biggest threat to voting rights in decades."[22] Their map of attack included the battleground states of Wisconsin, Pennsylvania, Ohio, and Virginia, and six of the seven states in the old Southern strategy (now cult-gen gap) arc from South Carolina to Texas. Voter fraud was like beheaded bodies in the Arizona desert—a cognitive illusion. Demographic change was real.

Republicans quickly passed twenty-five voter suppression laws and two executive actions in nineteen states, including limitations on early and absentee voting, new restrictions on voter registration drives, and polling-day photo I.D. and proof-of-citizenship requirements. The Brennan Center noted that the laws could have disenfranchised five million voters. In fourteen states, the courts recognized the partisan overreach, and reversed or defanged the new laws.

The summer would bring more party discontent. During the 2012 Republican convention, some attendees pelted a Black CNN camerawoman with peanuts, shouting, "This is how we feed animals." Not long afterward SB 1070 author Russell Pearce went down to double-digit defeat in an Arizona primary. South Carolina congressman Lindsey Graham told the *Washington Post*, "We're not generating enough angry white guys to stay in business for the long term."[23]

The gap between the party's image of itself and its reality pushed the spectacle of the Republican convention to a strange climax. On a night of pomp and platitudes during which Romney was to accept the nomination—he would vow to "restore" Americans to an uncomplicated Reaganite past in which they might revert to their natural state, "optimistic and positive and confident in the future"—he would be derailed by what Jon Stewart called "a twelve-minute, improvised, avant-garde performance of 'One Angry Man'" staged by Clint Eastwood.

In it, Eastwood spoke to an empty chair he imagined inhabited by President Obama, accusing him of, among other things, starting the war in Afghanistan. Ralph Ellison would not have missed the symbolism—the ghost in the chair, a screen for their fears. "I could never wrap my head around why the world and the president that Republicans describe bears so little resemblance to the world and the president that I experience," Jon Stewart mused. "And now I know why. There is a President Obama that only Republicans can see. [24]

On election night in Costa Mesa, California, at the Westin South Coast Plaza, the state's Republican Party had gathered to celebrate the Romney landslide that nearly all of the right-wing media had predicted. Party faithful—the women in red suits, the men in blue with red ties, the odd person dressed as Paul Revere—sat before a large flat screen broadcasting Fox News. A large flag hung on a back wall, and a small forest of flag stands were bunched forlornly in a corner.

Just fifteen minutes after the polls closed across the Golden State, Fox News, following every major network, declared Obama the winner. The crowd stared, stunned, as Karl Rove—who had leveraged and spent $390 million of conservative super PAC money attacking Obama and won exactly zero of his races—began arguing with newsroom staff that the election was not over. "That's awkward!" laughed anchor Megyn Kelly.

A small tide of panic swept through the hotel ballroom. One legislative aide told an *Orange County Register* reporter, "These next four years are going to be about Obama's revenge. We're going to see the elimination of our freedom. It's going to be like communist Vietnam."[25] On the small stage a local rock band launched into a loud, epic-length version of the Rolling Stones's "You Can't Always Get What You Want." The ballroom began emptying very quickly.

Obama's victory was less decisive than it had been in 2008, and the mood this time was decidedly sober. President Obama had been reelected with 51 percent of the popular vote and 332 electoral votes. Mitt Romney won a poetic 47 percent. Over 7 in 10 Latinos and Asians, and 3 of 4 gays, lesbians, and bisexuals voted for Obama. Romney won 6 in 10 whites, but 3 in 10 voters were now nonwhite.

Seven months later, the conservative-led Supreme Court all but invoked the demographic shifts underpinning Obama's victory when they declared portions of the Voting Rights Act unconstitutional. Chief Justice John Roberts wrote, "Things have changed dramatically."

In her dissent, Justice Ruth Bader Ginsburg scoffed at the majority's logic. They had relied, she wrote, "on increases in voter registration and turnout as if that were the whole story. One would expect more from an opinion striking at the heart of the Nation's signal piece of civil-rights legislation." Voiding the antidiscrimination preclearance portion of the act, she added, was "like throwing away your umbrella in a rainstorm because you are not getting wet."

Within hours of the decision, the storms moved in again. The Republican-led legislature in Texas approved a voter ID law and redistricting maps that feds had blocked for discriminating against Black and Latino voters. In six more states—including Arizona, South Dakota, and four Southern states—politicians began preparing to do the same.

The campaign had been brutal, the nation more divided, and more conflict lay ahead.

THE QUALITY OF EMPATHY

In 2006, then-senator Obama was in high demand as a speaker, and before audiences of young people at conferences and university commencements he presented himself in a way that his later successes would no longer allow—as a pure idealist. He seemed to have inherited from Martin Luther King Jr., the multiculturalists, and even the post-multiculturalists an expansive faith in American democracy.

At Xavier University in New Orleans almost exactly a year after Hurricane Katrina, Senator Obama admitted to graduates that he might have given a speech on challenges, on courage, or on community—but that nothing he could say would be better than what the students and residents had taught him about those topics over the previous year. So instead he asked them to think about their future and how it related to what they had learned in the previous year.

"After graduating from a great school like Xavier, you'll pretty much be able to punch your own ticket," he said. "You can live in neighborhoods with people who are exactly like yourself, and send your kids to the same schools, and narrow your concerns to what's going on in your own little circle.

"Pundits and politicians will affirm that the problems of the nation and the world are," he said, "someone else's fault and someone else's problem to fix. They'll tell you that the Americans who sleep in the streets and beg for food got there because they're all lazy or weak of spirit. That the immigrants who risk their lives to cross a desert have nothing to contribute to this country and no desire to embrace our ideals. That the inner-city children who are trapped in dilapidated schools can't learn and won't learn and so we should just give up on them entirely."

"And when you hear all this, the easiest thing in the world will be to do nothing at all."

But he challenged them to take a more difficult path, "to leave here and not just pursue your own individual dreams, but to help perfect our collective dream as a nation."

"There's a lot of talk in this country about the federal deficit," he said. "But I think we should talk more about our empathy deficit—the ability to put ourselves in someone else's shoes; to see the world through the eyes of those who are different from us." He concluded:

> I ask you to take this second path—this harder path—not because you have
> an obligation to those who are less fortunate, although you do have that
> obligation. Not because you have a debt to all of those who helped you get
> to where you are, although you do have that debt.

I ask you to take it because you have an obligation to yourself. Because our individual salvation depends on our collective salvation.[26]

Obama had drawn on King's idea of the nation as "an inescapable network of mutuality." Katrina reminded us that our destiny depended upon how we treated each other. If we could dissolve our illusions, overcome our blindnesses, and end our silences with real talk, we might still hope to find that beloved community.

INTO THE DARKNESS

But then there were these pictures.

There was the picture of George Zimmerman in his red jacket, his nose bloodied. And there was another, taken of the back of his shaven head, two abrasions with blood fanning down in drips.

There was the picture of Trayvon Martin, covered by a yellow bag, lying to the right of a wet sidewalk, a number 6 placed next to his inert body, just one high-top Nike poking out into the dark night.

And finally, most shockingly, there was the picture of Trayvon Martin before the bag had been placed over him. He lay on the same grass on which he had played pickup football games with the kids in the gated community of the Retreat at Twin Lakes.

His body, which had been found facedown, had been turned over. His arms were askew. One of his legs was crossed under the other, a small ankle peeking out of skinny, cuffed khakis. His gray hoodie, decorated with a memorial button of a friend, had a hole to the left of the button, where he had been shot through the heart. His eyes were half-shut, his mouth locked in its last gasp.

In the end, when a verdict came down, the easiest questions to answer were how George Zimmerman saw Trayvon Martin and how the law failed to see Trayvon Martin.

Behind the gates of the Retreat at Twin Lakes, on a rainy Sunday evening in late February, just three weeks before his eighteenth birthday, Trayvon Martin had come from Miami to visit the home of his father Tracy's fiancée, Brandy Green. The adults were out having dinner. Martin and Green's son were settling in to watch the game. But first Martin decided to make a solo snack run to the nearby 7-Eleven. As he returned, he looked up the number of an old friend he had known since second grade, a Haitian American girl named Rachel Jeantel. The moon was waxing crescent. The rain and wind picked up. He put up his hood to protect himself from the cold.

He was walking back past the townhouse community's gated entrance—slowly limbering home in his long six-foot-plus, 150-pound frame, his earbuds in and $22, a pack of

Skittles, and an AriZona watermelon-flavored drink in his pockets—when George Zimmerman, the community's neighborhood watch leader, spotted him. Zimmerman had been driving toward the entrance in his truck, getting ready to leave on an errand, but now he stopped to call 911.

Race begins in the gap between appearance and the perception of difference.

"Hey we've had some break-ins in my neighborhood, and there's a real suspicious guy," Zimmerman told the dispatcher in a low whisper. "This guy looks like he's up to no good, or he's on drugs or something. It's raining and he's just walking around, looking about."

The young Black boys in the neighborhood were already familiar with Zimmerman. "He would circle the block and circle it; it was weird," a seventeen-year-old told Frances Robles of the Miami Herald. "If he had spotted me, he'd probably asked me if I lived here. He was known for being really strict."[27] Now Zimmerman, a Kel-Tec PF9 9 mm handgun holstered and concealed at his waist, decided to tail Martin in his truck.

The Retreat at Twin Lakes was located on the far western end of the Florida suburb of Sanford, just a half hour north from Orlando, where the 2012 NBA All-Star Game had just started. In the mid-1940s a mob had come to the mayor, demanding that he run a young Black baseball player named Jackie Robinson out of town. As late as 1982, students at the local high school elected two homecoming queens—one white, one Black.[28] By the 2000s, Sanford was over 40 percent nonwhite.

The gated community had opened in 2006 at the height of the market with 263 modest townhome condos that included granite countertops, hardwood floors, and walk-in closets. "With its modern Florida architecture," a spokesmodel told buyers in a promotional video, "this secluded, gated community is like living in a resort."[29] But the Great Recession had hit the area hard and left many mortgages underwater and units foreclosed. Buyers scooped up units on short sales.

For Frank Taaffe—Zimmerman's neighbor, a former block captain, and a white-power activist who would become one of Zimmerman's biggest media defenders—that was the beginning of the end. The demographics of the gated community shifted, tipping past half nonwhite. He complained to the *Miami Herald*'s Robles that the homes were being rented to "low-lifes and gangsters."[30]

The Zimmermans, Tracy Martin, and Brandy Green were middle-class strivers and renters. Tracy Martin was a truck driver. Green worked as a juvenile detention officer. Zimmerman had been a mortgage broker in the early 2000s. But after the market tanked, he spun through odd jobs before finally landing a job at Digital Risk, a "mortgage-risk firm." His job was to comb through borrowers' data to ferret out potential loan fraud, helping big banks file claims against debtors.

Zimmerman aspired to become a cop. He studied criminal justice. After moving in to the Retreat at Twin Lakes in 2009, he became a frequent 911 caller. Lane DeGregory of the *Tampa Bay Times* wrote, "The transcripts of Zimmerman's 911 calls during the more than 2 years he lived on Retreat View Circle fill 28 pages."[31]

In September 2011, after a series of burglaries, including one in which a white mother hid in a bedroom with her infant as two African American men robbed their home, Zimmerman organized a Neighborhood Watch meeting and was voted the captain. He knocked on doors and advised his neighbors to buy guns. Around that time Zimmerman's 911 calls, DeGregory wrote, "seemed to shift, zeroing in on Black males."[32]

Zimmerman's Black neighbors began changing their routines. Ibrahim Rashada stopped his casual walks around the community. "I fit the stereotype he emailed around," he told the *Miami Herald*'s Robles. "Listen, you even hear me say it: 'A Black guy did this. A Black guy did that.' So I said, 'Let me sit in the house. I don't want anyone chasing me.'"[33] Two weeks before the killing, the Retreat at Twin Lakes's Twitter feed was updated: "Our Neighborhood Watch leads to four arrests in burglaries in the RTL. Great job!"

Much of what we know of the murder comes from phone calls—in succession, Zimmerman's 911 call, Martin's call to his elementary school friend Rachel Jeantel, resident Jenna Lauer's 911 call, and then a sudden flurry of 911 calls from other residents.

Zimmerman's call begins at 7:09 p.m. Zimmerman tells the dispatcher, "He's got his hand in his waistband." Then, "Something's wrong with him. Yup, he's coming to check me out, he's got something in his hands. I don't know what his deal is."

As Martin nears the truck, he notices Zimmerman staring at him and looks back at him. For a moment they lock eyes. Zimmerman says, "These assholes, they always get away." Then, "Shit, he's running."

The car doorbell rings. Zimmerman is leaving his truck to follow Martin on foot. Then, three lines around which destiny turns.

The dispatcher asks, "Are you following him?"

"Yeah."

"OK we don't need you to do that."

In his call to Jeantel, Martin tells her that a "creepy ass cracka" is watching him. They try to talk about the All-Star Game. "The nigga is following me now," he says to her. She says, "Run!" And he does. She hears a whoosh of wind and loses his call. When she calls back, he tells her, "The nigga still behind me." She listens, and hears this:

Martin: "Why are you following me for?"
Zimmerman: "What are you doing around here?"
A thump, and then what Jeantel will later describe as "wet grass sounds."
Martin: "Get off, get off." Silence.

Jenna Lauer makes her 911 call. As she speaks, a voice can be heard in the background screaming something. Then, "Help!" A gunshot. Silence.

At this point the calls multiply. There are six more of them. The voices are scared, shocked, fearful, hysterical. All the conversations are private, individuated, separated, vectoring past each other into the wintry night.

Six minutes after Zimmerman's call, Trayvon Martin is dead. The police arrive at 7:17, handcuff and detain Zimmerman for questioning, but release him without charging him. Trayvon Martin's body is sent to the morgue as a John Doe.

Racial injustice is fed by the denial of difference.

For over six weeks, George Zimmerman was not charged in the killing. Sanford PD had just come through two separate brutality scandals—in two separate cases, sons of police officers were left uncharged in a beating of a homeless man and a killing of a Black teen. Yet Sanford police chief Bill Lee, brought in to restore confidence after those scandals, refused to file charges against Zimmerman, first citing a lack of probable cause and then arguing that the department needed to complete its "color blind" investigation.[34]

The murder of Trayvon Martin went largely unremarked, a back-page police blotter item, until lawyers Benjamin Crump and Natalie Jackson took on the case, and communications expert Ryan Julison began telling the story to the media. Nine days after the shooting the Reuters wire service picked up the story.[35] Quickly it went viral.

If Fairey's Obama HOPE image had been the image of rising idealism, four years later two images of Trayvon Martin—a small black-and-white of him in a hoodie peering upward, and another of him in a red Hollister shirt smiling like a schoolboy—would become the images of brittle precarity. Into these low-res images generations would pour all of their frustration over racial profiling, the sadness and rage over all those who had been impacted by the politics of fear, and the thousands of lives ended too soon.

In a month, a million people had signed an online petition authored by Trayvon's father Tracy Martin and his mother Sybrina Fulton to ask state attorney Angela Corey to prosecute George Zimmerman. Million Hoodie Marches popped up all across the country. On March 22, the case hit an inflection point. That morning Geraldo Rivera went on Fox to declare, "I think the hoodie is as responsible for Trayvon Martin's death as George Zimmerman was."[36]

In response, Dwyane Wade posted on Twitter and Facebook a photo of himself wearing a hoodie. By midday, LeBron James had tweeted a picture of himself and his Miami Heat teammates gathered in hoodies, their heads downcast and covered, their hands in their pockets.[37] His tweet read: "#WeAreTrayvonMartin #Hoodies #Stereotyped #WeWantJustice." By the afternoon, President Obama had ended a press conference on his World Bank appointee by addressing the case, the first time that he had openly stepped into a high-profile race incident since his remarks early in his first term on the detaining of Professor Henry Louis Gates Jr. had left him battered and reeling.

"When I think about this boy I think about my own kids," he said. "I think all of us have to do some soul-searching to figure out how something like this happened. That means that we examine the laws and the context for what happened as well as the specifics of the incident."

He added, "If I had a son, he would look like Trayvon."

From around the country, protestors marched to the Sanford Public Safety Complex—a gleaming new $16 million building for the police and fire department dropped right into the center of Sanford's historic Black community—and shut it down. The Department of Justice, FBI, and Florida Department of Law Enforcement soon launched their own investigations. Finally, Governor Rick Scott ordered the case transferred from Sanford PD to Corey for review. On April 11, she charged Zimmerman with second-degree murder.

By then, Zimmerman had long since bolted town, gone into hiding, quit his lawyers, and begun raising hundreds of thousands of dollars for "his living expenses and legal defense" through a Web site emblazoned with American flags, quotes from Edmund Burke and Thomas Paine, and a photo of Ohio State University's Hale Black Cultural Center, which had been vandalized with the words "Long Live Zimmerman."[38]

An illegal leak of Trayvon Martin's protected school records disclosed that Martin had been suspended for tagging "WTF" on a locker, another time for possession of a pipe and a Baggie with marijuana residue, and a third time for tardiness and truancy. Once, when school officers searched his backpack, they found pieces of jewelry and a screwdriver, and sent these items to the Miami-Dade police for investigation. But the police never found any evidence that the jewelry had been stolen. Martin's parents were certain that the leak was meant to show that their child fit a kind of a profile—a criminal, a junkie, a lowlife. His mother, Sybrina Fulton, said, "They killed my son, and now they are trying to kill his reputation."[39]

None of these facts—the institutional facts of a teen's life ended unmercifully soon—were pertinent to how the conflict had begun that rainy night in February, when Zimmerman knew nothing of Martin but what he saw before him. Corey and the prosecution team needed to decide what Zimmerman's initial gaze meant. In their affidavit, they chose to argue that Zimmerman had profiled, but not *racially* profiled Martin.

Perhaps they were worried that they would burden their case. Perhaps they were sensitive to the appearance of bowing to protesters. Whatever the case, when Corey announced the charges, she told the press, "We only know one category as prosecutors, and that's a V. It's not a B, it's not a W, it's not a H. It's a V, for 'victim.'"[40] Colorblindness and colormuteness had framed the Sanford Police Department's decision not to charge Zimmerman, and they would also frame the prosecution's case.

When the trial commenced in June 2013, defense attorney Mark O'Mara asked Judge Debra Nelson to bar the prosecution from using the word "profiling," arguing that the term was potentially explosive and that race was not at issue. Prosecutor John Guy responded, "That is not a racially charged term unless it's made so, and we don't intend to make it racially charged."

He added, "There are a number of avenues someone can be profiled in any one way or combination. We don't intend to say he was solely profiled because of race."

O'Mara responded that profiling and racial profiling went together "like peanut butter and jelly."[41]

Judge Nelson gave the defense a victory by accepting the prosecution's argument. She barred the prosecution from telling the jury that Zimmerman had racially profiled Martin. The prosecution was allowed, as they had put it in their affidavit, to use the word "profiling." But they were uninterested in exploring even this theory. Although tapes of Zimmerman's 911 calls regarding suspicious persons—all of whom were Black males— were at their disposal, the prosecution would never use them.

But if the prosecution would pretend not to see race, the defense had no such qualms. They dropped the jury inside the moment of conflict—into the darkness, stripped of context, thin of facts. In the darkness the defense would ensure that the jurors could not see Trayvon Martin at all. The defense would get the jury to see only Trayvon Martin's surroundings, themselves, figments of their imagination.

They introduced the jury to the woman whose home had been burglarized—a young, blond, self-described "stay-at-home mom" named Olivia Bertalan. She gave a horrifying account of locking herself in her infant son's upstairs bedroom, rusty scissors in one hand and her baby pressed close in the other, as two young African-American men broke into her home downstairs and stole a camera and a laptop. She described Zimmerman to reporters as a kind and concerned neighbor, bringing over a new lock for her back door. She later learned that one of the robbers lived at the Retreat at Twin Lakes.

The prosecution never objected, never asked what Bertalan's story had to do with Trayvon Martin. The teenager merely happened to share the burglars' gender, youth, and race, and for that weekend, he was resting in the same gated community where both the victim and the suspect lived. But the defense understood that the jury of six women—five of whom were white—could connect the dots themselves.

Olivia Bertalan was, *The Nation*'s Mychal Denzel Smith wrote, "the 'perfect victim,' which Trayvon could never be: a white woman living in fear of Black criminals."[42] The defense had evoked an old racial narrative: George Zimmerman was not only defending himself and his neighborhood, he was defending white womanhood. They had justified the murder of Martin, Smith noted, in exactly the same way Southern defense lawyers had justified the killing of Emmett Till.[43]

In his closing, defense attorney Mark O'Mara returned to Bertalan as "the face of the frustration that George was feeling." He reminded the jury that all those arrested at the Retreat at Twin Lakes for various crimes had been young, Black males. He presented them with a six-foot-high cutout silhouette of Trayvon Martin, and placed it next to a five-foot-eight silhouette of George Zimmerman. He spoke of Martin's "muscle tone," saying that autopsy photos could not capture it, because Martin's body had lost half its blood.

Then O'Mara showed two more pictures. The first was a surveillance shot of the hooded Martin purchasing his Skittles and fruit drink, appearing as a dark shadow in the fluorescent convenience store glare. The second was perhaps a selfie, taken from a low angle. Trayvon loomed large, half-lit, cap high, chin up, lips tight, shirtless. "This is the person who George Zimmerman encountered that night," said the defense lawyer. "This is the person who attacked George Zimmerman."

O'Mara then showed a final photo from that dark, fatal night—stunning in both its banality and inscrutability—the kind of photo that might have been taken by mistake, as if a cellie's camera function had been pressed accidentally. In this photo, the only visible objects were a thin gray line across the middle—perhaps the sidewalk through the Retreat at Twin Lakes or the yellow police tape stretched across the back porch of a townhouse—a square light in the top right-hand corner—perhaps someone's lit window—and a small indistinct gray rectangle in the bottom corner—perhaps an electrical box. Most of the photo was an impenetrable black. Out of this darkness, the defense could conjure demons.

"It was out of this darkness that Trayvon Martin decided to stalk—I guess—plan, pounce, I don't know," O'Mara said. "Out of the darkness, Trayvon Martin came towards George Zimmerman."

"Out of *this*," he said, waving the photo. "And *we know* what happened."

O'Mara brought out a large, sharp-edged cement block, carried it over carefully like a workman hauling a heavy paver, and deposited it in front of the jury. "Now that is cement, that is a sidewalk, and that is *not* an unarmed teenager with nothing but Skittles trying to get home," O'Mara said. "That is somebody who used the availability of dangerous items, from his fists to the concrete, to cause great bodily injury."

The wet pathway was no longer a wet pathway, it was Martin's deadly weapon. The teen himself was a deadly weapon.

Rock paper scissors. He deserved his fate. Fist concrete handgun.

And so the jurors would come to see the events of this almost moonless night solely through George Zimmerman's eyes. Late on July 13, George Zimmerman was found not guilty both on the charge of second-degree murder of Trayvon Martin, and on a lesser, hastily added charge of manslaughter.

Per Judge Nelson's basic jury instructions, O'Mara and the defense team only had to show that Zimmerman had not demonstrated "a depraved mind without regard for human life."[44] On the charge of manslaughter, they simply had to prove that Zimmerman had not intended to kill Martin—that he had fired by accident or under the threat of serious injury. They did *not* need to prove their wild assertion that it was *Martin* who had been stalking Zimmerman.

After the case, one of the jurors, a white female dubbed Juror B-37, went on CNN to speak to Anderson Cooper—her identity shrouded in partial darkness. She made clear where her empathy lay. Of Trayvon Martin, she said, "Oh, I believe he played a huge role in his death. He could, he could have—when George confronted him, and he could have walked away and gone home. He didn't have to do whatever he did and come back and be in a fight."

George Zimmerman, she said, "started the ball rolling. He could have avoided the whole situation by staying in the car. But he wanted to do good. I think he had good in his heart."[45]

Cooper asked her: "Even though it's he who had gotten out of the car, followed Trayvon Martin—that didn't matter in the deliberations? What mattered was those final seconds, minutes, when there was an altercation, and whether or not in your mind the most important thing was whether or not George Zimmerman felt his life was in danger?"

"That's how we read the law. That's how we got to the point of everybody being 'not guilty,'" she said. "I had no doubt George feared for his life in the situation he was in at the time.

"I think he was frustrated with the whole situation in the neighborhood, with the break-ins and robberies," she said. "I think he's learned a good lesson."

Cooper asked her if she minded that he would be getting his gun back. She said, "It doesn't worry me. I think he would be more responsible than anyone on the planet now."[46]

Soon another juror—the panel's only woman of color—also stepped into the media spotlight. She had been known as Juror B-29, and ABC's Robin Roberts introduced her as Maddy. She was Puerto Rican—she called herself, in contrast to George Zimmerman, "a Black Hispanic."

She had eight children, including teenagers around Trayvon's age. She said she had threatened to hang the jury because she wanted to see Zimmerman punished. But she gave in because she could not find a way to meet the standards of the law. And she stood by her decision.

Yet Maddy had been overcome by strong feelings of guilt, especially at the thought of Trayvon's mother's anguish over her son's death. After the verdict, she said, "I literally fell on my knees and I broke down. My husband was holding me. I was screaming and crying and I kept saying to myself, 'I feel like I killed him.' And I feel that if maybe if they would put the law and a lot of people would read it they would understand the choices that they gave us."[47]

Both the verdict and the jurors' public statements regarding the law consoled conservatives who believed the case had come to trial only because of the despicable efforts of the professional racial grievance class. Cornell law scholar and blogger William Jacobson argued, "[I]f the jury were correct under the law, how can the case be about race since the law is race neutral?"[48] But this hermetic, circular logic suggested that legal formalism was not unlike art-world formalism—it denied its blindness even as it infected the entire discourse with the same blindness.

Maddy told ABC's Robin Roberts that she had stepped forward to speak publicly because she felt Juror B-37 implied that she wanted to quit the jury rather than acquit Zimmerman because of her racial sympathies.[49] "The way she made a lot of it sound was, 'We walk by color,' and that's not what I do," Maddy said. When Roberts asked her what she wanted to tell Trayvon's parents, she answered, "I didn't know how much importance I was in to this case because I never looked at color. And I still don't look at color."[50]

In his closing, Prosecutor John Guy repeated his claim that the case was not about race. He asked the jury to consider the question, "What if it was Trayvon Martin who shot and killed George Zimmerman? What would your verdict be?" He then concluded, "*That's* how you know it's not about race."

At the time many liberal pundits praised Guy's gambit. Any rational person, they said, would immediately know the answer to Guy's question—Martin would be found guilty. In the same sense, the jury would have to find Zimmerman guilty. It was a classic "post-racial" reversal—one had to think race to deny race. It flattered the race-conscious-yet-colorblind conscience. But Guy and his fellow prosecutors had only twisted themselves up in their own logic. They never saw it coming.

In this verdict, the casual violence of racial profiling, the formal violence of color-blindness, and the physical violence afforded by a loaded semiautomatic had converged. Now the question of how to build "beloved community" seemed suspended. The race conversation that national leaders would inevitably call for, raged the cultural critic Frank Rich, was a farce. "We've had that conversation," he said. "It's gotten us nowhere."[51] Indeed if the race conversation could only be had in the context of court cases—as in the killing of Emmett Till or the beating of Rodney King—defined by formal blindness and set within an oppositional mode, how much could it really accomplish?

In 1966, James Baldwin had written, "The law is meant to be my servant and not my master, still less my torturer and my murderer."[52] Nearly a half-century later, the Zimmerman verdict suggested hopelessness. You could try to change the images people saw, but how could you change the images people already held of you in their minds?

But through a twist of history, Ryan Coogler's film *Fruitvale Station*—an affecting portrait of an Oakland youth, Oscar Grant, shot dead in the back on New Year's Day 2009 by BART policeman Johannes Mehserle—had opened the day before the verdict. Coogler presented Grant as a young man often given over to his demons yet struggling to quell them, cut down before he could find his redemption. That Sunday, thousands gathered in the darkness of the movie houses to make sense of Grant's and Martin's brutally foreshortened lives and what they meant for all those still living.

And as the new week began, young people would step out with a renewed determination—not to burn this time, but to challenge and provoke, to ask difficult questions. In

1968, the Memphis sanitation workers had raised placards that read, "I Am a Man." Now, around the country, young boys of color raised picket signs that read, "Am I Next?" As they grew into their world, they asked, would that world grow toward them? The crisis of inclusion had become a crisis of mutuality.

Three days after the verdict, about five weeks before the fiftieth anniversary of Martin Luther King Jr.'s "I Have a Dream" speech at the March on Washington for Jobs and Freedom, a nine-year-old child stepped into Florida governor Rick Scott's office. Hundreds of people—Black, Latino, and white, mostly young but some with graying hair—followed him, starting what would become a monthlong, around-the-clock occupation.

The youths were urging Governor Scott and the Florida legislature to pass a piece of legislation they called the Trayvon Martin Civil Rights Act. It would repeal Stand Your Ground laws and school zero-tolerance policies; require law enforcement agencies to define, prohibit, and train their officers around racial profiling; and promote youth restorative justice programs.

They called themselves the Dream Defenders. In their manifesto they declared:

> Our America is bewitched by labels: Black, Brown, White, Gay, Criminal,
> Illegal, Monster, Vigilante, Nigger, Cracker. These labels cover us.
> They conceal our similarities. They divide us. They have rendered us
> inhumane. They have allowed us to turn the murder of one of our brothers
> by one of our brothers, into a media spectacle. We can no longer see
> ourselves in others. We can no longer believe in each other. We are afraid to
> connect. We are bewildered by difference. We are fearful of all things
> foreign. The murder of a child before they've seen womanhood or manhood
> should shake each of us to the core of our being. A society that convinces
> a man or woman to live in fear of that child should leave us all baffled and
> heartbroken....
>
> They expect us to riot; to torch cities and burn bridges. They expect us to
> disperse; to wait for the next ambulance. But we challenge you to build.
> Real Power. We challenge you to channel your anger, your confusion, and
> your angst into a passion for positive action. We challenge you to question
> your truths. We challenge you to organize. We challenge you to see this
> case for what it truly is: a beginning.[53]

Six days after the verdict, Obama surprised reporters in the White House Briefing Room. He wanted to say something about Trayvon Martin. He explained that he, too, had been racially profiled many times in his life. It was part of the reason he had sponsored legislation in Illinois to collect data and support police training around the problem. It was also the reason, he said, that the African American community was now responding to the verdict with anguish and pain.

"When Trayvon Martin was first shot, I said this could have been my son. Another way of saying that is Trayvon Martin could have been me thirty-five years ago," he said. "Now the question for me, at least, and I think, for a lot of folks is, where do we take this?"

Obama dismissed the notion of having another grand conversation on race. "They end up being stilted and politicized, and folks are locked into positions they already have," he said. "On the other hand, in families and churches and workplaces, there's a possibility that people are a little bit more honest, and at least you can ask yourself your own questions about, am I wringing as much bias out of myself as I can? Am I judging people, as much as I can, based on not the color of their skin but the content of their character?"

He concluded on a note of hope. "Each successive generation seems to be making progress in changing attitudes when it comes to race. It doesn't mean that we're in a post-racial society. It doesn't mean that racism is eliminated. But you know, when I talk to Malia and Sasha and I listen to their friends and I see them interact, they're better than we are. They're better than we were on these issues."[54]

But back at the Retreat at Twin Lakes, where Sanford police had been deployed to surround the gates the night Zimmerman was set free, the community inside seemed to be coming apart. Some stockpiled guns. Young males of color were still being profiled. Mothers and fathers locked their dark-skinned boys in when the sun began to set and worried over what they should advise them to do if they were ever confronted.[54]

In the warm easing dusk, when the lakes of Central Florida reflected an endless sky unfurling in torsade strands of orange and purple, the green lawn where the kids used to play football with Trayvon Martin sat silent and empty.

I am here
No more fear
No more dark shadows
Let it come
Let me talk to you
See the face of your future

—Savages, "I Am Here," *Silence Yourself*

Snapshots of Lancaster, November 2008. Photos by B+ for mochilla.com.

DREAMING AMERICA

I

Seventy miles north and twenty-five hundred feet above Los Angeles, the image-producing capital of the world, stands the invisible city of Lancaster. It is set at the western edge of the high Mojave Desert where the Tehachapi and San Gabriel Mountains meet, in a valley named for the running antelope that were hunted to extinction over a century ago. Its residents like to refer to Lancaster as "Up Here" and to LA as "Down Below." Up Here, an unseen town built upon American dreaming.

It is the winter of 2008, two weeks after Obama's election and nine since the implosion of Lehman Brothers set off the markets' domino fall. At dawn the lawns of Lancaster suddenly burst with hissing sprinkler heads crisscrossing the fescue at six-inch gaps. Each blade of grass is bathed thrice. Sidewalks and curbs run dark with water.

Green grass is a point of civic pride—mandated, even—for Lancaster's remaining residents. Yet on every block there are homes where wild parched cotton clings to its branch in the morning gust, where grass splays yellow like a silent protest, where tumbleweeds gather in the thin shadow of lonely doorways. Taped official city notices warn against entry. Cards hang on mailboxes—"Do Not Place Mail in This Box VACANT." Sometimes these reminders come four or five houses in a row.

Here on the west side of the city, signs point the way to abandoned developments, blue arrows emblazoned with names of real estate companies like KB Home, Pacific Communities, American Premiere, and K. Hovnanian. At the peak of the boom twenty-four long months before, young families used them like the aisle signs in Walmart, guides through the wide streets to promising new subdivisions hidden behind cinderblock walls. Now they seemed like gravesite memorials to the city's failed private planners.

Developers had been building new subdivisions on all sides of Lancaster's grand monument to 1990s government largesse—the six hundred acres that include the Challenger Memorial Youth Center, the county's largest juvenile detention center; the Mira Loma Detention Center, an immigrant jail; High Desert Health, the county health clinic; and the California State Prison. The prison alone accounts for more jobs than the school district. Steel concertina fences have become just another feature of suburban life.

Agustin Rodriguez, working in his garage, appears to be the last person in this brand new subdivision across the road from the prison complex. An immigrant from Durango, Mexico, he had come six months ago up the Antelope Valley Freeway from the San Fernando Valley. When his masonry skills were no longer in demand, he helped people move out of their foreclosed homes. Many of his friends had returned to Mexico. Now that there is no work, he says, the only good thing is that he can finally afford to rent a new five-bedroom house.

At this point in 2008, 5,500 homes—over 10 percent of Lancaster's entire housing stock—are in foreclosure. The median home price has plunged from a peak of $340,000 to $202,000, and the bottom is not near. In the coming months, the price will continue to slide to the low hundred thousands. Hundreds more homes, worth less than their mortgages, have simply been abandoned. In real estate parlance, they are "underwater," desert homes submerged.

Dreams were supposed to have bloomed Up Here, rising from the arid sediment of the centuries. But as Ishmael Reed once wrote, "Deserts are for visions not materialists." In the 1800s Spanish missionaries removed the four indigenous peoples—the Serrano, Kitanemuk, Tataviam, and Kawaiisu—to their missions, leaving behind only traces of the rich exchanges along this Indian trading route to the coast. The Southern Pacific Railroad retraced these routes in 1876. Within a decade, half of the three thousand laborers in the area were Chinese, and Lancaster had its own Chinatown built of tents.[1]

The railroad began selling plots of land to grand schemers from as far away as Mississippi and England.[2] One ad, published in London, promised field plots as fertile as those in the San Fernando Valley. Another offered free land with newspaper subscriptions. An investment group wanted to export paper made of desert flora back to the *Daily Telegraph* in London, and procured Chinese laborers laid off by the railroad or fleeing the white mobs of Los Angeles, San Francisco, or the Sierras to clear the steel-sharp yucca and Joshua trees.[3] The business failed quickly and miserably, and both the nascent globalizers and their immigrant work force vanished. By then the town had built its first jail.

Two decades after the railroad tracks were first laid, amid a punishing drought, the city had been all but abandoned—dust to dust—until discoveries of borax and gold ensured Lancaster's survival into the twentieth century. But fires raged through the heart of the town center regularly, taking down saloons, hotels, and the newspaper.[4] It was as if Lancaster had no need for those needing respite or passing through, nor for the tellers of tales. There was only hard work for the devoted and the fast.

The desert floor was a blank canvas, suitable for socialist utopians and space travelers, high-flying top guns and hard-eyed dreamers. As Mike Davis noted in his classic study of Los Angeles, *City of Quartz*, a short-lived socialist "garden city" called Llano del Rio opened in 1914 and thrived until the river plain ran dry when its colonists lost access to water through political intrigue and geological drift.[5] The stone ruins of the Great Assembly Hall still stand against the sweep of tan and percylite.

Lancaster has known booms. At the height of the Great Depression the air force moved in and on a bright morning in 1947, Chuck Yeager flew out of Muroc Air Force Base and through the sound barrier. The first sonic boom echoed across the desert floor, the sound of militarist Keynesianism and Cold War triumphalism in a place that thought itself exceptionally American. The city grew quickly afterward. In the center of the modest downtown area, a decommissioned airplane was mounted at an angle of rocketing ascent. A plaque marking an "Aerospace Walk of Honor" celebrated the town's values: "Imagination Reason Skill."

By the 1980s, the combination of urban unrest, prison expansion, grinding underemployment, and inner-city gentrification pushed a new generation of diverse families out of Los Angeles. Lancaster was working-class aspirational, offering sizable homes for purchase or rent at a fraction of the cost. In 1980, it was 86% white. Three decades later, the city is 34% white. It is also 38% Latino and 21% Black. Lancaster's elected officials are almost all white, Republican, and tend to be related to each other.

At the dawn of Reagan's morning, Muroc—long since renamed Edwards Air Force Base—was chosen as the landing site for the space shuttle. But the bust soon followed, when feds shifted aerospace money to Texas and Florida. In 1990, California's first Walmart opened in Lancaster. The huge prison complex soon sprouted, a razor link between urban poverty (the prisoners) and a suburban middle class (the guards). Finally there was all of that pent-up housing demand. Retail, prisons, and construction were the future.[6]

The hitch to living in Lancaster is that you must commute three-plus hours down the freeway to Los Angeles and back up each day. "If you can get a job it is cheaper and easier to live here," says resident Shannon Clairemont. "*If* you can get a job here." In November 2008, the local unemployment rate is 12.5 percent, almost double the national rate. In a year, it will rise to 17.7 percent, still almost double the national rate.[7] One in five Lancaster residents will be living under the poverty line.

Across from Amargosa Creek Middle School, in a neighborhood of American flags, Ford F-150 pickups, and camper-trailers, four two-story homes out of a John Hughes film are for sale. "I'm Gorgeous Inside," reads one sign. Bill Westover and his son Eddie are edging the lawn on one of the homes. Work has slowed in the ski resort town of Big Bear Lake, so they have come back to clean and winterize all the unsold homes, homes where the tenants departed in a hurry, leaving half-finished food on the counters and DVD cases strewn across the room, garages filled with motorcycles and toolboxes.

They have eight pages of addresses that need work, including many in the well-to-do section of Quartz Hill. "It's hitting people on all levels," Bill says. To the banks and reconveyance companies, Bill and Eddie—with their antifreeze cans and their grass blowers—are the last men standing against broken windows, squatters, and thieves.

The predatory capitalism of the boom is being replaced by the vulture capitalism of the bust. Lenders are now real estate companies. Real estate agents are now short-sellers. Everyday folks are trying to figure out the new hustle.

During the boom, Shannon Clairemont made a decent living sewing window curtains. Now she and her husband, Dave, a carpenter, are trying their hand at short-selling as well. They have discovered quickly it's a world of deceptions and lies. They point down the block to a group of homes where lawn signs read "Sold." "Those signs went up four months ago," Clairemont says. "No one has moved in."

It's about appearances. City leaders—largely rubber-stamping development in the earlier free-market frenzy—are now spending $8 million to buy vacant homes, refurbish them, and resell them at low cost. These flipped homes will not likely show up on HGTV.

And as in other desert cities, city leaders have found a useful scapegoat for their woes. At the same moment falling rents are allowing low-income renters of color to improve their housing conditions, they are aggressively deploying sheriff's deputies and county housing agents to investigate low-income renters of color for Section 8 "compliance abuse," such as keeping extra tenants. They argue that these renters are turning Lancaster into a "dumping ground" for the dregs of Down Below.

"It is a problem that is crushing our community," Mayor R. Rex Parrish says. He has nothing to say of the developers who have overpromised, overbuilt, and skipped town.[8] The NAACP will soon file a lawsuit challenging what it calls the criminalization of low-income Black and Brown residents, and the unfair termination of the Section 8 rental assistance vouchers.

Driving east through downtown, sprawling buildings and their vast parking lots stand empty. Once they had been lively retail storefronts selling furniture or carpeting or mattresses. Now their windows display lonely scrawls against dark interiors: "Sale!" "Sale!" "Sale!" "Why Wait?" Another promises "GOODWILL Coming Soon," but there is no one around to register disbelief.

There is no street art in Lancaster. In an older section east of downtown, aggressive tags are scrawled across an abandoned house in a quiet cul-de-sac. Someone has built a skate ramp from particleboard panels ripped from the house's broken windows. Youth continues.

This neighborhood of modest ranch homes—some featuring cabled driveways that once covered Ford Fairlanes—were built in the real estate boom following Yeager's sonic boom, Ruscha's California. Standing on a corner shaded by mature oaks, Rafael Villanueva points out the empty houses. The yellow one across the street has been deserted for months. Two more down that block are also empty. The blue one across the street, with a large felled tree branch uncleared from the last storm, has been foreclosed.

Thieves had broken into the yellow house and ripped out the copper piping and wiring. Some had even tried to climb over his fence to steal his recycled cans and bottles before he scared them away. One morning he watched a woman and a man fight over the block's weekly harvest of glass and aluminum. "This is my turf," the man told her.

Villanueva had come up from Santa Clarita to drive a cement mixer in Lancaster. "When I moved here, it was empty. Then it was full, it was a boom town," he says. In 2004, he was working six days and sometimes more than sixty-five hours a week. "Now it's empty again."

A few blocks away the neighborhood changes again, into broad-fronted homes where there are fewer trees, but with yards that are better tended, and bushes and fences that rise much higher. Andy Jowyk steps into the morning heat for his daily walk in high tan shorts and Reeboks. He is a Ukrainian immigrant who had come through Bremen to New York City, he says, in clogs, "knowing two words of English: yes and no." He had since, he proudly adds, been shot at by commies in Vietnam and Laos.

This neighborhood, he says, waving his hand, was full of air force retirees like himself, people who worked at Edwards during the boom years. The economic crisis remains a popular topic among his friends. "You look at the top. How in the hell can they give billions to AIG and go have a party? What kind of shit is that? Pardon my language," he says. "But you know what? You never borrow more than you can pay. The worse thing I see is: they don't just lose a home, they destroy the thing."

Farther south, off East Avenue K and 20th Street East, in a sparkling new section of four-bedroom homes, an ice-cream truck with a USMC flag in its window cruises slowly past the fire station through wide new streets where homes were selling in the mid-$400,000s three years ago. No children come out to greet it.

Down around a turn, where the subdivision that American Premiere Homes advertises as Eastbrook Estates begins, the reception office is closed in the high light of a weekday. Attractive model homes—with names like Aspen Creek, Willow Edge, Cedar Brooke—are dressed up with low-water grass, three-car garages, high tan front doors, and Craftsman-style details. But they sit locked behind low black iron gates, like pageant contestants who have failed to place.

To the right the street disappears. There is no subdivision, just sidewalks cut to suggest where cars might go, and markings in the shifting sand that imply property boundaries. In the distance, a long cinderblock wall and the low line of roofs behind it mark the end of the development. There is only the bridled desert breeze and the wide insouciant sky, until a couple appears at the curve of the street.

Eileen and John Zanderzuk have ended up in Lancaster from stops in New York City and Pennsylvania and Simi Valley. They bought their home three blocks away on a short-sale, happy to secure an extra half-acre on which they could build a greenhouse for their bonsai business. "It's quiet," Eileen says. "We don't feel lonely."

"Are you from American Premiere?" she asks. "We never see anyone from there and lots of people ask us questions."

The silent streets of Lancaster form an unlikely early-twenty-first-century counterpoint to the silent streets of the late-twentieth-century South Bronx. From the inner cities to the colorized suburbs, abandonment is a form of destruction, a willed blindness.

At this moment, on the other side of town, the California state prison—which dropped "Lancaster" and then "Antelope Valley" from its name to satisfy residents worried about the area's reputation—is facing a court order to reduce its severe overcrowding. The prison holds five thousand mostly Latino and Black inmates, double its design capacity.[9] Its health services are under severe strain. Even the state's top prison administrator agrees that conditions are an unsafe embarrassment.[10] He is campaigning to add even more prisons to the largest system in the nation with the largest system in the world.

Mira Loma Detention Center, with its nine hundred immigrant detainees, is still cooling off after April uprisings ended in a mass tear-gassing.[11] Reports have not yet surfaced that a series of teenage riots at Challenger Memorial Youth Center kept the facility in lockdown for most of December 2007.[12] The Department of Justice is investigating mistreatment of students there, the Los Angeles Probation Commission will soon issue a report calling its educational facilities "broken," and the ACLU will file a complaint arguing that Challenger is denying basic educational opportunities and due process to its youths.[13]

A year later, as the Tea Party and its movement for "limited government and free markets" is roaring to life, Kenneth E. Hartman, a prisoner convicted of murder and sentenced to life without parole in the California State Prison, writes in a piece for the *New York Times*,

> From the four-inch-wide window in the back of my cell, I watched, for
> seven years, the construction of a housing tract across the street—a
> subdivision we call Prison View Estates. We marvel at the hubris of building
> chockablock stucco mini-mansions within shouting distance of a maximum-
> security prison. Today, a year after the gaudy balloons from the grand
> opening deflated, the row of houses directly across from my window looks
> to be unoccupied.[14]

II

Tucson. Almost noon in the desert sun.

They are running. But it feels like—perhaps for the first time—they are not running from something, but *toward* something. Voice. Control. The future. With one hand, they press their mortarboards to their heads as they dash for the door. The satin folds of their blue graduation gowns billow and catch the light. They shine.

Lizbeth still has a pancake in her other hand. Yahaira had warned her, *You'd better eat before this all starts*. Now Lizbeth's going, *What do I do with this pancake?* They're yelling back, half-annoyed and half-amused, *Just throw it on the fucking ground!*

Their hearts are speeding. Adam—a Japanese American ally, the only one not in a cap and gown—buzzes the intercom with a perfect ruse: an appointment for a legislative internship. It all might have become a set of likable Facebook posts—mortarboards, graduation gowns, an uneaten pancake, punking a powerful senator.

If time was something they still had. "Status update" has added meaning to those without nine-digit numbers, those who are undocumented. At this moment there are 11.5 million of them—invisible Americans, part of a global population derisively called "illegal," which really means "condemned by others to live as less than human."

Laws are constructs. Laws can be changed. So they have put their hopes into one called the Development, Relief, and Education for Alien Minors Act—the DREAM Act—introduced in 2001 by Senators Richard Durbin (D-Illinois) and Orrin Hatch (R-Utah), and reintroduced in every session of Congress since. The bill would allow undocumented youths who had met certain requirements—they had arrived as minors, lived in the United States for at least five years, and completed two years in the military or college—to apply for citizenship. It will not take care of all the 11.5 million, but as Yahaira tells people, *It will allow many of us to move forward with our futures and fulfill the dreams we have of bettering our communities and fully integrating as the Americans we are.*

Change happens in expressions of unrest and risk, in explosions of mass creativity. For over a decade the undocumented youth movement has been growing. But until now the activists have not put their American lives on the line, gambling on permanent exile from their communities, their homes. But they have pled. They will no longer plead. They have waited. They can no longer wait.

Adam speaks into the intercom. The door clicks, then it gives. He holds it for them. Each takes a breath and files in. Yahaira Carrillo, 25, Kansas City. Tania Unzueta Carrasco, 26, Chicago. Lizbeth Mateo, 25, Los Angeles. Mohammad Abdollahi, 24, Ann Arbor. There is also a documented ally from Tucson, Raul Al-qaraz Ochoa.

They do not all remember the details of what they said at the beginning. Only that it has begun. That they are there and they are not leaving until Senator McCain supports the DREAM Act. They sit on the floor of the reception area.

It is May 17, 2010, the forty-sixth anniversary of the decision in *Brown v. Board of Education*. The energies of the state once directed toward ending racial segregation are now being marshaled to crack down on immigrants. In fewer than two years, President Obama has deported over a million of them—he has become the fastest deporter-in-chief in U.S. history.[15] His clampdown is broad, indiscriminate, and brutal. Thousands of children have been separated from their parents.[16] Thousands of citizens and legal residents have been detained and some deported, too.[17]

Immigration policy is now largely about enforcement and punishment—saturation border policing, high-volume capture, and processing efficiency. The forces of—oxymoron alert—government innovation once focused on putting a man on the moon now serve the goal of updating the formal status of large numbers of people from "illegal" to "removed" in as little time as possible.

But little is being exerted to cut the red tape an immigrant faces in applying for naturalization. "People ask me, 'Why don't you just go through the process?'" says the Pulitzer Prize–winning journalist and undocumented immigrant Jose Antonio Vargas. "They don't understand. There is no process, not any rational one." The waiting line for some Filipinos to receive a family visa stretches back a quarter of a century. For a Mexican petitioning to be reunited with a citizen who is a sibling, the wait is 164 years.[18]

This summer will be scorching. Governor Jan Brewer has just signed HB 2282, banning ethnic studies. The legislature has passed SB 1070 and she vows to sign that as well. The week before, the young protestors had been young lobbyists in Washington, DC, asking senators to move the DREAM Act, telling them that right after their meetings they would be flying to Arizona, the most hostile state in which to be an immigrant in America, to raise the stakes around this debate. Nobody believed them then.

Conformity, their leaders had long told them, was the only way to pass the camel of a reform bill through the eye of the congressional needle. Don't be too radical, too queer, too loud, they warned. Don't stray off message. But that strategy had failed.

In 2007, millions around the country had rallied for the second year in a row to demand immigration reform. Immigrant stories had moved Congress to take up a bill. But both the Comprehensive Immigration Reform Act and the DREAM Act went down in legislative flames. By 2010, formalist language had eclipsed human narrative, and the debate had been effectively reduced to two words. "Legal" was one. The other had been mainstreamed in the racist question—what part of *"illegal"* don't you understand?

Turning toward civil disobedience in Arizona, the DREAM activists agree, raises questions of access to education and calls attention to Senator McCain's flip-flops on immigration. But it might also force open the question of what it means to be visible, mobile, and whole in a world defined by flows of capital and bodies. More to the point, what other choice do they have but to fight?

The sociologist Robert S. Gonzales describes how the lives of undocumented youths depart from their peers. By their teens, undocumented immigrants are being diverted toward a grimmer future. Between sixteen and eighteen years old, they go through a "discovery" phase in which they become aware of their status. From eighteen to twenty-four, they see their opportunities dissolving before their very eyes. They cannot vote. They cannot secure financial aid. Getting a driver's license or a job is complicated. They "learn to be illegal." And as their peers transition into full adulthood in their late twenties, they resign themselves to an existential state of "coping."[19]

"My life has been on pause, rewind, or replay for years," Yahaira writes in a letter to President Barack Obama during the summer of 2010. "Waiting is not an option."[20]

Tania was one of the earliest poster-children for the DREAM Act. The daughter of community organizers, she arrived in Chicago at ten. At Lincoln Park High, she was captain of the swim team, a star student, and an acknowledged leader. When one of her friends was unfairly arrested outside of school, she organized classmates to challenge police brutality and school militarization.

But as she approached her high school graduation in 2001, she began to understand what it meant not to have papers. First her mother had told her she could not go to France with her classmates: "I don't know that you can come back if you go." Tania thought her mother was simply being overprotective. But in time she saw that her status was separating her from her peers. "I didn't want to be different," Tania said. "I didn't want them to think that I had special needs of any kind. I just wanted to be 'normal.'"

But she would not be able to attend any of the colleges of her choice unless she applied as an international student, which seemed absurd. She accepted a scholarship to a private college conditional upon securing a Mexican student visa. In the summer after graduation, she left for Mexico, angry and frustrated, to try to get one. But officials confiscated her passport and told her that her parents owed American taxes as illegal immigrants. At eighteen, she was suddenly stateless.

Her case came to the attention of Illinois senator Richard Durbin, who had recently introduced the first version of the DREAM Act. Reporters came calling. In one of those articles, Tania read that at least 65,000 other undocumented students graduated in the United States each year. She began to feel like she wasn't alone.

Repatriated to Chicago under a one-year grant of humanitarian parole, Tania was slated to be Durbin's star witness at a hearing for the DREAM Act. "I had my plane ticket for September 11, 2001," she said. The hearing was canceled. "And the government's response was to turn everything around immigration into a conversation of national security and terrorism."[21]

Her scholarship fell through, her parole lapsed, and she was once again undocumented. After 9/11, she enrolled at the University of Illinois at Chicago, a school that allowed her to pay resident tuition. She found an outlet for her activism among LGBT students and at a bilingual community radio station, Radio Arte. She came out, and she began reading Audre Lorde, bell hooks, and Harvey Milk. She recalled, "I remember highlighting so much stuff—like, this is *exactly* how it feels to be undocumented."

Radio Arte's philosophy was to explore the power of narratives from the unheard. As an announcer and a production workshop leader, she said, "I really tried to push that, to tell people, 'Your story is important.' And we started talking about immigration a lot in class, and queer stuff."

Soon Tania realized that half of the students in her Radio Arte classes were, in official parlance, "out of status." One day, a student came into the office wanting to talk to Tania about a dream she had the previous night. There had been an immigration raid at the radio station, and they all needed to run somewhere. They stuffed themselves into a closet in Tania's office and waited fearfully. The student had described a nightmare that felt all too real to many of the Radio Arte youths.

In early 2009, Rigo Padilla, a soft-spoken male student, told Tania after class, "I have my own story." He pulled up a jean leg and showed her his ankle bracelet monitor. The twenty-one year old had been watching a football game with friends, and had downed a few beers. Driving home, he rolled through a stop sign and was pulled over. He was charged with misdemeanor drunken driving. When police learned he had no driver's license, they turned him over to Immigration and Customs Enforcement (ICE) officials. He was convicted and placed into deportation proceedings. A judge ordered him to return to Mexico by December 16, a country he had left at age six.

With a new name—the Immigration Youth Justice League—and nothing else but Rigo's story, they began to build a campaign. But although Rigo had been an honors student with a spotless record before the arrest, many immigration reform activists refused to support his case. To them, his drunken driving conviction put him in the same category as the criminals President Obama wanted to deport—he was no longer a "good DREAMer," but the picture of a "bad illegal."

Undocumented Radio Arte staffer and IYJL organizer Reyna Wences argued, "What happened to Rigo could happen to me if I made a mistake, if I was at the wrong place at the wrong time." This argument convinced a broad coalition—including mainline immigration organizations, the Chicago City Council, and Representative Jan Schakowsky—to support his bid to vacate his removal order. In December 2009, the Obama administration granted a one-year reprieve to Rigo. They had won with the power of a single story, and now they could turn to transforming the national undocumented movement.

The national failures of 2007 had spurred more intense national organizing among the DREAMers. In December of that year, Mohammad Abdollahi, Maria Marroquin, Juan Escalante, and Prerna Lal launched the Web site DREAMActivist.org where undocumented youths met, collaborated, shared information, and collected stories. United We Dream—a national confederation of organizations—began convening thousands of youths for trainings, and cultural and political campaign planning.

Together the two organizations launched the Education Not Deportation (END) initiative to rally support for people in deportation proceedings. They also sponsored annual DREAM Graduations, media events that highlighted that hinge moment where undocumented youths' futures departed from their peers. From 2007—when German-born Tam Tran, Costa Rica–born Marie Gonzalez, and Zambia-born Martine Kalaw headlined a House Judiciary Subcommittee hearing on undocumented students—to the start of 2010, the national youth underground had molded itself into a story machine.

On New Year's Day, four undocumented youths—Gaby Pacheco, Felipe Matos, Carlos Roa, and Juan Rodriguez—began walking 1,500 miles from Miami to Washington, DC, to call for immigration reform, naming their journey the Trail of DREAMs. As they marched through the South they summoned images of the civil rights movement. In Greensboro, North Carolina, they met with veterans of the lunch counter sit-ins. In Nahunta, Georgia, they confronted a Ku Klux Klan counterdemonstration.

In Chicago, the IYJL organizers had discovered a collective identity, and through that, a way forward. "We realized it had been really empowering to be in a room where other people had said that they were undocumented," recalled Tania. They could also see how their vision might be informed not only by civil rights and immigrant rights history, but by the history of the gay liberation movement.

Rigo asked the group, "Doesn't the LGBT community have a 'coming out' thing? What if we were to have a coming out day for undocumented people?" This idea excited the group. Someone asked, "Gay people come out of the closet. But what do undocumented people come out of?" The answer was clear: the shadows. Not long after the Trail of DREAMs began, IJYL held its first Coming Out of the Shadows event at the Radio Arte building.

Inspired, Tania and Reyna made a presentation in February to United We Dream's national convening of organizers. They said they wanted to do an action in Chicago's Federal Plaza, in front of Senator Durbin's office, across the street from ICE offices—they would loudly announce their status within shouting distance of Immigration officers. They encouraged others to do the same; it could be called "National Coming Out of the Shadows Day." Yahaira recalled the shockwaves the idea sent through the room: "Half of us panicked and half of us were like, 'Yes! That's awesome!'"

It had become common for undocumented activists announce themselves in the media one night—omitting details like their full names that might incriminate them—only to see their families' homes raided the next. Documented allies saw their job as shielding the undocumented activists. Their allyship was based on the idea of defending the right of the undocumented to stay. What would it mean if undocumented youths decided to sacrifice their futures by placing themselves, unprotected, on the front line?

Many undocumented activists had come to feel they were running out of time. It had been three years since Comprehensive Immigration Reform had tanked. No new immigration bill had been announced, and the DREAM Act was now stalled, too. Each year they waited, they got closer to aging out of the window to qualify. What good was it to wait for an all-clear signal from Washington, DC? They were tired of being spoken for, talked to, and trotted out for press conferences. No more fear, no more shame, no more shadows.

The gathering voted to support a National Coming Out Day. On March 10, demonstrations were held across the country. In Chicago's Federal Plaza, Tania rose to speak:

What does it mean to "come out"? *¿Qué quiere decir "salir de las sombras"?* "Coming out" means telling a friend, a loved one, a classmate, a teacher, something that otherwise you would have kept private. It is using our lives and stories as a political tool for change....

"Brothers and sisters, we must come out," said Harvey Milk in 1978. "Come out to your relatives, come out to your friends, if indeed they are your friends, come out to your neighbors, to your fellow workers, to the people who work where you eat and shop, but once and for all, let's break down the myths, destroy the lies and distortions."

Inspiring, you know?

Except, except that we want to make it very clear that we are not here asking for acceptance. We are asking for change. We are asking for a chance to be able to contribute fully to our communities and our societies. We are asking for legalization.

I am going to ask you to imagine for a minute a country where twelve million people decide to come out of the shadows—an unstoppable movement of immigrants turned storytellers turned political activists for change.

Can you imagine living in a country where you can walk out of your house without wondering if you will ever come back?

When you can answer the door without fearing that it's Immigration knocking and they have finally come for you?

Where you can vote?

Where you are allowed to be careless every once in a while because one mistake will not get you deported?

Where you can travel without having to make plans for which lawyer you're going to call and who will tell your brothers and sisters or children or mother that you are not coming home as scheduled?

Can you imagine a country where we are free?

Last night—last night, when we were coming up with this list of possibilities I wish you could have seen the smiles on our faces. This world *is* possible.

So undocumented brothers and sisters, let's come out and organize. Come out in your church. Tell your teachers, tell your friends. Ask the DJ for a mic at your next party and announce it over the speakers: *I Am Undocumented*.

The same day, from Los Angeles to Kansas City to Little Rock, undocumented youths were coming out to tell their stories. They introduced themselves and they stated—in another IYJL-coined-slogan—that they were "undocumented and unafraid." The movement had found its voice.

Mohammad—a gay Iranian American whose family's immigration application had been denied because their attorney had not informed them the fees had increased by $20—began quietly organizing the core of those who would end up in McCain's office in Tucson. He sought out the activists who were especially energized by Tania's proposal.

Lizbeth Mateo was the daughter of a taxi driver who had fled political unrest in Mexico. Her parents had received their green cards, but she had aged out of qualifying for her own as their child. She put herself through Cal State Northridge by working at restaurants, and began organizing undocumented classmates.

Yahaira had come to the United States for the first time with her seventeen-year-old single mother as an infant. After a second crossing at the age of eight, she settled in Napa Valley, where her mother found work doing housekeeping in a nursing home. The third time, she nearly drowned in the river passage.

She came of age in Kansas City, and even as her family disintegrated, she graduated near the top of her class. But when her peers went to college, Yahaira went to work. Only later did she find private universities that welcomed undocumented students. It took her eight years—and countless jobs—to receive her bachelor's degree. She had also begun her activism, and soon found her way into the burgeoning national network of young organizers.

Mohammad posed a simple question: "What do you think would happen if a bunch of DREAM Act leaders got placed into deportation proceedings?" All of their work around deportations had confirmed that people could be mobilized to save leaders from deportation. Each of them had come to the same conclusion: the next stage of escalation would be to purposefully seek arrest and risk deportation.

Mohammad was persuading them *they* could be those leaders. They could sacrifice themselves. They could galvanize people. They might even be able to document conditions in the immigration detention centers, and organize detainees around human rights issues. The idea was insane, they all agreed, and it had to be done. And so they decided they would leave for Arizona after their May lobbying visit to Washington, DC.

But first, Yahaira needed to talk to her mother.

One afternoon, Yahaira had been driving home from an event when she came upon a DUI checkpoint. She panicked. For a moment she was certain she would be pulled over and it would all end, her entire American life. But she passed through, and the next morning when she was at her law office job, Mohammad reached her on Google Chat. The topic of their discussion was "This Crazy Idea."

Now she had to tell her mother about her decision.

Why you? her mother asked.

She answers, *If it's not us, then who is going to do it? I am tired. I am tired of living like this. If I am going to leave, it is going to be on my terms. It won't be at a driver's license checkpoint, it won't be outside a grocery store. I can't do it anymore. And whether it's now or whether it's later, I'm going to be outta here by the time I'm 30 if something doesn't change. I want to make sure I can leave knowing I did everything I could to change it, to fix my situation, in a sense. To have a shot, to say that I tried until I couldn't try anymore. And there would be no additional questions, nothing else that I could ask myself. Really, is there anything else that is more in my control than that?*

Her mother says, *But you have a good job, you are getting paid $11.25 an hour. You are working in an office, air-conditioned. You're doing really well.*

But this isn't the life I wanted for myself. I want more. You taught me that. You taught me to fight for my happiness. And you said that you brought me here because you wanted me to be happy. I'm trying.
Ok. I don't like it. But it's your life. You make that choice. I just really want you to think about it.

I have, Mom. Yeah.

Yahaira gave her Kansas City group final instructions on how to take care of her mother, to make sure that if it all went awry she would have a support system, that she would be fine. Then she left.

Now the press release has gone out, the social media activated, the Web site launched, the groups are at home on high alert. The demonstration has begun.

McCain's secretary is making it easy. *Clear a path for fire access*, she says. *And all those press people can't come in all at once. Let them in one at a time.* Everyone in the media will get their interview, their photo op. The reporters and photographers and cameramen line up for their turns. A policeman brings the DREAMers cookies.

At that moment, across the street, in Tucson's gleaming new federal building, an immigration judge is presiding over a model of bureaucratic efficiency bluntly known as the "Streamline."

Every weekday at 2:00 p.m., a line of a dozen orange-jumpsuited immigrants—shackled at the wrists and ankles and chained to each other, many of whom do not even speak Spanish but languages indigenous to villages from southern Mexico to Nicaragua—shuffles into a courtroom well to face the judge, their skins dark from the desert sun, chapped by wind and heat.

Lawyers and translators move into position as the judge reads the immigrants their charges. Each pleads guilty. All of them are then quickly shuffled off, for the next dozen to step in. Within the past forty-eight hours, these invisible men and women have been spotted and captured by ICE. Within another forty-eight hours all of them will be disappeared, most likely on a bus to the other side of the wall in Nogales, left to the goodwill of Catholic soup kitchens in a teeming city some of them have never seen.

The DREAMers know this is happening. They yearn to intertwine themselves with these immigrants' stories and longings. They know they have the privilege to ask: who is American? Who is human?

A Tucson police sergeant is mediating between them and the McCain staff. Five o'clock passes. 5:30. He looks at Mohammad. *You remind me of my son.* He says to them all, *You have to think about your futures. What if you want to get jobs? What if you want to vote? What if you ever want to run for office?*

At 6:30, the sergeant gives a final warning. The group has been deliberating over the complexities of Tania's case, and convinced her it's OK for her not to be arrested, but instead to be their spokesperson. She stands to depart.

The sergeant says, *I just want you to know there will be no handcuffs unless you resist. I'm not interested in making this a show. You can come willingly or not.*

They follow him to the police van. Mohammad and Raul are separated from Lizbeth and Yahaira. Lizbeth waves in thanks to the hundreds of supporters who have gathered outside McCain's office. The van pulls out toward the federal detention center. Yahaira looks through the caged window at the long line of police cars behind, their lights flashing. *Oh my God, we're actually going to jail,* she thinks to herself. *This is happening.*

By the evening the women are in their prison white, sitting in the holding pen of the Pima County jail, a place called "The Pit," where all overnight prisoners are held. There are benches but they are not allowed to lie down. It is cold but they will not be offered blankets. Still, there is TV, they will be given sandwiches, and there are people to talk to. Outside their supporters are holding a vigil. Yahaira thinks of her mother. She closes her eyes.

In the morning they can hear the ICE officials through the doors. *Who are they? Where is their Web site? They made the cover of the* New York Times? *What are we supposed to do with them? What is DC saying?*

One by one they are called in to see a judge, who reviews their charge—misdemeanor trespassing. Is there an ICE hold? he asks. There is none. Then each is called in to see Department of Homeland Security officials. Yahaira thinks, We're about to get deported. She thinks about where she may be headed—perhaps Eloy or Florence. She goes over what she is supposed to and not supposed to say.

But DHS is friendly. The hardest question is what she wants from McDonald's. Then they are being taken into the van, again uncuffed. At 8:30 p.m. they are released from the ICE processing center. They had planned to be in detention for two weeks. They had planned to be placed into deportation proceedings. None of that will happen. After less than thirty-six hours they are, in a sense, free. There will be a night to celebrate. They will sleep, they will dream. And then they will awake the next morning to plan.

Three days later, undocumented activists shut down Wilshire Boulevard. Hunger strikes break out in six states, including a sit-in at New York senator Charles Schumer's office. On July 20, twenty undocumented youths from across the country, all in blue gowns and caps, are arrested in Washington, DC, after a day of demonstrations in the Hart Senate Office Building.

By December, with the president's backing and with Comprehensive Immigration Reform nowhere in sight, the DREAM Act has moved further than it ever has before, passing the House on a close vote. But on the eighteenth, the Act is filibustered by Senate Republicans, effectively killing the bill for yet another Congressional session.

There will be more discord in the movement. "In tears, rage, and love," Raul Al-qaraz Ochoa will withdraw his support for the DREAM Act over its military service requirement, and the way that politicians use it to justify border militarization and demonize DREAMers' parents. United We Dream will splinter over tactics, funding, and ideology. The militant DREAMers will be told by the reformers, *You are being selfish. You are not thinking of your families, your communities.*

But they have also confirmed the wisdom of Lorde's and Milk's lessons: *Your silence will not protect you. You must come out.* Mohammad begins telling activists, *If you organize you are safe.*

As states like Georgia, Indiana, and Alabama pass copycat SB 1070 laws, a new generation of activists committed to civil disobedience emerges. Protests in Atlanta, Indianapolis, and Montgomery, result in hundreds of arrests of undocumented youths.

The Obama administration gradually eases deportation enforcement against some groups, including DREAM Act–eligible youths, those convicted of minor offenses or traffic violations, and victims of domestic violence and human trafficking. It also allows officials the discretion to consider factors such as "the person's ties and contributions to the community, including family relationships," and "whether the person or the person's spouse suffers from severe mental or physical illness." In the summer of 2012, activists start to test the gap between federal policy and practice. They follow through on their original idea by getting arrested and infiltrating immigrant detention centers.

The singular image of caps and gowns has become a flood of new images: T-shirts that say "Undocumented Unafraid Unapologetic"; a picket sign that mocks the authorities: "Jail the Worst You Have? Because Our Organizing Starts in Jail!"; posters of all kinds of faces and bodies that simply state "I Exist"; a butterfly with the words "Migration Is Beautiful."[22]

On June 4, 2012, two activists walk into an Obama campaign office in Denver—in the heart of a swing state with a big cultural generation gap—and begin a hunger strike. They will leave, they say, when the president agrees to stop deportations. The Undoccupations, as they are called, spread to Obama campaign offices in Los Angeles, Cincinnati, Oakland, and Dearborn.

At the same moment, in New York City, the journalist Jose Antonio Vargas has completed a cover story for *Time* magazine, a deeply personal piece on the absurdity of the immigration system. His life has been defined by two big secrets. The first he had long reconciled. He had come out as gay in a high school history class. The second threatened to unravel his promising career. The year before, inspired by the youth movement, he had come out as undocumented in a *New York Times Magazine* article.

His immigration lawyers had worried over the consequences of that article. They counseled him not to reveal so much, that he was committing "legal suicide." But Jose felt freed. He had shed all his illusions. He had told the truth. He announced that he was forming a nonprofit organization called "Define American" to help other undocumented immigrants tell their story as well. "When we 'come out,' we not only liberate ourselves. We ask you to imagine yourselves in our shoes," he said. "It's a question of empathy."

Now the *Time* staff is asking him about a cover image. They want a portrait of him. He demurs. *Why not do a photo*, he asks them, *that represents the 11.5 million?* The staff looks at him dumbfounded. *Where are they?* they ask. *Can we even find any of them?* Jose laughs.

Dreaming America

On the cover he is surrounded by thirty-five young undocumented immigrants from fifteen countries, including South Korea, Brazil, Israel, Nigeria, Mexico, the Dominican Republic, Germany, and Peru, the faces of colorized America. They are all in low light. They seem to be coming out of the shadows. The cover line reads:

WE ARE AMERICANS

It is midnight the day the story is posted online. Jose had begun the week editing round-the-clock, helping organize the photo shoot, and doing media rollout. He has interviews scheduled the entire weekend. He is exhausted. But his phone is ringing. One of his close friends from the Beltway is calling. He says,

Jose, I have good news and bad news for you. Which do you want first?

The good news.

Obama has decided to defer action on the deportation of 800,000 to 1.4 million DREAMers.

Jose processes what his friend is telling him. Through presidential directive Obama has done exactly what the DREAMers had asked he do, exactly what Congress had failed to do. It is not a pathway to citizenship. But perhaps it is a start.

What's the bad news?

You don't qualify.

Obama's directive makes thirty the cutoff. Jose had turned thirty-one four months earlier.

He puts down the phone and punches the wall. He cries tears of anger. He slumps into his couch.

His eyes catch the stack of magazines fresh from the printer. He picks one up and starts counting the faces. Thirty-two of the thirty-five people will qualify for deportation relief and a temporary work permit. He sits back.

Through his tears, he smiles.

←Previous page: National Coming Out Of The Shadows Day, Chicago. March 10, 2011. Immigrant Youth Justice League. Photo by Peter Holderness.

III

On a cold morning in Washington, DC, the Capitol dome gleams bright in the winter sun. School buses pull up to the National Gallery of Art's East Building. Inside the museum, a visitor turns a corner to face a black-and-white Norman Lewis painting called *Untitled (Alabama)*. He stares.

Three fields of solid black give the painting shape—a band stretching across the top, a triangle in the left corner, and a square with a slightly tilted top in the right one. From the left middle of the canvas, Lewis has filled a cone with geometric shapes of rigorous strokes. The cone stretches across the canvas, terminating just right of the center in a dramatic vertical line dropping off the bottom of the painting. Toward the middle, the strokes begin to cohere: a Klansman's hood, a horse's head, abstractions of threat. Where the cone ends, a narrower band begins—civil rights marchers, action/reaction—its arrowlike strokes pulling in from the right edge of the canvas.

The painting is smaller than the visitor imagined it. The idea of it had swelled in his mind. Yet he is still mesmerized by its movements and codes. He thinks of Lewis's 1965 masterpiece, *Processional*, with its stormy hope, unveiled not long after the marchers moved from Selma to Montgomery. He thinks of Phase 2's graffitied subway cars of Bronx-liberated hieroglyphs.

"Do you know what you are looking at?" a voice says behind him.

The visitor finds himself stammering, "Um well, yes, I…"

He had been waiting to see a real Norman Lewis painting up close for years. He knows this painting is from 1967, two years after Spiral's *Black and White* show, a year after Spiral's demise, a year before Norman Lewis donned a protest placard before the entrance to the Metropolitan Museum of Art. The visitor turns to answer, "I mean, I've been studying Norman Lewis."

The security guard smiles. He is bald with a high forehead, his skin an ocher tone. "So you know this painting is about the artist's experiences with the night riders." He points—and the visitor gestures along with him—at Lewis's two black downstrokes against the white background forming a triangle, two more dabs for the eyes, almost a cartoon: the hood. The guard says, approvingly, "I see you've done your homework."

He explains, "When I was a young boy, when I was twelve, I used to go in the woods with my friend. Sometimes we'd watch these night riders doing their meetings."

"I saw my boss there once. I used to work at a grocery store," he continues. "He'd drive up in his truck, get out and put his hood on, go and light a cross with all the rest of them, then he'd get back in his truck and go home."

Now the visitor gawks at the guard. "How did you feel? I mean, were you scared?"

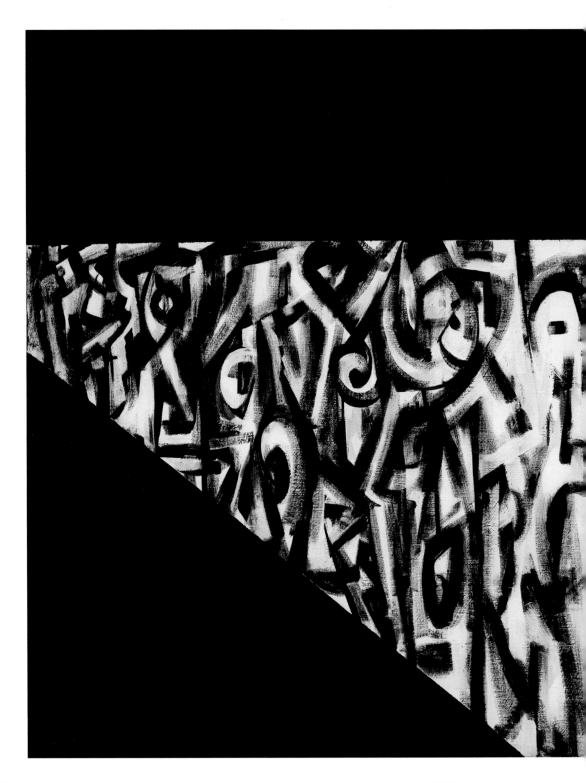

Dreaming America

"We didn't know what it was back then," he says, then pauses in thought. "You know, nothing ever happened to me in my town. It was more like they were carrying on the traditions of their forefathers."

The visitor considers this. "Um, where did you grow up?"

"Small town in Virginia, about twelve miles from the North Carolina state line," the guard says. He holds up his hands. "I'm saying this was just me. I was a young boy. Up to the early sixties they were doing stuff like this. But now? Now they're a joke."

The guard looks to his right, alerted by some noises. Two girls are posing by the Roy Lichtenstein painting of Mickey Mouse and Donald Duck. In front of Donald's word balloon—"Look Mickey, I've Hooked a Big One!!"—a wiry blond boy in a green beanie and a black Pittsburgh Steelers hoodie looks as if he is preparing to bomb the photo, a coiled spring of potential disaster.

"I'm sorry," the guard says, "let me get back to my babysitting here."

The visitor nods. He tilts his head and takes in another look at the painting. It appears different, deeper, more real. Then he turns back around the corner.

There a red-haired, middle-aged schoolteacher and her five students stare up at a high wall. On it, 429 chipboards of wood are arranged closely, each eight inches by ten inches. Up close the chips reveal subtle textures: some show their grain, others their brushstrokes, a few disclose the scratches from before they had been painted. Most are evenly colored, but some are shiny, some are flat; others have hotspots of gloss, variations like shadows on the barks of old trees. Each chip is colored within the spectrum from pink to bister.

The group stands before the wall with furrowed brows, puzzling it all out. They're magnetized but they can't say why. The teacher walks to the wall labels. There is a stenciled diagram of boxes and within each box is a person's name. Their first names are arranged alphabetically from left to right. She looks back at the wall. "Oh!" she says. "These are skin colors!"

"Ooooooooooh," coo the four girls and the boy in the hoodie, who has joined them. They stare with fresh eyes at Byron Kim's *Synecdoche*. Then they each begin to move toward the wall.

"I'm *that*," says the first girl, holding her fist up toward a cocoa-colored chip.

"That's me," says another, glasses high over her soft cheekbones, pulling along a friend as she points her fist toward a russet chip.

Her friend—brown hair pulled back in thick pigtails, long thin brown eyes framing a fair face—skips toward a dark brown chip, declaring as she raises her own fist to it, "I'm so *black*!" The two giggle with delight.

←Previous page: *W (Alabama)* by Norman W. Lewis. 1967. Oil on canvas. Courtesy of the Estate of Norman W. Lewis and Iandor Fine Arts, New Jersey.

"Help me find my color!" shouts a blond girl in Ugg boots, grabbing the hand of the boy in the hoodie. They draw close to the wall, waving their hands, eyes darting across the grid.

"You're doing it wrong," says a bronze-skinned guard in tinted glasses, gold tassel hanging off the right shoulder of his uniform, a grin lingering in his baritone voice. He strides back to a spot distant from the center of the wall and declares, "Let me show you all how."

The group gathers around him. "Here," he says. They watch as he brings his hand up to his eye line, his fingers spread casually, his palm facing away. He says, "First you hold your hand out."

And each of the six raise their open hands, seeing the colors of their fingers and the colors of the painting through them, searching for themselves and for each other, seeing together anew, as if they are reaching out to touch the future.

Dreaming America

←Previous page: *Synecdoche* by Byron Kim. 1991–present. Oil and wax on panel. 429 10 × 8 in. panels (as of 2009). In the collection of the National Art Gallery. Photo by Dennis Crowley. Courtesy James Cohan Gallery.

Acknowledgments

The tragedy of life is that you never know all the things you're supposed to know when you're supposed to know them. The best part is that you will have the chance to catch up and make some things right, or at least to recognize how much less certain about everything you really ought to be, like Dylan in "My Back Pages."

This book offers a closure of sorts to the long burst of energy and inquiry that began with *Can't Stop Won't Stop* and continued in *Total Chaos*. In the odd way that all history writing is autobiographical, this book took me back through my own process of finding and forming my own identity. It's been an opportunity to figure out what I got right and what I still need to get right.

The title came of course from the DMX song—a suitably middle-finger response to the anti-multiculturalists, I once thought, before growing younger. But I think these three words—and the four that follow—still fit. The language is still forming for the world we need to be in, and crazy as dog is, he wasn't wrong.

Who We Be was really sparked by three events that blew my mind after I finished *Can't Stop Won't Stop*. So here's where my acknowledgments must begin.

On May 18, 2005, I was privileged to curate a panel at the Ford Foundation called "Got Next: Identity and Aesthetics After Multiculturalism." The discussion, commissioned by Roberta Uno at Ford, led by Greg Tate, and featuring Vijay Prashad, Mark Anthony Neal, and Brian Cross, meant to focus on hip-hop. But it quickly spun into a wide-ranging conversation on the legacies of multiculturalism. It was a head-spinning session that reframed so much recent history many of us had so quickly forgotten.

Later that evening, we went to the Bronx Museum of the Arts for another panel, this time on hip-hop in the visual arts, curated and moderated by Lydia Yee. She framed the talk by first acknowledging the impact that the mid-1990s backlash against identity had on the contemporary art world and young artists of color of the Post Generation. This discussion panel, featuring the artists Nadine Robinson, Sanford Biggers, Jackie Salloum, and Luis Gispert, helped me to think harder about the role that the arts and artists played as targets of reaction and agents of change.

Both of these panels happened at a point when few were talking about the culture wars of the 1990s. 9/11 had created a patriotic kind of multiculturalism, and pop culture itself was still in the thrall of hip-hop's millennial takeover. No one knew that the return of the culture wars was right around the corner.

In 2009, Hua Hsu's cover story in the inauguration-month issue of the *Atlantic*, "The End of White America?", captured the paradox of the post-racial moment and pointed suggestively at the return of the culture wars. Hua's essay endures. It has helped frame media discussions around race in the Obama era. Hua and his essay made me feel that writing about the colorization of America wasn't actually that insane.

So in addition to all those generously brilliant people I mentioned above, my thanks also go to those who helped manifest these moments—San San Wong, Christine Balancé, Margaret Wilkerson, Dr. Allison Bernstein, Tricia Rose, and the 2005–2006 staffs at the Ford Foundation, the Bronx Museum of the Arts, and La Peña Cultural Center.

OK. Y'all ready? This book took forever, so the list is gonna be mad long. Adjust your reading glasses.

In no particular order, I would like to share my gratitude with all those who helped me on this long journey.

Thank you to Joy Yoon, Trevor Schoonmaker, Isolde Brielmaier, Jennifer Fallago Monahan, Kinshasha Holman Conwill, John Jay, Laura Kina, Kai Ma, Sin Yen Ling, Jane Kim, David Leonard, Judilee Reed, the late inspirational Karin Higa, Martin Perna, Connie Wolf, Elisabeth Sussman, Kori Newkirk, Daniel Joseph Martinez, Nizan Shaked, Helene Winer, and Ala Ebtekar.

Thank you to the late great Morrie Turner, Karol Trachtenberg, Aaron McGruder, Andrea Fraser, Ali Wong, Keri Smith Esguia, W. Kamau Bell, Hari Kondabolu, Marlene Cancio Ramirez, Alan Wallach, Byron Kim, Carol Duncan, Charles Stone III, Claude Grunitzky, Cornell Belcher, David Ross, Gravity Goldberg, James Leventhal, Donald Newman, Faith Ringgold, Grace Matthews, Franklin Sirmans, Gaby Pacheco, Glenn Ligon, Thelma Golden, Hank Willis Thomas, and his entire studio staff.

Thank you to Howardena Pindell, Ishmael Reed, Tennessee Reed, Al Young, Janine Antoni, Jamel Shabazz, Peter Holderness, Janet Henry, Angela Fullen, Jessica Hagedorn, John Hanhardt, John Lee and Jiae Kim, john a. powell, Jose Antonio Vargas, Tania Mitchell, Judy Baca, Chris Eisenberg, Miles Bennett-Smith, Jerome Reyes, Gina Hernandez Clarke, Chris Gonzalez Clarke, Elvira Prieto, Al Camarillo, Ramón Saldívar, José David Saldívar, Kathy Coll, and Steve Phillips.

Thank you to Andrew Leland, Vendela Vida, Izabela Moi, Karrie Jacobs, Oliviero Toscani, Kay WalkingStick, Laura Trippi, Frances Phillips, Alexandra Chang, Linda Craighead, James Rucker, Gary Simmons, Lucy Lippard, Margo Machida, Coco Fusco, Billy Wimsatt, Davey D, Matt Revelli, Maya Soetoro, Harry Gamboa Jr., Juan Capistran, Melanie Cervantes & Jesus Barraza of Dignidad Rebelde, Mark Gonzales, Aaron Perry-Zucker, Ernesto Yerena, Melissa Chiu, Susette Min, James Bernard, Baye Adofo, Josh MacPhee, Aura Bogado, Arlene Goldbard, Brett Cook, Paul McMahon, Christine Kim, and Ragland Watkins.

Thank you to Angela Davis, Reggie Hudlin, Touré, Neil Arthur, John Jay, Lorrie Boula, Richard Wayner, Rita Gonzalez, Susan Wyatt, Rosa Clemente, Bakari Kitwana, Tania Unzueta, Tony Whitfield, Tyrone Forman, Vijay Iyer, Jennifer Brody, Aleta Hayes, Amita Manghnani, DJ Rekha, Dounia Mikou, Arcade Fire, Erykah Badu, Savages (Gemma Thompson and Jehnny Beth), Big Dipper Management, Thomas Dillon, Dave Twombly, Tom Gagnon, Katie Thomson, Gord Mazur & the Lavin Agency staff, Julia Martyn, Holly

Caracappa, Rachel Rosenfelt, Elizabeth Keating, and the planning committee of NCORE.

Thank you to Rinku Sen & the ARC staff, Kai Wright, Jamilah King & the entire *ColorLines* staff, Tommer Peterson & Grantmakers In the Arts staff, Alan Jenkins & the Opportunity Agenda staff, Betsy Theobald Richards & the Creative Change staff, Malkia Cyril & the Center for Media Justice Staff, Vincent Pan & the CAA and AACRE staffs, Anne Pasternak, Laura Raicovich, Nato Thompson, and the Creative Time staff.

Thank you to Eugene Kuo, Shinji Kuwayama, Kristina Rizga, Mike Stern, Maribel Alvarez, Sharon Zapata, Jose Antonio Vargas, Logan Phillips, Kat Rodriguez, Lindsay Marshall, Raul Alqaraz, Alfredo Gutierrez, Isabel Garcia, Carlos Garcia, Jeff Biggers, Roberto Bedoya, Leilani Clark, Deyden Tethong, Susan Davis, Elizabeth Kabler, Binta Brown, Fernando Garcia-Dory, Rick Lowe, Olga Garay, Maori Holmes, Tariq Trotter, Rich Nichols, Chinua Thelwell, and the Mochilla fam—Eric Coleman, Luke Lynch, and Mike Park. Thank you to Dustin Cable, Meredith Gunter, Amy Muldoon, and the Weldon Cooper Center for Public Service for allowing us to use their Racial Dot Map, which grabbed many hours of our curiosity and time.

Thank you to Scott Kurashige, Tim Noakes, Daniel Hartwig, Alex Tom, jelani Cobb, Teju Cole, Daniel Alarcon, Anna Deavere Smith, and Rebecca Solnit.

I am constantly inspired by my CultureStrike fam—Andy Hsiao, Ken Chen, Favianna Rodriguez, Yahaira Carrillo, Julio Salgado, Michelle Chen, Sharmila Venkatasubban, Kemi Bello, Marco Flores, Sonia Giunansaca, Oree Original, Cynthia Brothers, and all our past and present staff members, board members, participants, and supporters.

To the Culture Group for the intellectual intensity and the not-so-intellectual stuff, too—Brian Komar, Erin Potts, Liz Manne, Ian Inaba, Alexis McGill Johnson, Yosi Sergant, Gan Golan, Emily Smith, Jessy Tolkan—thank you.

For their invaluable research help, thanks to Jess Wilcox and the entire Artists Space staff, Camille Billops and James Hatch from the Camille Billops and James V. Hatch Archives, and Kristen Leipert at the Whitney Museum Archives.

For their generous support, thanks to Cora Mirikitani and the Center for Cultural Innovation for their Investing in Artists grant, to the United States Artists program for their generous fellowship, and to the Gaea Foundation for the Sea Change Residency, during which I finished the first complete draft of this book. Thanks to Peggy, Chris & Carla, Durga, and Gaylord for letting me soak up the creative vibes in that amazing cottage and for making my time there exactly what I needed.

To the Youth Speaks/Brave New Voices/Life Is Living fam, you give me hope.

I could not have completed this book without having a special team to work with. To Carlo De La Cruz, Denise Beek, Freddy Anzures, Anna Alves, and especially the super-clutch Gabrielle Zucker and Stephen Serrato, my gratitude is bottomless.

Robert Karimi gave me the right advice at the right moment. Adam Mansbach, Elizabeth Mendez Berry, Oliver Wang, Sharon Mizota, Harry Elam, David Leonard, Kiese

Laymon, Charles Yao, Kristina Rizga, Mike Stern, Joan Morgan, and Jungwon Kim were brave enough to read the book when I was doubtful it would ever amount to anything. If this was all they did, I would be forever indebted. But theirs was also a well that was always full.

B+ was the patron saint of this book.

My IDA family has kept me in motion. I am grateful for their boundless energy and easy genius. A big thank you to the brilliant H. Samy Alim, Ellen Oh, Elizabeth Quinlan, and the entire IDA fam for always having my back. Samy, thanks for taking a chance.

To the St. Martin's Press, Picador, and Macmillan family, especially James Meader, Alexandra Sehulster, Stephen Morrison, David Rogers, James Iacobelli, and Josh Kendall, thank you for always making great things happen.

To Surie Rudoff and Diana Frost, thanks for keeping me honest and correct. To Josh Karpf for expert copyediting.

To all those I forgot, it was my head, not my heart. My head will be buying the food and drinks.

To Victoria Sanders, for never giving up and always knowing what's next. As the kids say, you Tha Bawse.

To Benee Knauer, Chris Kepner, Bernadette Baker-Baughman, Gillian Barnard, and everyone who has worked in that office for the trust, honesty, and the open door.

To Monique Patterson, for believing. It's been an incredible ride. Here we go again!

To the Changs, the Chais, the Pagaduans, and the Andayas, I will *always* represent.

To Lourdes, Jonathan, Solomon, it's always all for you.

Grace Lee Boggs says, "We are the children of Martin and Malcolm, and our duty is to shake the world a new dream."

She also says, "I don't know what the American revolution will look like but you might be able to imagine it, if your imagination were rich enough."

I am one of the children of Grace, and I be dreaming togther with you.

—J

Notes

Seeing America

1. Jennifer N. Gutsell and Michael Inzlicht, "Empathy Constrained: Prejudice Predicts Reduced Mental Simulation of Actions During Observation of Outgroups," *Journal of Experimental Social Psychology* 46 (2010): 841–45.
2. Vijay Iyer, "Improvisation, Rhythm, Empathy, and Experience: A Perspective from Embodied Music Cognition," unpublished paper, February 2013.
3. Raymond Wiliams, *Keywords: A Vocabulary of Culture and Society* (New York and London: Routledge, 1976), 76.
4. Eduardo Galeano, *Days and Nights of Love and War* (London: Monthly Review Press, 2000), 138.
5. I am indebted to Brian Komar for this idea. Abraham Lincoln once said, "Public sentiment is everything. With public sentiment, nothing can fail; without it nothing can succeed." He added, "Consequently he who moulds public sentiment goes deeper than he who enacts statutes or pronounces decisions. He [who moulds public sentiment] makes statutes and decisions possible or impossible to be executed." See Jeff Chang and Brian Komar, "Culture before Politics," *American Prospect,* December 6, 2010, http://prospect.org/article/culture-politics.
6. Patrick J. Buchanan, *Suicide of a Superpower: Will America Survive Until 2025?* (New York: St. Martin's Press, 2011), 5.
7. Andrew Malcolm, "Obama Joker Artist Unmasked: A Fellow Chicagoan," *Los Angeles Times*, August 17, 2009.
8. "Glenn Beck: Obama Is a Racist." CBS News Web site. July 29, 2009, http://www.cbsnews.com/news/glenn-beck-obama-is-a-racist/.
9. Toni Morrison, *Playing in the Dark: Whiteness and the Literary Imagination* (Cambridge: Harvard University Press, 1992), 9.
10. Susan Sontag, *On Photography* (New York: Farrar, Straus and Giroux, 1977), RosettaBooks e-book edition (2005), 15.

Part One: A New Culture, 1963–1979

Chapter One
Rainbow Power: Morrie Turner and the Kids

A Note on Interviews
For this book I conducted dozens of personal interviews. In instances where a quote is not accompanied by a footnote, it comes from a personal interview.

1.   Franklin's father was serving in the war. But Schulz never really developed the Franklin character, perhaps stung by Black criticism that Franklin (at least in the black-and-white dailies) did not look much different from Pigpen. In 1977, he admitted to an interviewer, "I think it would be wrong for me to attempt to do racial humor because what do I know about what it is like to be black?"
Mort Walker also consulted with Turner before introducing Lt. Jack Flap in 1970. Walker was a Nixonite but clearly loved Flap's character. In Flap's very first appearance in October 1970, the goateed, Afroed, fist-pumpingly proud officer yelled at Sarge, "How come there's no Blacks in this honkie outfit?!" It reportedly remains one of Colin Powell's favorite comic strips of all time. Walker says he immediately lost ten to fifteen newspapers with that strip.

2.   Christopher P. Lehman, *The Colored Cartoon: Black Representation in American Animated Short Films, 1907–1954* (Amherst: University of Massachusetts Press, 2007), 1, 3–4.

3.   The shaved head was the mark of a lice-prone ghetto child.

4.   Outcault's later strip *Pore Lil Mose*, starring a Black country boy come to the big city, simply made plain the debt early comics owed to minstrelsy.

5.   Herriman's biraciality—his birth to Creole New Orleans parents was confirmed twenty-five years after his death—has recently caused a reassessment of his entire corpus of work. It became a cause célèbre when Ishmael Reed dedicated his classic 1972 novel *Mumbo Jumbo* to "George Herriman, Afro-American, who created Krazy Kat." The last word on the topic could be Jeet Heer's essay "The Kolors of Krazy Kat" in *Krazy and Ignatz: The Complete Full-Page Comic Strips, 1935–1936* (Seattle: Fantagraphics, 2005), 8.

6.   For a fascinating genealogy of how the name "Mose" passed from signifying "a particular type of rough, rowdy, and often dandified urban white youth," "an American urban hero," to becoming the domesticated blackface husband to Aunt Jemima, see David Roediger's *The Wages of Whiteness* (New York: Verso, 1991), 99–100.

7.	In 2009 Niall Ferguson launched a blogworthy dustup when he compared Obama to Felix the Cat, saying, "Felix was not only black. He was very very lucky." When some called him on it, Ferguson got none other than Henry Louis Gates Jr. to clear him of racial wrongdoing. Gates wrote, "Felix's blackness, like Mickey's and Minnie's, was like a suit of clothes, not a skin color…You are safe on this one." But cartoon historians might point Gates and Ferguson to such late-1920s and -1930s cartoons as *Uncle Tom's Crabbin'* or *Mickey's Mellerdrammer*, just two examples of the ways blackface design and blackface minstrelsy easily fed each other.

8.	Henry T. Sampson's survey *That's Enough, Folks! Black Images in Animated Cartoons, 1900–1960* (Lanham, MD: Scarecrow Press, 1998) summarizes hundreds of examples, including the most famous of them, Warner Bros.' so-called Censored Eleven. Many of the most offensive cartoons of this era have been suppressed since the late 1960s. Their presence remains controversial, as evidenced in a 2008 YouTube controversy in which many of the Censored Eleven cartoons were removed from the site. A large underground market has developed among animation enthusiasts for bootlegged copies of these cartoons and hundreds more like them. Some call their inaccessibility censorship and blame a regime of multiculturalist corporate political correctness. Others collect them like some do racist toys, as reminders of how times have changed. The NAACP's position was "that the cartoons are despicable. We encourage the films' owners to maintain them as they are—that is, locked away in their vaults."

9.	Lehman argues in *The Colored Cartoon* that jazz was key to both characters. Mickey's famous first sound appearance in *Steamboat Willie* (1928) was set to a tune based on the minstrel song "Zip Coon." He also argues that Tex Avery infused Bugs with a Black aesthetic of folktale trickster moxie and urban bebop cool.

10.	Characters of color did still appear in the adventure comics, mostly as bumbling sidekicks, primitive enemies, or both. In this sense, they often followed the European comics, such as Hergé's *Tintin* series, informed by an imperialist imagination. Milton Caniff's invention of the salacious *hapa*-Chinese pirate leader the Dragon Lady for *Terry and the Pirates* took race-typing in a different direction.

11.	The rise of the Asian American movement was still three years into the future as well.

12.	In that regard Campbell was following in a tradition that had dated back to eighteenth-century Black painters like Joshua Johnson and Robert Duncanson.

13.	In a May 1970 strip for *Negro Digest*, Turner had a white man at the beach hearing the same words from a conch shell!

14.	Chester Himes, *My Life of Absurdity: The Autobiography of Chester Himes*, vol. 2 (Garden City, NY: Doubleday), 1.

15.	Caniff's creation George Webster Confucius was a quintessentially American invention, the Yellow Kid made yellow. In his work for *Terry and the Pirates* and *Steve Canyon*, Caniff was not allowed by his syndicates to identify the Japanese antagonists as anything but "the invaders." This ended when World War II kicked in. Caniff then did a strip for an armed forces training manual that has become a minor Internet sensation. It meant to clue the boys into how to tell the difference between Chinese and Japanese soldiers, and it was called *How to Spot a Jap*.

16. In 1980, Bronx activists protested the Paul Newman vehicle *Fort Apache, The Bronx* over its depictions of Blacks and Puerto Ricans, the start of a decade of protests against Hollywood representations. See *Can't Stop Won't Stop* (New York: Picador, 2005), 145.

17. Jerry Craft, creator of *Mama's Boyz*, posted the cartoons at http://www.mamasboyz.com/news/protest.html along with a passionate essay on why he joined the protest.

18. "But Is It Racist?", post by Karisue Wyson, February 8, 2008, *Washington Post* Writers Group Blog, archived at https://web.archive.org/web/20101009101901/http://postwritersgroup.com/BlogArchives/200802.html.

Chapter Two
After Jericho: The Struggle Against Invisibility

1. Martin Luther King Jr., "Statement on Ending the Bus Boycott," December 20, 1956, speech delivered in Montgomery, AL, http://mlk-kpp01.stanford.edu/index.php/encyclopedia/documentsentry/statement_on_ending_the_bus_boycott/.

2. *Jet*, March 17, 1955, 33.

3. Martin Luther King Jr. "Facing the Challenge of a New Age," January 1 1957, speech delivered at NAACP Emancipation Day, Washington, DC, Papers of Martin Luther King Jr., http://mlk-kpp01.stanford.edu/primarydocuments/Vol4/1-Jan-1957_FacingtheChallenge.pdf.

4. Martin Luther King Jr., "Desegregation and the Future," December 15, 1956 speech delivered at the Annual Luncheon of the National Committee for Rural Schools, New York, NY. From the Martin Luther King Jr. Papers Project, *The Papers of Martin Luther King, Jr.: Birth of a New Age, Volume III, December 1955–December 1956* (Berkeley: University of California Press, 1997), 475, http://mlk-kpp01.stanford.edu/primarydocuments/Vol3/15-Dec-1956_DesegregationAndTheFuture.pdf.

5. Ibid.

6. Ibid.

7. Ibid.

8. Ibid.

9. Elsa Honig Fine, *The Afro-American Artist: A Search for Identity* (New York: Holt, Rinehart and Winston, 1973), 154.

10. Sharon F. Patton, *African-American Art* (Oxford and New York: Oxford University Press, 1998), 185.

11. Ralph Ellison, "If the Twain Shall Meet," in *The Collected Essays of Ralph Ellison*, edited by John Callahan (New York: Modern Library, 1995), 567.

12. Ralph Ellison, "Chant of Saints: The Art of Romare Bearden." *The Massachusetts Review* 18:4 (1977), 674, 675, 678; first published in 1968.

13. Patton, *African-American Art*, 197. In 1970, she would be arrested and jailed for her participation in "The People's Flag Show." The charge was "desecrating the flag." See Faith Ringgold, *We Flew Over the Bridge: The Memoirs of Faith Ringgold* (Durham, NC: Duke University Press, 2005), 181–86.

14. Bill Moyers, *Moyers on America: A Journalist and His Times* (New York: Anchor Books, 2005), 167.

15. Ibid., 167.

16. Rick Perlstein, *Nixonland: The Rise of a President and the Fracturing of America* (New York: Scribner, 2008), 79.

17. Ibid., 202. See also Richard Nixon, "What Has Happened to America?", *Reader's Digest*, October 1967, http://college.cengage.com/history/ayers_primary_sources/nixon_1967.htm.

18. James Boyd, "Nixon's Southern Strategy: It's All in the Charts," *New York Times Magazine*, May 17, 1970.

19. Ibid.

20. E. W. Kenworthy, "Nixon: A Tightrope in the South," *New York Times*, September 29, 1968.

21. Perlstein, *Nixonland*, 341.

22. Barbara Ehrenreich, *Fear of Falling: The Inner Life of the Middle Class* (New York: Pantheon Books, 1989), 130.

23. Ibid., 141.

24. H. R. Haldeman, *The Haldeman Diaries: Inside the Nixon White House* (New York: P.G. Putnam's Sons, 1994), 53.

25. Thomas A. Johnson, "Negro Leaders See Bias in Call of Nixon for 'Law and Order,'" *New York Times*, August 13, 1968, 27.

26. E. W. Kenworthy, "Nixon Strategy in South: Humphrey Attack on Wallace Causes G.O.P. Nominee to Shift His Tactics," *New York Times*, October 5, 1968, 20.

27. Lawrence's presence was important: his Migration series had been purchased jointly by the MOMA and the Phillips Collection in 1941, and he became the first Black artist to have his works bought and exhibited in the MOMA.

28. Ringgold, *We Flew Over the Bridge*, 167.

29. Its reputation would be resuscitated a generation later by Henry Louis Gates Jr.

30. Most photos and slides were from the collection of James Van Der Zee.

31. Grace Glueck, "The Total Involvement of Thomas Hoving," *New York Times Magazine*, December 8, 1968.

32. Ibid.

33. "The Black Artist in America: A Symposium," *The Metropolitan Museum of Art Bulletin* 27:5 (January 1969) 246. http://resources.metmuseum.org/resources/metpublications/pdf/The_Metropolitan_Museum_of_Art_Bulletin_v_27_no_5_January_1969.pdf.

34. Before the exhibition closed, Hoving faced controversies over a catalog essay by a Black high school student some thought was anti-Semitic, and a vandal carving letters into a Rembrandt painting. It culminated for Hoving with a full-fledged trustee revolt.

35. "The Shame of the Art World," manifesto printed in *East Village Other*, February 14, 1969, reprinted in Art Workers' Coalition, *Documents: Open Hearing*, originally published in 1969, reprinted by Editorial Doble J, 2010, 19–21.

36. In a statement signed by the United Black Artists Committee, Lloyd and Ringgold demanded that the wing be created within eighteen months, that MOMA acquire at least one hundred works of Black artists, create a Black artist advisory board, and mount special exhibitions, including ones of African art and Bearden's work. The list of signers included Bearden, Oscar Brown Jr., Ossie Davis, and eighteen others. See United Black Artists Committee and other Black Artists, letter of "Students and Artists United for a Martin Luther King Jr. Study Center for Black Art at the Museum of Modern Art in New York City," n.d., 1969, courtesy of the Camille Billops and James V. Hatch Archives.

37. Grace Glueck, "Negroes' Art Is What's In Just Now," *New York Times*, February 27, 1969, D34.

38. Sharon F. Patton, "The Search for Identity, 1950–1987," in *African-American Artists 1880–1987: Selections from the Evans-Tibbs Collection* (Washington, DC: Smithsonian Institution Traveling Exhibition Service, in association with the University of Washington Press, 1989), 100.

39. Frances Fox Piven and Richard A. Cloward, *Poor People's Movements: Why They Succeed, How They Fail* (New York: Vintage Books, 1977), 269.

Chapter Three
"The Real Thing": Lifestyling and Its Discontents

1. Bill Backer, *The Care and Feeding of Ideas* (New York: Crown, 1993), 5.

2.   Ibid., 251.

3.   Richard S. Tedlow, *New and Improved: The Story of Mass Marketing in America* (New York: Basic Books, 1991), 50.

4.   Ibid, 54. See also Tristan Donovan, *Fizz: How Soda Shook Up the World* (Chicago: Chicago Review Press, 2014), 80.

5.   E. J. Kahn, "The Universal Drink III: A Matter of Syllables," *New Yorker*, February 28, 1959, 56.

6.   E. J. Kahn, "The Universal Drink IV: An Innocent Friendship," *New Yorker*, March 7, 1959, 64.

7.   Tedlow, *New and Improved*, 101.

8.   For more about Pepsi's pioneering efforts to reach Black consumers after World War II, see *The Real Pepsi Challenge*, Stephanie Capparell (New York: Free Press, 2008).

9.   Mark Pendergrast, *For God, Country and Coca-Cola*, 2nd ed. (New York: Basic Books, 2000), 253, 266. The battle heated up once again in the mid-sixties when Pepsi hired a Black vice president of corporate planning, prompting KKK-led protests. Pepsi responded with a "Fight the Klan, Drink Pepsi" campaign. See also Donovan, *Fizz*, 164.

10. Pendergrast, *For God, Country and Coca-Cola*, 266.

11. Ibid.

12. *Ebony*, November 1959, 15.

13. *Ebony*, November 1959, 167.

14. Bob Stoddard, *Pepsi: 100 Years* (Santa Monica, CA: General Publishing Group, 1997), 133.

15. *Ebony*, February 1960, 24.

16. Stoddard, *Pepsi: 100 Years*, 141.

17. "New Faces: Sommers Is Icumen On," *Time*, December 15, 1961.

18. Backer, *Care and Feeding of Ideas*, 238.

19. Stanley C. Hollander, *Was There a Pepsi Generation before Pepsi Discovered It? Youth-based Segmentation in Marketing* (Lincolnwood, IL: NTC Business Books, 1992).

20. John Paul Freeman, "The Real Thing: 'Lifestyle' and 'Cultural' Appeals in Television Advertising for Coca-Cola, 1969–1976," PhD diss., University of North Carolina at Chapel Hill, 1986, 14. Emphasis added.

21. Backer, *Care and Feeding of Ideas*, 271.

22. Frederick L. Allen, *Secret Formula: How Brilliant Marketing and Relentless Salesmanship Made Coca-Cola the Best-known Product in the World* (New York: HarperCollins, 1994), 322. During the next decade Bryant would become notorious for her antigay activism.

23. Freeman, "The Real Thing," 113.

24. Allen, *Secret Formula*, 353–54.

25. This is detailed in Pendergrast, *For God, Country and Coca-Cola*, 293–97, 370–71.

26. Pendergrast, *For God, Country and Coca-Cola*, 301.

27. Freeman, "The Real Thing," 175–79.

28. Renato Rosaldo, *Culture & Truth: The Remaking of Social Analysis* (Boston: Beacon Press, 1989), 69.

29. Freeman, "The Real Thing," 220.

30. For its part, BBDO went on to design Nixon's silent-majority campaign.

31. Backer, *Care and Feeding of Ideas*, 7.

32. Ibid., 8.

Chapter Four
Every Man an Artist, Every Artist a Priest:
The Invention of Multiculturalism

1. Ishmael Reed, "Ishmael Reed on the Miltonian Origin of the Other," East Village: The Local Blog, January 28, 2012, http://eastvillage.thelocal.nytimes.com/2012/01/28/ishmael-reed-on-the-revolutionary-satanic-origin-of-the-other/.

2. Shamoon Zahir, "An Interview with Ishmael Reed," *Callaloo* 17:4 (Autumn 1994), 1136.

3. Ishmael Reed, "An Interview with Franklin Sirmans," in *NeoHoodoo: Art for a Forgotten Faith* (Yale University Press, 2008), 77.

4. Rickey Vincent, *Funk: The Music, the People, and the Rhythm of the One* (New York: St. Martin's Griffin), 175-77.

5. Vine Deloria Jr., *Custer Died for Your Sins: An Indian Manifesto* (New York: Macmillan, 1969), 174.

6. Alan Lomax, "Appeal for Cultural Equity," *Journal of Communication* 27:2 (Spring 1977), 137.

7. See her story "The Apprentice" in *The Seabirds Are Still Alive* (New York: Random House, 1977), her foreword in Cherrile Moraga and Gloria Anzaldula, eds., *This Bridge Called My Back: Writings of Radical Women of Color* (Watertown, MA: Persephone Press, 1981). Also, "At a writers' conference at Howard University sponsored by the Institute for the Arts and Humanities in April of 1976, Sister Toni Cade Bambara said: 'The responsibility of a writer representing an oppressed people is to make revolution irresistible.'" John Oliver Killens, "Lorraine Hansberry: On Time!", in *Freedomways Reader: Prophets in Their Own Country*, ed. Esther Cooper Jackson and Constance Pohl (Boulder, CO: Westview Press, 2000), 335, originally

published in 1979.

8.   Ray Riegert, "Ishmael Reed Hoo-Doos the Cultural Nazis," *Berkeley Barb*, December 12–18, 1977, 8–9.

9.   Malcolm X, "A Message to the Grassroots," speech delivered in Detroit, MI, November 10, 1963, http://xroads.virginia.edu/~public/civilrights/a0147.html.

10.   Ishmael Reed, "Integration or Cultural Exchange?," *Yardbird Reader* 5 (1976), 3.

11.   Riegert, "Ishmael Reed Hoo-Doos the Cultural Nazis," 8–9.

Chapter Five
Color Theory: Race Trouble in the Avant-Garde

1.   "Trudie Grace and Irving Sandler," interviewed by Joan Rosenbaum, in Claudia Gould and Valerie Smith, eds., *5000 Artists Return to Artists Space: 25 Years* (New York: Artists Space, 1998), 21.

2.   Legs McNeil and Gillian McCain, *Please Kill Me: The Uncensored Oral History of Punk.* (New York: Penguin Books, 1997), 275.

3.   A few years later, he sang "I'm Against It" on their album *Road to Ruin*, which could be called the Ramones's manifesto. Technically it leans right. In reality it calls for nothing. Politics wasn't the point.

4.   Lucy Lippard, ed, *Six Years: The Dematerialization of the Art Object from 1966 to 1972* (Berkeley: University of California Press, reprint edition, 1997), 75.

5.   In 2010, the advertising agency OgilvyOne Worldwide sponsored a contest on YouTube called "The Search for the World's Greatest Sales Person," offering a job to the winner. Their task? Sell a brick.

6.   Alan Wallach, "Furor Continues over Exhibit of 'Nigger Drawings,'" *Art Workers News*, May 1979, 7.

7.   Paul McMahon in *5000 Artists Return to Artists Space*, 85.

8.   His work was often hilarious, and included a 1984 Fab-5-Freddy-and-Charlie-Ahearn-sendup music video called *Mild Style*.

9.   Dick Gregory with Robert Lipsyte, *Nigger: An Autobiography* (New York: Dutton, 1964), 209.

10.   Jerry Farber, *The Student as Nigger: Essays and Stories* (North Hollywood: Contact Books, 1969). "Artists are the Blacks of the white intelligentsia," Lucy Lippard had written in an Art Workers' Coalition manifesto, "A bright, angry Black woman artist may be the most explosive factor around." Lucy Lippard, ed., *Get the Message? A Decade of Art for Social Change* (New York: Dutton, 1984), 17.

11.   David Driskell once told Esther Iverem a story about speaking to his friend Georgia O'Keeffe at the opening to her Whitney retrospective in October 1970. He com-

plained that there were no places for African American artists to show. O'Keeffe told him, "What are you complaining about? You're a man! If there's any such thing as the niggers of the art world, it's women. It's not any man." Esther Iverem, "David Driskell's Big Picture: A Connoisseur of African American Art Frames His Collection in a Broader Context," *Washington Post*, November 23, 1998, D1.

12. Richard Goldstein added in his piece, "The Romance of Racism," "If neutralizing language is what their work has been about, then shouldn't the victim be let in on the joke?" Goldstein, "The Romance of Racism," *Village Voice*, April 2, 1979.

13. For a thorough and compelling unpacking of the white radical/avant-garde fascination with the notion of "the nigger," see Stephen Duncombe and Maxwell Tremblay, eds., *White Riot: Punk Rock and the Politics of Race* (New York: Verso, 2011). The antithesis of this position is in the shock-value aesthetic of pioneering punk zinester John Holmstrom. "I mean, we weren't racists. But we were unashamedly saying, 'We're white, and we're proud. Like, they're black and they're proud. That's fine. We were totally into that, you know? I always thought, if you're black and you want to be hip you're a Black Panther, and you tell whitey to go fuck off. And you carry a gun. That's what I thought was cool. And if you're white, you're like us. You don't try to be black. What I thought was stupid was white people trying to act black. Like Lester. His use of the word 'nigger' was his way of trying to act black. He was trying to be the 'white nigger.' The 'white nigger' idea was Norman Mailer's fifties lesson in how to be cool. And we were really rejecting that. We were rejecting the fifties and sixties instructions on how to be cool." McNeil and McCain, *Please Kill Me*, 278.

14. Philip J. Deloria, *Playing Indian* (New Haven: Yale University Press, 1999), 9.

15. McNeil and McCain, *Please Kill Me*, 371.

16. Wallach, "Furor Continues," 7.

17. "Open Letter to Artists' Space," March 5, 1979, courtesy of the Artists Space Archive. The signers were: Carl Andre, Amy Baker, Rudolf Baranik, Edit DeAk, Cliff Joseph, Kate Linker, Lucy Lippard, Howardena Pindell, Faith Ringgold, Ingrid Sischy, May Stevens, and Tony Whitfield.

18. Kellie Jones, "Howardena Pindell: Painter," interview conducted April 2, 1989, *Artist and Influence* 9 (1990), 114.

19. Ibid.

20. Western Union Mailgram to Helene Winer from the New York State Council on the Arts, March 5, 1979. Sourced from the Camille Billops and James V. Hatch Archives.

21. Letter from Linda Goode Bryant to Kitty Carlisle Hart, Chairperson, New York State Council on the Arts, March 14, 1979, sourced from both the Artists Space Archive and the Camille Billops and James V. Hatch Archives. This quote also headlined

a flyer from Action Against Racism in the Arts, undated. Sources from the Artists Space Archive.

22. Letter from Janet Henry to James Reinisch, Program Associate, Visual Arts Services, New York State Council on the Arts, March 6, 1979, sourced from both the Artists Space Archive and the Camille Billops and James V. Hatch Archives.

23. Henry to Reinisch.

24. Donald Newman, "In Response to the Open Letter (Attached) You Sent to Artists' Space on March 5th," March 8, 1979, sourced from the Artists Space Archive.

25. Artists Space public letter, March 10, 1979, sourced from the Artists Space Archive and the Camille Billops and James V. Hatch Archives. The letter read, in part: Artists Space made a commitment to the artist and his work, and as in other instances, respected his right to present his work unedited. Artists Space and the artist acknowledge that greater and different consideration should have been given to the title in this case. We made an error in assuming that this word could be legitimately used in an art context. In fact, it appears to many its use is categorically unacceptable. . . . It is our sincere wish that this incident not affect our ability to continue to provide a viable program.

26. Groan! Goldstein, "Romance of Racism."

27. The full list of signers is: Carl Andre, Benny Andrews, Rudolf Baranik, Joan Braderman, Horace Brockington, Linda Bryant, Donna DeSalvo, Carol Duncan, Mel Edwards, Leon Golub, Paul Goode, David Hammons, Janet Henry, Cliff Joseph, Janet Koenig, Sol LeWitt, Lucy Lippard, Howardena Pindell, Charles Simonds, Ingrid Sischy, Michelle Stuart, Joyce Timpanelli, Alan Wallach, Randy Williams. See also "Letters: Art and Language Divorced," *Village Voice*, April 9, 1979.

28. Unaddressed open letter from Donald Newman, April 7, 1979, sourced from the Artists Space Archive. The critic Craig Owens echoed this argument almost word for word in a defense of Newman in the April issue of *Skyline* magazine. It's not clear who wrote the passage first. "Is it not ironic that those 'liberals' who in the sixties, when government support of the arts was hotly debated, warned against the danger of censorship, turn out to be precisely those who attempt to use the governmental agency as an instrument of repression." From "Black and White," *Skyline*, April 1979, 16.

29. E-mail letter to author, February 10, 2010.

30. Jacqueline Trescott, "Minorities and the Visual Arts: Controversy Before the Endowment," *Washington Post*, May 2, 1979.

31. Goldstein, "Romance of Racism."

32. Douglas Crimp, "Commentaries on Artists Space's Exhibit of 'Nigger Drawings,'" *Art Workers News*, June 1979.

33. Elizabeth Hess, "Art-World Apartheid," *Seven Days* 3:6 (May 18, 1979), 27.

34.   Roberta Smith, "Donald at Artists Space," *Art in America*, July–August 1979.

35.   Letter from Alan Wallach to James Reinisch, Visual Arts Services, New York State Council on the Arts, March 19, 1979.

36.   Hess, "Art-World Apartheid."

37.   Goldstein, "Romance of Racism."

38.   Lawrence Alloway, "Art," *Nation*, May 26, 1979, citing a study by Nancy Jervis and Maureen Schilds published in the April 1979 issue of *Art Workers News*.

39.   Goldstein, "Romance of Racism."

40.   My deepest gratitude to Camille Billops and James Hatch, who took these photos and taped this meeting. They are available at the Camille Billops and James V. Hatch Archives, New York City.

41.   Elizabeth Hess, "Art-World Apartheid."

42.   "An Open Letter to all Artists," Artists Space, April 28, 1979, sourced from the Artists Space Archive.

43.   Mitchell Algus, "Donald's 'The Nigger Drawings,'" unpublished review, undated, probably mid-1990s, courtesy of the author.

44.   Lester Bangs, *Psychotic Reactions and Carburetor Dung* (New York: Anchor, 1987), 276. The original piece actually ran in the *Village Voice* on the pages immediately preceding Richard Goldstein's second story on Donald Newman, Helene Winer, and the *Nigger Drawings* controversy at Artists Space, in the April 30, 1979 issue. 1979 was a crucial year for discussing punk culture and racism. Bad Brains appeared on the New York scene later that year. Bangs also wrote that Ivan Julian, the Black guitarist for Richard Hell's band the Voidoids, had given him perspective: "Once when I was drunk I told Hell that the only reason hippies ever existed in the first place was because of niggers, and when I mentioned it to Ivan while doing this article I said, "You probably don't even remember—" "Oh yeah, I remember," he cut me off. And that was two years ago, one ostensibly harmless slip. You take a lifetime of that, and you got grounds for trying in any way possible, even it's only by convincing one individual at a time, to remove those words from the face of the earth," 277.

45.   Newman cofounded Sonicnet.com, a music Web site bought by MTV, and oversaw tech for a few Silicon Alley startups.

46.   Letter from Linda Goode Bryant to Kitty Carlisle Hart, March 14, 1979.

Part Two: Who Are We? 1980–1993

Chapter Six
The End of the World As We Know It:
Whiteness, the Rainbow, and the Culture Wars

1. David Treuer, "Kill the Indians, Then Copy Them," *New York Times*, September 29, 2012.

2. *Boogie Man: The Lee Atwater Story*, directed by Stefan Forbes (2008).

3. Thomas Byrne Edsall and Mary D. Edsall. *Chain Reaction: The Impact of Race, Rights, and Taxes on American Politics* (New York: W. W. Norton, 1991), 221–22.

4. Ibid., 145

5. Alexander Lamis, *The Two-Party South*, 2nd ed. (Oxford and New York: Oxford University Press, 1990), 26. This interview—revealed in an asterisked note in its original context—has been much cited and even more broadly debated. Less often noted is the late political scientist Lamis's own note: "Needless to say, how much one is doing away with the race issue in this context is debatable." As an addendum, the actual tape of the interview itself has now been released by Rick Perlstein on the Web site of *The Nation*: http://www.thenation.com/article/170841/exclusive-lee-atwaters-infamous-1981-interview-southern-strategy.

6. Edsall and Edsall, *Chain Reaction*, 11.

7. David Roediger, *How Race Survived U.S. History: From Settlement and Slavery to the Obama Phenomenon* (New York: Verso, 2008), 205.

8. Stuart Butler, Michael Sanera, and W. Bruce Weinrod. *Mandate for Leadership II: Continuing the Conservative Revolution* (Washington, DC: Heritage Foundation, 1984), 155.

9. Ibid.

10. John Brady, *Bad Boy: The Life and Politics of Lee Atwater* (Boston: Addison-Wesley, 1996), 183

11. Eric Alterman, "G.O.P. Chairman Lee Atwater: Playing Hardball," *New York Times Magazine*, April 30, 1989.

12. Brady, *Bad Boy*, 181.

13. Alterman, "G.O.P. Chairman Lee Atwater."

14. Ehrenreich, *Fear of Falling*, 144.

15. Ehrenreich, *Fear of Falling*, 15.

16. Scott Kraft, "Were Foreclosure Pressures to Blame? Farm Family Deaths Shock Hamlet," *Los Angeles Times*, January 10, 1986, http://articles.latimes.com/

print/1986-01-10/news/mn-839_1_farm-crisis.

17. Jeffrey S. Nordhaus, "Farm Foreclosures Will Increase," *Harvard Crimson*, April 11, 1986, http://www.thecrimson.com/article/1986/4/11/farm-foreclosures-will-in-crease-pforeclosures-on/.

18. Gary Orfield and John T. Yun, "Resegregation in America's Schools," Harvard University: The Civil Rights Project, June 1999, 12.

19. Ibid., 14.

20. Steven M. Gillon, *"That's Not What We Meant to Do": Reform and Its Unintended Consequences in Twentieth-Century America* (New York: W. W. Norton, 2000), 163–64.

21. Lyndon B. Johnson, "Remarks at the Signing of the Immigration Bill, Liberty Island, New York," October 3, 1965, http://www.lbjlib.utexas.edu/johnson/archives.hom/speeches.hom/651003.asp.

22. Office of Immigration Statistics, *2009 Yearbook of Immigration Statistics,* (Washington, DC: Department of Homeland Security, August 2010), http://www.dhs.gov/xlibrary/assets/statistics/yearbook/2009/ois_yb_2009.pdf.

23. Marshall Frady, *Jesse: The Life and Pilgrimage of Jesse Jackson* (New York: Simon & Schuster, 1996), 306.

24. All Jackson quotes are from Josh Gottheimer, ed., *Ripples of Hope: Great American Civil Rights Speeches* (New York: Basic Books, 2003), 375–76.

25. Ishmael Reed, Kathryn Trueblood, and Shawn Wong, eds., *The Before Columbus Foundation Fiction Anthology* (New York: W. W. Norton, 1992), xi.

26. Ishmael Reed, "America: The Multinational Society," in Rick Simonson and Scott Walker, eds., *The Graywolf Annual Five: Multicultural Literacy: Opening the American Mind* (St. Paul, MN: Graywolf Press, 1988), 160.

27. John F. Kennedy. "Remarks at Amherst College, October 26, 1963," http://arts.gov/about/kennedy.

28. As quoted in Michael Brenson, *Visionaries and Outcasts: The NEA, Congress, and the Place of the Visual Artist in America* (New York: New Press, 2001), 15.

29. Kennedy, "Remarks at Amherst College."

30. Stephen C. Dubin. *Arresting Images: Impolitic Art and Uncivil Actions* (Oxon and New York: Routledge, 1992), 96.

31. See Richard Bolton, ed., *Culture Wars: Documents from the Recent Controversies in the Arts* (New York: New Press, 1992), 338–42.

32. Omari H. Kokole, "The Master Essayist," in Omari H. Kokole, ed., *The Global African: A Portrait of Ali A. Mazrui* (Trenton, NJ: Africa World Press, 1998), 14. See also Jon Weiner, "'Hard to Muzzle': The Return of Lynne Cheney," *Nation*, October 2, 2000.

33. Hilton Kramer, *The Revenge of the Philistines: Art and Culture, 1972–1982* (New

York: Free Press, 1985), 335–41. See also Daniel A. Seidell, *God in the Gallery: A Christian Embrace of Modern Art* (Grand Rapids, MI: Baker Academic, 2008), 121.

34. The exhibition had previously been canceled at the Corcoran Gallery of Art. It had included the work *Man in Polyester Suit*, among many other images of Black men he had taken over the years.

35. In protest, Papp and others refused their grant awards and the oath was soon ruled unconstitutional.

36. It was the first public controversy for the author of *Push*, later renamed *Precious* for its movie adaptation.

37. Joyce Price and George Archibald, "Frohnmayer's Out at the NEA," *Washington Times*, February 22, 1992, A1.

38. John Frohnmayer, *Leaving Town Alive* (Boston: Houghton Mifflin, 1993), 324–27.

39. Robert M. Andrews, "Poll Says Majority Supports Federal Aid for Controversial Art," Associated Press, April 19, 1990.

40. Michele Wallace, "The Culture War within the Culture Wars: Race" in Julie Ault, Brian Wallis, Marianne Weems, and Philip Yenawine, eds., *Art Matters: How the Culture Wars Changed America* (New York: New York University Press, 1999), 180. Also in Michele Wallace, *Dark Designs & Visual Culture*. (Durham, NC: Duke University Press, 2004).

41. Bureau of the Census. *We the American ... Children* (Washington, DC: U.S. Department of Commerce, September 1993), https://www.census.gov/prod/cen1990/wepeople/we-10.pdf.

42. Allan Bloom, "Our Listless Universities," *National Review,* December 10, 1982, http://www.nationalreview.com/articles/218808/our-listless-universities/flashback.

43. Allan Bloom, *The Closing of the American Mind* (New York: Simon & Schuster, 1987), 147.

44. George Lowery, "40 Years Ago, a Campus Takeover that Symbolized an Era of Change," *Ezra* 1:3 (Spring 2009), http://ezramagazine.cornell.edu/SUMMER09/CampusLife.html.

45. Joseph Berger, "Scholars Attack Campus 'Radicals,'" *New York Times*, November 15, 1988.

46. Quoted from his newsletter, *From the Right*, by Nancy Murray, "Columbus and the USA: From Mythology to Ideology," *Race & Class* 33:3 (1992), Curse of Columbus issue, 55.

47. Buchanan, *Suicide of a Superpower*, viii.

48. William H. Honan, "Schlesinger Sees Free Speech in Peril," *New York Times*, May 27, 1994.

49. Richard Bernstein, *Dictatorship of Virtue: How the Battle over Multiculturalism Is Reshaping Our Schools, Our Country, Our Lives* (New York: Random House, 1995), 11.

50. Ibid., 8.

51. Ibid., 3–5.

52. Ibid., 11.

53. Ibid., 7.

54. Kwame Anthony Appiah, "The Politics of Identity," *Daedalus*, Fall 2006, 15.

55. Buchanan, *Suicide of a Superpower*, 229.

56. Malcolm X, "The Ballot or the Bullet," April 3, 1964, speech delivered in Cleveland, in *Malcolm X Speaks: Selected Speeches and Statements* (New York: Grove Press, 1990), 26.

57. Ibid.

58. Paul Beatty, *The White Boy Shuffle* (New York: Picador, 1996), 53.

59. Patrick Buchanan, "1992 Republican Convention Speech," August 17 1992, http://buchanan.org/blog/1992-republican-national-convention-speech-148.iRick Orlov, "L.A. Residents say Pat's 'Force' Story Is Fiction," *Los Angeles Daily News*, August 19, 1992, http://articles.philly.com/1992-08-19/news/25991511_1_mob-vermont-knoll-retirement-center-jewell-anderson.

Chapter Seven
Unity and Reconciliation: The Era of Identity

1. Catharine R. Stimpson, "On Differences: Modern Language Association Presidential Address," *Papers of the Modern Language Association* 106:3 (May 1991), 403.

2. Henry Louis Gates Jr., "Writing 'Race' and the Difference It Makes," *Critical Inquiry* 12:1 (Autumn 1985), 6, 12, 13.

3. Cornel West, "The New Cultural Politics of Difference," in *Out There: Marginalization and Contemporary Cultures* (New York: New Museum of Contemporary Art and Massachusetts Institute of Technology Press, 1990), 19.

4. Mary Rourke. "Marcia Tucker, 66; Curator Championed Emerging Artists," *Los Angeles Times*, October 27, 2006.

5. Nilda Peraza, "A Conversation," in Louis Young, ed., *The Decade Show: Frameworks of Identity in the 1980s* (New York: Museum of Contemporary Hispanic Art, New Museum of Contemporary Art, and Studio Museum in Harlem, 1990), 10.

6. Cited in Elaine Kim, "Interstitial Subjects: Asian American Visual Art as a Site for New Cultural Conversations," in Elaine H. Kim, Margo Machida, and Sharon Mizota, eds., *Fresh Talk/Daring Gazes: Conversations on Asian American Art* (Berkeley: University of California Press, 2003), 7.

7. "Cultural Diversity Based on Cultural Grounding II: Ratification Statement, October 19, 1991," Wn Marta Moreno Vega and Cheryll Y. Greene, eds., *Voices from the*

Battlefront: Achieving Cultural Equity, (Trenton, NJ: Africa World Press, 1993), 177.

8. Elinor Bowles, *Cultural Centers of Color: Report on a National Survey* (Washington, DC: National Endowment for the Arts, 1992), 7.

9. Ibid., 21.

10. The definitive account of the CARA exhibition and its decision-making process is Alicia Gaspar de Alba's *Chicano Art: Inside/Outside the Master's House: Cultural Politics and the CARA Exhibition* (Austin: University of Texas, 1998).

11. Gaspar de Alba, *Chicano Art*, 161.

12. Elaine Kim, "Interstitial Subjects," 7–8.

13. Eric Gibson, "Politically Correct 'Chicano' Is a Radical Dud," *The Washington Times*, June 21, 1992, D8.

14. Hilton Kramer, "Studying the Arts and Humanities: What Can Be Done?", *New Criterion*, February 1989, http://www.newcriterion.com/articles.cfm/Studying-the-arts-and-humanities--what-can-be-done--5788.

15. Clement Greenberg, "Towards a Newer Laocoon," *Partisan Review* 7:4 (July–August 1940).

16. Linda Gordon and Gary Y. Okihiro, eds., *Impounded: Dorothea Lange and the Censored Images of Japanese American Internment* (New York.: W. W. Norton, 2006), 12. Citing Lange, interview by Suzanne Reiss, "Dorothea Lange: The Making of a Documentary Photographer," 1968, transcript, University of California Regional Oral Office, Berkeley, 181.

17. W. E. B. DuBois, "Criteria of Negro Art," originally published in *The Crisis*, October 1926, http://www.webdubois.org/dbCriteriaNArt.html.

18. Hilton Kramer, "Differences in Quality," *New York Times*, November 24, 1968. There Kramer had written, "It wasn't easy for anyone to be an artist in America in the thirties. For a black artist, the situation was infinitely more arduous and problematical. No one with a sense of history and a sense of justice can feel anything but sorrow, indignation, and guilt that this should have been the case and that it may very well still be the case. But these feelings, though they have an important role to play in the redress of social grievances, are of little use in judging the quality of works of art."

19. Ibid.

20. Hilton Kramer, "Black Art or Merely Social History?", *New York Times*, June 26, 1977.

21. Greg Tate, *Flyboy in the Buttermilk: Essays on Contemporary America* (New York: Simon & Schuster, 1992), 243.

22. From PESTS flyer dated December 6, 1986.

23. Howardena Pindell, *The Heart of the Question: The Writings and Paintings of Howardena Pindell* (New York: Midmarch Arts Press, 1997), 7.

24. Pindell also compiled a list of hundreds of artists of color who lived in the New York area and sent them to galleries and museums.

25. Maurice Berger, *How Art Becomes History* (New York: HarperCollins, 1992), 146.

26. Tucker admitted to Conwill, "[O]nce you saw that the New Museum's mission was to try to break apart the 'canon,' so to speak, to position itself in opposition to or outside of the mainstream, you joked, 'Well you guys want to get rid of the canon just at the moment when we are about to enter it!'"

27. Michael Brenson, "Quality and Other Things," *American Art* 6:4 (Autumn 1992), 6–7.

28. Alexandra Chang, *Envisioning Diaspora: Asian American Visual Arts Collective* (Hong Kong: Timezone 8, 2009), 36.

29. Karin Higa, "Origin Myths: A Short and Incomplete History of Godzilla," in Karin Higa, Melissa Chiu, and Susette Min, eds., *One Way or Another: Asian American Art Now* (New Haven: Yale University Press, 2006), 22.

30. From "Is There an Asian American Aesthetics?", taken from a plenary session at Defining Our Culture(s), Our Selves conference, June 8, 1991, Hunter College, transcribed by Gargi Chatterjee and edited by Augie Tam, in Min Zhou and James V. Gatewood, eds., *Contemporary Asian America: A Multidisciplinary Reader* (New York: New York University Press, 2000), 631.

31. Kay WalkingStick, "Native American Art in the PostModern Era," *Art Journal* 51:3 (Autumn 1992), 15.

32. Ibid.

Chapter Eight
Imagine/Ever Wanting/to Be: The Fall of Multiculturalism

1. Steven Kaplan, "New York: The Whitney Biennial 1991," *ETC* 15 (1991), 91.

2. John Yau, "Official Policy: Toward the 1990s with the Whitney Biennial," *Arts* 64:1 (September 1989), 51, 54.

3. Robert Hughes, "The Whitney Biennial: A Fiesta of Whining," *Time*, March 22, 1993.

4. Judd Tully, "The Multicultural Biennial," *Art & Auction*, March 1993, 91.

5. See Gilbert Coker, "The Whitney's Golden Years," *International Review of African American Art* 15:4 (1999).

6. Thelma Golden in "The Theater of Refusal Roundtable," April 16, 1993, Humanities Research Institute, University of California. See also Catherine Lord, ed., *The Theater of Refusal: Black Art and Mainstream Criticism* (Irvine: Fine Arts Gallery, University of California, 1993), 62–63.

7. Jean Nathan, "Silence Is Not Golden," *New York*, January 11, 1993.

8. Paul Richard, "Scrawling in the Margins," *Washington Post*, March 4, 1993.

9. Thelma Golden, "What's White?", in *1993 Biennial Exhibition* (New York: Whitney Museum of American Art, 1993), 35.

10. Coco Fusco, "Passionate Irreverence: The Cultural Politics of Identity," in *1993 Biennial Exhibition* (New York: Whitney Museum of American Art, 1993), 75.

11. Guerrilla Girls poster, "Whitey Biennial," 1993, http://www.guerrillagirls.com/posters/whitey.shtml. See also Eleanor Heartney, "Identity Politics at the Whitney," *Art in America* 81 (1993).

12. Tully, "The Multicultural Biennial," 89.

13. David Ross's quote is taken from "Whitney Biennial Audiotape," a performance audio piece, 1993. © Andrea Fraser. Permission granted courtesy of Andrea Fraser.

14. Thelma Golden, ed., *Black Male: Representations of Masculinity in Contemporary American Art* (New York: Whitney Museum of American Art, 1994), 29.

15. Lorna Simpson's piece inspired an influential debate in the art journal *October*. See "The Politics of the Signifier: A Conversation on the Whitney Biennial," *October* 66 (Fall 1993), 3–27. Nizan Shaked's research on this debate is especially illuminating: Nizan Shaked, "The Paradox of Identity Politics as an Agent in Critical Art: 1970s to the 1990s," PhD diss., Claremont Graduate University, 2007, 208–20.

16. Requoted in Eugenie Tsai, "Between Heaven and Earth," in *Threshold: Byron Kim, 1990–2004* (University of California, Berkeley Art Museum, and Pacific Film Archive, 2004), 17.

17. Harry Gamboa Jr., "In the City of Angels, Chameleons, and Phantoms: Asco, a Case Study of Chicano Art in Urban Tones (or Asco Was a Four-Member Word)," in Richard Griswold Del Castillo, Teresa McKenna, and Yvonne Yarbro-Bejarano, eds., *Chicano Art: Resistance and Affirmation: An Interpretive Exhibition of the Chicano Art Movement, 1965–1985* (Los Angeles: Wight Art Gallery, 1991), 124.

18. Ibid., 125

19. Chon Noriega, "The Orphans of Modernism," in Rita Gonzalez, Howard Fox, and Chon A. Noriega, eds., *Phantom Sightings: Art after the Chicano Movement* (Berkeley: University of California Press, 2008), 24.

20. Max Benavidez quoting Chon Noriega in Max Benavidez, *Gronk* (Los Angeles: UCLA Chicano Studies Research Center and University of Minnesota Press, 2007), 47.

21. Filippo Tommaso Marinetti, "The Foundation and Manifesto of Futurism," in Charles Harrison and Paul Wood, eds., *Art in Theory: An Anthology of Changing Ideas, 1900–2000*, (Malden, MA: Wiley, 2003), 148.

22. Daniel J. Martinez, Artist's Statement from 1993 Whitney Biennial files, Whitney Museum of American Art.

23. Fusco, "Passionate Irreverence," 76.

Notes

24. Ibid., 85.

25. Jan Avgikos, "Kill All White People," *Artforum* 31:9 (May 1993), 11.

26. Langston Hughes, "The Negro Artist and the Racial Mountain," *Nation* 122:3181 (June 23, 1926), 694.

27. Langston Hughes, "I, Too," in Arnold Rampersad, ed., *The Collected Poems of Langston Hughes* (New York: Vintage Books, 2004), 46.

28. Deborah Solomon, "A Showcase for Political Correctness," *Wall Street Journal*, March 5, 1993. See also John Taylor, "Mope Art: Deconstructing the Biennial," *New York*, March 22, 1993; Richard Caseby, "PC—or Racism?", *The Sunday Times*, April 4, 1993; Bill Van Siclen, "Get the Message?", *Providence Journal*, March 28, 1993.

29. Ross answered, "It couldn't have been done because it wouldn't have been about the position of dominance." Peter Plagens and Carolyn Friday, "From Hopper to Hip-Hop," *Newsweek*, November 8, 1993, 76.

30. He later recanted. And Danto praised Martinez's tags in a retrospective book of his work. The tags, Danto later said, revealed Martinez not so much as an activist but as "an anti-formalist, making an art whose force and meaning did not rest upon getting the design formally right." Arthur Danto, "Daniel Joseph Martinez's *Museum Tags* as Anti-formal Performances," in *Daniel Joseph Martinez: A Life of Disobedience* (Ostfildern, Germany: Hatje Canz, 2009), 201.

31. Jed Perl, "From Tung Ch'i-Ch'ang's China to David Ross's Manhattan," *New Criterion*, April 1993. See also Andrew Graham-Dixon, "Still Alive, But Only Just," *Independent*, March 9, 1993; Christopher Knight, "Crushed by Its Good Intentions," *Los Angeles Times,* March 10, 1993.

32. John Taylor, "Mope Art"; Deborah Solomon, "A Showcase."

33. Paul Richard, "Scrawling in the Margins"; John Taylor, "Mope Art"; Bill Van Siclen, "Get the Message?"; Carol Strickland, "Politics Dominates Whitney Biennial," *Christian Science Monitor*, March 26, 1993; Fredric Koeppel, "Art Tirades at Biennial Simply Get Tiresome," *Memphis Commercial Appeal*, March 28, 1993; Peter Plagens, "Fade from White," *Newsweek*, March 14, 1993.

34. John Leo, "Cultural War at the Whitney," *U.S. News & World Report*, March 22, 1993.

35. Hilton Kramer, "The Biennialized Whitney: Closed for Deconstruction," *New York Observer*, March 29, 1993.

36. Ibid.

37. Ronda R. Penrice, "The Whitney's 'Black Male': It's a Shame, Girl," *Routes, the Biweekly Guide to African-American Culture* 4:15 (December 6–19, 1994), 7.

Chapter 9
All the Colors in the World: The Mainstreaming of Multiculturalism

1. Lewis Blackwell, "Casual but Smart," *Creative Review*, April 1991.

2. Randall Rothenberg, "Benetton's Magazine to Push Vision, Not Clothing," *New York Times*, April 15, 1991.

3. William Leith, "The Observer Interview: Oliviero Toscani, the Wild Man of Italian Knitwear," *Observer*, March 16, 1997.

4. Theodore Levitt, "The Globalization of Markets," *Harvard Business Review*, May–June 1983, 94.

5. Ibid., 93.

6. Ibid., 93, 102.

7. Jonathan Mantle, *Benetton: The Family, the Business, and the Brand* (New York: Warner Books, 2000), 142, 208.

8. Keith Robertson, "On White Space In Graphic Design," Originally published in *Émigré* No. 26, 1993.

9. One could write a history on the use of the white backdrop. Penn, Avedon, George Lois, David Bailey, Robert Mapplethorpe, and others had made their names with minimalist work. The cover designer of the 1970 Pocket Books editions of Vance Packard's *The Hidden Persuaders* and *The Status Seekers* had, with casual irony, wrapped the white background around Packard's takedowns of the ad industry and the 1 percent. Even Saatchi & Saatchi's galvanizing "Labour Isn't Working" poster for Margaret Thatcher's 1978 Tory campaign had long dole lines stretching toward the horizon against a white background. Then in 2000, Bruce Mau and Barr Gilmore would use white space for their cover of Naomi Klein's anti-branding classic *No Logo*, echoing the cover of Notorious BIG's *Ready to Die* done by Cey Adams.

10. Noreen O'Leary, "Benetton's True Colors," *Adweek*, August 24, 1992.

11. Patricia Clough, "The Posters Shock … But We All Buy the Knitwear," *Independent*, December 16, 1992.

12. Oliviero Toscani in Benetton, *Global Vision: United Colors of Benetton* (Tokyo: Robundo, 1993).

13. Judith Graham, "Benetton 'Colors' the Race Issue," *Advertising Age*, September 11, 1989.

14. Ibid.

15. "An Interview with Oliviero Toscani," *The Florentine*, September 21, 2006.

16. Martha T. Moore, "Controversial Adman Bares His Concept," *USA Today*, July 25, 1991.

17. Russell Ferguson, William Olander, Marcia Tucker, and Karen Fiss, eds., *Discourses: Conversations in Postmodern Art and Culture* (New York: New Museum and MIT

Press, 1990), 198.

18. Alison Simko, "Do the Left Thing," *Advertising Age*, January 13, 1992, S22.

19. Tibor Kalman in Peter Hall and Michael Bierut, eds., *Tibor Kalman: Perverse Optimist* (New York: Princeton Architectural Press, 2000), 26.

20. Nicholas Mirzoeff, *An Introduction to Visual Culture*, 2nd ed. (New York: Routledge, 2009), 3.

21. Mantle, *Benetton*, 218.

22. Bruce Horovitz, "Shock Ads: New Rage that Spawns Rage," *Los Angeles Times*, March 22, 1992.

23. Hall and Bierut, *Tibor Kalman*, 266.

24. Farrell Crook, "Angry Readers Protest Photo of Black Queen," *Toronto Star*, March 28, 1993.

25. Sontag, *On Photography*, 140.

26. Ibid.

27. Adrienne Ward, "'Socially Aware' or 'Wasted Money': AA Readers Respond to Benetton Ads," *Advertising Age*, February 24, 1992, 4.

28. Randall Scotland, "Benetton's 'Black' Queen Sparks Ad Debate," *The Financial Post*, April 17, 1993.

29. Jean Baudrillard, *Simulacra and Simulation*, trans. by Sheila Faria Glaser (Ann Arbor: University of Michigan Press, 1994), 87.

30. "Benetton Gets Case of the Blues Following Run of Bad Publicity," *South China Morning Post*, February 26, 1995.

31. Naomi Klein, *No Logo: Taking Aim at the Brand Bullies* (New York: Picador, 1999), 114.

32. Hall and Bierut, *Tibor Kalman: Perverse Optimist*, 302–3.

Chapter Ten
We Are All Multiculturalists Now: Visions of One America

1. David A. Hollinger, "Amalgamation and Hypodescent: The Question of Ethnoracial Mixture in the History of the United States," *The American Historical Review* 108:5 (December 2003), 1364.

2. Daniel Pope, *The Making of Modern Advertising* (New York: Basic Books, 1983), 258.

3. Michael J. Weiss, *The Clustering of America* (New York: Harper & Row, 1988), 144.

4. Mark Fisher, *Capitalist Realism: Is There No Alternative?* (Hants, UK: Zero Books, 2009), 8.

5. Raymond A. Bauer, Scott M. Cunningham, and Lawrence H. Wortzel, "The Market-

ing Dilemma of Negroes," *Journal of Marketing*, 29:3 (July 1965), 1.

6. Henry Allen Bullock, "Consumer Motivations in Black and White," *Harvard Business Review* 39 (May–June 1961), 93.

7. Ibid., 95.

8. Ibid., 91.

9. Bauer, Cunningham, and Wortzel, "Marketing Dilemma of Negroes," 2.

10. D. Parke Gibson, *The $30 Billion Negro* (New York: Macmillan, 1969), 20.

11. Gibson, *$30 Billion Negro*, 9.

12. Ralph Lee Smith, "The Wired Nation," *Nation*, May 18, 1970, 584.

13. Juan Gonzales and Joseph Torres, *News for All the People* (New York: Verso, 2011), 318.

14. Harold H. Kassarjian, "The Negro and American Advertising, 1946–1965," *Journal of Marketing Research* 6:1 (February 1969), 29.

15. Arnold M. Barban, "The Dilemma of 'Integrated' Advertising," *Journal of Business* 42:4 (October 1969), 477–96.

16. Dorothy Cohen, "Advertising and the Black Community," *Journal of Marketing* 34:4 (October 1970), 4.

17. Emphasis added. Joseph Turow, *Breaking Up America: Advertisers and the New Media World* (University of Chicago Press, 1997), 19.

18. Turow, *Breaking Up America*, 37.

19. Robert Johnson and Brian Dumaine, "The Market Nobody Wanted," CNN Money, October 1, 2002, http://money.cnn.com/magazines/fsb/fsb_archive/2002/10/01/330571/index.htm.

20. Brett Pulley, *The Billion Dollar BET: Robert Johnson and the Inside Story of Black Entertainment Television* (Hoboken, NJ: Wiley & Sons, 2004), 32.

21. Turow, *Breaking Up America*, 26.

22. Johnson and Dumaine, "Market Nobody Wanted."

23. Jason Chambers, *Madison Avenue and the Color Line: African Americans in the Advertising Industry* (Philadelphia: University of Pennsylvania Press, 2008), 226.

24. The Madison Avenue Project continues to call attention to racial discrimination in the advertising industry. See http://www.madisonavenueproject.com.

25. Table 1, "U.S. Buying Power Statistics by Race, 1990, 2000, 2009, and 2014," in Humphreys, Jeffrey M., "The Multicultural Economy 2009," *Georgia Business and Economic Conditions* 69:3, Selig Center for Economic Growth, University of Georgia, third quarter 2009, 3.

26. Johnson and Dumaine, "Market Nobody Wanted."

27. Pulley, *Billion Dollar BET*, 53–54.

28. Ibid., 200

29. Ibid., 112.

30. Ibid., 111.

31. Ibid., 6–7.

32. Italics mine. Paul Gilroy, *Darker than Blue: On the Moral Economies of Black Atlantic Culture* (Cambridge: Harvard University Press, 2010), 11–12, 20–22.

33. Peter Francese, "A Symphony of Demographic Change," *Advertising Age*, November 9, 1988.

34. Kristal Brent Zook, *Color by Fox: The Fox Network and the Revolution in Black Television* (New York: Oxford University Press, 1999), 5.

35. George Gerbner, "Women and Minorities on Television: A Study in Casting and Fate: A Report to the Screen Actors Guild and the American Federation of Radio and Television Artists," June 1993.

36. "How Blacks' TV Viewing Habits Differ From Whites'," *Jet*, April 26, 1993, 38.

37. Daniel M. Kimmel, *The Fourth Network: How Fox Broke The Rules and Reinvented Television* (Lanham, MD: Ivan R. Dee, 2004), 199.

38. Kimmel, *The Fourth Network*, 199.

39. Zook, *Color by Fox*, 10.

40. Ibid., 11.

41. Ibid., 106.

42. "Three-Fourths of People Polled Oppose Affirmative Action," Associated Press, March 24, 1995.

43. Ward Connerly, interview by Brian Lamb, *Booknotes*, C-SPAN, April 30, 2000, http://www.booknotes.org/Watch/155997-1/Ward+Connerly.aspx.

44. Dinesh D'Souza, *The End of Racism* (New York: Simon & Schuster, 1996), 24.

45. Daniel T. Rodgers, *Age of Fracture* (Cambridge: Harvard University Press, 2011), 128–29.

46. Rene Sanchez, "Black, Hispanic Admissions Plunge at 2 Calif. Campuses," *Washington Post*, April 1, 1998, A1.

47. In this, American liberal intellectuals like Lind, Todd Gitlin, and others went considerably further than many of their British counterparts, such as Terry Eagleton, who despite his criticism of identity movements argued, "Any socialism which fails to transform itself in the light of this fecund, articulate culture will surely be bankrupt from the outset.... At its most militant, postmodernism has lent a voice to the humiliated and reviled, and in doing so has threatened to shake the imperious self-identity of the system to its core. And for this one might also forgive it the whole of its egregious exercises." Terry Eagleton, *The Illusions of Postmodernism* (Oxford and Cambridge, MA: Blackwell Publishers, 1996), 24.

48. Michael Lind, "The End of the Rainbow," *Mother Jones*, September–October 1997, http://www.motherjones.com/politics/1997/09/end-rainbow.

49. Lind, "End of the Rainbow."

50. Nathan Glazer, *We Are All Multiculturalists Now* (Cambridge: Harvard University Press, 1997), 33.

51. Ibid., 13–14.

52. Ronald Brownstein, "Clinton: Parties Fail to Attack Race Divisions," *Los Angeles Times*, May 3, 1992, http://articles.latimes.com/print/1992-05-03/news/mn-1956_1_los-angeles.

53. John F. Harris, *The Survivor: Bill Clinton in the White House* (New York: Random House, 2005), 264.

54. Perhaps only the Whitney Museum would have been a better venue.

55. William J. Clinton, "Commencement Address at the University of California San Diego in La Jolla, California," June 14, 1997, http://www.presidency.ucsb.edu/ws/?pid=54268.

56. Claire Jean Kim, "Clinton's Race Initiative: Recasting the American Dilemma," *Polity* 33:2 (Winter 2000), 175–97.

57. Jodi Enda, "Racial Advisory Board Focuses on Education, Economic Opportunity," *Philadelphia Inquirer*, July 15, 1997, A5, http://articles.philly.com/1997-07-15/news/25548347_1_board-members-advisory-board-racism.

Part Three: The Colorization of America, 1993–2013

Chapter Eleven
I Am I Be: Identity in Post Time

1. Kwame Anthony Appiah, *The Ethics of Identity* (Princeton University Press, 2005), 5.

2. Simon Hattenstone, "Whassup?," *Guardian*, October 25, 2000, http://www.theguardian.com/print/0,,4081177-103680,00.html.

3. Michael McCarthy, "Budweiser's 'Whassup?!' TV Ads Claim Grand Prix in Cannes," *USA Today*, June 26, 2000.

4. Taylor in Gutmann, ed., *Multiculturalism: Examining the Politics of Recognition* (Princeton University Press, 1994), 25.

5. Gutmann, *Multiculturalism*, 73.

6. Gutmann, *Multiculturalism*, 71.

7. Chappelle told Oprah Winfrey, "I was doing sketches that were funny, but socially irresponsible. I felt like I was deliberately being encouraged [by his network, Comedy Central] and I was overwhelmed, so, it's like you get flooded with things and you don't pay attention to things like your ethics when you get so overwhelmed. It was

like you'd won the lottery." *Oprah*, aired February 3, 2006.

8. "Between the Studio and the Street: A Roundtable Curated by Lydia Yee," in Jeff Chang, ed., *Total Chaos: The Art and Aesthetics of Hip-Hop* (New York: Basic Civitas, 2006), 135.

9. Ligon in *Glenn Ligon: America* (New York: Whitney Museum of American Art, 2011), 244.

10. George S. Schuyler, "The Negro-Art Hokum," *Nation* 122:3180 (June 16, 1926), 662.

11. Alain Locke, "Art or Propaganda?", in Henry Louis Gates Jr., ed., *The New Negro: Readings On Race, Representation, and African-American Culture, 1892–1938* (Princeton University Press, 2007), 260.

12. Raymond Saunders quoted in Elvan Zabunyan, *Black Is a Color: A History of African American Art* (Paris: Éditions Dis Voir, 2005), 92.

13. Raymond Saunders quoted in Sharon F. Patton, *African-American Art* (Oxford and New York: Oxford University Press, 1998), 227–28.

14. Saunders in Patton, *African-American Art*, 228.

15. Kehinde Wiley in *Kehinde Wiley: The World Stage: Lagos-Dakar* (New York: Studio Museum in Harlem, 2008), 11.

16. Richard Duncan, Duncan McKenzie, and Amy Mooney, "Interview with Kehinde Wiley," interview conducted September 2010, *Art Practical.*, Bad at Sports podcast episode 263, http://www.artpractical.com/feature/interview_with_kehinde_wiley/.

17. Touré, *Who's Afraid of Post-Blackness? What It Means to Be Black Now* (New York: Free Press, 2011), 37.

18. Glenn Ligon, "Thelma Golden," *Bomb Magazine*, March 2004, http://bombsite .com/issues/999/articles/3588.

19. Zadie Smith, *Changing My Mind: Occasional Essays* (New York: Penguin Press, 2009), 7–8.

20. Ibid., 12.

21. Darby English, *How to See a Work of Art in Total Darkness* (Cambridge: MIT Press, 2010), 206.

22. Appiah in Gutmann, *Multiculturalism*, 163.

23. Ibid.

24. Franklin Sirmans in *Glenn Ligon: America*, 168.

25. Thelma Golden interview with Kori Newkirk in *Kori Newkirk: 1997–2007* (Los Angeles: Fellows of Contemporary Art, 2008), 15.

26. "Screen Doors on Submarines: Dave McKenzie in Conversation with Ryan Inoue," n.d., likely April 2008, http://www.barbarawien.de/artists/mckenzie_tex.php.

27. Holland Cotter, "Beyond Multiculturalism, Freedom?," *New York Times*, July 29, 2001, http://www.nytimes.com/2001/07/29/arts/art-architecture-beyond-multiculturalism-freedom.html.

28. Cynthia Houng, "Ala Ebtekar Interview," Fecal Face Web site, December 18, 2007, http://www.fecalface.com/SF/features-mainmenu-102/938-ala-ebtekar-interview.

29. Higa, Chiu, and Min, *One Way or Another*, 27.

30. Ibid., 28.

31. Ibid., 38.

32. Ibid., 35.

33. Howard N. Fox, "Theater of the Inauthentic," in *Phantom Sightings: Art after the Chicano Movement* (Berkeley: University of California Press, 2008), 81.

34. Chon Noriega, Howard N. Fox, and Rita Gonzalez, "Introduction," in *Phantom Sightings*, 13.

35. See the essay "Light at the End of Tunnel Vision," and the short story "Where They Found Javier," Harry Gamboa Jr., in Chon A. Noriega, ed., *Urban Exile: Collected Writings of Harry Gamboa, Jr.* (Minneapolis: University of Minnesota Press, 1998).

36. Chon Noriega, "The Orphans of Modernism," in *Phantom Sightings*, 18.

37. *Los Angeles Times* art critic Christopher Knight would write of Valdez in the photo, "Like the museum as art object, she's also the objectified 'picture' artistically 'signed.'" Christopher Knight, "'Phantom Sightings' at LACMA," *Los Angeles Times*, April 15, 2008, http://www.latimes.com/entertainment/news/arts/la-et-phantom15apr15,0,2921844.story.

38. Natalie Haddad, "Phantom Sightings," *Frieze* 117 (September 9, 2008), http://www.frieze.com/issue/review/phantom_sightings/.

39. Agustin Gurza, "Chicano Art, Beyond Rebellion," *Los Angeles Times*, April 6, 2008, http://www.latimes.com/entertainment/la-ca-chicano6apr06,0,7737991.story.

40. Ken Johnson, "They're Chicanos and Artists. But Is Their Art Chicano?," *New York Times*, April 9, 2010, http://www.nytimes.com/2010/04/10/arts/design/10chicano.html.

41. Gurza, "Chicano Art."

42. Duncan, McKenzie, and Mooney, "Interview with Kehinde Wiley."

43. Cuauhtémoc Medina, "High Curios," in *Brian Jungen* (Vancouver: Vancouver Art Gallery, 2005), 28.

44. Brian Jungen, "In Conversation with Simon Starling," in *Brian Jungen*, 135.

45. Kim, *Threshold*, 32.

Chapter Twelve

Demographobia: Racial Fears and Colorized Futures

1. "Hamilton College National Youth Poll: Racial Attitudes of Young Americans," August 1999, http://www.hamilton.edu/news/polls/racial-attitudes-of-young-americans.

2. Louis Menand, "Patriot Games," *New Yorker*, May 17, 2004.

3. In fact federal interrogation experts had watched the show for ideas about how to treat prisoners of war. Justice Antonin Scalia and "torture memo" architect John Yoo would defend the fictional agent Jack Bauer's extralegal methods. Dalia Lithwick, "The Fiction behind Torture Policy," *Newsweek*, July 25, 2008, http://www.newsweek.com/lithwick-how-jack-bauer-shaped-ustorture-policy-93159.

4. Tram Nguyen, *We Are All Suspects Now: Untold Stories from Immigrant Communities after 9/11* (Boston: Beacon Press, 2005), 19.

5. Ibid., xv.

6. Lothrop Stoddard, *The Rising Tide of Color Against White World Supremacy* (New York: Charles Scribner's Sons, 1922), 297.

7. Samuel P. Huntington, *Who Are We? The Challenges to American Identity* (New York: Simon & Schuster, 2004), 254–55.

8. Mahzarin Banaji and Thierry Devos, "American = White?," *Journal of Personality and Social Psychology* 88:3 (March 2005), 447–66.

9. Samuel P. Huntington, "The Hispanic Challenge," *Foreign Policy*, March–April 2004, http://www.foreignpolicy.com/articles/2004/03/01/the_hispanic_challenge.

10. Menand, "Patriot Games."

11. In 2012, this tipping point was crossed.

12. Ronald Brownstein, "The Gray and the Brown: The Generational Mismatch," *National Journal*, July 24, 2010, http://www.nationaljournal.com/magazine/the-gray-and-the-brown-the-generational-mismatch-20100724.

13. Fairey in Shepard Fairey and Jennifer Gross, eds., *Art for Obama: Designing Manifest Hope and the Campaign for Change* (New York: Harry Abrams, 2009), 7. Chris McGreal, "Texas Schools Board Rewrites US History with Lessons Promoting God and Guns," *Guardian*, May 16, 2010, http://www.theguardian.com/world/2010/may/16/texas-schools-rewrites-us-history.

14. Curtis Prendergast, "Narratives in the News: The Death of Robert Krentz," *Sonoran Chronicle*, March 19, 2011, http://sonoranchronicle.com/2011/03/19/narratives-in-the-news-the-death-of-robert-krentz/.

15. Jan Brewer, *Scorpions for Breakfast* (New York: Broadside Books, 2011). For an excellent account of the reign of Jan Brewer in Arizona, see Jeff Biggers, "Manufacturing the Crisis" in his book *State out of the Union: Arizona and the Final Showdown over the American Dream* (New York: Nation Books, 2012).

16. Michael Hoefer, Nancy Rytina, and Bryan C. Baker, *Estimates of the Unauthorized Immigrant Population Residing in the United States: January 2010*, Department of Homeland Security, Office of Immigration Statistics, February 2011, http://www.dhs.gov/xlibrary/assets/statistics/publications/ois_ill_pe_2010.pdf.

17. Biggers, *State out of the Union*, 59, 64. See also Dennis Wagner, "Violence Is Not

Up on Arizona Border," *Arizona Republic*, May 2, 2010, http://www.azcentral.com/arizonarepublic/news/articles/2010/05/02/20100502arizona-border-violence-mexico.html.

18. Data is from Lindsay Marshall of the Florence Immigrant and Refugee Rights Project. Interview with Lindsay Marshall, August 7, 2012.

19. "FY 2011: ICE Announces Year-End Removal Numbers, Highlights Focus on Key Priorities Including Threats to Public Safety and National Security," U.S. Immigration and Customs Enforcement, press release, October 18, 2011, http://www.ice.gov/news/releases/1110/111018washingtondc.htm.

20. Detention Watch Network, "The Influence of the Private Prison Industry in the Immigration Detention Business," May 2011, http://www.detentionwatchnetwork.org/sites/detentionwatchnetwork.org/files/PrivatePrisonPDF-FINAL%205-11-11.pdf.

21. Doris Meissner, Donald M. Kerwin, Muzaffar Chishti, and Claire Bergeron, "Immigration Enforcement in The United States: The Rise of a Formidable Machinery," Migration Policy Institute, January 2013, 7, http://www.migrationpolicy.org/pubs/enforcementpillars.pdf.

22. Ibid, 9. Criminal enforcement includes the FBI, DEA, Secret Service, U.S. Marshals Service, and the Bureau of Alcohol, Tobacco, Firearms and Explosives.

23. Christine Sleeter, "Ethnic Studies and the Struggle in Tucson," *Education Week*, February 15, 2012, http://www.edweek.org/ew/articles/2012/02/15/21sleeter.h31.html.

24. Emphasis added. Biggers, *State out of the Union*, 181

25. Biggers, *State out of the Union*, 196.

26. Interview with Marshall.

27. "Interactive Map: America's Changing Demographics," Center for American Progress Web site, April 2011, http://www.americanprogress.org/issues/2011/04/census_map.html.

28. Brownstein, "The Gray and the Brown."

29. Michael Hardt and Antonio Negri, *Empire* (Cambridge: Harvard University Press, 2000), 399.

30. Hua Hsu, "The End of White America?", *Atlantic*, January–February 2009, http://www.theatlantic.com/magazine/archive/2009/01/the-end-of-white-america/307208/.

31. Ibid.

32. William H. Frey, "A Demographic Tipping Point among America's Three-year-Olds," Brookings Institution, February 7, 2011, http://www.brookings.edu/research/opinions/2011/02/07-population-frey.

Chapter Thirteen
The Wave: The Hope of a New Cultural Majority

1. "Shepard Fairey: Mayday: The Politics of Street Art," interview by Aaron Rose at Los Angeles Public Library, presented by ALOUDLa and Los Angeles Weekly, event held March 7, 2011, http://vimeo.com/34112077.
2. Ibid., 18.
3. Courtney Comstock, "Fairey Dusts Off Charges," Forbes.com, July 15, 2009.
4. "Shepard Fairey: Mayday."
5. Fairey in *Obey: Supply & Demand: The Art of Shepard Fairey* (Corte Madera: Gingko Press in association with Obey Giant, 2006), 94.
6. Christopher Knight, "Review: Shepard Fairey at ICA Boston," LA Times Culture Monster blog. March 23, 2009, http://latimesblogs.latimes.com/culturemonster/2009/03/shepard-fairey.html.
7. Mark Vallen, "Obey Plagiarist Shepard Fairey: A Critique by Artist Mark Vallen," The post states "Published on the occasion of Fairey's Los Angeles solo exhibition, (Dec. 2007)," http://www.art-for-a-change.com/Obey/index.htm.
8. Josh MacPhee, "A Response to OBEY Plagiarist," Just Seeds Blog, December 14, 2007, http://www.justseeds.org/blog/2007/12/a_response_to_obey_plagiarist_1.html#more.
9. Both quotes from Fairey, *Obey: Supply & Demand*, 139–40. Originally published in *Tokion*.
10. Aura Bogado, "I Have a Name: An Open Letter to Shepard Fairey," To the Curb blog, May 29, 2008, http://tothecurb.wordpress.com/2008/05/.
11. Fairey, *Obey: Supply & Demand*, 139–40.
12. Fairey in Shepard Fairey and Jennifer Gross, eds., *Art for Obama: Designing Manifest Hope and the Campaign for Change* (New York: Harry Abrams, 2009), 7.
13. Noam Cohen, "Viewing Journalism as a Work of Art," *New York Times*, March 23, 2009, http://www.nytimes.com/2009/03/24/arts/design/24photo.html. AP later sued Shepard Fairey for copyright infringement. The case settled out of court.
14. Bruce E. Boyden, "The Obama 'Hope' Poster Case: Mannie Garcia Weighs In," Marquette University Law School Faculty Blog, July 13, 2009, http://law.marquette.edu/facultyblog/2009/07/13/the-obama-hope-poster-case-mannie-garcia-weighs-in/.
15. Shepard Fairey interview with Wendy Wick-Reaves, National Portrait Gallery podcast, January 17, 2009, http://www.npg.si.edu/audio/blog_fairey_int_011709.MP3.
16. Ibid.
17. Fairey and Gross, *Art for Obama*, 8.
18. Shepard Fairey interview with Wendy Wick-Reaves.

19. "Penn Strategy Memo, March 19, 2008," *Atlantic*, August 11, 2008, 3, http://www.theatlantic.com/politics/archive/2008/08/penn-strategy-me-mo-march-19-2008/37952/.

20. Richard Morin and Christopher Muste, "The Enthusiasm Gap," *Washington Post*, September 30, 2004, http://www.washingtonpost.com/wp-dyn/articles/A61725-2004Sep30.html.

21. Foon Rhee, "McCain Ad Hits Obama's 'Celebrity,'" *Boston Globe*, July 30, 2008, http://www.boston.com/news/politics/politicalintelligence/2008/07/mccain_ad_hits_2.html.

22. Angela Davis, *The Meaning of Freedom: And Other Difficult Dialogues* (San Francisco: City Lights, 2012), 151.

23. Data available at http://www.ropercenter.uconn.edu/elections/how_groups_voted/voted_08.html.

24. Emily Hoban Kirby and Kei Kawashima-Ginsberg, "The Youth Vote in 2008," Center for Information & Research on Civic Learning & Engagement, April 2009, 5, http://www.civicyouth.org/PopUps/FactSheets/FS_youth_Voting_2008_updated_6.22.pdf.

25. "The Diversifying Electorate: Voting Rates by Race and Hispanic Origin in 2012 (and Other Recent Elections)," U.S. Census Bureau report, May 2013, http://www.census.gov/prod/2013pubs/p20-568.pdf.

26. Marc Ambinder, "Race Over?", *Atlantic*, January–February 2009, http://www.theatlantic.com/magazine/archive/2009/01/race-over/307215/.

27. "Inside Obama's Sweeping Victory," Pew Research Center, November 5, 2008, http://www.pewresearch.org/2008/11/05/inside-obamas-sweeping-victory/.

28. Claude Steele, *Whistling Vivaldi: And Other Clues to How Stereotypes Affect Us* (New York: W. W. Norton, 2010), 219.

29. Andrew Sullivan, "Goodbye to All That: Why Obama Matters," *Atlantic*, December 2007, http://www.theatlantic.com/magazine/archive/2007/12/goodbye-to-all-that-why-obama-matters/306445/.

30. Ambinder, "Race Over?"

31. Ann Friedman, "All Politics Is Identity Politics," *American Prospect*, July 29, 2010, http://prospect.org/article/all-politics-identity-politics-0.

32. Hsu, "End of White America?"

Chapter Fourteen
Dis/Union: The Paradox of the Post-Racial Moment

1. Lawrence Bobo, "Somewhere Between Jim Crow and Post-Racialism: Reflections

on the Racial Divide in America Today," *Daedalus* 140:2 (2011), 29, http://www
.mitpressjournals.org/doi/pdf/10.1162/DAED_a_00091.

2. Cathy Cohen, "Millennials & the Myth of the Post-Racial Society: Black Youth,
    Intra-generational Divisions & the Continuing Racial Divide in American Politics,"
    Daedalus 140:2 (2011), 200–202.

3. Gallup Poll on race relations, data from polls taken on June 5–6, 2008 and October
    16–19, 2009, http://www.gallup.com/poll/1687/race-relations.aspx.

4. *New York Post*, December 23, 2008.

5. *The Colbert Report*, aired December 21, 2011.

6. *The Colbert Report*, aired January 20, 2009.

7. Patrice O'Neal, *Elephant in the Room*, DVD, 2011.

8. Hsu, "End of White America?"

9. Gary Younge, "The Obama Effect," *Nation*, December 13, 2007, http://www.then-
    ation.com/article/obama-effect.

10. Gwen Ifill, *The Breakthrough: Politics and Race in the Age of Obama* (New York:
    Doubleday, 2009), 49.

11. In 2008, Connerly's anti–affirmative action measure in Colorado went down to
    defeat, as the state voted blue for only the second time in four decades.

12. Lawrence Auster, "What Is Post-Racial America?", View from the Right blog, Febru-
    ary 25, 2008, http://www.amnation.com/vfr/archives/010000.html.

13. Buchanan, *Suicide of a Superpower*, 133.

14. Buchanan, *Suicide of a Superpower*, viii.

15. "From Kids on Bus to Kanye West: Race Rules All in Obama's America," transcript
    of Rush Limbaugh show, September 15, 2009, http://www.rushlimbaugh.com/
    daily/2009/09/15/from_kids_on_bus_to_kanye_west_race_rules_all_in_obama_s_
    america.

16. Gallup Poll on race relations.

17. Po Bronson and Ashley Merryman, *NurtureShock: New Thinking about Children*
    (New York: Twelve, 2009), 52. See also Tony Brown, Emily Tanner-Smith, Chase L.
    Leane-Brown, and Michael E. Ezell, "Child, Parent, and Situational Correlates of
    Familial Ethnic/Race Socialization," *Journal of Marriage and Family* 69:1 (February
    2007), 17–19.

18. Morrison, *Playing in the Dark*, 9–10.

19. Eduardo Bonilla-Silva and Tyrone A. Forman, "'I Am Not a Racist But …': Map-
    ping White College Students' Racial Ideology in the USA," *Discourse & Society*
    11:1 (2000), 75–78. http://sites.psu.edu/kielceskirclblog/wp-content/uploads/
    sites/863/2013/04/bonilla-silva_forman_2000_i__m_not_a_rac.pdf.

20. Morrison, *Playing in the Dark*, 9.

21. Bronson and Merryman, *NurtureShock*, 56.

22. Steele, *Whistling Vivaldi,* 206.

23. Richard Thompson Ford, *The Race Card: How Bluffing about Bias Makes Race Relations* (New York: Farrar, Straus and Giroux, 2008), 335.

24. Howard Schuman, Charlotte Steeh, Lawrence Bobo, and Maria Krysan, "Trends in White Racial Attitudes," in *Racial Attitudes in America: Trends and Interpretations,* rev. ed. (Cambridge: Harvard University Press, 1997), 140–41, 148.

25. Paul Taylor, Rich Morin, D'Vera Cohen, and Wendy Wang. "Americans Say They Like Diverse Communities; Election, Census Trends Suggest Otherwise," Pew Research Center, December 2, 2008, http://www.pewsocialtrends.org/2008/12/02/americans-say-they-like-diverse-communities-election-census-trends-suggest-otherwise/.

26. Sean Reardon and Kendra Bischoff, "Growth in the Residential Segregation of Families by Income, 1970–2009," US2010 Project, November 2011, 15–16, http://www.s4.brown.edu/us2010/Data/Report/report111111.pdf.

27. Gary Orfield, John Kucsera, and Genevieve Siegel-Hawley, *E Pluribus ... Separation: Deepening Double Segregation for More Students*, Los Angeles, The Civil Rights Project/Proyecto Derechos Civiles at UCLA, September 2012, 9–10. See also Gary Orfield, *Reviving the Goal of an Integrated Society: A 21st Century Challenge*, Los Angeles: The Civil Rights Project/Proyecto Derechos Civiles at UCLA, January 2009, 9, http://civilrightsproject.ucla.edu/research/k-12-education/integration-and-diversity/reviving-the-goal-of-an-integrated-society-a-21st-century-challenge/orfield-reviving-the-goal-mlk-2009.pdf.

28. UCLA Institute for Democracy, Education, and Access, *Separate and Unequal: 50 Years after Brown: California's Racial "Opportunity Gap,"* May 6, 2004, 17, http://idea.gseis.ucla.edu/publications/files/brownsu2.pdf.

29. Ibid., ii.

30. Orfield and Yun, *Resegregation*.

31. Sheryll Cashin, *The Failures of Integration: How Race and Class Are Undermining the American Dream* (Cambridge: PublicAffairs, 2004), 3.

32. Douglas Massey and Nancy Denton, *American Apartheid: Segregation and the Making of the Underclass* (Cambridge: Harvard University Press, 1993), 50–53.

33. "Former Wells Fargo Subprime Loan Officer: Bank Targeted Black Churches as Part of Predatory Subprime Lending Scheme," *Democracy Now* news program, August 28, 2009, http://www.democracynow.org/2009/8/28/former_wells_fargo_subprime_loan_officer.

34. "The State of the Nation's Housing 2008," Joint Center for Housing Studies of Harvard University, 2, http://www.jchs.harvard.edu/research/publications/state-nations-housing-2008.

35. See Jacob S. Rugh and Douglas S. Massey, "Racial Segregation and the Ameri-

can Foreclosure Crisis," *American Sociological Review* 75:5 (2010), http://blogs. reuters.com/felix-salmon/files/2010/10/10ASR10_629-651_massey-2.pdf; Richard Rothstein, "A Comment on Bank of America/Countrywide's Discriminatory Mortgage Lending and Its Implications for Racial Segregation," Briefing Paper #335, Economic Policy Institute, January 23, 2012, http://www.epi.org/publication/ bp335-boa-countrywide-discriminatory-lending/.

36. Margery Austin Turner, Rob Santos, Diane K. Levy, Doug Wissoker, Claudia Arana, Rob Pitingolo, and the Urban Institute, "Housing Discrimination against Racial and Ethnic Minorities 2012," U.S. Department of Housing and Urban Development, 2013, http://www.huduser.org/portal/publications/fairhsg/hsg_discrimination_ 2012.html.

37. "Mayor and City Council of Baltimore v. Wells Fargo Bank and Wells Fargo Financial Leasing, Inc." Attachment A, "Declaration of Tony Paschal" and "Declaration of Elizabeth Jacobson," filed June 1, 2009, http://www.nclc.org/images/pdf/ unreported/paschal-decl-balt.pdf.

38. Rugh and Massey, "Racial Segregation."

39. Gregory D. Squires, Derek S. Hyra, and Robert N. Renner, "Segregation and the Subprime Lending Crisis," Economic Policy Institute, Briefing Paper #244, November 4, 2009, 3, http://www.epi.org/publication/segregation_and_the_subprime_ lending_crisis/.

40. Jo Becker, Sheryl Gay Stolberg, and Stephen Labaton, "White House Philosophy Stoked Mortgage Bonfire," *New York Times*, December 20, 2008, http://www .nytimes.com/2008/12/21/business/21admin.html.

41. Adam Davidson, "How AIG Fell Apart," Reuters, September 18, 2008, http://www .reuters.com/article/2008/09/18/us-how-aig-fell-apart-idUSMAR85972720080918.

42. Becker, Stolberg, and Labaton, "White House Philosophy."

43. "State of the Nation's Housing 2008," 20.

44. Debbie Gruenstein Bocian, Wei Li, and Keith S. Ernst, "Foreclosures by Race and Ethnicity: The Demographics of a Crisis," Center for Responsible Lending, June 18, 2010, 10, http://www.responsiblelending.org/mortgage-lending/research-analysis/ foreclosures-by-race-and-ethnicity.html.

45. Ibid., 17.

46. Tim Sullivan, Wanjiku Mwangi, Brian Miller, Dedrick Muhammad, and Colin Harris. *State of the Dream 2012: The Emerging Majority*, Boston, United for a Fair Economy, January 12, 2012, 14, http://faireconomy.org/dream/2012/executive_summary.

47. Rakesh Kochhar, Richard Fry, and Paul Taylor, "Wealth Gaps Rise to Record Highs Between Whites, Blacks and Hispanics," Pew Research Center report, July 26, 2011, 15, http://www.pewsocialtrends.org/2011/07/26/wealth-gaps-rise-to-record-highs-between-whites-blacks-hispanics/.

48. Becker, Stolberg, and Labaton, "White House Philosophy."

49. Ta-Nehisi Coates, "Fear of a Black President," *Atlantic*, September 2012, http://www.theatlantic.com/magazine/archive/2012/09/fear-of-a-black-president/309064/.

50. Cashin, *Failures of Integration*, 38.

51. Coates, "Fear of a Black President."

52. Ibid.

Chapter Fifteen
Who We Be: Debt, Community, and Colorization

1. Martin Luther King Jr., "The Birth of a New Nation," speech delivered at Dexter Avenue Baptist Church, April 7, 1957, Martin Luther King Jr. Papers Project Web site, http://mlk-kpp01.stanford.edu/kingweb/publications/speeches/The_birth_of_a_new_nation.html.

2. Quoted here from David Graeber, *Debt: The First 5,000 Years* (Brooklyn: Melville House, 2012), 372–73.

3. Ibid.

4. Ibid., 389.

5. Ibid., 379.

6. Ibid., 378–79.

7. Ibid., 382.

8. Judith (Jack) Halberstam, *The Queer Art of Failure*. (Durham: Duke Univeisty Press, 2011.)
   Ibid., 383.

9. Micah M. White, "Cognitive Illusions," Adbusters Web site, June 22, 2012, https://www.adbusters.org/magazine/102/cognitive-illusions.html.

10. Matthias Schwartz, "Pre-Occupied," *New Yorker*, November 28, 2011, http://www.newyorker.com/reporting/2011/11/28/111128fa_fact_schwartz.

11. Quoted in "#OCCUPYWALLSTREET," Adbusters Web site, July 13, 2011.

12. "A Modest Call to Action on This September 17th," Occupy Wall Street Web site, September 17, 2011, http://occupywallst.org/archive/Sep-18-2011/.

13. John Paul Montano, "An Open Letter to the Occupy Wall Street Activists," Zashnain @bedlamfury blog, http://www.zashnain.com/2011/09/open-letter-to-occupy-wall-street.html.

14. See Ronald Takaki, *A Different Mirror: A History of Multicultural America* (New York: Back Bay Books, 1993), 14.

15. Angela Davis, "(Un)Occupy," in Keith Gessen and Astra Taylor, eds., *Occupy!*

Scenes from Occupied America (New York: Verso, 2011), 133.

16.   Mike Davis, "The Last White Election?", *New Left Review*, January–February 2013, 19, http://newleftreview.org/II/79/mike-davis-the-last-white-election.

17.   Matt Taibbi, "Greed and Debt: The True Story of Mitt Romney and Bain Capital," *Rolling Stone*, September 13, 2012, http://www.rollingstone.com/politics/news/greed-and-debt-the-true-story-of-mitt-romney-and-bain-capital-20120829.

18.   David Corn, "Secret Video: Romney Tells Millionaire Donors What He Really Thinks of Obama Voters," *Mother Jones*, September 17, 2012, http://www.motherjones.com/politics/2012/09/secret-video-romney-private-fundraiser.

19.   Peter Roff, "Enthusiasm Gap Means Mitt Romney Could Blow Out President Obama," *U.S. News & World Report*, August 13, 2012, http://www.usnews.com/opinion/blogs/peter-roff/2012/08/13/enthusiasm-gap-means-mitt-romney-could-blow-out-president-obama.

20.   Jacob K. Javits, "To Preserve the Two-Party System," *New York Times*, October 27, 1963.

21.   Wendy Weiser and Diana Kasdan, *Voting Law Changes: Election Update*, Report by the Brennan Center for Justice, October 2012, 1, http://www.brennancenter.org/sites/default/files/legacy/publications/Voting_Law_Changes_Election_Update.pdf.

22.   Rosalind S. Helderman and Jon Cohen, "As Republican Convention Emphasizes Diversity, Racial Incidents Intrude," *Washington Post*, August 29, 2012, http://www.washingtonpost.com/politics/as-republican-convention-emphasizes-diversity-racial-incidents-intrude/2012/08/29/b9023a52-f1ec-11e1-892d-bc92fee603a7_story.html.

23.   "RNC 2012: The Road to Jeb Bush 2016: Invisible Obama," *The Daily Show*, August 21, 2012, http://www.thedailyshow.com/watch/fri-august-31-2012/rnc-2012---the-road-to-jeb-bush-2016---invisible-obama.

24.   Martin Wisckol, "O.C. GOP licks Wounds, Eyes Future," *Orange County Register*, November 7, 2012, http://www.ocregister.com/totalbuzz/gop-469555-obama-ocregister.html.

25.   Barack Obama, "Xavier University Commencement Address: New Orleans," August 11, 2006, http://obamaspeeches.com/087-Xavier-University-Commencement-Address-Obama-Speech.htm.

26.   Frances Robles, "Shooter of Trayvon Martin a Habitual Caller to Cops," *Miami Herald*, March 21, 2012, http://www.mcclatchydc.com/2012/03/19/142416/shooter-of-trayvon-martin-a-habitual.html.

27.   Jeff Kunerth, "Trayvon Martin Case Reveals Undercurrent of Racial Tension, Distrust in Sanford," *Orlando Sentinel*, August 29, 2013, http://articles.orlandosentinel.com/2012-07-21/news/os-trayvon-racial-tension-sanford-20120721_1_new-sanford-sanford-restaurant-theo-hollerbach.

28.   Lane DeGregory, "Trayvon Martin's Killing Shatters Safety within Retreat at Twin

Lakes in Sanford," *Tampa Bay Times*, March 24, 2012, http://www.tampabay.com/news/humaninterest/trayvon-martins-killing-shatters-safety-within-retreat-at-twin-lakes-in/1221799.

29. Robles, "Shooter of Trayvon Martin."

30. Ibid.

31. DeGregory, "Trayvon Martin's Killing."

32. Robles, "Shooter of Trayvon Martin."

33. Frances Robles, "Sanford Police Chief Under Fire amid Trayvon Martin Case," *Miami Herald*, March 21, 2012, http://www.miamiherald.com/2012/03/21/2706876/sanford-commission-votes-no-confidence.html.

34. Daniel Trotta, "Trayvon Martin: Before the World Heard the Cries," Reuters, April 3, 2012, http://www.reuters.com/article/2012/04/03/us-usa-florida-shooting-trayvon-idUSBRE8320UK20120403.

35. Hillary Busis, "Geraldo Blames Trayvon Martin's Hoodie, Feels Internet's Wrath," *Entertainment Weekly*, March 23, 2012, http://popwatch.ew.com/2012/03/23/geraldo-rivera-trayvon-martin-hoodie/.

36. "Miami Heat Don Hoodies after Teen's Death," ESPN News Services, March 24, 2012, http://espn.go.com/nba/truehoop/miamiheat/story/_/id/7728618/miami-heat-don-hoodies-response-death-teen-trayvon-martin.

37. Thomas Bradley, "'Long Live Zimmerman' on Hale Hall, Ohio State's Black Cultural Center," *The Lantern*, April 4, 2012, http://thelantern.com/2012/04/long-live-zimmerman-on-hale-hall-ohio-states-black-cultural-center/. School officials agreed that the symbolism seemed intentional. President Gordon Gee stated, "Let me be very clear: this is not who we are at Ohio State. Racism will not be tolerated on our campus."

38. In the coming months, Seminole County Court Judge Kenneth Lester would set his bail at $1 million, citing Zimmerman's plan not to disclose the money he had raised, and a related plot to flee the country.

39. Frances Robles, "Multiple Suspensions Paint Complicated Portrait of Trayvon Martin," *Miami Herald*, March 26, 2012, http://www.miamiherald.com/2012/03/26/v-print/2714778/thousands-expected-at-trayvon.html.

40. Toluse Olorunnipa, Erika Bolstad, and Frances Robles, "George Zimmerman Could Face Life in Prison for the killing of Trayvon Martin," *Miami Herald*. April 11, 2012, http://www.mcclatchydc.com/2012/04/11/144855/report-george-zimmerman-to-be.html.

41. Michael Muskal, "Judge Bars Some Words in George Zimmerman Murder Trial," *Los Angeles Times*, June 21, 2013, http://articles.latimes.com/2013/jun/21/nation/la-na-nn-george-zimmerman-trial-20130621.

42. Mychal Denzel Smith, "Trayvon Martin: From Lament to Rallying Cry," *Nation*, July

15, 2013, http://www.thenation.com/blog/175274/trayvon-martin-lament-rally-ing-cry.

43. Sonali Kolhaktar interviewing Mychal Denzel Smith, "Trayvon Martin and Emmett Till, and How Concrete Became Martin's 'Weapon,'" Uprising Radio, July 15, 2013, http://uprisingradio.org/home/2013/07/15/trayvon-martin-and-emmett-till-and-how-concrete-became-martins-weapon/.

44. *State of Florida v. George Zimmerman*, "Instructions Read to Jury by the Honorable Debra S. Nelson, Circuit Judge," July 12, 2013.

45. "Stand Your Ground Scrutinized," CNN, July 17, 2013, transcript, http://edition.cnn.com/TRANSCRIPTS/1307/17/cnr.09.html.

46. "Exclusive Interview with Juror B-37," *Anderson Cooper: 360 Degrees*, CNN, July 15, 2013, http://transcripts.cnn.com/TRANSCRIPTS/1307/15/acd.01.html.

47. Transcribed by author, Video of Interviews aired on *Good Morning America* and ABC News Web site, July 26, 2013.

48. William A. Jacobson, "The 'What if Trayvon Were White' Logical Fallacy," Legal Insurrection blog, July 15, 2013, http://legalinsurrection.com/2013/07/the-what-if-trayvon-were-white-logical-fallacy/.

49. Maddy may have been reacting to this exchange between Anderson Cooper and Juror B-37:

COOPER: Can you tell me just a little bit about that last day in the jury room deliberating? I mean, you went for so long. Did you know you were close?

JUROR B-37: We knew we were close. We knew we were close five hours before we got to where we were because we were slowly making progress the entire time. We didn't come to a stumbling block. We were reading and reading and reading and reading and knew we were progressing.

COOPER: And did the jurors, did you all get along well? I mean, was there conflict? Was there—how did the deliberation process? How was being together this long?

JUROR B-37: The deliberation was—it was tough. We all pretty much get along. It's hard sometimes to let other people talk, you know, at one time and then have somebody else talk instead of adding your comments to whatever they were saying trying to help figure it out what we were trying to figure out. At times, I thought we might have a hung jury because one of them said they were going to leave, and we convinced them that you can't leave. You can't do this. You have been in this too long to walk out now.

COOPER: They were going to leave for personal reasons, family reasons?

JUROR B-37: Mm-hmm. Mm-hmm.

Anderson Cooper: 360 Degrees, CNN, "Interview of Zimmerman Juror-B37," aired July 16, 2013, http://transcripts.cnn.com/TRANSCRIPTS/1307/16/acd.01.html. Ibid., author's transcript.

50. Frank Rich, "Frank Rich on the National Circus: National Conversations Can't Fix What Killed Trayvon," *New York,* July 18, 2013, http://nymag.com/daily/intelligencer/2013/07/frank-rich-talk-cant-fix-what-killed-trayvon.html.

51. James Baldwin, "A Report from Occupied Territory," *Nation*, July 11, 1966, http://www.thenation.com/article/159618/report-occupied-territory.

52. Thanks to the critic Gary Younge for reviving this quote in his excellent 2012 and 2013 writings on Trayvon Martin, Mamie Till, racial murders, and urban segregation. See Gary Younge, "Mamie Till's Warning Still Holds True in a Racist World," *Guardian*, April 8, 2012, http://www.theguardian.com/commentisfree/2012/apr/08/rooting-out-racism-us-uk-black. Also, Gary Younge, "Law and Disorder: The Destructive Dynamic of America's Segregated Cities," *Guardian*, April 5, 2013, http://www.theguardian.com/commentisfree/2013/apr/05/law-disorder-destructive-dynamic-segregated-cities.

53. "America in the Mirror," Dream Defenders Web site, July 9, 2013, http://dreamdefenders.org/america-in-the-mirror/.

54. Barack Obama, "Remarks on Trayvon Martin," July 19, 2013, http://www.whitehouse.gov/the-press-office/2013/07/19/remarks-president-trayvon-martin.

55. DeGregory, "Trayvon Martin's Killing"; Robles, "Shooter of Trayvon Martin"; "Sanford Police Surround Community Where George Zimmerman Shot Trayvon Martin," WKMG, July 13, 2013, http://www.clickorlando.com/news/sanford-police-surround-community-where-george-zimmerman-shot-trayvon-martin/-/1637132/20969242/-/12ro846z/-/index.html.

Dreaming America

1. Norma H. Gurba, *Images of America: Lancaster* (Charleston: Arcadia Publishers, 2005), 7, 11.

2. "1876–1910: The Beginning," City of Lancaster website. http://www.cityoflancasterca.org/index.aspx?page=219

3. Ibid.

4. Gurba, p. 49.

5. Mike Davis, *City of Quartz: Excavating the Future in Los Angeles* (New York: Verso, 1991), 3–6.

6. Matt J. Albert, "Up Above," http://www.mattjalbert.com/radical-urban-theory/AntelopeValley/06.html.

7. Google Public Data from Department of Labor Services. Data is not seasonally adjusted. http://www.google.com/publicdata/explore?ds=z1ebjpgk2654c1_&met_y=unemployment_rate&idim=city:CT067800&fdim_y=seasonality:U&dl

=en&hl=en&q=lancaster+california+unemployment+rate#!ctype=l&strail=false&bcs=d&nselm=h&met_y=unemployment_rate&fdim_y=seasonality:U&scale_y=lin&ind_y=false&rdim=country&idim=city:CT067800&ifdim=country&hl=en_US&dl=en&ind=false.

8. Jennifer Medina, "Subsidies and Suspicion," *New York Times*, August 10, 2011, http://www.nytimes.com/2011/08/11/us/11housing.html.

9. California Department of Corrections and Rehabilitation, Monthly Report of Population as of Midnight September 30, 2007.

10. Gideon Rubin, "Tilton Calls for Prison Reform; Lancaster Lockup is Overcrowded," *Los Angeles Daily News*, March 3, 2007.

11. "Authorities Investigating Gang-related Riots at LA Detention Center for Illegal Immigrants," Associated Press, April 24, 2008.

12. Tracy Manzer, "Camp Challenger: Giving Structure to Felony Offenders," *Press-Telegram*, May 21, 2008, http://www.presstelegram.com/general-news/20080521/camp-challenger-giving-structure-to-felony-offenders.

13. "Landmark Federal Class-Action Lawsuit Charges Los Angeles County with Failure to Educate Youth in Probation Camps," American Civil Liberties Union, press release, January 12, 2010, https://www.aclu.org/racial-justice/landmark-federal-class-action-lawsuit-charges-los-angeles-county-failure-educate-yout.

14. Kenneth E. Hartman, "The Recession Behind Bars," *New York Times*, September 5, 2009, http://www.nytimes.com/2009/09/06/opinion/06hartman.html.

15. Aarti Kohli, Peter L. Markowitz, and Lisa Chavez. "Secure Communities by the Numbers: An Analysis of Demographics and Due Process," the Chief Justice Earl Warren Institute on Law and Social Policy, University of California, Berkeley Law School, research report, October 2011, https://www.law.berkeley.edu/files/Secure_Communities_by_the_Numbers.pdf. Jacqueline Stevens, "U.S. Government Unlawfully Detaining and Deporting U.S. Citizens as Aliens," *Virginia Journal of Social Policy and the Law* 18:3 (Spring 2011), http://jacquelinestevens.org/StevensVSP18.32011.pdf.

16. Seth Freed Wessler, *Shattered Families: The Perilous Intersection of Immigration Enforcement and the Child Welfare System*, Applied Research Center, November 2011, 5, http://www.raceforward.org/research/reports/shattered-families.

17. Stevens, "U.S. Government Unlawfully Detaining," 618–624.

18. Vargas was speaking specifically of green-card applicants filing for a visa under a family clause—as the spouse, parent, child, or sibling of a citizen. Data for factoid on Mexican Americans from "But Where Is the Back of the Line?," Asian Law Caucus Infographic, produced March 25, 2013, http://www.asianlawcaucus.org/sites/asian-law-caucus/files/INFOGRAPHIC%20-%20Back%20of%20the%20Line-01%20(1).jpg

19. Robert S. Gonzales, "Learning to Be Illegal: Undocumented Youth and Shifting Legal Contexts in the Transition to Adulthood." *American Sociological Review* 76:4 (2011), 602–619, http://www.asanet.org/images/journals/docs/pdf/asr/Aug11 ASRFeature.pdf.

20. Yahaira Carrillo, "DREAM Now Letters: Yahaira Carrillo," Citizen Orange Blog, July 21, 2010, http://www.citizenorange.com/orange/2010/07/dream-now-letters-yahaira-carr.html.

21. Tania Unzueta, "Netroots Nation Closing Session," C-SPAN, June 18, 2011, http://www.c-spanvideo.org/program/Nation6.

22. The images can be seen at http://juliosalgado83.tumblr.com/archive. See also Steve Pavey and Marco Saavedra, *Shadows then Light* (Lexington, Kentucky: One Horizon Institute, 2012); Culturestrike, http://www.culturestrike.net.

Index